Born Innocent

Born Innocent

Protecting the Dependents of Accused Caregivers

MICHAEL J. SULLIVAN

OXFORD
UNIVERSITY PRESS

Oxford University Press is a department of the University of Oxford. It furthers
the University's objective of excellence in research, scholarship, and education
by publishing worldwide. Oxford is a registered trade mark of Oxford University
Press in the UK and certain other countries.

Published in the United States of America by Oxford University Press
198 Madison Avenue, New York, NY 10016, United States of America.

© Oxford University Press 2023

All rights reserved. No part of this publication may be reproduced, stored in
a retrieval system, or transmitted, in any form or by any means, without the
prior permission in writing of Oxford University Press, or as expressly permitted
by law, by license, or under terms agreed with the appropriate reproduction
rights organization. Inquiries concerning reproduction outside the scope of the
above should be sent to the Rights Department, Oxford University Press, at the
address above.

You must not circulate this work in any other form
and you must impose this same condition on any acquirer.

Library of Congress Cataloging-in-Publication Data
Names: Sullivan, Michael J., author.
Title: Born innocent : protecting the dependents of accused caregivers / Michael J. Sullivan.
Description: New York : Oxford University Press, 2023. |
Includes bibliographical references and index.
Identifiers: LCCN 2023004779 (print) | LCCN 2023004780 (ebook) |
ISBN 9780197671238 (hardback) | ISBN 9780197671245 (epub)
Subjects: LCSH: Children of prisoners—United States. |
Prisoners—Family relationships—United States.
Classification: LCC HV8886.U5 S855 2023 (print) | LCC HV8886.U5 (ebook) |
DDC 362.82/950973—dc23/eng/20230320
LC record available at https://lccn.loc.gov/2023004779
LC ebook record available at https://lccn.loc.gov/2023004780

DOI: 10.1093/oso/9780197671238.001.0001

Printed by Integrated Books International, United States of America

Contents

1. Introduction: Born Innocent and the Vicarious Punishment of Dependents   1

2. A Broader View of Punishment   14

3. In Defense of Birthright Citizenship   48

4. Restoring Offenders as Citizens and Caregivers   75

5. The Collateral Consequences of Banishment   101

6. Collective Intergenerational Responsibilities   126

7. Conclusion: Addressing State-Mandated Family Separation in the 2020s   164

Acknowledgments   183
Notes   185
References   199
Index   249

1

Introduction

Born Innocent and the Vicarious Punishment of Dependents

The United States has the highest incarceration rate in the world, with 639 per 100,000 U.S. residents in prison (Sentencing Project 2021, 1). Over 7 percent of all children in the United States—more than 5 million children—have experienced a parental incarceration, and an estimated 2.7 million children currently have a parent who is incarcerated (Knopf 2018, 3; Arditti 2018, 41). An additional 5 million children under age 18 live with at least one parent without authorization to be in the United States facing deportation (Passel, Cohn, and Gramlich 2018, 2–3). These collateral consequences of mass incarceration and immigration detention are the subject of growing concern among scholars working at the nexus of political science, criminology, and law. Broader, linked issues involving the collateral consequences of preventive justice measures like denationalization and anti-terrorism legislation, including the impact of the denationalization of the parents of immigration detainees, are of concern to the same scholars, but less explored and undertheorized.

Within the incarcerated population, there are stark racial disparities that are not unique to the United States. In the United States, 38.3 percent of inmates incarcerated in May 2022 were Black, even though only 13.4 percent of the U.S. population is African American (Bureau of Prisons 2022; U.S. Census Bureau 2022). While the United States has the highest incarceration rate in the world, it is not unique in its disproportionate incarceration of subaltern minority groups. In North America, Canada has a much lower overall incarceration rate than the United States, with 127 per 100,000 residents incarcerated (Malakieh 2020). But like the United States, Canada is also marked by stark racial disparities in its incarcerated population. In Canada, the largest group of incarcerated persons are of Indigenous origin. Thirty percent of incarcerated Canadians are Indigenous, even though Indigenous people only make up 5 percent of the total population of Canada

Born Innocent. Michael J. Sullivan, Oxford University Press. © Oxford University Press 2023.
DOI: 10.1093/oso/9780197671238.003.0001

2 BORN INNOCENT

(Office of the Correctional Investigator 2020).[1] As of May 2022, 50 percent of federally sentenced women in Canada were Indigenous, a percentage that has been steadily increasing over the past decade (Office of the Correctional Investigator 2021; White 2022). Many of these women are mothers who are separated from their children while incarcerated, perpetuating a multigenerational cycle of family separation in Indigenous communities which Canada is only beginning to reckon with.

This book advances a normative argument that vicarious punishment is re-emerging in a variety of state actions involving the detention of individuals for a range of reasons, including immigration and anti-terrorism detentions not described in law as criminal punishments. States deny individuals birthright citizenship based on the actions, behaviors, status, or group identity of their parents. Economically disadvantaged and minority citizens suffer the collateral consequences of mass incarceration when the state detains their parents or caregivers. Children in mixed-citizenship status families are experiencing the loss of a parent or caregiver through detention and deportation. The children of foreign fighters are suffering the vicarious punitive effects of denationalization and other state actions targeting their parents for their actions in a conflict zone as an anti-terrorism measure by their former country of citizenship. Vicarious punishment never went away in the case of Indigenous children separated from their families to punish their community for resisting assimilation and the extinguishment of their land claims. Their families continue to suffer from intergenerational trauma and child welfare interventions.

Beneath these policy problems and legal issues lie two deeper ethical dilemmas that are the focus of my book. The first question asks what the state and its citizens owe to the individuals it detains (whether as suspects, offenders, or without formal charges), given their ongoing contributions in relationships to dependents. The second question asks what the state and its citizens owe to innocent dependents in view of the collateral consequences of their caregivers' detention.

The Binding Tie: The Injustice of Family Separation

A common theme throughout this book involves the ways in which states use family separation in punitive ways toward parents, and indirectly as vicarious punishment for their children. Although family separation is ordinarily a violation of international law and human rights guarantees (Starr and Brilmayer 2003), I argue in Chapter 2 that states use family separation in punitive ways to deter unauthorized immigration and residence. Citizenship at birth is granted according to two principles: *jus soli*, or in the country where the child is born, or *jus sanguinis*, by descent based on the citizenship of a child's parents. In Chapter 3, I show how states are penalizing unauthorized and temporary resident parents for giving birth to citizens in *jus soli* countries in proposals to deny their children citizenship there. A related argument extends to *jus sanguinis* countries that penalize their citizens for living abroad by denying their children citizenship by descent. Deportation and imprisonment separate families in avoidable ways that harm children deprived of the care of a deported or incarcerated parent. In Chapter 4, I consider how the incarceration and separation from family members undermine the hope, outside ties, and sense of obligation that inspires prisoners to seek rehabilitation and to work toward reintegrating into the community. Anti-terrorism prosecutions do not just target guilty parties. They also impose disabilities on their innocent children. In Chapter 5, I consider how anti-terrorist operations against parents harm the innocent children of suspected terrorists through intergenerational denationalizations and the refusal by countries of origin to repatriate the children of suspected terrorists. Finally, family separation is used as an instrument of cultural genocide by states that seek to extinguish minority communities and their land claims. In Chapter 6, I show how the policies of forced residential school attendance away from families, followed by the removal of children from fit Indigenous parents in the child welfare system served to undermine the sovereignty and integrity of Indigenous communities. These punitive actions resulted in the incarceration of Indigenous parents and the institutionalization of their children in residential schools. In these carceral facilities, abuse, violence, and forced industrial labor were rife, resulting in intergenerational harms by breaking the transfer of parenting and survival skills from one generation to the next, undermining victims' life prospects (Sawatsky 2009, 107–108). Immigrants and settlers sometimes think of themselves as being born innocent of past policies like the removal of Indigenous peoples from their lands and the separation of their families through residential schooling and child welfare removals. But everyone in a settler society is part of an intergenerational community that shares in the burdens of these past policies which have ongoing consequences. Racism motivated family separations designed to undermine the intergenerational continuity of Indigenous families and

4 BORN INNOCENT

communities, and ethnocentrism continues to shape Indigenous child welfare policies.

Overall, this book considers the ways in which states can and should protect dependents from punishment directed at a caregiver. A secondary concern involves looking at whether the forms of punishment directed at the primary offender are in fact just. Here, I ask whether punishment is being pursued in a way that facilitates the goals of rehabilitation and reintegration, which can help offenders and family members alike. Finally, I consider the forms of redress that can rectify the intergenerational losses suffered by Indigenous peoples in which settler states seized and divided their ancestral homelands. Citizenship grants in both countries and other forms of rectification by these states can serve as an important way to reunite families and communities bisected by settler state boundaries, as a remedy which Indigenous people should be able to choose or reject.

"The Sins of Parents Should Not be Visited on Their Children"

The general principle underlying modern criminal responsibility is the retributive principle that "punishment should not be applied except to an individual who has broken the law" (Hart 1968, 81). This principle is meant to respect persons as agents capable of choice by distributing punishment only to those who have already chosen to offend, protecting "the individual from society" and its desire to obtain security above all else (Hart 1968, 44, 49, 81). Deontological legal theorists adhere to this principle even though they recognize the social utility of deterring more persons from crime if family members and associates of offenders were punished vicariously for their crimes (Rawls 1955, 10–12; Hart 1968, 11; Boonin 2008, 41).

Utilitarian legal theorists continue to defend vicarious punishment as a means of minimizing both current and future risks as a matter of preventive justice. They point to examples in civil law (torts) and social behavior where collective sanctions are used as regulatory strategies to monitor and control the actions of individuals (Lucas 1993, 91–92, 113; Levinson 2003, 427). They also highlight areas of the law where vicarious responsibility is a common and accepted part of the law, such as civil liability on the part of an employer for the torts of an employee. Levinson suggests that law enforcement and judicial officials should apply the same principles to hold innocent associates and dependents of suspects responsible, because they are "well-positioned to monitor and control" hard-to-reach offenders, and the end of deterrence justifies the means of punishing the innocent (Levinson 2003, 349). Here, the argument for collective punishment is not justice but rather deterrence, an end that justifies the means of punishing the innocent (Fletcher 2004, 166). Scholars of law and economics maintain that "in situations where detection is difficult or impossible, or when punishing the innocent is not seen as costly, group punishment might offer an acceptable alternative to individual punishment" (Miceli and Segerson 2007, 81). They focus on the most cost-effective strategy of deterring anti-social behavior and encouraging compliance. In the process, they sidestep the question of whether these sanctions are justifiable punishments given the higher standard of modern individual accountability. In international humanitarian law, for instance, there is a prohibition on the imposition of penal and quasi-penal punishment based on association rather than individual criminal responsibility as specified in Article 33 of the Geneva Convention (IV) (Bell 2010, 80; Sivakumaran 2010, 1020).

While vicarious responsibility is an accepted part of the law of contracts and torts, the concept is much more problematic when applied to criminal and moral responsibility (Darcy 2007, xix–xx). Vicarious criminal liability draws condemnation by modern legal and political philosophers as a "barbarous regression" to "such primitive notions as vendetta, noxal surrender, and substitute sacrifice" (Feinberg 1968, 676). In the ancient world, Roman, Greek, and Hebrew law all used collective responsibility as a means of seeking punishment through revenge, in the absence of a centralized responsibility mechanism, by absolute power holders who were unconcerned with sparing the innocent in the pursuit of private vengeance (Miceli 2014). As societies have moved away from ascribed to achieved status, responsibility has come to rest on a person's own actions and choices, rather than their relationship to others or the position into which they were born (May 1992, 156). To this end, theologians who rely on ancient scriptures as a guide to modern behavior deemphasize doctrines of illegitimacy that punish descendants for the deeds of their ancestors (Witte 2009, 4–5; Deuteronomy 23:2). Instead, they underscore passages consistent with modern views of individual criminal responsibility, whereby "the son shall not suffer for the iniquity of the father" (Feinberg 1970, 227; Witte 2009, 5; Weiss 2017; Ezekiel 18:19–20).

Vicarious punishments target offenders that are difficult to capture or deter. They attack family members or dependents that enforcement officials

6 BORN INNOCENT

can more readily access and target, and whom the suspect would want to protect from hardship, such as their spouse or children. Even if this strategy may be useful as a means of minimizing societal risk by deterring serious crimes and acts of terror, vicarious punishments run afoul of the legal principle that only individuals who commit offenses should be subject to hard treatment or censure. While it is tempting for a society that is fearful of crime and acts of terror to use whatever tools necessary to prevent the possibility of a future crime by targeting nonoffenders, security considerations should not take precedence over the rights of individuals to be punished only for acts *they* committed (Husak 2008, 43, 190, 293). Similarly, state authorities sometimes use collective sanctions to delegate punishment to the offender's community as a whole, irrespective of the guilt or innocence of its members. They do so to try to enlist the offender's community resources toward monitoring, controlling, and sanctioning the offender at a lower cost to the punishing state (Levinson 2003, 427). As a deterrent strategy, this theory fails as collective sanctions fall on vulnerable parties that do not have the power to influence the targeted individual's actions, such as dependent children in families, or powerless subjects in political communities. This tactic objectionably makes innocent family members, including children, into mere pawns at the mercy of the state's crime control strategy. Even if this strategy deterred offenders, it comes at the unconscionable expense of a normative conception of justice defined in terms of individual responsibility for past offenses (Fabricant 2011, 391; Heffernan 2019, 28–29). For this reason, political philosophers like Avia Pasternak (2021) rightly argue that sentencing authorities should consider the impact of a punishment on a perpetrators' dependents. Sentences should be tailored to allow offenders to continue to discharge their duties of care toward their children whenever possible (Pasternak 2021, 30, 179, 183).

These objections do not stop law enforcement and military officials from resorting to vicarious punishments directed at innocent family members both as a preventive measure to deter suspects from committing offenses, and as a way of eliciting information and compliance to aid in the apprehension of suspects who have committed crimes. In the U.S. criminal justice context, the Anti-Drug Abuse Act of 1988 authorizes the eviction of entire families from Section 8 public housing if one or more of the occupants engages in drug-related criminal activity (*Department of Housing and Urban Development v. Rucker* 2002; Silva 2015, 789–799; Hoskins 2019, 171). In immigration enforcement, former President Trump justified family separations as a "disincentive" deterrent measure designed to prevent migrants from claiming asylum in the United States (Kindy, Miroff, and Sacchetti 2019; Shear and Kanno-Youngs 2019). Department of Homeland Security memos justify family separations for their "substantial deterrent effect on those seeking to enter the United States" as asylum-seekers (DHS 2017). This policy has not had the desired impact even when asylum-seekers are aware of the policy given the overriding risks of remaining in their country of origin (Ryo 2019, 247).

In international relations, collective punishment persists when states use sanctions and target civilian populations in military strikes to weaken or punish regimes without incurring the political and military costs of targeting insulated responsible political elites (Miceli 2014). Narrowly targeted sanctions may still be defensible when they are used to deescalate a military conflict to avoid further harm, as with their application by Ukraine's allies against Russia following its invasion and brutal occupation in 2022. At the same time, the international community has a moral obligation to support political dissidents from the targeted country. They should mitigate the costs of sanctions on innocent civilians whenever possible, recognizing that innocent civilians in authoritarian states do not necessarily condone their leaders' war crimes. Simply stating that it is difficult but permissible to justify distributing the costs of sanctions to dissenters is an incomplete answer, though their exclusion from liability for reparations is a helpful starting point (Fleming 2020, 156, 165). At the very least, dissenters fleeing a targeted state who are seeking to avoid political persecution or conscription into an unjust war should be offered asylum in the sanctioning countries, subject to security screening. In 2022, this would mean granting asylum to potential Russian conscripts who refuse to fight in the unjust occupation of Ukraine to support the opposition, encourage civil disobedience against the war, and protect dissenters against reprisals (Cortright 2022).

Within states, but outside the ordinary criminal justice system, security forces use vicarious punishment as an anti-terrorism measure. For instance, Israel demolishes the houses of suspected Palestinian terrorists to impose costs upon their family members, justifying this measure to prevent and deter terrorism (Fassin 2018, 42; Fletcher 2020, 60–61; Hatz 2020, 521; Klocker 2020, 44). As an anti-terrorism measure, the Israeli Supreme Court has ruled against similar vicarious punishments, arguing that forcing the families of Palestinian militants from their homes is a violation of the doctrine of individual responsibility rooted in Israel's Jewish and liberal democratic principles (*Ajuri v. IDF Commander in West Bank* 2002).

8 BORN INNOCENT

In other contexts in criminal law, immigration enforcement, and anti-terrorism, family members of suspects end up suffering collateral consequences of state action directed at suspected individuals, even when law enforcement does not directly target their dependents.

Organization of the Book

The following chapters argue for limitations on preventive justice measures that are increasingly used by liberal democratic countries to combat a broad range of suspected offenses including alleged immigration violations and affiliations with terrorist groups. States should direct punishment and administrative sanctions at the individual offender who violates the law. Vicarious forms of punishment that aim to deter crime, immigration violations, or anti-state actions including terrorism by targeting the children and family members of offenders should be avoided. For offenders in the criminal justice system, reintegration should be the goal of punishment for offenders, allowing them to reassume roles as caregivers, providers, and contributing members of society. The criminal justice system should shield children and other dependents of offenders from the collateral consequences of punishing an offender who is a caregiver and provider wherever possible. Collateral consequences of state sanctions extend beyond the domestic criminal justice system to include deportations and denials of citizenship and its protections to children of irregular migrants and persons suspected of anti-state offenses and affiliations. The dependents of suspects are also wrongly harmed when their immigration or citizenship status and rights are removed because of a proceeding targeting their parents or caregivers. "Preventive" child welfare interventions that involve seizing children from their families and communities should be replaced in many cases by community-based assistance for at-risk families that will allow them to remain in their communities.

In Chapter 2, "A Broader View of Punishment," I argue that state actions that undermine caregivers' capacities to provide for their children inflict undeserved collateral hardship on the children and family members of offenders. Scholars of political science, criminology, and immigration have expanded our understanding of what it means to experience punishment. There is a cross-national trend toward the criminalization of regulatory offenses such as immigration violations. The United Kingdom and the United States have each used inchoate offenses that amount to thought or allegiance crimes as anti-terrorism measures (Robinson 2012, 190; Roach 2011; Corda 2019, 168–173). To this end, an interdisciplinary group of scholars is developing a new field of inquiry to understand punitive consequences at the intersection of criminal justice and immigration (crimmigration) and national security and criminology (preventive justice). Despite formal divisions in the law between administrative sanctions and criminal punishment, immigration enforcement actions, denials of citizenship, denationalizations, and preventive detentions for inchoate offenses are equally punitive. Suspects, offenders, and those who depend on them should be entitled to counsel and other protections reserved for offenders in the criminal justice system. The state should assume responsibility for ensuring the adequate protection and well-being of those who are dependent on persons detained on immigration and terrorism charges. The consequences of failing to provide protection for the dependents of detainees is all too evident in the detention of asylum-seekers and in preventive anti-terrorism prosecutions.

In Chapter 3, "In Defense of Birthright Citizenship," I argue that political communities should not be free to decide whether to deny citizenship and its substantial protections to infants based on their parents' actions or behaviors, including immigration status, place of residence, or where they work at the time of their child's birth. Despite exceptions that bind some children to the status of their parents based on their employment or conduct, for most native-born children, territorial birthright citizenship contains the promise of integration on equal terms with other citizens for second-generation immigrants that does not indefinitely tie them to the immigration status of their parents. In the United States, equal protection of the law for the children of irregular immigrants means a free public education, on the grounds that "legislation directing the onus of a parent's misconduct against his children" that "does not comport with fundamental conceptions of justice" (*Plyler v. Doe* 1982, 220). Similar justifications have been made for granting young immigrant children protections from deportation, arguing that immigrants who entered a country without authorization as children should not be held culpable for their parents' immigration violations. Children of irregular immigrants deserve separate consideration for immigration benefits and citizenship apart from the status and conduct of their parents. Legislation that punishes children for the conduct of their parents "classifies on the basis of an immutable trait" that is "entirely out of the child's control" (Stier 1992, 736–737; Carvalho and Chamberlen 2018). On the whole, children who arrive in a country shortly after they are born

10 BORN INNOCENT

are similarly situated to native-born children who remain in their country of birth. They deserve the protections of citizenship where they live irrespective of citizens' judgment of their parents' conduct as irregular entrants or visa overstayers.

In Chapter 4, "Restoring Offenders as Caregivers and Citizens," I argue in favor of restorative justice approaches that aim to rehabilitate and reintegrate offenders into their communities whenever possible (Braithwaite 2002; Golash 2005). This marks a departure from the imposition of collateral consequences and "preventive" sanctions that some legal scholars have compared to the colonial sanction of "civil death," by preventing those whom have served their sentence from assuming productive roles in society (Ewald 2002, 1059; Manza and Uggen 2006, 23, 210; Chin 2012; Mayson 2015, 303). Reintegration involves preparing a former offender to take on more productive roles and responsibilities in society. To minimize the collateral consequences of punishment for dependents, offenders should be able to maintain caregiving relationships with the goal of restoring offenders to their roles as providers upon release (Lippke 2007, 185; Muth 2018, 17–18). Second, I argue that the criminal justice and child welfare systems should facilitate family unity wherever possible through visitation, flexible sentencing, and sanctions that aim at reintegration, rather than retribution toward offenders (Lippke 2007, 183–188; Brownlee 2020, 173, 191). The goal here is to break the cycle of family dissolutions and distrust in authority among the children of incarcerated parents that increases the chance that they will commit criminal offenses (Fassin 2018, 114; Levine and Topalli 2019).

In Chapter 5, "The Collateral Consequences of Banishment," I argue that political communities should not be free to decide whether to deny citizenship and its protections to children based on their parents' allegiances or alleged offenses at the time of their child's birth. Citizenship deprivation is an intergenerational punishment when children lose entitlement to citizenship at birth based on their parent's denationalization, as is the case for stateless children born to ISIS-affiliated parents (Zedner 2019a, 328). Citizenship deprivation is also a possible intergenerational punishment for children born to spies posted in countries with *jus soli* birthright citizenship. As for the collateral consequences of anti-terrorism sanctions, my primary concern in this chapter is to ensure that the dependents of suspects and offenders do not lose status-based entitlements to citizenship and its rights based on their parents' actions. Second, I question whether harsh retributory punishments including citizenship deprivation, banishment, and execution are warranted

INTRODUCTION 11

for political crimes (Beck, Britto, and Andrews 2007; Lenard 2018; Gibney 2020a). Distinctions in law and policy must be made between beliefs and actions, or rather, suspicions and thoughts of disloyalty, and acting upon these beliefs in a way that causes harm to individuals (Lacey 2016, 152–154).

In Chapter 6, "Collective Intergenerational Responsibilities," I ask how the current generation might accept responsibility for the injustices of its forebears in a way that helps all citizens to progress toward reconciliation. The objective is to avoid simply penalizing the children of immigrants and settlers who have not committed an offense themselves. In settler states like Canada, Australia, and the United States, agents of the state removed children from their parents to residential schools where their caretakers abused them.[2] Later, child welfare agencies took the place of residential schools, removing Indigenous children from caring and supportive parents for cultural reasons. The legacy of these actions endures for Indigenous families and children to this day, and the harms inflicted upon them by previous generations of officials remain with our fellow citizens. Few current citizens participated in these harms directly. Yet as the descendants of settlers and recent immigrants, they continue to benefit from access to property and resources that resulted first from the dispossession of Indigenous residents. Here, I argue that the collective path forward involves addressing the intergenerational legacy of past injustices through criminal justice, child welfare, and immigration and citizenship policy reforms. The citizen-to-citizen path involves the descendants of immigrants drawing from their resources of empathy to join their Indigenous neighbors' struggle for justice, to share in the burdens and benefits of citizenship in their adopted country.

For the First Nations of North America, national borders can be daily impositions that divide their traditional homelands and separate family and kinship groups. As settler states, Canada and the United States had similar policies that resulted in the separation of Indigenous families through enforced residential schooling and child welfare interventions. This underscores the importance of studying these two cases together (Jacobs 2014, xxviii; Woolford 2015, 2–5).[3] To this end, I argue for immigration and citizenship policy interventions that would break down barriers bisecting Indigenous polities, strengthen their sovereignty claims, and reunite family and kinship groups.

In Chapter 7, "Conclusion: Addressing State-Mandated Family Separation in the 2020s," I provide a summary and postscript to my discussion of state-mandated family separation and remedies to this problem as they relate to

12 BORN INNOCENT

immigration detentions, citizenship, criminal justice, the fate of the children of foreign fighters, and the legacy of Indigenous child welfare removals.

In the United States, I cover the first year of President Biden's administration and evaluate his administration's approach to reuniting immigrant families, criminal justice reform, and the impact of the war on terror on the children of foreign fighters stranded abroad. In Canada, I cover the same themes with an emphasis on recent developments in Indigenous child welfare protections that could serve as a model for other jurisdictions. More broadly, I address the ongoing impact of the COVID-19 crisis on issues related to immigration, citizenship, criminal justice, and Indigenous rights from a comparative North American perspective. Here, I focus on the ongoing vulnerabilities faced by families separated by the immigration, criminal justice, and child welfare systems.

Overall, this book confronts the problem of state-mandated family separation in its various forms that endanger the well-being of dependents of condemned caregivers. It shows how children and other vulnerable persons are suffering from intergenerational punishment directed at their parents, guardians, and communities. This includes immigration and anti-terrorism detentions not described in law as criminal punishments. States deny individuals birthright citizenship based on the actions, behaviors, status, or group identity of their parents. Economically disadvantaged and minority citizens suffer the collateral consequences of mass incarceration when the state detains their parents or caregivers. Children in mixed-citizenship status families are experiencing the loss of a parent or caregiver through detention and deportation. The children of foreign fighters are suffering the vicarious punitive effects of denationalization and other state actions targeting their parents for their actions in a conflict zone as an anti-terrorism measure by their former country of citizenship. In the Indigenous case, they are suffering as members of vulnerable communities, with high incarceration rates linked to a legacy of state-sponsored family separation and abuse.

This book argues for replacing punitive measures defined in terms of deterrence, incapacitation, and retribution of caregivers in immigration detention, incarceration, anti-terrorism proceedings, and child welfare interventions with rehabilitation and reintegration. The goal in all cases is to help at-risk persons who face state-mandated separation from their dependents, other family, and communities. Instead of punishment, they need support and resources to help them to flourish as caregivers and citizens. In the process, this book builds upon my previous argument in *Earned Citizenship* (2019) about the civic value of caregiving in new contexts involving the criminal justice system, anti-terrorism prosecutions, and child welfare removals. *Earned Citizenship* took a critical stance against existing state practices, whereby I argued that those who had already undertaken costly sacrifices on behalf of the state should be rewarded with citizenship, instead of facing deportation and denationalization.[4] Here, as in *Earned Citizenship*, I argue that parenting has an important civic value. Polities should allow parents the chance to earn their rehabilitation and reintegration into society, rather than separating at-risk parents from their children. Where immigration and citizenship status separates families, the solution is to allow families to live together in the country where they currently reside with the opportunity to become citizens there. Criminal justice policies should facilitate the preservation of caregiving relationships wherever possible through sentencing, visitation, rehabilitation, and deradicalization programs that are in the interests of parents and their innocent children. For persons without children, other caregiving relationships may serve a similar purpose, albeit not for the benefit of a developing and dependent citizen-in-becoming. In Indigenous communities, rehabilitation through restorative justice and healing circles promotes reintegration that strengthens intergenerational care and bonds within tribal communities.

2

A Broader View of Punishment

International security responses to the September 11, 2001 terrorist attacks hastened a cross-national trend toward criminalizing regulatory offenses, such as immigration violations, and inchoate offenses that amount to thought or allegiance crimes in the case of anti-terrorism legislation (Robinson 2012, 190; Corda 2019, 168–173). In response, scholars of political science, criminology and immigration are expanding our understanding of what it means to experience punishment. New fields of inquiry are probing the punitive consequences at the intersection of criminal justice and immigration (crimmigration) and national security and criminology (preventive justice) (Stumpf 2020b, 93). Scholars of law and society have long described immigration enforcement actions, denials of citizenship, denationalizations, and preventive detentions for inchoate offenses as punitive actions. As punitive actions, those who suffer hard treatment by the state merit greater legal protections. In each case, state actions undermine caregivers' capacities to provide for their dependents, inflicting collateral hardship on children and family members. Drawing from studies at the intersection of criminal justice and immigration (crimmigration), preventive justice (terrorism), and migration and citizenship studies (denationalization), I uncover the interconnection between disparate forms of state punishment in the criminal justice system, immigration enforcement, and anti-terrorism law, policy, and enforcement measures. Here, I critically assess the impact of state punishment on the innocent dependents of the accused, challenging the morality of these vicarious forms of punishment that are often overlooked, or justified as unavoidable collateral consequences.

What Is Punishment?

H. L. A. Hart provides the classic retributivist definition of punishment, and the problems associated with vicarious punishment in his book *Punishment and Responsibility* (1968). Here, he defines the central case of punishment

Born Innocent. Michael J. Sullivan, Oxford University Press. © Oxford University Press 2023.
DOI: 10.1093/oso/9780197671238.003.0002

in terms of five elements. First, it must involve pain or other consequences normally considered unpleasant. Second, it must be for an offense against legal rules. Third, and most importantly for distinguishing between individual and collective responsibility, "it must be of an actual or supposed offender for his offense" (Hart 1968, 4). Fourth, human beings other than the offender must administer the punishment, and fifth, authorities must follow the regulations set out by a legal system in administering the sanction (Hart 1968, 4–5). Hart contrasts this standard or central case of punishment against defective sanctions, including "vicarious or collective punishment of some member of a social group for actions done without the former's authorization, control, or permission," and the "punishment of persons who neither are in fact nor supposed to be offenders" (Hart 1968, 5). The latter two categories of substandard punishment are the focus of my concern in this chapter, where family members and associates of an offender suffer vicarious punishment even though they did nothing wrong. This can occur either when the criminal justice system does not alleviate the collateral damage of punishing a caregiver on his dependents, or by design, when authorities target family members to deter crime, to augment the suffering of the offender, or to target a person who is easier to reach than the offender. Hart associates the targeting of family members with a simplistic utilitarian justification for punishment: that if harm to others, including those dependent on an offender, causes someone to reconsider a criminal offense, then it is justified to improve the security of the community (Hart 1968, 6; Tonry 2020a, 15). Hart then asks, "If this is the justification of punishment, why not apply it, when it pays to do so, to those innocent of any crime, chosen at random, or the wife and children of the offender" (Hart 1968, 6)?

Hart answers these questions and condemns vicarious punishment in the following terms. First, punishment ought to respect the individual, and his or her capacity for choice. A legal system should direct individuals toward obedience but leave them free to choose. By contrast, officials illegitimately direct vicarious punishment at those who could not have chosen to do wrong, including children with limited agency, and associates that did not take part in the crime (Hart 1968, 44). Collective punishments like house demolitions that are directed at families and communities of terrorism suspects rather than offenders run afoul of the same principle of individual liability (Klocker 2020, 29). States are tempted to turn to vicarious punishment in their unrestrained zeal to condemn a violation of their norms, and to restore their sense of security at the expense of the innocent (Hart 1968, 81; Tonry 2020a, 15).

16 BORN INNOCENT

This is particularly true in the case of offenses that strike at the community's identity, boundaries, and sovereignty, such as immigration violations and terrorism offenses. This also includes inchoate "allegiance crimes" in preventive justice that penalize offenders before harmful acts take place. In this case, justice in punishment requires restraint, placing a higher priority on protecting innocent individuals from society, rather than ensuring "moral evil should meet its return in punishment" (Hart 1968, 81).

Hart's hypothetical concern about utilitarian justifications for punishment is grounded in practice. For instance, Israel demolishes the homes of non-combatant Palestinians for their associations with family members suspected of terrorism, and in the United States, family members of drug offenders are evicted from public housing (Fletcher 2020, 60–61; Hatz 2020, 521; Klocker 2020, 44). Vicarious punishment also occurs without the express intention of the state when family members suffer the loss of their parent or guardian's income and nonfinancial forms of caregiving upon their incarceration. A retributivist would argue that it is only fair that everyone receives the same penalty for a crime regardless of their other roles, responsibilities, and circumstances (Markel, Collins and Leib 2009, 29–32). This is not happening in practice. In immigration enforcement, policymakers highlight the prospect of collateral consequences for dependents to deter families from entering the United States to claim asylum. The state calls the detention of immigration offenders "administrative custody," rather than a punishment. This label is facetious. To the people affected, punishment feels like punishment, whatever its rationale or name (Tonry 2020a, 15). Second, states and correctional officials can take steps to mitigate harms to blameless dependents while still punishing offending caregivers. Offenders can be detained closer to their families, with expanded visitation opportunities. Except in cases of abuse, offenders should be able to retain custody over their children, with the opportunity for remunerative work to pay for child and spousal support. When states do not take steps to mitigate collateral hardships on the dependents of offenders, they indirectly inflict vicarious punishment upon innocent family members. Social services agencies then must take up the burden of supporting the dependents of offenders at a long-term cost to taxpayers and society.

Uncovering Stealth Punishments: Formalism versus Function

In most legal systems, states attempt to categorize some sanctions as "nonpunitive," which has the effect of denying those sanctioned due process rights for administrative convenience. In the ordinary criminal justice system that applies to all residents, a wide range of sanctions classified as "preventive measures" fall under this classification. These include anti-social behavior orders in the United Kingdom, pretrial detention (*United States v. Salerno,* 1987), involuntary commitment of sex offenders (*Kansas v. Hendricks,* 1997), and delinquency (*In Re Gault,* 1967). Each is a longstanding example of false formalism in criminal procedure that denies an individual due process rights. These measures serve the punitive function of incapacitating an offender. Outside the ordinary criminal justice system, immigration offenses that apply only to noncitizens are among the most frequently cited examples of sanctions that serve the incapacitatory and deterrent functions of punishment identified in precedent across jurisdictions and legal theory (Chiao 2019, 211–213). Finally, since September 11, 2001, law enforcement agencies have acquired new powers to detain persons without formal criminal charges on national security grounds to deter and incapacitate potential terrorists, based on their beliefs and affiliations rather than actions (Ashworth and Zedner 2014, 182).

One way to define punishment is to take a functional approach by attempting to determine what the state is either attempting to accomplish, or the outcome it is bringing out in practice by limiting an individual's liberty in response to a violation of its laws. In its negative form, punishment incapacitates, deters, and expresses retribution. In its positive form, punishment can also have a rehabilitative and restorative dimension, reconciling offenders and victims. In *Golden Gulag* (2007), Ruth Wilson Gilmore argues that of these three functions of punishment, incapacitation best explains the growth of the U.S. carceral state. She explains that incarceration as incapacitation takes people "from disordered, deindustrialized milieus and deposit[s] them somewhere else." The U.S. criminal justice system does not devote enough resources to rehabilitation, changing nothing "about people except where they are" (Gilmore 2007, 14, 246). The same can also be said about the immigration detention and deportation system, which dispenses with the remaining vestiges of the rehabilitative function of the domestic prison system in favor of incapacitating noncitizens by removing them from the country. Incapacitation has also taken the place of rehabilitation with the denationalization of accused terrorists by Western states that refuse to accept the responsibility of judging and rehabilitating their own citizens. They have shifted this burden to the struggling governing authorities managing refugee camps in former ISIS-controlled areas of Syria and Iraq.

Another way to determine what is punishment is to ask how this practice is different from other limitations that a state imposes on an individual's

18 BORN INNOCENT

freedom (Tripkovic 2019, 48). Punishment involves both the imposition of hard treatment on a person who violates a law, and a stigma, or an expression of the state's moral condemnation of an individual for intentionally acting in a prohibited manner (Husak 2010, 1182). To take an example from what is now a widely shared experience to differentiate punishment from other restrictions on individual liberty, many jurisdictions have imposed public health quarantines and lockdowns on their citizens to mitigate the transmission of COVID-19.

First, punishment does not just have a harmful effect; it is an official measure designed to harm a law violator (Boonin 2008, 15). By contrast, though quarantines and lockdowns limit individual liberty and corporate economic activity in ways that have incited protests, they were never intended to harm anyone. Quite the opposite, public health officials sought to protect individual health in the short term and the public health infrastructure over time.[1] Unlike in the case of punishment, officials are frequently at pains to apologize for the inconveniences they require of quarantined individuals (Tonry 2020b, 179).

Second, quarantines and lockdowns are primarily forward-looking, in that they seek to prevent harm to the individuals they affect in the future. Punishment in its focal sense is primarily backward looking, as a mechanism for society to communicate censure for an act that has already taken place, for which an individual is responsible. From a retributivist perspective, an offender must deserve his punishment for willfully committing an offense. This sense of desert comes from being morally, rather than just inadvertently responsible for some act or omission (Brooks 2021, 19). Punishment then comes as a disadvantage prescribed by the state for a breach of duty (Lamond 2000, 58). To this end, Hart holds that officials should only detain persons not responsible for a guilty act "to avoid damage of a catastrophic character." In this class, he includes "the detention of persons of hostile origin or association in wartime" as noncitizens who have not committed a crime, "the insane," and persons suffering from an infectious disease (Hart 1968, 17). Following this logic, immigration detainees and terrorist suspects who have yet to commit a crime are like quarantine patients, who can be held to prevent harm to society, but only as a last resort, and by arranging compensation and comforts that distinguish their detention from hard treatment allotted to guilty actors.

Third, quarantines and lockdowns incapacitate by limiting movement and deter interaction, which is also a function of punishment, but officials intend these measures to incapacitate a virus and an involuntary health condition that is beyond an individual's control. Even when specific individuals are quarantined after contracting the virus, the stated aim of public health actions is not to condemn an individual for a condition that could happen to anyone. This has not stopped citizens and public officials from scolding quarantined individuals for not being careful enough as though their condition was the result of culpable recklessness. This results in stigma that doubly harms COVID-19 victims, complicating the efforts of public health officials to elicit cooperation with self-isolation and contact tracing measures (Dwyer 2020).

Fourth, punishment is expressive. States design punitive measures to express official condemnation of a person who violated a law, while the stigma attached to quarantine is unofficial, unintended, and counterproductive to the aims of public health officials (Boonin 2008, 22). Fifth, insofar as public health measures rehabilitate, they do so by providing time and resources to help physical bodies to recover, rather than to change behavior and attitudes, as is the aim of penal rehabilitation. Sixth, both public health quarantines and punishment are concerned with proportionality, but not with deservingness. Officials attempt to prioritize the individual liberties of blameless affected citizens in the balance between controlling the disease and minimizing the restrictiveness and inconvenience of the action to what is necessary to control the contagion (Childress et al. 2002, 173).

Finally, whereas penal restoration aims to reconcile offenders with the victims they have intentionally wronged by their actions, quarantined citizens have no need to repent or make restoration to those they may have unknowingly infected before they became aware of their condition, so long as they abide by the terms of their isolation. Punishment arises from a moral breach, while quarantine results from a morally neutral assessment of an involuntary condition and the risks of contagion (Kleinig 2012, 66). The quarantined COVID-19 patient may have become infected even after taking every precaution outlined by public health authorities. COVID-19 patients are not blameworthy or morally responsible for their disease, but they still must isolate, under the best conditions the government can offer to compensate for the inconvenience, and to protect others from also falling ill. As C. L. Ten describes quarantine, there "is the infliction of some unpleasantness or suffering, but it is only in the case of punishment that the unpleasantness is essential to what is to be done" (Ten 1987, 15).

It is even more important in a correctional setting to distinguish between solitary confinement, which is designed to punish, and medical quarantines, which serve to protect prisoners, staff, and the safety of the facility. To make quarantines nonpunitive, some measure of compensation for the prisoner is needed. For instance, quarantine patients should be allowed to communicate with dependents who cannot visit with them for free (Cloud et al. 2020, 1734). In short, unlike punishment, quarantine mandates recognize the moral innocence of those constrained, and seek to avoid harming them for a condition that is both outside their control and imposed upon them for the welfare of the community. Quarantines are coercive preventive measures, but they assign no culpability upon those whom officials temporarily incapacitate to contain a pandemic, as "one cannot be held criminally responsible for being sick" (Cole 2015). The same cannot be said about laws governing those who later act to knowingly violate quarantine laws, in which officials impose fines and jail sentences upon violators to incapacitate offenders, deter others from doing the same, and express society's condemnation of those who would put the community at risk.[2] Some citizens perceive quarantines to be a form of punishment. This perception can translate into reality when citizens breach public health guidelines and receive steep fines for their noncompliance. In Canada, for instance, these fines can reach $750,000 (Government of Canada 2022).

As a matter of public health ethics, the onus is on officials to distinguish quarantines from punishments by mitigating hardships resulting from these emergency measures and tailoring them to monitor and improve the health of those who are isolated. Whereas incapacitation is a goal of punishment, it is an undeserved consequence of quarantine, and those affected should be compensated for their inconvenience (Bayer et al. 2007, 270; Ashworth and Zedner 2014, 263). Drawing lessons from the practice of quarantines as emergency public health measures, legal philosophers led by Derk Pereboom devised a more humane alternative to retributive punishment. This model draws a close analogy between measures designed to protect society from risk and contagion in physical health and behavioral health. Its advocates hold that just as quarantines are a last resort as a public health measure to prevent an uncontrollable and untreatable disease, punishments that involve incapacitating offenders should also be a last resort, reserved for the worst offenses for which there is no effective treatment (Pereboom 2014, 156). In physical and behavioral health, early diagnosis, prevention, and treatment are always to be preferred to incapacitation, whether through quarantine in the case of diseases, or incarceration in the case of violations of the law.

The public health-quarantine model goes beyond simply questioning the need to incapacitate low-level offenders. It also has more controversial features that can be discarded without rejecting the model altogether. Pereboom's version of criminal quarantine starts from a "fundamental skepticism about free will," "that since what we do and the way we are is ultimately the result of factors beyond our control, we are never morally responsible for our actions" (Caruso and Pereboom 2021, 356). From this standpoint, those who commit crimes are more like carriers of disease than willful violators of legal rules and social norms. As a result, dangerous criminals are not as responsible for their behavior as retributivists believe, making punishments that castigate their behavior less defensible. The degree of skepticism about free will that accompanies Pereboom's public health-quarantine model is highly controversial and not widely shared among criminal justice practitioners (Tonry 2020b, 180).

As my favorable assessment of Hart's defense of individual responsibility in punishment demonstrates, my argument in this book does not question free will or deny that adults have the rational capacity to deserve praise or blame for their actions. It condemns vicarious punishment directed at dependents for the choices and actions of their caregivers or family members. It also preserves the element of retributivist thought that emphasizes that ordinary mature adults have some degree of choice and agency in their decisions, which is a source of human dignity. Indeed, some individuals actively resist moral and legal norms because they conscientiously disagree with them as a matter of faith or philosophical conviction. For instance, when border citizens of faith affiliated with the Sanctuary Movement leave out water jugs on trails frequented by irregular migrants and asylum-seekers, and shelter them in their homes and churches, they do so with the full knowledge that their actions are illegal. They also act from the conviction that the laws that would forbid them from helping and sheltering persons seeking refuge from political violence in their homeland are wrong. They strive to change the law in the long term, but also to protect vulnerable migrants in their moment of need. Some citizens and officials may view these offenders as dangerous criminals because they are deviant in ways that undermine the optimal functioning of their social order. This form of civil disobedience can point to errors in conventional moral norms and existing legal rules, where the problem is not with the so-called offender, but with the society and regime that would seek to punish them. It would be disadvantageous for social progress, and belittling to potential conscientious dissenters, to treat conscientious persons who break the law as persons in need of treatment and rehabilitation. The public health-quarantine model may unwittingly provide defenders of unjust social conventions with tools to diminish the force and undercut the agency of conscientious objectors. This would undercut the social justice concerns of public health quarantine model advocates who are troubled by overcriminalization and who seek alternatives to punishment.

Leaving aside total free-will skepticism, the public health-quarantine model still helps us to consider the ways in which systemic causes diminish the agency of some offenders and make them less able to abide by social norms and legal rules. It points the way to policy solutions that emphasize social responsibility to protect, treat, and rehabilitate persons that are vulnerable to offending for reasons they cannot control. First, we need to take *mens rea* or the capacity to act with a guilty mind more seriously when finding blame and assigning responsibility (Serota 2020). This means recognizing the many behavioral issues that offenders are afflicted with, which are no more worthy of moral condemnation than physical sickness. In some cases, public policy failures are the cause of physical and mental health ailments that increase a person's propensity to offend. The now well-recognized link between lead exposure during childhood and higher crime rates in exposed adults is just one example where systemic health factors mitigate individual responsibility for deviant behavior (Martin and Wolfe 2020, 17–19). This example also points to the culpability of elites for decisions that are socially irresponsible and undermine public health, such as the officials responsible for Flint, Michigan's toxic water supply (Hughes 2021, 1222). More importantly, in terms of helping those "born innocent" of the biosocial risk factors that lead to offending after the harm has already been done, children-at-risk need the benefit of remediation throughout life, including targeted rehabilitation if they commit crimes later in life, rather than retributive punishment (Choy 2021, 225). Policymakers cannot hide behind personal responsibility tropes that place all of the blame on the offender. They must accept responsibility for the structural causes of crime.

The public health-quarantine model's focus on diagnosing and preventing behavioral health ailments from manifesting themselves in criminal behavior could help to protect society from crime without harming offenders. Here, psychiatrists and social workers have an important role to play in preventing crime and recidivism where offenders are suffering from mental health disorders that lessen their ability to abide by social and legal norms. This is part of the impulse underlying calls to replace police crisis responses with mental health intervention teams. Criminal behavior can also result from formative social determinants. Some of these deep-seated contextual elements include socioeconomic and educational inequities and family of origin challenges (including parental incarceration). Here, early intervention by educators and social workers has a place in preventing crime. Finally, criminal behavior results from public policy failures to address current systemic challenges that precipitate offenses, including "mental illness, homelessness, poor environmental health, addiction," and for immigrants, dangerous conditions in their country of origin (Caruso and Pereboom 2021, 361). In short, in a society that emphasizes an ideology of "personal responsibility" and blame, the principal contribution of the public health-quarantine model is to call attention to the social determinants of crime. Like those who are physically ill, society has a responsibility to help those who are at risk of offending, to treat their behavioral illnesses, and to rehabilitate them into productive social roles.

Immigration Detention and Deportation

One goal of punishment is the rehabilitation and reintegration of offenders into society. Often states prefer to remove deportable noncitizens rather than incurring the costs of reintegration, denying that noncitizen offenders are prospective contributing members of society. To this end, countries including the United Kingdom and the United States withhold rehabilitative social services in prison and in the community from noncitizen offenders (Aliverti 2017; Bosworth 2019). The United States has prisons specifically designated for incarcerated noncitizens, where immigrant prisoners are denied rehabilitative programs like drug treatment, job training, and counselling (Kaufman 2019, 1383). They are exempt from U.S. Bureau of Prisons guidelines that prisoners should be held "within 500 miles of the location where they have the most community and/or family support," making it more difficult for their U.S. family members to visit and maintain ties with them (1414). Unlike citizens who commit crimes, noncitizens who have served their sentence for their criminal offense are not released on parole. Instead, they are transferred to the custody of immigration enforcement officials, who hold them pending their deportation. While this measure is treated as an administrative sanction rather than a punishment, this is merely a definitional sleight of hand.

24   BORN INNOCENT

In the U.S. context, Sarah Song (2018) reminds us that deportation practice is governed by a precedent set in the context of anti-Asian animus of the 1890s. At that time, the Supreme Court ruled that "deportation is not punishment for a crime," and so constitutional protections against cruel and unusual punishments, among other safeguards, did not apply (*Fong Yue Ting v. United States* 1893, 730; Song 2018, 23). Even amidst the virulent anti-Chinese sentiment of their time, in three vigorous dissents, Justices Brewer, Field, and Fuller called this theory into question. They condemned the majority's decision as an unjust punishment akin to the most egregious acts of ethnic and racial hatred. Justice Brewer called the majority of the Court out for their racism, permitting "whole classes in our midst" to be "driven from our territory" for no crime but that of their race and nationality (*Fong Yue Ting* 1893, 738). Field compared the government's removal of Chinese immigrants to acts of despotic European regimes, including the brutality of the Spanish Inquisition, the expulsion of Protestants by France's absolutist monarch Louis XIV, and the removal of the Jewish people by the Russian Tsar in his own time (*Fong Yue Ting* 1893, 757). For Song, *Fong Yue Ting* and the other Chinese Exclusion Cases of the same period established that "preservation of a white national identity is offered up as a legitimate ground for exclusion" (Song 2018, 25). And yet despite marked advances in civil rights protections for minorities in U.S. constitutional law in the ensuing period, *Fong Yue Ting* and the doctrine that deportation is not a punishment remains with us. This precedent serves as a reminder of the ongoing disfavored status of noncitizens in U.S. immigration and nationality law, and the racial animus underlying the illusion that deportation is not a punishment meriting the full gamut of constitutional protections for the accused.

If immigration enforcement agencies are detaining and deporting noncitizen offenders because they have committed an offence, they are in effect suffering more punishment than citizen offenders for the same crime. This raises the prospect of double jeopardy, and disproportionate punishments for noncitizens relative to their crimes (Bauböck and Paskalev 2015, 17; Duff 2018, 125–126). Here, states are in effect applying a separate criminal law for noncitizens that follows the same logic as the *feindstrafrecht* or criminal law for enemies of the state proposed by German legal scholar Gunther Jakobs (Zedner 2013, 50). Jakobs's "criminal law for enemies" dispenses with due process protections for noncitizens the state classifies as security threats, as if we are at war with them (Rosenberg Rubins 2022, 274).

Most jurisdictions, including Canada and the United States, classify immigration inadmissibility, detention, and deportation as administrative measures, which are not punitive (Campesi 2020, 528). Legislation and U.S. Supreme Court rulings characterize immigration detention in the United States as civil, rather than criminal custody designed to facilitate the removal of individuals without permission to remain in the country (Ryo 2019). Officially, immigration detention centers are "places to quarantine individuals who are awaiting a legal process that will determine if they are imprisoned, deported, or released" (Lopez 2019, 110).[3] One way to respond to this characterization of immigration detention is to demand that officials treat immigration detainees like other persons confined to serve a nonpunitive public order purpose, akin to quarantined patients (Ashworth and Zedner 2014, 263). Following this line of reasoning, if a state is serious about its claim that immigration detainees are not being punished, they should be treated like quarantine patients. This means only detaining them when no other alternative exists, and minimizing the hardship of their detention (Ashworth and Zedner 2019, 441). To this end, detention facilities should be as comfortable as possible, with open visitation, and the state should compensate detainees for their foregone liberty (ibid.). Following the quarantine analogy, following the least restrictive appropriate alternative, states should offer community-based alternatives to immigration detention. Ashworth and Zedner's analogy between quarantines and immigration enforcement measures is conceptually interesting, as it forces us to think of what a civil immigration detention regime might look like if states were serious about their claim that immigration enforcement measures are not punitive.

In reality, states treat actions that lead to immigration detention and deportation as crimes. Most states regard persons who enter a country without authorization, even to seek a claim to asylum recognized under international law, as intentional violators of the law who are guilty of a crime that can lead to an arrest and prison time. Hence, criminologists, legal philosophers, and human rights tribunals increasingly regard the "nonpunitive" classification of immigration detention and deportation as a slight of hand that subverts the criminal process and its human rights protections (Zedner 2015, 4, 10; Benslimane and Moffette 2019, 52; Lopez 2019, 110). A person detained for an immigration offense experiences his detention as a weighty sanction. Yet when officials characterize his detention as an administrative procedure, he does not have recourse to safeguards against cruel and unusual punishment and other criminal procedure protections. Parsing out the ways in which immigration detention is functionally similar to criminal punishment is not a matter of semantics. Scholars working at the intersection of criminal and immigration law hope that by drawing attention to the punitive characteristics of immigration confinement, they will be able to move toward an immigration law enforcement regime in which confinement is the exception (García Hernández 2014, 1350–1351).

Some communitarian political theorists still accept and try to defend existing immigration regulation practices as a nonideal but unavoidable feature of living in political society in a world of sovereign nation-states, albeit with limitations that differentiate them from restrictionist policymakers. To this end, Philip Pettit accepts the status quo position that while the "state can and should allow you emigration, it cannot give you or anyone else the right to live in one state rather than another" (Pettit 2012a, 75). Pettit further justifies immigration enforcement, claiming that "no state can open its borders to nonresidents in general, on pain of internal malfunction and collapse" (Pettit 2012b, 161). This view may have been justified as a temporary matter during a national public health emergency, as when Australia barred most noncitizens from entering from March 2020 to November 2021 to control the spread of COVID-19 (Hunt 2022; Sullivan 2022c). But as part of a theory of nondomination, Pettit's view falls short by not accounting for the extreme coercion that noncitizens face when they cannot flee and enter another country. Receiving states have a strong moral obligation to take in migrants, particularly asylum-seekers fleeing violence and persecution in their homelands.

David Miller questions this alleged "right to control borders" to "see whether this practice is justified or not, and on what conditions" (Miller 2016, 58). Ordinarily, Miller does not see border control as being necessarily coercive, but rather preventative, "removing one option from the existing set," leaving "many others available to be selected" (74). That said, Miller accepts that there are some migrants, whom he calls "particularity claimants," with a special moral right to enter a particular state given what that country has done to their people in the past, or because they performed some service for that state (77, 113). This applies to countries that are "at least in part responsible for making her into a refugee" by their intervention in the migrants' country of origin (90). Miller believes that if states enter into relationships with migrants by accepting their services or harming their interests this limits their moral right to exclude them, a position that tracks my own standpoint on earned legalization and citizenship (Sullivan 2019, 17–18). This position differentiates Miller from the views of policymakers like his own country's Home Secretary, Priti Patel, who developed a strategy to deport asylum-seekers to Rwanda to deter future entries and prevent migrants from seeking protection in the United Kingdom at the government's expense (Patel 2022). Patel's policy is not being applied to refugees arriving in the United Kingdom from Russia's invasion of Ukraine, which raises concerns about the U.K. government's racial prejudice against non-European asylum-seekers (Yousaf 2022). Patti Tamara Lenard goes a step further to question existing immigration enforcement practices. She reminds communitarians like Pettit and Miller who believe that "states have at least some right to control their borders" that they cannot "do anything they like to enforce the policies they adopt to control admission to territory and membership" (Lenard 2021, 241).

Here, I argue that the U.S. policy of family separation at the southern border is a key example of a violation of a minimum standard of justice that states should observe in their enforcement policies, even during emergencies like a pandemic. These and other immigration detention and deportation practices that use family separation as instruments of deterrence are serious problems for a theory of freedom as nondomination as coercive exercises of state power. They deprive individuals of their liberty and separate them from their families and communities without the due process rights accorded to persons in the ordinary criminal justice system. This also results in significant hardship for the dependents of detainees. Noncitizen prisons and detention facilities deny offenders access to resources aimed at rehabilitating prisoners to function as caregivers and contributing members of their societies (Kaufman 2019, 1383; Brouwer 2020; Rosenberg Rubins 2022, 276). Unauthorized entry (or re-entry) into a country is punished as a crime with an incapacitory, deterrent, and expressive function, signaling the state's disapproval of the individual's presence. Law enforcement officials arrest immigrants in their homes and workplaces and place them in custody, sometimes alongside violent offenders, all without the right to legal counsel. Deportation permanently removes immigrants from their communities, separating them from family members without the legal right to join them abroad, and leaving them in a country where they have limited ties or the ability to secure a livelihood.

The Meaning of Punishment in U.S. Immigration and Citizenship Jurisprudence

One way to determine the legitimacy of a punishment is to examine the purposes that it is supposed to serve for society. From a utilitarian perspective, the threat of punishment is justified because it promotes ongoing cooperation and reciprocity between members of society (Chiao 2019, viii). Deterrent views of punishment assume in theory that offenders are rational, willing, and able to consider the costs of their actions (Hallevy 2013, 25). Punishment may serve an expressive function if it indicates the state's perspective about the severity of the offense. The problem is that this view may be unstable, and not equally shared by a wide cross section of citizens (Hallevy 2013, 9). For instance, most U.S. residents favor the legalization of marijuana and disapprove of existing penalties in U.S. federal law for mere possession (Van Green 2021). Cruel punishments do not serve the expressive function of addressing the offender as a member of the moral community that needs to be corrected (Laufer and Hughes 2021, 196–197).

The severity and illegitimacy of nonconsensual denationalization as a baseline status-related punishment has long been widely shared by theorists and legal commentators. They point to the irrevocable role of denationalization in depriving individuals of any basis for claiming other rights, particularly when that person has no other country of citizenship (Bauböck and Paskalev 2015, 16; Cohen 2016). Cesare Beccaria, in his influential reformist treatise *On Crimes and Punishment* ([1764] 1995), warned of the particular severity of banishment, as "death and banishment are identical in the eyes of the body politic" (Beccaria [1764] 1995, 58). Understanding that banishment could carry unjust collateral consequences, Beccaria insisted that its effects be limited to the guilty party. Any related confiscations imposed on dependents "make the innocent suffer the punishment of the guilty, and they force on the innocent the desperate necessity of committing crimes" (ibid.). Families, in particular, should be shielded from the effects of the "disgrace and destitution by the crimes of its head" (59). This warning about intergenerational collateral consequences of nonconsensual citizenship deprivations remains pertinent today, amidst the denial of citizenship to innocent children born of involuntarily denationalized parents languishing stateless and abandoned in refugee camps (Doherty 2020).

In the United States, the Supreme Court has consistently maintained since the mid-twentieth century that the nonconsensual denationalization of citizens is a particularly cruel and unusual punishment. In *Trop v. Dulles*

(356 U.S. 86, 1957), Chief Justice Earl Warren wrote for the majority that nonconsensual denationalization is barred by the Eighth Amendment to the U.S. Constitution, because:

> There is instead—the total destruction—of the individual's status in organized society. It is a form of punishment more primitive than torture, for it destroys for the individual the political existence that was centuries in the development. The punishment strips the citizen of his status in the national and international political community. His very existence is at the sufferance of the country in which he happens to find himself. (ibid., 101)

In a related case centered on the constitutionality of denationalization as a punishment, the majority of the Court noted that "banishment and exile have throughout history been . . . adjudged a harsh punishment even by men who were accustomed to brutality in the administration of criminal justice" (*Kennedy v. Mendoza-Martinez* 1963, 168).[4] From the starting point that banishment as involuntary denationalization constitutes a paradigmatic example of a punitive sanction, the Supreme Court in *Kennedy v. Mendoza-Martinez* employed a seven-factor test that remains authoritative in determining whether a sanction constitutes a punishment requiring constitutional due process protections. The first two factors focus on the sanction itself, asking if the action has a penal effect, and if it is the type of action that has historically been used as a punishment, namely, "retribution and deterrence." The other factors focus on the government's intention in applying the sanction. The test asks whether the action involves a finding of guilt; applies to behavior that "is already a crime"; is rationally connected to "an alternative purpose" other than punishment; and "appears excessive in relation to the alternative purpose assigned" (*Kennedy v. Mendoza-Martinez*, 372 U.S. 144, 168–169 [1963]). This test is still in place, although U.S. courts rarely use this measure to override a legislature's characterization of a sanction as nonpunitive, leaving sanctioned individuals without due process protections (Hoskins 2019, 64).

Deportation
Given the U.S. Supreme Court's reasoning for determining that "banishment" understood as a nonconsensual denationalization is a baseline cruel and unusual punishment, we may question why the court refuses to characterize deportation in the same manner. Granted, unlike Warren's

30 BORN INNOCENT

characterization of denationalization, deportation does not strip an individual of a status in the political community that he never enjoyed as a noncitizen. But in other ways, deportation is functionally similar to banishment for noncitizen long-term residents, involving the breach of longstanding community and family ties to one's country of permanent residence. When the state is successful in removing an immigration detainee from his country of long-term residence, the practice of deportation functionally resembles exile, which has a long history of usage as a particularly harsh punishment sundering the individual from all of his connections (Walters 2002). When noncitizen permanent residents face deportation subsequent to incarceration, deportation is a form of double jeopardy, or a punishment added to a criminal sentence when law enforcement transfers an ex-offender into immigration custody following the completion of his sentence. For the noncitizen ex-offender, deportation for post-entry criminal conduct serves several of the functions of punishment, including incapacitation, deterrence, and retribution (Kanstroom 2000, 1894). Transferring a noncitizen who served his sentence from prison to immigration detention to await deportation has an additional penal effect, by restricting an ex-offender's liberty beyond his original sentence without an additional finding of guilt for a new offense (Stinneford 2020, 11). Deportation's impact on the sanctioned individual is experienced as a deprivation of the offender's freedom that is at least as severe as incarceration, separating a deportee from his family, community, and other social connections.

Even so, the courts are reluctant to review the legislature's understanding of the sanction as part of its ostensible plenary power to regulate immigration, with minimal judicial interference. Hence, in a 1984 case, the Supreme Court referred to a "deportation proceeding" as "a purely civil action to determine eligibility to remain in this country, not to punish an unlawful entry, though entering or remaining unlawfully in this country is itself a crime." Here, the majority of the Court allowed the legislature to have it both ways: to categorize the offense as a crime, but a crime not meriting due process protections for the defendant who is sanctioned (*INS v. Lopez-Mendoza* 1984, 1038). The Court later expressed a willingness to reconsider its characterization of deportation in a 2011 case that more closely resembled the fact pattern of citizen banishment that gave rise to the *Kennedy v. Martinez-Mendoza* test. In *Padilla v. Kentucky* (2011), the U.S. Supreme Court ruled that the deportation of a lifelong permanent resident is "an integral part—indeed, sometimes the most important part—of the penalty that may be imposed on noncitizen

A BROADER VIEW OF PUNISHMENT   31

defendants who plead guilty to specified crimes," as has been the case for nearly a century (*Padilla v. Kentucky* 2011, 1481). Here, the U.S. Supreme Court ruled that criminal procedural protections should apply in at least some deportation cases.

Immigration Detention and Family Separation

The "civil" detention of immigrant families by the U.S. government has legal and ideological precedents in other forms of family detention including Indigenous removal campaigns in the nineteenth century and Japanese internment in the twentieth century (Jordán Wallace and Zepeda-Millán 2020, 30). Since the beginning of immigration enforcement in the late nineteenth century, Chinese Americans have been held apart from their families for extended periods. The family ties of alleged "paper sons" of U.S.-born citizens and legal immigrants were subject to extended scrutiny. After the extension of immigration enforcement at the border and the interior to a wider range of groups in the 1920s, undocumented immigrants and asylum-seekers became more vulnerable to family separation (Briggs 2020, 132). In mixed-citizenship families in the United States, undocumented immigrant parents are faced with a Hobson's choice if they are deported. They must either take their citizen-child away from his community to live with them in a place where they have few ties, or leave the child with relatives or in foster care, and separate the family (*Acosta v. Gaffney* 1997; *Oforji v. Ashcroft* 2003; Sullivan 2019, 119–131). At the height of the Trump administration's "zero-tolerance" policy toward asylum-seekers in Spring 2018, asylum-seeking families did not even have this choice.

The foundation for the Obama and Trump administrations' large-scale deterrence-based family detention policies was set by previous administrations beginning with the Carter administration's response to an influx of Haitian and Cuban migrants. Later presidential administrations across party lines including Reagan, Bush Sr., Clinton, and Bush Jr. expanded mandatory detention facilities in an attempt to deter asylum-seekers by detaining everyone, including unaccompanied children and families (Jordán Wallace and Zepeda-Millán 2020, 31–34). When the first caravans of asylum-seekers arrived at the U.S.–Mexico border in 2014, Jeh Johnson, Secretary of Homeland Security during the Obama administration, characterized enforcement actions directed at migrant families as deterrent measures. He sent a message to future migrants "that our border is not open to illegal migration, and if you come here, you should not expect to simply be released"

32 BORN INNOCENT

or otherwise permitted to remain (Preston 2014). This deterrent message was reinforced through a media campaign in migrant-sending countries warning of the dangers of the journey (Hamlin 2021, 141). By December 2014, the Department of Homeland Security implemented a policy of "general deterrence," keeping families in detention to discourage new asylum-seekers from coming to the United States (*R.I. L-R v. Jeh Johnson* et al. 2015, 1–2, 10; Schrag 2020, 148–149). This Obama-era policy of deterrence through family detention constituted a violation of the U.S. government's legal obligation to allow migrants to make a claim for asylum in the United States (*R.I. L-R v. Jeh Johnson* 2015, 33). The United States District Court for the District of Columbia ruled that since the government claimed that the detainees were being held in civil rather than criminal confinement, a position which allows them fewer procedural protections, their detention could not become "a mechanism for retribution or general deterrence" (*R.I. L-R v. Jeh Johnson* 2015, 35). To avoid granting asylum-seekers procedural protections, the government claimed it was not punishing them. But their detention conditions and the government's justification for detaining them served deterrent, incapacitory, and retributive functions of punishment. Under the Obama administration's post-2014 deterrence-based detention policy, detained asylum-seeking families were already enduring stealth functional punishments (Schrag 2020, 147–150, 163).

The Trump administration amplified the Obama administration's earlier deterrent messaged directed at prospective asylum-seekers, to the point of intentionally separating families to deter parents from coming with their children to enter without prior authorization to seek asylum in the United States (Trump 2018; Johnson 2019; Dickerson 2020). On May 7, 2018, during a speech in San Diego, California, then Attorney General Jeff Sessions announced that he "put in place a zero tolerance policy for illegal entry on our Southwest border. If you cross the border unlawfully, then we will prosecute you. It's that simple. If you are smuggling a child, then we will prosecute you and that child will be separated from you as required by law" (Sessions 2018). Four days later, in a conference call to U.S. attorneys, Sessions stated, "we need to take away children" for the deterrent element of asylum-seeking prevention policy to work (Office of the Inspector General 2021, 39). This policy statement was a marked departure from previous practice, in which immigration officials provided the family unit adult with a Notice to Appear, and then released the family to remain in the United States until their date in immigration court (6). Both the proponents and opponents of the administration's family separation policy understood it as a form of punishment aimed at deterring and penalizing parents for entering the United States to seek asylum (Policy Options 2017, 1; Office of the Inspector General 2021, 20, 23, 54). Immigration enforcement officials separated over 3,000 children from their parents under the Trump administration's zero-tolerance policy in May and June 2018 (Office of the Inspector General 2021, 2). Medical researchers have documented significant psychological and physical harm to the children that immigration officials separated from their parents and placed in Office of Refugee Resettlement facilities without their caregivers (Matlow and Reicherter 2019, 5). Some children remained separated from their families three and a half years later, under a new presidential administration that is committed to reversing this policy (DHS 2022b).

Immigration detentions and family separations of asylum-seekers on the U.S. border are expressly justified by the federal government as deterrent measures. The mental distress of family separation is a painful consequence that U.S. authorities communicate to prospective migrants in their home countries to deter them from leaving (Johnson 2019; Baylis 2022). By itself, the *Kennedy v. Mendoza-Martinez* test should be enough to categorize the detention of asylum-seekers as serving a penal function that merits greater criminal procedure protections. Beyond a test that defers to legislative intent, courts should employ a functional definition of punishment to ensure that immigration detainees and those facing deportation are accorded criminal process protections. In legal theory, punishment ordinarily serves the following functions: incapacitation, deterrence, rehabilitation, and retribution. In the absence of additional offenses, immigration enforcement is not primarily retributive or backward-looking, but forward-looking. Immigration enforcement's place in penal theory also must reflect the practice on the ground, rather than the law on the books, which does not mandate the detention of unauthorized immigrants pending a hearing (Gerson 2022, 1225). The intent of U.S. immigration detention is to incapacitate those who may constitute a flight risk to facilitate their removal from the United States, and to deter future offenders by sending a message that unauthorized entry and residence will result in family separation, detention, and removal (Gerson 2022, 1225, 1239–1240; Stumpf 2020a, 1066–1067).

Immigration detention is functionally similar in some ways to criminal punishment and its collateral consequences. Civilly detained immigration law violators and criminally incarcerated inmates are held in functionally similar conditions, and sometimes in the same facilities (Schriro 2010, 1442;

34 BORN INNOCENT

Bensadoun 2019; Brownlee 2020, 183). In Canada, immigration detainees are being detained in provincial prisons, and held alongside violent offenders in crowded conditions where COVID-19 outbreaks have taken place during a global pandemic (Arbel and Joeck 2021, 5).[5] Similarly, in the United States, immigration detainees are held in crowded facilities where the COVID-19 case rate was an average of 13.4 times the overall U.S. infection case rate during the initial wave of the pandemic from April to August 2020 (Erfani et al. 2021). Two years into the pandemic in 2022, physicians working in U.S. Department of Homeland Security facilities blamed an outbreak of the Omicron variant among immigration detainees on the lack of availability of booster shots and other treatment options for persons in custody (Allen and Rich 2022; Sacchetti 2022). Their initial infections and subsequent risks of developing long COVID symptoms constitute a debilitating collateral consequence of their detention. Prisons have a long history of infectious disease outbreaks that spread outside the institution to the broader community (Hooks and Libal 2020, 6).

U.S. Immigration and Customs Enforcement and its private prison contractors frequently hold immigration detainees in remote conditions without the ability to contact their family or counsel (Sullivan and Enriquez 2016). Like incarcerated criminal offenders, immigration detainees face a permanent loss of custodial rights over their children under the provisions of the U.S. Adoption and Safe Families Act (*In Re Interest of Angelica L.* 2009; *In Re the Adoption of C.M.B.R., A Minor* 2011; Sullivan and Enriquez 2016, 56; Amrami and Javier 2020, 258–261). Under the terms of the Adoption and Safe Families Act, the convergence of immigration detention for parents and foster care means losing custody of their children permanently, which is experienced by many parents as the most severe punishment that the state can inflict upon them. Even when custody is not at issue, dependents and other family members of immigration detainees experience collateral consequences of punishment arising from systemic institutional barriers to visitation (Patler and Branic 2017, 33).

In some ways, immigration detention is even harsher than short-term criminal punishment. First, immigration detention has no positive or rehabilitative function. Rehabilitation, reintegration, and restorative justice are all positive objectives of criminal punishment for those convicted of ordinary crimes who serve a community sentence or incarceration with a fixed release date. At its best, punishment with a restorative element offers offenders the opportunity to repair the conflict with society arising from their violation of the law rather than excluding them permanently (Duff 2003, 90). Understood this way, criminal punishment serves as a means of moral education that invites offenders to repent and change, with a pathway to restored citizenship as a reward upon their release (Duff 2003, 175). To promote rehabilitation, correctional officials can help maintain family ties through visitation as a positive factor that facilitates rehabilitation, re-entry, and reduced rates of recidivism (Brunton-Smith and McCarthy 2017, 464–466). Immigration detention operators do not have this incentive to promote reintegration when they are simply holding an offender for removal from the country (Bosworth, Franko, and Pickering 2018, 43; Brouwer 2020, 707). Second, immigration detainees can be held without representation. Third, immigration detention may be indefinite, resulting not from the severity of the detainee's immigration violation, but factors over which he has no control, including his country of origin's willingness to repatriate him. Finally, immigration detainees cannot look forward to rejoining society at the end of their sentence like criminal offenders, since the objective of their detention is their removal from the country, without the opportunity to return in the future. Most offenders are still regarded as potential contributing citizens whose roles and relationships in the outside world ought to be nurtured, to afford them "meaningful opportunities both to try to contribute and to learn from others how to contribute" (Brownlee 2020, 192). With that in mind, the state invests in rehabilitation and educational services denied to noncitizen offenders who face deportation after their sentence is completed. In this way, immigration detention and deportation are akin to the worst aspects of criminal punishment. It merely subjects them to the state's oppressive power and reinforces their exclusion from society, without the possibility of redemption there (Duff 2003, 33).

Canada: Humanitarian Aspirations and Punitive Realities

Canada has a humanitarian reputation as a country that is more tolerant and accepting of irregular migrants seeking refuge abroad than the United States, buoyed recently by its acceptance of tens of thousands of Syrian refugees in 2015 and 2016 (Okafor 2020, 241–244; Fleming 2020, 26). This reputation stands in contrast to Canada's treatment of asylum-seekers, who have been subject to similar deterrent and incapacitory measures as their counterparts in the United States, including prolonged detention and family separation. As in the United States, Canadian officials do not view deportation as a punishment that gives rise to criminal process protections. Only ten years after

36 BORN INNOCENT

Canada's Charter of Rights and Freedoms came into force, the Supreme Court of Canada rejected the application of Section 12 of the Charter of Rights and Freedoms barring cruel and unusual punishment to deportation cases, holding that "deportation is not imposed as a punishment" (*Chiarelli v. Canada* 1992, 735). Despite the administrative convenience involved in not classifying deportation as a punishment, inadmissibility rulings, detention, and deportation serve some of the same formal goals and purposes as punishment in legal theory, including incapacitation and deterrence (Hudson 2018, 41–42).

As in the United States, the Canadian government uses family separation to deter irregular migration and human smuggling. Under the Designated Foreign National (DFN) designation, children under age sixteen are forced to "choose" detention or removal from their parents into state custody (Kenney 2012; Arbel 2015, 200–201; Kronick and Rousseau 2015, 18–20; Gros and Song 2016, 10; Houle and MacAllister 2022, 185, 194). In this case, children, including Canadian citizens, suffer punishment drift aimed at placing pressure on immigration detainees to self-deport to their country of citizenship, even if their children may not be citizens there (Gros 2017). While the current Liberal government has pledged to "stop detaining or housing minors and family separation" procedures initiated by its predecessor, the practice continues to be widespread, particularly among migrants detained after crossing the U.S.–Canada border (Canada Council for Refugees 2019). In fiscal year 2019–2020, a total of 138 children spent time in detention, including 73 children under six years of age, which represented a 17 percent increase over the previous year (Human Rights Watch 2021, 16, 73). The U.N. Office of the High Commissioner on Human Rights and the U.N. Committee on the Elimination of Racial Discrimination condemn Canada's continued detention of children in immigration holding facilities (Amir 2019; Human Rights Watch 2021, 77–78). Both bodies are asking Canada to develop alternatives to detention for families awaiting immigration appeals decisions.

Canadian immigration enforcement practices governing the detention and family separation of asylum-seekers are still defined by the former Conservative government and the Canada Border Services Agency's (CBSA) response to the arrival of two ships: the *Ocean Lady* and the *Sun Sea*, carrying asylum-seekers in 2009 and 2010.[6] First, in anticipation of the arrival of the Sun Sea vessel carrying asylum-seekers from Sri Lanka, the CBSA outlined a strategy centered on "proposing a more aggressive approach to create a deterrent to future arrivals," through detention, inadmissibility proceedings, prosecutions, and challenging all claims to refugee status regardless of merit (Hill 2010). Then, in subsequent legislative debate in 2012 on provisions governing the detention of asylees, the Conservative Minister of Public Safety, Vic Towes, proposed separating innocent children from their "guilty" parents by placing them in foster care (Towes 2012). In doing so, he recognized the principle that "children should not bear the responsibility of crimes that their parents may have committed . . . but they are obviously under the care and control of their parents" (Towes 2012). In the same hearing, another Conservative Member of Parliament attested to the deterrent force of the measure, placing it squarely within a recognized function of state punishment. Detention and family separation was cast as "a parental decision to be made by them, and it is part of their parental responsibility when they decide to get on a boat and bring their children over. That is going to be clearly outlined so that parents know before they get on the boat that these are their choices" (Smith 2012). The problems with this deterrence through family separation policy is first, it is not a crime for anyone to seek asylum in Canada, and second, removing children from the care of their parents is an extreme hardship for young children, and an act with punitive effect for the parents.

Older children and adults suspected by the Minister of Public Safety of entering Canada as human smuggling victims have been detained without a right to an appeal (Atak 2019, 466–467; Labman 2019, 51). The stated aim of the program was to deter human smuggling, even though asylum-seekers, and children in particular, are generally viewed under U.N. refugee and children's rights conventions as victims (Atak 2019, 475). The DFN designation and its role in immigrant family separation has caused the U.N. Committee on the Rights of the Child to question Canada's commitment to its international obligations as a United Nations Convention on the Rights of the Child (UNCRC) signatory, citing the UNCRC's commitment to family unity, the scale of detention, and the psychological impact on the children who "choose" detention.[7] The DFN designation is an example of vicarious punishment that harms innocent parties, including children, as a way to deter families from seeking asylum in Canada.

A state and its immigration enforcement authorities cannot always remove every noncitizen they want to deport. If the state cannot establish the identity of the migrant, it cannot secure identity papers and permission from another state to receive a deportee. In this case, Canadian officials have

38 BORN INNOCENT

subjected noncitizens to indefinite detention. This measure is difficult to distinguish from punishment as incapacitation and deterrence, whereby the state is incarcerating a migrant alongside other prisoners for what it regards as intentional guilty acts: noncooperation and resistance (Anstis and Joeck 2020, 58). Some noncitizens cannot be deported because their country of presumed citizenship will not receive them back, due to a lack of a repatriation agreement between the two countries, or an unwillingness by a state to acknowledge that a particular individual is a citizen of that country. The U.S. Supreme Court in *Zadvydas v. Davis* (2001) ruled that the indefinite detention of noncitizens whom the state cannot deport due to the noncooperation of a foreign state is unconstitutional under the Fifth Amendment's due process clause, absent a determination that the noncitizen constituted a flight risk or a danger to society (690–691). As a result, noncitizens who are stateless or citizens of a country with whom the United States does not have removal arrangements are allowed to remain indefinitely under orders of supervision until such time as a country is found that will take them back, if ever (Kerwin et al. 2020, 193). In Canada, the Supreme Court considered the U.S. Zadvydas decision but ultimately rejected its reasoning in *Charkaoui v. Canada* (2007). The Canadian decision justified indefinite detention regime and rendition to torture if a country was willing to accept a detained noncitizen for removal.[8] The Supreme Court considered the Charter rights of the detainees against arbitrary detention and cruel and unusual treatment as questions of fundamental justice, but ultimately dismissed the challenge insofar as detainees have "regular opportunities for review of detention" (*Charkaoui v. Canada* 2007, ¶110). In this sense, then, the United States has gone further than Canada to guarantee due process civil rights for immigration detainees who cannot readily be deported, to preserve the pretense that the proceedings are "nonpunitive in purpose and effect" (*Zadvydas v. Davis* 2001, 677).[9] During the Trump administration, the United States maintained its "supervised release" program for noncitizens whom it cannot deport despite calls from President Trump to "provide a legislative fix for the Zadvydas loophole" that would authorize ICE to retain custody of noncitizens "whose home countries will not accept their repatriation" (Trump 2017). Supervised release is still problematic, as it comes with onerous monitoring conditions and leaves nondeportable noncitizen residents "in limbo," without a pathway to legal permanent residence (Kerwin et al. 2020, 193, 200). But even as a nonideal policy, it remains a less restrictive alternative to detention, allowing noncitizens the ability to work and care for their families, while maintaining state interests in locating noncitizens to ensure that they participate in immigration proceedings.[10]

Security Related Detention: Preventive Justice

Preventive justice approaches prioritize risk management over individual civil liberties and the presumption of innocence. Outside of law and philosophy, Philip K. Dick's short story *The Minority Report* (1956), adapted as a movie in 2002, offers a well-known illustration in American popular culture about the dangers of preventive justice approaches when officials prioritize risk management over the presumption of innocence and other individual civil liberties. The story envisages a fanciful dystopia where officials can predict crime and apprehend suspected offenders before they act, and at times, before they even think of the offense. Coupled with the authority to apprehend and incapacitate suspects, officials are seemingly able to prevent most crime before it happens. The story then dramatically reveals the shortcomings of the enterprise, calling into question the accuracy of the predictions, serving as a cautionary tale to dispel the utopian vision of a perfect crime prevention and risk management tool that avoids false positives. Alternately, in times of societal insecurity, areas of attenuated constitutional protections like national borders, and in authoritarian states, officials continue to pursue this vision by applying predictive technological capacities with built-in biases, raising new civil liberties concerns (Barrett 2017, 344–358; Ferguson 2017, 1149–1161; Li 2021).

With respect to the danger of preventive injustices posed by indefinite immigration detention shorn of due process protections, the United States Supreme Court's ruling in *Zadvydas v. Davis* (2001) maintained the pretense that "the proceedings at issue here are civil, not criminal" and "they are nonpunitive in purpose and effect" by setting limits on the preventive detention of immigrants. At the same time, the majority allowed that it might rule differently in cases involving "terrorism or other special circumstance where special arguments might be made for forms of preventive detention and for heightened deference to the judgments of the political branches with respect to matters of national security" (696). Here, I turn my attention to the proliferation of security related detentions that have taken place since the terrorist attacks of September 11, 2001 for what amount to inchoate "thought crimes," where individuals are detained before they act to violate a law simply on

40 BORN INNOCENT

suspicion of their sympathies and associations (Roach 2011, 449; Mendlow 2019, 127). Individuals become suspect for reasons that are very remote from an action or intention to cause harm, including their family ties and identities.

Similar measures pre-date the events of September 11, 2001 in European countries with a long history of anti-state violence and counterinsurgency policing, such as the United Kingdom and France (McCulloch and Pickering 2009, 636). In the United Kingdom, not reporting a family member whom officials suspect of terrorist involvement could lead to prosecution for an association offense, even if the individual is not fully aware of their relative's activities (Terrorism Act 2000, Section 38B; Ashworth 2013, 59–60; Walker 2014, 148). The goal on the part of officials is to prevent crime from happening by shifting enforcement from punishing after the fact to anticipating what has not yet happened and may never occur (Zedner 2007, 262). The pre-crime venture sacrifices the presumption of innocence and the procedural safeguards of the criminal process to *potentially* prevent harm and promote national security. Detaining persons for their sympathies, allegiances, and ties to known terrorists can result in the punishment of individuals for their connections to relatives, caregivers, and others with a more direct link to the criminal activity in question, raising concerns about punishing the innocent. Under the U.K. Prevention of Terrorism Act, citizens and nondeportable immigrants whom the Home Secretary deems to be a threat are being forcibly relocated hundreds of miles from their community, family, and friends. The government requires them to live under a curfew in isolation or internal exile (Ashworth and Zedner 2014, 184–185). For deportable noncitizens, preventive detention is a precursor to removal to places where they may be tortured, contrary to international nonrefoulement laws.

There are four major criticisms of preventive justice. First, it imposes hard treatment for crimes individuals may commit rather than for ones they have committed. Though officials claim pre-crime approaches are prophylactic, rather than punitive, the official act of depriving a person of their liberty for sympathies, allegiances, and affiliations the state condemns fulfills both the expressive and deterrent functions of punishment (McCulloch and Wilson 2015, 21–23).

Second, like immigration detention, it erodes due process and the procedural safeguards attached to criminal process, including the presumption of innocence (Ashworth and Zedner 2014, 13). Pre-crime approaches do not seek to balance an individual's civil liberties and national security, or to determine whether the sanction is proportionate to an individual's responsibility for causing harm. Rather, preventive justice makes the sentence proportional only to the possible risk of harm that a society faces if the sanctioned individual or his associates decide to carry out an offense for which a criminal sanction applies. Pre-crime anti-terrorism measures are designed to preempt threats and prevent possible incidents from occurring from the moment an individual clicks on a questionable website or plans a journey that may lead to travel through a conflict zone, without the need for extensive and costly investigations or the benefit of due process for those targeted (U.K. Government 2018b, 2). For instance, the U.K. Counter-Terrorism and Border Security Act contains provisions prohibiting U.K. citizens from "entering or remaining in an area outside the United Kingdom that has been designated in regulations by the Secretary of State," or viewing terrorist propaganda online (U.K. Government 2019). The stated intent in "introducing the ability to prosecute individuals for travelling to or remaining in a designated area" is to "have a deterrent effect, with individuals less inclined to travel to a designated area," even if their intent has no possible connection to any possible harm to U.K. security interests (U.K. Government 2018b, §44). Both measures are designed to allow for additional prosecutions for activity that may or may not lead to subsequent terrorist activity (U.K. Government 2018b, §44). Similar measures are in place in Australia, with no exceptions for legal, business, and religious purposes unrelated to terrorism, and are under consideration in other European countries (Hofman 2019; Australian Government 2020). The state's goal is simply to minimize risk and increase prosecutions (Gailberger 2020). Both security experts and human rights advocates have criticized declared area offences for stigmatizing, deterring, and punishing humanitarian workers who seek to do development work that might help stabilize and deradicalize the population in conflict zones (McCulloch 2019; Wright 2020; Gailberger 2020). Despite limited exemptions, these pre-crime measures also raise the risk of widening the inquisitorial net to target individuals travelling to affected zones for humanitarian reasons, outside the scope of expressly exempted groups, and having a chilling effect on those engaged in legal aid, and journalistic or academic research (Hofman 2019; De Coensel 2020, 291; Wright 2020). When coupled with the state's power to denationalize suspects, these measures run the risk of granting security officials the capacity to take away a person's citizenship based on a secret risk assessment without due process (Austin 2019). Here, suspicion is enough for coercive action. Evidence, charges, and conviction for an intentional harmful

42   BORN INNOCENT

action are not necessary. On the whole, these pre-crimes expand the scope of the criminal law by satisfying the demands of officials for security that "dictates earlier and earlier intervention to reduce opportunity" (Zedner 2007, 265).

Third, pre-crime offenses undermine both the presumption of innocence and the possibility for positive interventions leading to de-radicalization. One particularly egregious example involves U.K. legislation that allows prosecutors to charge a person for a single click on a terrorist-related site online (Zedner 2021, 69–70). There are broader philosophical reasons for being concerned with pre-crime, or rather, strict liability offenses that anticipate, but will not necessarily lead to an intentionally harmful act. The presumption of innocence entails showing respect due to the moral personality of an agent who has yet to commit a harmful intentional act, and whom we should respect as being capable of choice and not proceeding any further. Leaving aside legitimate exemptions, with pre-crimes there is a window of moral opportunity for the would-be offender to change her mind. One visit to a site associated with terrorism does not constitute a commitment to radicalization. Pre-punishment for a possible harmful act that may occur denies an individual the moral opportunity to choose to veer off a dangerous path (Smilansky 1994, 52; Cole 2009, 696).[11] Law enforcement officials can choose to monitor a person who displays warning signs and to intervene before she acts on her beliefs by placing her on a course toward rehabilitation, rather than incapacitation or other forms of punishment. This means intercepting the person who plans to travel to a conflict zone without an excuse with no prior offense, and mandating participation in counterradicalization courses and initiatives. As it stands, a lengthy prison sentence for a person curious about radicalization in an institution with other radicalized individuals stands the greater risk of hardening the sanctioned individual's anti-state views and undermining the security objectives sought through preventive punishment.

Finally, pre-crime and preventive justice approaches undermine individual responsibility by assigning culpability to individuals based on their group identity, or whom they are associated with and the actions of some of those individuals. In this way, otherwise innocent family members of suspected terrorists are cast into the net of state surveillance and detention for acts they are not responsible for, leaving unassociated family members at risk for social stigma and radicalization (Hill 2017, 27).

One way in which pre-crime approaches undermine individual responsibility for harm in the name of risk prevention is by targeting spouses, children, and other relatives for their family member's suspected ties to an organization associated with criminal or anti-state activity. Ignorance of the family member's activities is not always sufficient as a defense. The fact that the organization may serve a dual purpose, with legal humanitarian and unlawful violent aims, is often irrelevant as a defense. Preventive justice approaches that ascribe guilt by association to uninvolved relatives of suspected gang members, terrorists, or other criminal or anti-state organizations are in tension with principles of individual responsibility that scholars and courts often describe as a central feature of the U.S. constitutional freedom of association (Cole 1999, 206). In the United States, derogations of the principles of individual culpability and the aversion to guilt by association invite heightened judicial scrutiny, which can diminish during periods of national insecurity. Even amidst concerted anti-communist legislative activity, the United States Supreme Court maintained the principle that "in our jurisprudence guilt is personal, and guilt by association alone is unconstitutional" (*Scales v. United States*, 1961, 367 U.S. 225).[12] In a case connected to the U.S. Civil Rights movement, the U.S. Supreme Court unanimously upheld the principle that "guilt by association alone, without [establishing] that an individual's association poses the threat feared by the Government, is an impermissible basis upon which to deny First Amendment rights" (*NAACP v. Claiborne Hardware Co.*, 1982, 458 U.S. 886, 919). However, in the wake of the September 11, 2001 terrorist attacks, and the subsequent enactment of the Patriot Act, a narrow, 5–4 conservative majority of the Supreme Court weakened the bar against guilt by association by upholding the constitutionality of a "material support" ban in the Patriot Act. Citizens who wished to support the "lawful, nonviolent activities" of a group designated by the Attorney General as a foreign terrorist organization were not free to do so under a First Amendment right to association (*Holder v. Humanitarian Law Project*, 2010, 561 U.S. 1).

The Patriot Act goes further to undermine the associational freedoms of noncitizens using immigration law, in which noncitizens have fewer constitutional protections and sanctions are alleged to be nonpunitive. Its provisions attribute guilt by association to noncitizen family members of persons suspected of any ties with a designated terrorist organization by rendering them inadmissible and deportable from the United States.

44 BORN INNOCENT

A second way that preventive justice approaches undermine individual responsibility for harm is by targeting parents and other caregivers for providing financial assistance to children who travel to conflict zones, and/or become affiliated with terrorist organizations. A parent overcome with grief about their teenage son's unwise choices and circumstances may be willing to do anything in an attempt to help him to leave a dangerous situation and to come home. In the eyes of counterterrorism officials, the parent's intent does not serve as an excuse. The case of the Letts family in the United Kingdom is a prominent example where counterterrorism officials targeted parents who attempted to help their child, Jack Letts, to extricate himself from ISIS and leave the conflict zone by providing him with financial support. The parents, Sally Lane and John Letts, were convicted in the United Kingdom in 2019 on a charge of funding terrorism for sending a payment of £233 to a Syrian man in Lebanon at their son's request, after U.K. officials refused to provide them with any assistance with their case (Hopper 2020). Jack Letts, a dual national of the United Kingdom and Canada at birth, was denationalized by the United Kingdom in 2019 and left to languish in a Kurdish prison without any Canadian consular assistance (Blackwell 2021).

The head of the United Kingdom's Special Crime and Counterterrorism Division cast the incident as one whose "lessons are simple: individuals should not travel to fight in war zones and those at home should not send them money," as if there is anything simple about the moral quandary of parents in this situation (U.K. Crown Prosecution Service 2019). In essence, the parents were held to blame, first for their wayward teenage son's unwise choices, and second, for not abandoning him to face torture in Syria. His parents now want him returned to Canada and accept that he should face justice for any alleged crimes he may have committed abroad (Adams 2022). The Letts family's plight became an example and a moral tale to instruct the nation, and the thousands of other parents whose teenagers were lured to conflict zones by ISIS recruiters. If they were not prepared to sacrifice their disloyal children for the good of the nation, they would bear the iniquity of their sons and daughters. The broader community could then attempt to absolve itself of any further responsibility for the structural causes motivating the radicalization of its youth.

A third way that preventive justice approaches undermine individual responsibility for harm is by targeting entire religious and ethnic communities and holding them responsible for the actions of affiliated individuals associated with anti-state groups (Cole 2003, 2; Guru 2012). This is the form of collective punishment and guilt by association exemplified by internment camps operated by liberal democratic countries including Canada, the United States, Australia, and New Zealand during the First and Second World Wars (Palk 2015, 19–20; Sullivan 2018, 329–330). In Northern Ireland, the British government cast much of the Catholic population in Belfast and Derry/Londonderry under surveillance while interning suspects whom it did not have sufficient evidence to convict under ordinary criminal procedures (Diplock 1972, 14, 21, 35; Kennedy-Pipe 2004, 67–68).[13] In each case, officials detained citizens and legal permanent residents without charges, based on their ethnicity, national origin, or community affiliations (Lowry 1976; Bashford and Strange 2002, 517–522; Kordan and Mahovsky 2004; Stibbe 2019). Everyone belonging to a targeted group was subject to preventive detention, regardless of their individual allegiances or actions. The states in question did not acknowledge that internment is punitive (*Korematsu v. United States* 1944, 323 U.S. 214). But internment nonetheless was functionally punitive, as it served the incapacitory, deterrent, retributive, and expressive functions of a penal sanction (Lowry 1976, 261–262). Those who were confined experienced internment as a nonjudicial punishment inflicted upon them for their group membership by a state that viewed them collectively as a political and security threat (Stibbe 2019, 7). While the same states later expressed remorse for interning their citizens, they continue to subject persons to ongoing profiling, surveillance, and guilt by association for both the alleged and actual crimes of those who happen to share their faith, ethnicity, or national origin.

In the twenty-first century, officials in liberal democratic countries regularly engage in religious profiling by singling out Muslim citizens for monitoring in their houses of worship and other facets of their associational life for the crimes of a few of their co-religionists (CLEAR 2013, 12–15; Sentas 2014, 205–208; McCulloch and Wilson 2015, 125–126; Cherney and Murphy 2016). The issue is not with community policing and asking Muslim citizens and religious leaders to be vigilant with respect to threats to the broader community, which many imams and other community leaders are willing to do to combat radicalization and help vulnerable youth to make positive choices (Jiménez 2006). Rather, civil rights attorneys and Muslim community representatives are concerned that informants are entrapping vulnerable young people by persuading them to plan terrorist acts that they would have not otherwise countenanced. The result is the arrest and conviction of persons with no independent inclination or capacity to harm others

46 BORN INNOCENT

(Norris 2019). Allegations of entrapment undermine the trust of community leaders that would otherwise be valuable assets for ascertaining risk and detecting and reporting active threats (Aziz 2014, 196–202).

In summary, preventive measures including immigration detention, and pre-crime anti-terrorism detentions are punishments in the sense that they serve the socially coercive functions associated with punishment in legal theory, including deterrence and incapacitation. They do so without regard for the positive, transformational benefits of punishment for the individual that come with rehabilitation and reintegration into society. Immigration detention does not include any rehabilitative features that will help to prepare a detainee for a life of contributory citizenship in any country. Pre-crime approaches aim to convict and imprison potential offenders rather than steering persons with anti-state inclinations away from radical ideology and rehabilitating them in the community. Their intent is to remove a person from society. The same is true of indefinite preventive detention orders that do not provide offenders with the chance to demonstrate their rehabilitation to earn the right to reintegrate into society as an equal citizen.

Conclusion

In this chapter, by considering what punishment consists of in terms of the purposes and functions of punishment, I uncovered stealth punishments disguised as administrative sanctions, including immigration detention, deportation, and security related offenses. Across national borders, there is a trend toward the criminalization of immigration violations, as well as thought and allegiance crimes through anti-terrorism preventive justice legislation (Robinson 2012, 190; Corda 2019, 168–173). Despite formal divisions in the law between administrative sanctions and criminal punishment, immigration enforcement actions and preventive detentions for inchoate offenses are equally punitive. Suspects, offenders, and those who depend on them should be entitled to counsel and other protections currently reserved for offenders in the criminal justice system. States should reserve preventive detention for persons who pose a clear and present danger to society based on a record of past actions. Where preventive justice measures are used, they ought to serve the same purposes as other forms of punishment, which means moving beyond just incapacitation and deterrence to include a focus on rehabilitation and reintegration.

For immigration related offenses, this means providing services including education, job training, and family visitation that will help the detainee to grow as a human being. If states claim that they are not punishing immigration detainees, they should be compensated for the time and earning potential the state is taking from them while they are confined. For those who are being punished for a crime related to terrorism, education, vocational support, and de-radicalization in the case of terrorist offenses should be important facets of the offender's sentence with the end goal of rehabilitation. The state should shield innocent family members from scrutiny and punishment for ordinary acts of support for offenders under their care and assume responsibility for ensuring the adequate protection and well-being of those who are dependent on persons detained on immigration and terrorism charges. In the chapter that follows, I will consider why the deprivation of citizenship is a punishment in more detail, with a focus on ensuring that children are regarded as innocent from birth. They should be assured of state protection that comes with secure citizenship status and shielded from official judgment for their parent's status or offenses. Then I will examine the consequences of failing to provide protection for the dependents of offenders within states (Chapter 4), and across borders, in detainment camps (Chapter 5).

3

In Defense of Birthright Citizenship

The practice of birthright citizenship, whether by territorial birth (*jus soli*) or descent (*jus sangunis*), is the subject of ongoing political controversy related to concerns about immigration and the prospect that parents can circumvent immigration laws through the citizenship claims of their children. Political objections to birthright citizenship are primarily targeted at parents by citizens who want to condemn their irregular migration, deter others from coming, or call their attachment to the country in question. Proposed changes to limit birthright citizenship are meant to condemn their parents, but their punitive impact would fall on their innocent children.

Policy proposals targeting so-called anchor babies, a derogatory term used to describe the native-born children of undocumented immigrants (Chavez 2017), would cause innocent children to suffer indirect and vicarious punishment by denying them citizenship where they were born and raised because of their parent's irregular immigration status there. In the United States, Brittany R. Leach (2022) shows how the coalition between pro-life activists and ethnonationalists in the Republican Party uses "anchor baby rhetoric" to construct "pregnant migrants and their fetuses/children" as "national security threats" (Leach 2022, 122). While they are detained, undocumented immigrant pregnant women are denied adequate medical care. This endangers the life of the fetus and the mother alike while the government incapacitates her for entering the country unlawfully (124). Advocates of punitive immigration control condemn both undocumented pregnant people and their fetuses. They claim they want to save lives, consistent with Justice Brett Kavanaugh's interest in "favoring fetal life" and "protecting the best interests of a minor," who, in this case, is a pregnant undocumented immigrant (Kavanaugh et al. in *Garza v. Hargan* 2017, 1). But they deny the dignity and value of an emergent child's life as a potential citizen in her country of birth, worthy of rights (Leach 2022, 121; Henderson in *Garza v. Hargan* 2017, 18).

Born Innocent. Michael J. Sullivan, Oxford University Press. © Oxford University Press 2023.
DOI: 10.1093/oso/9780197671238.003.0003

Attacks on *jus soli* birthright citizenship in Canada and the United States often work to scapegoat migrants with a precarious legal status, many of whom are racialized minorities (Abji and Larios 2021, 256–257). In Canada, pregnant visitors can receive medical care, although they are normally not covered by government health insurance. But asylum-seekers, undocumented, and out-of-status migrants face detention where denials of care resulting in miscarriages and deaths occur (257–258). Policy proposals that would deny entry or care to so-called birth tourists would impact other children born in the country while their parents are in the country with authorization but without citizenship or permanent resident status, including refugee claimants and parents on student visas.[1] Innocent children suffer indirect and vicarious punishment when they are denied citizenship in the country where they were born and raised because their parents were in the country without authorization at the time of their child's birth.[2] Children may also suffer if their parent's country of origin denies their claim to citizenship by descent, if this leaves them stateless at birth without access to *jus soli* citizenship in the country where they are born. Even though states do not formally characterize citizenship restriction measures as punitive, these measures are "experienced as punitive," by affected parents and children alike. They serve functions that both traditional legal theorists and critical race theorists identify with punishment including deterrence and incapacitation (Gilmore 2007, 14; Bowling 2013, 300). Here, I extend this literature to address the intergenerational consequences of denying a child citizenship based on their parent's actions or status, in particular, when they violate immigration laws or are present in an irregular status.

In this chapter, I argue that political communities should not be free to decide whether to deny citizenship and its substantial protections to infants based on their parents' actions or behaviors, including immigration status, place of residence, or where they work at the time of their child's birth. Children of irregular immigrants deserve separate consideration for immigration benefits and citizenship apart from the status and conduct of their parents. Legislation that punishes children for the conduct of their parents "classifies on the basis of an immutable trait" that is "entirely out of the child's control" (Stier 1992, 727). Moreover, noncitizen children who arrive in a country shortly after they are born are similarly situated to native-born children who remain in their country of birth, meriting the protections and

50 BORN INNOCENT

benefits of citizenship irrespective of citizens' judgment of their parents' actions and status.

To this end, I defend a broad application of *jus soli* and *jus sanguinis* birthright citizenship as it is now practiced in Canada and the United States, the two last highly developed countries of immigration with extensive *jus soli* citizenship policies, against restrictive policy initiatives and philosophical concerns about "overinclusive" citizenship policies.[3] These restrictive policy initiatives do not adequately address the vulnerabilities of children, particularly when their parents do not have a secure immigration or citizenship status where they reside. Birthright citizenship by territorial birth and descent is necessary to ensure the protection and inclusion of children in mixed-citizenship status families, whether they remain in their country of residence or they have to leave with their parents. My initial concern is with the protection of children in mixed-citizenship status transnational families from *de jure* and *de facto* statelessness. Here, I am speaking of citizenship in an elementary legal sense, using Linda Bosniak's definition of citizenship as "formal, juridical membership in an organized political community" (Bosniak 2008, 19). My secondary concern lies with ensuring that these children enjoy full civil, social, and political rights as adults in their countries of citizenship.

In a world of nation-states, the complementary and expansive practice of birthright citizenship by both territorial birth and descent is the best means of safeguarding the baseline claims to *a* citizenship status and its protections. When it is elevated into a constitutional principle, as in the U.S. Fourteenth Amendment, territorial birthright citizenship protects the citizenship claims of all children, regardless of their parents' immigration status. Birthright citizenship by descent ideally operates to protect the rights of children who are dependent upon deportable parents to return to their countries of origin if necessary, and to reintegrate there as full members of the community.

Finally, I respond to proposed amendments to *jus soli* and *jus sanguinis* that base citizenship attribution on alternate principles. Children cannot attain the protection of citizenship if it relies on their consent or a link they develop over time (Shachar 2009, 178). Young children need instruments of citizenship attribution that protect them as citizens before they are able to make choices or develop ties of their own. The best way to ensure that this occurs is to link their status both to their parents through an expansive interpretation of *jus sanguinis*, and to their place of birth and early residence through an expansive interpretation of *jus soli*, even if this comes at the risk of "overincluding" these children as citizens in multiple countries.

The Limited Inclusive Potential of Territorial Birthright Citizenship

Most Western Hemisphere countries automatically grant newborns citizenship at birth (*jus soli*), except if their parents are employed in the service of a foreign country with diplomatic immunities (Vonk 2015, 10). Territorial birthright citizenship also exists alongside citizenship by descent as a secondary mode of acquiring citizenship in most Western hemisphere countries for the children of their citizens who are born abroad.[4] By contrast, citizenship by descent or *jus sanguinis* is the primary basis by which citizenship is attributed to new members in most countries in the Eastern Hemisphere (Macklin 2017, 291).[5] *Jus soli* citizenship can encourage immigrant integration and bridge diverse ethnic groups into a common imagined political identity (Dauvergne 2016, 20; Macklin 2017, 292).

To reach its full inclusive potential, territorial birthright citizenship depends on universal birth registration. In practice, birth registrars do not always record noninstitutional births, births in border regions, rural areas, and among irregular migrants (Vonk 2015, 11; Rosenbloom 2017, 132–146; Kingston 2019, 67–72). Delays in birth registration have become more pronounced during the COVID-19 pandemic, making it even more difficult for children in marginalized communities to prove their citizenship to access basic social services (AbouZahr et al. 2021, 1123–1125; Shaw 2021, 1643). Irregular birth registration leaves native-born residents of otherwise inclusive *jus soli* countries with disputed citizenship claims (Price 2017, 35; Rosenbloom 2017, 133–138). Sometimes these registration deficiencies arise from a lack of state resources, and other times they intentionally target irregular migrants whose children are supposed to have a right to citizenship at birth (Overmyer-Velázquez 2018, 28). Still, the provision of territorial birthright citizenship to children irrespective of the national origins or immigration status of their parents in most countries of the Western Hemisphere has the advantage of making *de jure* statelessness comparatively rare in the Americas (Belton 2017, 18).

52 BORN INNOCENT

Policy Objections to Territorial Birthright Citizenship

Political debates about birthright citizenship often take place in the context of broader disputes about immigration policy (Schuck and Smith 2018, 61–62; Dickson 2018). Canada and the United States stand out as countries of mass immigration that have retained the British common law tradition of *jus soli* citizenship (Buhler 2002, 94; Shachar 2009, 114–116; *Wong Kim Ark* 1898, 682, 693–694). Britain (effective 1983), Australia (effective 1986), Ireland (effective 2005), and New Zealand (effective 2006) restricted *jus soli* birthright citizenship to the children of permanent residents or persons still continually resident in the country after ten years of age as an immigration control measure targeting noncitizen parents (Zappalà and Castles 1999, 273; Layton-Henry and Wilpert 2003, 69–73; Luibhéid 2013; Dauvergne 2016, 21; Macklin 2017, 293). Section 3 of Canada's Citizenship Act sets out the modern legal framework governing the acquisition of citizenship by birth on Canadian soil (*jus soli*) in subsection 3(1)(a). With the inclusion of an amendment to the citizenship act recognizing Indigenous persons born in Canada as Canadian citizens in 1956, the last remaining major exception to *jus soli* birthright citizenship in Canada was eliminated (Freckelton 2022, 705). This leaves only the comparatively rare cases of Canadian-born children of accredited diplomats or foreign agents outside the ambit of *jus soli* citizenship in Canada. In sum, subsection 3(1)(b) of Canada's Citizenship Act establishes that *jus soli* is the ordinary principle by which most newborns are deemed Canadian citizens at birth, and *jus sanguinis* is a complementary principle governing the less common incidence of citizenship by birth to a Canadian parent abroad.

In the United States, *jus soli* citizenship is entrenched in the Constitution, serving in the late nineteenth and early twentieth century as an inclusive counterpoint to immigration and naturalization laws that were racially exclusionary. Three generations after the ratification of the U.S. Constitution and more than a decade of bloodshed in America's Civil War, the U.S. Constitution was amended to include the U.S. children of former Black slaves as citizens (Haney López 2006, 29). In the United States, under Section 1 of the Fourteenth Amendment, "all persons born or naturalized in the United States, and subject to the jurisdiction thereof, are citizens of the United States and of the state wherein they reside." This requirement is codified in Section 301(a) of the U.S. Immigration and Nationality Act (INA) to include all persons born in the United States, except the children of foreign diplomats.

Section 1 of the Fourteenth Amendment was subsequently interpreted by the Supreme Court in 1898 to protect the citizenship claims of persons who were otherwise deemed ineligible for citizenship, including the U.S.-born children of unauthorized immigrants (*Wong Kim Ark v. United States* 1898).[6] Despite its other shortcomings, a recent circuit court case interpreting *Wong Kim Ark* frames one aspect of the historical context of that case accurately, at least as it applies to the mainland United States: "It was about a racist denial of citizenship to an American man born in an American state" (*Fitisemanu v. United States* 2021, 22).[7] The Supreme Court overruled this racist denial of Wong Kim Ark's birthright U.S. citizenship in a far-reaching inclusionary precedent that guides all subsequent interpretations of the Citizenship Clause to the present day.

However, the Supreme Court's ruling in *Wong Kim Ark* did not stop immigration inspectors from questioning the citizenship claims of native-born U.S. citizens of Chinese ancestry, or denying them their citizenship rights based on prevailing racial prejudices codified into law at the local and state levels (Salyer 1995, 150–152; Haney López 2006, 37). Also, after the *Wong Kim Ark* ruling, the United States acquired colonial possessions and ruled over their inhabitants as noncitizen nationals as part of an "unconstitutional exception to the principle of *jus soli* citizenship, invented by administrators and legislators operating under racialist presuppositions" (Brief of Citizenship Scholars 2021, 9). This status persists in American Samoa to the present day, and it is in tension with the Supreme Court's inclusionary interpretation of the Fourteenth Amendment's Citizenship Clause in *Wong Kim Ark v. United States* (ibid.). Moreover, naturalization laws continued to discriminate against East and South Asian applicants for citizenship until 1952 (Haney López 2006, 27–28). Racism continues to inform Donald Trump's questions about the birthright citizenship of Barack Obama and Kamala Harris as the multiracial son and daughter of immigrants, respectively (Rosenbloom 2020).

A separate but related provision in Section 301(b) of the U.S. INA addresses the status of "persons born in the United States to a member of an Indian, Eskimo, Aleutian, or other aboriginal tribe," which "provides that the granting of citizenship under this subsection shall not in any manner impair or otherwise affect the right of such person to tribal or other property" (8 USC §1401(b)). The language of this statute stands in contradistinction to nineteenth-century claims by the U.S. Supreme Court in *Elk v. Wilkins* (1884) that "directly contradicts the supposition that a member of an Indian

54 BORN INNOCENT

tribe can at will be alternately a citizen of the United States and a member of the tribe" (*Elk v. Wilkins* 1884, 103).

Native American U.S. residents were among the last communities of U.S. born persons to be recognized as *jus soli* citizens of the United States at birth on account of their race and political status. Even after the Fourteenth Amendment's Citizenship Clause was ratified in 1868 and interpreted by the U.S. Supreme Court to apply to the U.S.-born children of Chinese immigrants in 1898, the U.S. government generally rejected the citizenship claims of U.S. born Indigenous persons until 1924. A ruling by the U.S. Supreme Court, *Elk v. Wilkins* (1884) denied that the citizenship clause conferred *jus soli* citizenship on Indigenous people born in the United States on the theory that the United States did not consent to extending citizenship to them (*Elk v. Wilkins* 1884, 109; Schuck and Smith 1985, 83–84). The majority of the Court held that Indigenous U.S. residents could be naturalized as U.S. citizens under certain conditions confirming their assimilation and separation from their tribe, but only with the express consent of the U.S. government (*Elk v. Wilkins* 1884, 109). As a result, some U.S. born Native Americans continued to be denied U.S. citizenship status despite pledging and displaying their allegiance to the United States by enlisting in the U.S. military and serving in combat in the Spanish American War and First World War (Rollings 2004, 134). Their service-based claims to citizenship were only recognized after the First World War. The U.S. Congress enacted legislation on November 6, 1919 authorizing Indigenous veterans to apply for U.S. citizenship, "without in any manner impairing or otherwise affecting the property rights, individual or tribal, of any such Indian or his interest in tribal or other Indian property" (An Act Granting Citizenship to Certain Indians 1919).

Despite the theory of mutual consent that underlay the *Elk v. Wilkins* decision, the subsequent extension of U.S. citizenship to Indigenous residents of the United States took place without the consent of all Indigenous polities. This decision was made at the same time (1924) as the United States began to enforce border restrictions dividing First Nations along the U.S.-Canada border, further fragmenting Indigenous polities with traditional homelands that spanned across the boundary (Brunyeel 2004, 37–42). Some Native Americans rejected U.S. citizenship as an infringement on their tribal sovereignty. Others eagerly sought U.S. citizenship and served in the United States military in every conflict since the Revolutionary War, though their claims to earned citizenship went unrecognized until all Indigenous peoples in the United States were collectively granted citizenship in 1924 (Brunyeel 2004,

34–37; De Leon 2016, 220–222; Meadows 2017, 84–91). The Nationality Act of 1940 further clarified that Indigenous peoples born in the United States are *jus soli* citizens (Haney López 2006, 30). Today, only the residents of American Samoa continue to live under U.S. jurisdiction as noncitizen nationals (*Fitisemanu v. United States* 2021). The unilateral extension of citizenship to Indigenous persons raised controversies over tribal sovereignty that continue to this present day. I will address these issues in greater detail in Chapter 6.

Debates about Territorial Birthright Citizenship in Canada

In Canada, both Liberal and Conservative governments have considered changes to Section 3 of the Citizenship Act limiting citizenship by *jus soli* and *jus sanguinis* (Bethel 1994; Young 1997).[8] More recently, petitions have been presented to Parliament by Vancouver area Conservative and Liberal MP's in 2016 and 2018 respectively challenging the practice of birthright citizenship in light of allegations of birth tourism (Freckelton 2022, 708–709). These proposed policy changes are motivated by fears that nonresidents could obtain immigration benefits from Canada simply by giving birth to a Canadian child and then returning to their country of origin (birth tourism) (Bethel 1994, 15, 17, 19; Yeates 2014; Sullivan 2022b, 69). Seventy-one percent of Canadians polled in 2020 believe that "birth tourism can be unfairly used to gain access to Canada's education, health care and social programs" (Quan 2021).[9]

In reality, parents cannot actually access any immigration benefits by giving birth to Canadian-born children until they are eighteen years of age (Immigration, Refugees, and Citizenship Canada 2021). Mothers can access the Canada Child Benefit on behalf of their children so long as both the mother and the citizen-child remain in the country (Canada Revenue Agency 2022). Yet birth tourists by definition leave shortly after their child is born and do not gain access to any benefits reserved to resident children. Nevertheless, citing misleading political rhetoric about the potential for birth tourists to obtain immigration and social welfare benefits, Stephen Harper's Conservative government considered a proposal in 2014 to limit citizenship by territorial birth to the children of at least one citizen or permanent resident parent. This move was opposed by the provinces tasked with registering births on account of cost concerns (Yeates 2014, 1; Dauvergne 2016, 21; Macklin 2017, 293). The Conservative Party of Canada adopted a policy plank during its August 2018 convention renewing its support for limiting *jus soli* citizenship (Dickson 2018).

56 BORN INNOCENT

Overall, the media and policy debate in Canada focuses on wealthy nonresident parents who can afford the costs of travel, accommodation, and medical bills to give birth to a child in Canada, leaving shortly thereafter (Cosh 2019). Figures cited by the Standing Committee on Citizenship and Immigration in early March 2020 dispute the prevalence of this problem, pointing to Statistics Canada indicating that only 356 of 378,848 total Canadian births in 2018 were to a nonresident or noncitizen mother (Standing Committee on Immigration and Citizenship Canada 2020). Using hospital financial data, the Canadian Institute for Health Information (CIHI) reports that 3,628 births in Canada were coded as "other country resident self-pay" (Gaucher and Larios 2020). Opponents of birthright citizenship use this figure to support their argument that *jus soli* birthright citizenship should be restricted to the children of citizens and permanent residents (Griffith 2018). The CIHI figure does not disaggregate mothers coded under this billing category according to their degree of connection to their child's country of birth. The figure can include international students, expatriate citizens returning to Canada to give birth who are not eligible for provincial health insurance, or noncitizen spouses and partners of Canadian citizens, none of whom are birth tourists. In short, figures used to indicate the prevalence of "births to nonresidents" exaggerate the prevalence of birth tourism, whereby temporary visitors enter a country with nearly unrestricted *jus soli* citizenship solely to give birth and obtain that country's citizenship for their newborn.

Debates about Territorial Birthright Citizenship in the United States

In the United States, policy debates about birthright citizenship and the future status of irregular immigrants are closely connected. The Trump administration's January 2020 decision to deny visas to pregnant nonimmigrant visitors was the last salvo in that administration's efforts to limit birthright citizenship for the children of undocumented and legal nonimmigrants (Kanno-Youngs 2020). Territorial birthright citizenship is a key mechanism for the legal inclusion of the children of irregular immigrants as citizens, including 6.8 million U.S. citizen children born to irregular immigrants from 1980 to 2016 (Bloemraad and Sheares 2017, 830).

The academic debate about the legality and ethics of territorial birthright citizenship in the United States was reinvigorated by Peter Schuck and Rogers Smith's *Citizenship Without Consent: Illegal Aliens in the American*

Polity (1985). There, Schuck and Smith also expressed concerns about the potential for all *jus soli* citizenship regimes to incentivize irregular residence (Schuck and Smith 1985, 94). Ideally, Schuck and Smith argued that political communities should be able to grant or withhold citizenship to U.S.-born children with noncitizen parents, just as it does for new members by naturalization (Schuck and Smith 1985, 103). Opponents of consent-based citizenship fear that citizens and their representatives will use the consent principle to exclude U.S.-born children of parents whose loyalties are suspect because of their parents' group identity, national origin, or ideological beliefs (Chavez 2017, 13).

Given the failure of legislative efforts to repeal birthright citizenship in the United States, Smith has since adopted the position that "the nation can be said to have effectively consented to a reading of the Fourteenth Amendment that confers *jus soli* birthright citizenship on children of aliens never legally admitted to the United States" (Smith 2009, 1331). Similarly, Schuck now argues that Congress's lack of collective "inclination to eliminate the traditional rule" reflects "the advantages of the traditional rule" of territorial birthright citizenship (Schuck 2017, 168–169; Sullivan 2022b, 71). Legislative efforts to reinterpret the Citizenship Clause of the Fourteenth Amendment to the U.S. Constitution to exclude the children of irregular immigrants continue, supported by President Trump's threat to issue an executive order to this end in August 2019 (Birthright Citizenship Act of 2021; Lyons 2019). However, most legal analysts believe that a constitutional amendment would be required to alter U.S. territorial birthright citizenship (Dellinger 1995, 81; Joppke 2010, 38; Dauvergne 2016, 20–21, 103–105).

Unlike in Canada, in the United States, territorial birthright citizenship is explicitly entrenched in its Constitution as the lynchpin of the nation's commitment to legal equality emerging from its Civil War and Reconstruction. Even before the U.S. Civil War, the struggle by emancipated African Americans for recognition as free and equal citizens augmented existing legal arguments for *jus soli* citizenship in the United States (Jones 2018). Section 1 of the Fourteenth Amendment to the U.S. Constitution as ratified in 1868 guarantees *jus soli* citizenship for "all persons born and naturalized in the United States and subject to the jurisdiction thereof." A generation later, in 1898, the U.S. Supreme Court interpreted the clause "subject to the jurisdiction thereof" through the lens of precedents in English common law, excluding only children "born of alien enemies in hostile occupation, and children of diplomatic representatives of a foreign state" (*Wong Kim Ark*

58 BORN INNOCENT

v. United States 1898, 682). Pursuant to this ruling, the U.S. State Department maintains that

> acquisition of U.S. citizenship generally is not affected by the fact that the parents may be in the United States temporarily or illegally; and that; and (b) A child born in an immigration detention center physically located in the United States is considered to have been born in the United States and be subject to its jurisdiction. This is so even if the child's parents have not been legally admitted to the United States and, for immigration purposes, may be viewed as not being in the United States (U.S. State Department 2018).

Short-term visitors or irregular immigrants apprehended after crossing the border and held in an immigration detention center can give birth to a U.S. citizen-child. However, the vast majority of births to immigrants without citizenship or U.S. legal permanent resident status are to long-term U.S. residents (Passel, Cohn, and Gramlich 2018). In 2016, the Migration Policy Institute found that 86 percent of irregular immigrant parents who gave birth in the United States had resided there for more than five years (Capps, Fix, and Zong 2016, 9). Policy objections to U.S. citizenship for the children of irregular immigrants that portray the parents as birth tourists and the children as anchor babies do not account for their longstanding social membership. The country where they were born and raised is their home.

Underinclusiveness: Punishing Children for the Behavior/Actions of Their Parents

The caricature of the birth tourist who enters to give birth to a child who will be a citizen there, only to leave soon afterward is used as part of a political argument to persuade citizens to abandon territorial birthright citizenship for the children of nonpermanent resident parents. The reality is that most nonpermanent resident parents, including irregular immigrants and visa overstayers who have committed immigration violations, have enduring ties to the country where they gave birth. As a result, their children are likely to remain in that country, where in the absence of territorial birthright citizenship, they will not have the same civil, social, and later political rights as other native-born citizens. In effect, political communities are harming the children of irregular immigrants as a sanction directed at their parents out of a desire to encourage them to self-deport with their children. Here, I argue that political communities should not be free to decide whether to deny citizenship and its substantial protections to infants based on their parents' actions or behaviors. These include a parents' immigration status, their place of residence, or where they work at the time of their child's birth.

Denying children birthright citizenship is an example of vicarious punishment applied to a native-born child for a parent's immigration violations or, in the case of so-called birth tourists, the political perception that as nonimmigrant visa holders, their children do not deserve citizenship where they were born. The legitimacy of punishment is predicated upon its application to an actual offender for an offense for which he was tried and convicted (Hart 1968, 5). The requirement that punishment should only be applied to individuals who broke the law is meant to protect the individual from society, particularly those who are innocent but associated with the offender (Hart 1968, 81). By contrast, deterrence theorists value punishment not as a means of holding an individual accountable for past wrongdoing, but rather as a preventive measure to promote social safety and security by discouraging violations of the law (Hoskins 2019, 74). Efforts to deny birthright citizenship to the children of irregular immigrants in the United States are predicated on a desire by lawmakers to deter potential parents, including asylum-seekers, from coming to the United States without prior authorization (Ryo and Peacock 2020, 46). Former U.S. President Donald Trump and South Carolina U.S. Senator Lindsey Graham have described the policy as a "magnet for illegal immigration" that ought to be abolished (Edelman 2018; Lyons 2019). Such a measure would have minimal deterrent effect on the more recent wave of migrants from Central America to the United States who are facing political violence at home. A survey of studies of the effectiveness of deterrent enforcement measures on such migrants by Emily Ryo finds that the threat of state-levied sanctions has a minimal effect on their decision to enter or bring their families into a country without authorization (Ryo 2019, 244–248; Jordán Wallace and Zepeda-Millán 2020, 35–36). The number of families apprehended by Customs and Border Protection (CBP) increased during the zero-tolerance enforcement through family separation period in 2018, where the typical strategy of asylum-seekers is to surrender immediately to border enforcement officials upon entering the United States (Schrag 2020, 283). The anticipated rewards, including safety and a better life for their families outweigh their estimation of the risks involved. Political philosopher Chandran Kukathas (2021) takes this assessment of the futility

60 BORN INNOCENT

of deterrence a step further. Deterrence-based enforcement measures subject everyone to heightened surveillance away from the border, using racial and ethnic profiling that would be impermissible in other contexts and limiting the freedom of targeted citizens and immigrants alike (Kukathas 2021, 45–46, 70).

As part of an intentional effort to deter desperate parents from violating U.S. immigration laws, the United States Citizenship and Immigration Service under the Trump administration resorted to separating adults from their children. This measure inflicted hardship on both the parent who planned to enter the country without authorization, and the accompanying child who lacked the *mens rea* to intentionally plan to violate U.S. laws by entering the country illegally. The pain of contemplating one's child's suffering while she is detained away from her family is itself a form of state-inflicted hardship that when publicized may dissuade other migrant parents from entering the United States illegally. H. L. A. Hart envisioned the deterrent value of such an indirect sanction when he supposed, for the sake of argument, that "more persons may be deterred from crime if wives and children of offenders were punished vicariously for their crimes" (Hart 1968, 11). Even if the prospect of vicarious punishment deterred parents from violating the law to avoid the risk of state-sanctioned harm toward their innocent children, this course of action would undermine the legitimacy of a legal system premised on individual responsibility.

For nearly all children of immigrants born in Canada and the United States, territorial birthright citizenship there contains the promise of integration on equal terms with other citizens.[10] In the United States, equal protection of the law for the children of irregular immigrants means a free public education, on the grounds that "legislation directing the onus of a parent's misconduct against his children" that "does not comport with fundamental conceptions of justice" (*Plyler v. Doe* 1982, 220). Similar justifications have been made for granting children protections from deportation through the Deferred Action for Childhood Arrivals (DACA) program, arguing that immigrants who entered a country without authorization as children should not be held culpable for their parents' immigration violations (Sullivan 2019, 212, 223).[11] Overall, children who arrive in a country shortly after they are born are similarly situated to native-born children who remain in their country of birth.

DACA recipients in this position feel socially integrated into U.S. society and many have no other home but the United States. But they are constantly reminded of the insecurity of a status that could be rescinded in the future so long as they have no pathway to permanent residence (Chen 2020, 103–107). Many Americans only support the proposed DREAM Act (legislation that would go further than DACA's temporary deferred action from deportation by providing a pathway to legal permanent residence for undocumented immigrant youth) if there are service-based conditions attached to legalization. They simultaneously support this pathway to citizenship and punitive immigration policies for their so-called undeserving applicants (Matos 2021, 423). Based on continued support for this approach, a bipartisan group of senators introduced the America's CHILDREN Act in July 2021, following on twenty years of stymied legislative efforts to provide permanent residency and a pathway to citizenship for unauthorized immigrant youth (America's CHILDREN Act of 2021; Padilla 2021). Yalidy Matos insightfully connects simultaneous support for bills like the DREAM Act and punitive immigration policies motivated by racial resentment, and the deleterious impact that this policy stance has on DACA recipients and potential DREAM Act beneficiaries who stand to suffer family separation if their parents are deported, even as they are allowed to stay (Matos 2021, 436). Here, I emphasize the distance between that popular standpoint and my normative perspective on the claims of immigrant children to legal residence and citizenship. All undocumented immigrant youth deserve the protections and benefits of citizenship irrespective of citizens' judgment of their parents' conduct as irregular entrants or visa overstayers. Children of irregular immigrants deserve separate consideration for immigration benefits and citizenship apart from the status and conduct of their parents. Their parents' conduct may not be worthy of condemnation insofar as it involves nothing more than an immigration status violation, for which amnesties have been granted (1986) and proposed several times in the United States (Sullivan 2019, 190–195). If the Obama-era Deferred Action for Parents of Americans and Lawful Permanent Residents (DAPA) program enacted in 2014 was implemented, many of the parents of young U.S. citizens and immigrants would have been spared deportation to prevent family separations and in recognition of the civic value of their caregiving services (Office of the Press Secretary 2014). This is a normative stance that I continue to support as a positive feature of "earned citizenship" in legal immigration reforms, and one that I would extend to the parents of U.S. resident undocumented youth (Sullivan 2019, 221).

But even in the case of more serious infractions beyond mere immigration status violations, the gravity of the parents' alleged offense as a matter of

62 BORN INNOCENT

immigration law should not be taken into consideration in deciding whether a child is allowed to acquire citizenship by descent. Children of suspected terrorists should not be denied citizenship by descent in their parents' country of origin as a collateral consequence of punitive actions, including denationalization, levied upon their parents.[12] In sum, the state should avoid visiting harms upon children to condemn their parent's actions, over which they have no direct control.

Immigration laws that prevent minors from sponsoring their parents for immigration benefits undermine the protections of territorial birthright citizenship for children in mixed-status families (Sullivan 2016, 264). Young children have a strong developmental interest in forming intimate attachments to their parents to help them to develop modes of self-regulation necessary to function as autonomous and productive adult citizens (Brighouse and Swift 2014, 72–73). Federal immigration authorities routinely compromise young citizen-children's interests in continuity of care by detaining and deporting their noncitizen parents (Brock 2020, 95, 101–102). Local and state authorities do the same when they take a parent's custody away because of their immigration violations (Hacker 2017, 184–186). For instance, in *Harvest of Empire* (2011), Juan Gonzalez highlights the precariousness of the rights that come with U.S. citizenship for the U.S.-born children of undocumented immigrants. He points to the impact of workplace raids during the George W. Bush administration that separated thousands of U.S. citizen-children from their undocumented immigrant parents, even though the children were not the immediate target of the raids (Gonzalez 2011, 212). Many of their parents were arrested during the raids for being in the country without authorization, and for possessing false or loaned identity documents that they used to secure employment (Horton 2016, 88). The raids focused on immigrant workers while ignoring networks of citizens and immigrants who profit from the sale and loan of identity documents, and the employers who knowingly hire undocumented workers to lower regulatory and payroll costs (89–95). Their children suffered collateral consequences resulting from their parents' detention from the moment they came home from school to find their parents were not there. This was just the first step in a long process resulting in either their permanent separation from their parents, or their unwilling departure from the United States to remain united with deported caregivers in their parents' country of citizenship.

Jus sanguinis citizenship by descent allows many U.S.-born citizen children to return with their parents back to their ancestral country of origin when they are deported (Abrams 2018, 123). But this solution comes at a cost to older children who will have to leave their broader network of school and community-based care providers behind to maintain parental care in ancestral countries of origin where they have few ties and often experience social and legal barriers to reintegration (Heidbrink 2019, 140). Many deported parents do not have the financial means or institutional knowledge to register their U.S.-born children in Mexico so they can claim documents proving their *jus sanguinis* citizenship by descent there (Mateos 2019, 917).[13] Even when they can obtain the required documentation, they face further difficulties registering for public services and enrolling in the educational system as presumed foreigners, with limited Spanish language abilities (Mateos 2019, 930). In short, not all dual nationals benefit from a privileged position as compared to mono-nationals who never left their country of birth.

The Children of Diplomats, Consular Officials, and Spies

Even so, assigning citizenship by territorial birthright can eventually free native-born children as adults from the penalties that apply to their parents because of their citizenship or immigration status, conduct, or allegiance. Children of irregular immigrants can ordinarily obtain citizenship in the country of their birth irrespective of the immigration offenses of their parents. However, territorial birthright citizenship in Canada does not apply to diplomatic and consular officers and employees in their service (Canada Citizenship Act 2021 §3(2)). Both Canada and the United States do not allow the children of foreign diplomats to acquire citizenship by territorial birth, as they are deemed "not subject to the jurisdiction of the country" (Sullivan 2018, 337; Canada Citizenship Act 2021, §3(2), U.S. Citizenship and Immigration Services 2023).

Here, the state may call the citizenship of children into question for two reasons related to the parent's status and actions. First, bureaucrats may decide that the parents are not sufficiently attached to the polity, leading to deleterious consequences for their native-born children if they are not acknowledged as citizens in the country of their parent's birth. A prominent example of this exclusion from territorial birthright citizenship in Canada is the case of Deepan Budlakoti, an Ottawa, Ontario born stateless man who was denied Canadian citizenship because his parents were domestic servants

64   BORN INNOCENT

of the Indian High Commission to Canada before he was born (*Budlakoti v. Canada* 2015). His parents believed he was a Canadian citizen by birth since he was issued two Canadian passports. They never sought naturalization for Deepan like the rest of his family.

In the United States, Hoda Muthana, the Hackensack, New Jersey born daughter of the former First Secretary of the Permanent Mission of Yemen to the United Nations, was raised in the United States and believed she was a citizen there, having been issued two U.S. passports. U.S. authorities became aware of her status after she left for Syria to join ISIS, and then sought to return to the United States after the terrorist organization's defeat. The U.S. Circuit Court of Appeals for the District of Columbia Circuit ruled on January 19, 2021 that neither Muthana nor her Syrian-born son, who was born in a displaced persons camp holding ISIS affiliates, are U.S. citizens by birth or descent (*Muthana v. Pompeo*, 2021).

Both Budlakoti's case in Canada and Muthana's case in the United States came to the attention of authorities because of their crimes as adults. Their governments did not deny them citizenship because of their own actions, but rather because of their parents' affiliations and employment status, the facts of which are still subject to dispute. The Muthana case carries stronger political undertones, as the Trump administration had vowed not to provide her with any diplomatic assistance or support given her affiliation with ISIS as the wife of a combatant (Morin 2019). In Muthana's case, her innocent infant son, Adam was denied U.S. citizenship and its protections as a matter of law because his U.S.-born and raised mother was deemed a noncitizen (*Muthana v. Pompeo*, 2021), and because the Trump administration was unwilling to support her claim to protection as a lifelong U.S. resident (Al Faour et al. 2019). Hoda and Adam continue to languish in a displaced peoples' camp that is known as a hotbed for ISIS radicalization (Suliman 2022). This leaves her son, the grandson of U.S. citizens, prone to recruitment into ISIS or a successor movement (Speckhard and Ellenberg 2020).

Second, native-born children may suffer a loss of citizenship status based on their parents' affiliations and actions on behalf of an adversary state, which, however egregious, were entirely beyond their children's control. In the early 1990s, two Canadian-born children, Timothy and Alexander Vavilov, were born in Canada to presumed Canadian citizens who raised them without any knowledge of their parents' true identity as covert Russian agents until they were discovered and deported to Russia late in their adolescence. As adults, the Canadian-born Vavilovs sought to return to Canada as citizens. The Canadian government initially denied this request, contending that they were born subject to a provision in the Citizenship Act denying citizenship by birth to the children of representatives of a foreign government. In the process, the younger Vavilov's experienced a form of punitive incapacitation resulting from their parents' criminal activity, as they were prevented from returning to Canada and forced to remain in exile in Russia. In December 2019, the Canadian Supreme Court ruled that the revocation of the appellant's citizenship could not be sustained because their parents "did not enjoy such [diplomatic] privileges and immunities" while in Canada (*Citizenship and Immigration v. Vavilov* 2019, §334). In an earlier ruling, the Federal Court of Appeal supported its decision by invoking a normative claim "that the sins of parents ought not to be visited upon children without clear authorization by law" (*Vavilov v. Canada* 2017, §82). In this and similar cases, unconditional territorial birthright citizenship stands for the principle that children should be held innocent for their parent's conduct and allowed to live as equal citizens of the land of their birth.

Citizenship by Descent: Addressing Concerns about Overinclusiveness

Unconditional territorial birthright citizenship by descent serves as a backstop to prevent incidents of statelessness. In Canada and the United States, where most children become citizens by territorial birth in their country of residence, citizenship by descent or *jus sanguinis* helps ensure that the children of citizens born abroad have a claim to citizenship in their parent's country of origin (Canada Citizenship Act 2021, §3(1)(b); 8 U.S.C. 1401(c, d, e)). This helps to ensure family unity and protects children and subsequent generations of expatriates who cannot acquire the citizenship of the country where they were born from statelessness, such as what occurred when India denied Deepan Budlakoti a claim to the citizenship status of his parents.

Birthright citizenship by descent (*jus sanguinis)* can lead to political objections that children and subsequent descendants of citizens living abroad can obtain the benefits of citizenship without establishing connections to the polity arising from residence there. This objection was an important factor motivating changes in Canada's citizenship laws that took effect on April 17, 2009 as part of Bill C-37, limiting citizenship by descent to the first generation of Canadian citizens born abroad (Keon 2008, 1519–1520; Becklumb

2014, 13–14). This change was advanced by the Conservative Party, whose Minister of Citizenship, Immigration and Multiculturalism at the time, Jason Kenney, justified these changes to prevent people whom he believed had little connection to Canada from passing citizenship on to their descendants. The New Democratic Party immigration critic, Olivia Chow, warned that the minister was creating a second-class group of citizens and penalizing the children of Canadian parents who work overseas (Chow 2009).

Limitations on citizenship by descent have the potential of leaving children stateless, if they can no longer obtain citizenship either by descent or by birth according to the citizenship laws of the country where they are born (Siskay 2010; Harder and Zhyznomirska 2012). The Canadian restriction on citizenship by descent only partly addresses this problem. A grandchild of a Canadian-born citizen without a claim to citizenship elsewhere must apply for Canadian citizenship by age twenty-three and prove that she has resided in Canada for three out of the four years preceding her application (Immigration, Refugees and Citizenship Canada 2019). These restrictions may render descendants of Canadian citizens stateless at birth, with limited social rights and subject to deportation in Canada, and without diplomatic protection abroad (Brennan and Cohen 2018, 1309). Canada's limitations on citizenship by descent also do not consider the value of alternative ways that transnational families can maintain strong ties to Canada abroad apart from formal employment with the Government of Canada or a province or territory.

Most nations allow the children of native-born citizens born abroad to retain citizenship throughout their lives. One way to justify citizenship by descent using stakeholder theory is through the principle of biographical subjection. Once someone becomes a citizen by descent, they expect that country to continue to provide them with the right to return. They are subject to the political authority of a state that seeks to circumscribe this right (Bauböck 2009, 482). To denationalize an external citizen later in life amounts to banishment and involuntary exile, a severe penalty for any state to impose on its citizens simply for living abroad (Bauböck 2009, 483). The abstract principle of biographical subjection becomes more concrete when we consider why external citizens may need to return for the benefit of resident citizens. As children, they are dependent on their native-born parents. As adults, their native-born parents may return to their country of origin, and need their children born abroad to come home to provide care for them in their country of residence. In both cases, a native-born mono-citizens' interests in family unity and continuity of care may depend on their foreign-born children's lifelong right to return.

Normative Objections to Birthright Citizenship as Overinclusive

In normative political theory, objections to territorial and descent-based birthright citizenship are motivated by concerns about the supposed "overinclusiveness" of current citizenship laws (Schuck and Smith 1985, 121). Schuck and Smith's influential 1985 objection to *jus soli* birthright citizenship did not extend to claims to citizenship by descent by persons who "lives his entire life outside the United States," leaving this matter up to the consent of the "current American community" to decide (Schuck and Smith 1985, 128). Ayelet Shachar's *Birthright Lottery* (2009) is a more far-reaching project than Schuck and Smith's emphasis on birthright citizenship as framed in U.S. history and constitutional interpretation. Shachar offers a broader global normative indictment of all forms of birthright citizenship as inherited and unmerited privileges, whether by territorial birth, or by descent, encompassing the majority of citizenship attribution policies. The first half of *Birthright Lottery* focuses on the alleged distributive injustices of acquiring citizenship status at birth, while the second part of the book proposes that states adopt *jus nexi* or a center of life connections basis for distributing citizenship linked to residence and other ties to the political community. Shachar views a nonresident descendant of a citizen as a "nominal heir" of the benefits of citizenship, particularly when this "windfall beneficiary" is "born abroad to parents who merely inherited the title of citizenship by virtue of entail-like birthright, never themselves establishing a genuine connection to the home community the grandparents left behind" (Shachar 2009, 181). Overall, Shachar's objection to both *jus soli* and *jus sanguinis* is that both practices have the potential "to lead to the situation where persons with only minimal ties to the polity are granted all the rights and benefits of membership (overinclusiveness)" (Shachar 2009, 137).

Why Newborns Need the Protections of Birthright Citizenship

Shachar's *jus nexi* proposal is centered on connections established through long-term residence in a country, but she is also willing to consider attachments established through "related activities that indicate a person's connectedness and willingness to share both the risks and benefits of membership in a society in which he or she never lived" (Shachar 2009, 173).

68 BORN INNOCENT

This proposal goes further than the April 17, 2009 changes to Canadian citizenship law toward recognizing the possibility that external citizens living abroad may retain ties to Canada sufficient for indicating their connection to the political community, meriting claims to citizenship. The problem is that newborn children who are in immediate need of the protections of citizenship do not have the capacity or lived experience to establish a genuine connection to any country based on past participation, contributions, or behavior. It may be morally justifiable for states to take actions, behavior, and experiences developed over a lifetime into consideration when determining whether to admit *adults* as new legal permanent residents or naturalized citizens (Sullivan 2019, 49). Yet it is morally illegitimate to extend the same expectations to newborn infants who need of the protections of citizenship, denying them this security based on their parents' actions, or because citizens, legislators or bureaucrats believe they lack a genuine link to the country of their birth.

The legitimacy of judging newborns by factors like subjection to the laws, long-term residence and participation to civil society is dubious since they have no record that authorities can use to justify granting or denying them citizenship (Carens 2016, 206). Arguably, a state can withhold granting citizenship to the native-born children of noncitizen parents without lawful permanent resident status and still provide these children with the protection of their laws (Tanasoca 2018, 26). This is the policy that has been in place in Australia since 1986, when that country imposed a ten-year residency requirement for children of nonpermanent residents to obtain citizenship. While a child may enjoy some local legal protections during this time, ten years provides immigration authorities with ample time to deport nonpermanent resident parents with native-born children, which was why Australia imposed a lengthy residency requirement for birthright citizenship in the first place (Zappalà and Castles 1999, 284). If we are concerned with providing children with the protections that come with citizenship status at birth, the most efficient way to do this is to grant them citizenship where they are born, without exceptions. The practical dangers of leaving vulnerable individuals outside the protection of any state ought to supersede symbolic philosophical concerns that some children might be overincluded as citizens of more than one polity where they do not reside, leaving them ineligible for many of the benefits of citizenship there.

Luara Ferracioli makes an interesting argument for why children need both the protections of their parent's care and citizenship status where they reside that is relevant here. For Ferracioli, "citizenship is the functional equivalent of the family under current sociopolitical conditions." Just as "the family provides for the most robust protection and promotion of those interests of the child that are best advanced within the context of an intimate relationship, citizenship provides the most robust protection and promotion of those interests of the child that are best advanced by the coercive apparatus of the state of residence" (Ferracioli 2022, 22). To build on Ferracioli's point, it also matters which citizenship status a child has. Simply inheriting a citizenship status from one's parents as a theoretical right to return to another country does not protect her interests where she resides. If a school-aged child that is already situated in a web of relationships at school and in the community had to leave his country of citizenship because his parents were deported, his interests and civic formation would be undermined even if he was not separated from his parents. Gillian Brock further contends that forcing a child to leave with his parents "would destroy their status in their adopted society," and this constitutes "a harsh form of punishment, on a par with torture" (Brock 2020, 95). While many families choose to move their children between countries, in the immigration enforcement context, the state undermines the family's autonomy to make this decision for their children.

Ferracioli believes that children have the "right to be subjected to effective paternalism," as a developmental interest (Ferracioli 2022, 23–24). From the family to the school to the community to the state, this network of associations works together to help children to develop their capacities to contribute to society and live productive, meaningful lives (Ferracioli 2022, 21). Ferracioli helpfully shows how the family and the state work together. The family provides love, care, and close companionship. The state then offers public goods like education, public health provisions, regulation, and healthy public spaces to extend the family's capacity to help their children. She leaves aside the potential for the family and the state to come into conflict in areas where parents believe the state is overreaching or disrespecting their values, however, which complicate her narrative in practice. Still, guaranteeing a family's citizenship status in the country where their children permanently reside is the surest way to protect children's rights to continue to live in, and benefit from this network of community associations from the destructive and destabilizing impact of deportation. Of course, this does not preclude other forms of network disruption that would undermine the benefit of family-association-state paternalism in the interests of a child's

70 BORN INNOCENT

development. The parents can decide to choose to leave their community and country. The state can also disrupt citizen family unity by imprisoning parents, which is a harm I discuss and seek to mitigate in Chapter 4. But Ferracioli's point still stands—in an ideal world—when parents and children share the same citizenship status and are free from the threat of deportation, a child can benefit from the effective developmental assistance of the family and state institutions in unison.

Citizenship by Descent Helps Safeguard Family Unity

Citizenship by descent provides limited but important benefits to the children of deported parents who left their other country of citizenship under duress and must integrate in another country with few resources or ties of their own. It safeguards against statelessness and helps to protect family unity and the continuity of care for children in mixed-citizenship status families (Titshaw 2018, 98). Citizenship by descent does not protect children from barriers to integration in their parents' country of origin that often lead to educational setbacks, developmental disruptions, and discrimination (Zayas and Bradlee 2014, 171). Even so, political and legal theorists continue to question the moral legitimacy of citizenship by descent as though it were a form of inherited privilege, akin to a family heirloom rather than a public good regulated by a self-governing people (Shachar 2009; Stevens 2010; Tanasoca 2018, 29–32). One can provisionally acknowledge the legitimacy of those concerns by asking adults to assume more civic duties in exchange for inheriting the rights and status of citizenship. At the same time, we can still insist that children be entitled to the same citizenship status as their parents while they are dependents. Since what is most important is that children can live in the same country as their caregivers to ensure continuity of care, we can envision adapting *jus sanguinis* to ensure that children inherit the citizenship status of their primary caregivers so families can live and move together (Bauböck 2018, 85–86; Honohan 2018, 133).

Birthright Citizenship Does Not Necessarily Privilege Its Recipients

Some normative political theorists including Ayelet Shachar (2009) argue that birthright citizenship and access to dual citizenship is an unjust form of privilege. These claims depend on a child's potential ability to take advantage of their legal claim to citizenship in a developed country as an adult. They do not consider the ways in which a child's ability to act on this potential is linked to her parent's status and circumstances. In the United States, most of the children born to parents without U.S. citizenship or lawful permanent resident status are long-term irregular residents of limited economic means who live under a constant threat of detection and deportation. A child born in the United States to irregular immigrant parents is a citizen there by territorial birthright, but it will be difficult for her to take advantage of an education that will lead to opportunities there if her parents are deported. Mixed-status families with parents that cannot legally work in the United States already face obstacles to their socioeconomic advancement (Capps, Fix, and Zong 2016). Even in same-citizenship status families, children face wide disparities in opportunity based on their parents' socioeconomic status. These inequalities limit the advantages that come from birthright citizenship in a developed country. Though they are often dual citizens, U.S. children of irregular immigrants are rarely privileged compared to their peers who have only U.S. citizenship. The desperate circumstances that lead parents to risk migrating without authorization indicate their family's lack of privilege and status in both of their children's countries of citizenship. These families should not be penalized with a "birthright privilege levy" as a means of minimizing global inequality.

Costica Dumbrava proceeds a step further to argue that citizenship as membership in a political community should not depend on contingent facts of birth, such as their parents' immigration and citizenship status (Dumbrava 2018, 79). Yet arbitrary allocations of membership—in families no less than in states—are impossible to avoid at birth and for some time thereafter, as we are necessarily born into a web of relationships prior to attaining moral agency. What is essential is not the means of distribution but that we have agents to protect our vital interests in a period of minority or vulnerability (Blake 2003, 402). Birthright citizenship—whether assigned by territorial birth or descent, among other unchosen ties—provides individuals with a context for choice in which children can securely develop their capacity to become free moral agents in their own right (MacIntyre 1984, 221; Duff 2018, 196). The contingent nature of assigning citizenship based on one's place and jurisdiction of birth can also help to "avoid the trap of moral judgment about who (or more appropriately, the children of whose parents) deserves to be a citizen" (Shachar 2009, 146). Children should not be penalized for the polity's assessment of the actions, behavior, or status of their parents. They should have the opportunity to participate fully in the life of their country of birth and continued residence as citizens in their own right.

72 BORN INNOCENT

Beyond the First Generation: Including the Children of Expatriates as Citizens by Descent

Canada's post-2009 restriction on citizenship by descent to the first generation born abroad, as codified in subsection 5.1(4) of the Citizenship Act, is unusual among countries of mass immigration. Beyond the first generation, many countries allow the grandchildren of native-born citizens with a claim to citizenship provided they reside in the country for a specified period (Weil 2001, 20; Macklin and Crépeau 2010, 5). Ireland has a particularly expansive conception of citizenship by descent. Ireland's Department of Justice and Equality encourages the children and grandchildren of Irish-born citizens to claim Irish citizenship by registering in its Foreign Births register, and to do so "before the birth of the next generation (i.e. your children)" to "safeguard the Irish citizenship of future generations" (Department of Justice and Equality 2019). Registration of births with the Irish government allows each generation of the diaspora to pass down their entitlement to Irish citizenship from generation to generation, along with the right to live and work in other EU countries (Handoll 2006, 309). Further normative challenges to *jus sanguinis* citizenship result from the absence of a residency requirement for citizenship transmission by descent. These privileges for the diaspora are arguably unfair to immigrant residents of these polities (Shachar 2009, 121; Joppke 2010, 65–66).

Political communities offer two compelling reasons for granting intergenerational diasporic citizenship without a residence requirement. First, they want to protect their vulnerable nationals abroad who may not have access to citizenship in the country where they live (Fitzgerald 2008, 176; Waldinger 2015, 121–123). Second, a growing number of states with a history of forcibly denationalizing and exiling citizens are acting in atonement by granting their descendants a claim to citizenship by descent. This act also acknowledges the injustice of involuntary exile, and the costs that the preceding regime imposed on other states that accepted the moral obligation to shelter the original generation of refugees. These countries are accepting the particularity claims of former refugees and their descendants on the states that forced them into exile in the first place (Miller 2016, 77). For this reason, Germany and Austria offer citizenship to the descendants of citizens expelled by the Nazi regime (Harpaz 2013, 176; Cohen 2018, 42; Republic of Austria 2021). Spain offers citizenship to the descendants of Spaniards expelled from their country during and after Spain's civil war as a form of reparation for persecution by the Franco regime (Martín-Pérez and Francisco Moreno-Fuentes 2012; Escudero 2014, 142). In doing this, Germany, Austria, and Spain are fulfilling a moral duty incumbent on all states that have coercively constituted the identities of individuals and their descendants by renationalizing affected individuals (Smith 2015, 254). This duty to provide immigration and benefits to the descendants of deportees diminishes over time and as "responsibility for wrongdoing is more difficult to ascribe or is dispersed across several actors" (Espindola 2021, 10). For instance, we should welcome Spain's decision to provide immigration benefits to the descendants of Sephardic Jews over five hundred years ago (James 2022, 537). But the modern state of Spain is less directly accountable for this historical injustice than it is for more recent crimes of expulsion committed by Franco's regime.

Finally, the genuine connection criterion for defining citizenship does not necessarily lead us in the direction of curtailing citizenship by descent (Nottebohm Case 1955; Shachar 2009, 166). Instead, the International Court of Justice discussion of the "genuine connection criterion" states that nationality is a "legal bond having as its basis the social fact of attachment, a genuine connection of existence, interests and sentiments, together with the existence of reciprocal rights and duties" (Nottebohm Case 1955, 23). Nothing in this statement suggests that external citizens have to permanently live in a country to fulfill this requirement. A connection of existence, interests, and sentiments may be fulfilled by an individual who is motivated enough to learn the language, culture, and acquire the civics, administrative, and legal knowledge to make a claim to his ancestral country of origin. The language of the Nottebohm decision regarding the impact of naturalization on allegiance and the need for a closer connection to one nation than another is anachronistic (Nottebohm Case 1955, 23–24). Today, many countries accept dual nationality, with fewer compulsory military service requirements or other instances where one claim to nationality may come into conflict with another. Moreover, advances in communication enable motivated expatriate citizens to maintain ties with their country of origin and to acquire the current knowledge needed to be an informed participant in its evolving political affairs (*Frank v. Canada* 2019, ¶33–35, 69). In short, it is becoming easier for nonresident citizens and their descendants to demonstrate a "genuine connection" with their ancestral country of origin that merits a continued claim to citizenship there. Nonresident adult citizens by descent may have a further moral obligation to their compatriots to maintain their citizenship status

74 BORN INNOCENT

through contributions to the well-being of their ancestral country of origin and its citizens.

Conclusion

In this chapter, I have argued to ensure that children receive maximal protection as citizens of *a* state, countries should err on the side of including all persons born within their territorial jurisdiction as citizens, regardless of their parent's immigration and nationality status. The importance of ensuring that children are granted *a* citizenship status at birth is so essential to their future life prospects that it should be constitutionally protected. This is necessary to prevent a political majority from discriminating against children based on their parents' immigration or nationality status. It is also important to protect children's claims to citizenship in a country where they can return with their parents by ensuring that they can acquire citizenship by descent. Even beyond the first generation, descendants of children born abroad (external citizens) may have strong citizenship claims based on enduring ties to their ancestral country of origin. At the very least, every descendant of a citizen that would otherwise be stateless in his or her country of habitual residence should also be included as an external citizen by descent at birth.

4

Restoring Offenders as Citizens and Caregivers

There are two major problems at issue related to punishment drift for the children of imprisoned parents.[1] First is a theory of the objectives and principles of punishment that aims at retribution for all offenders, rather than reintegration. Second is a criminal justice system that is inflexible in incarceration and sentencing arrangements, without consideration for an offender's familial or community ties. Empirical research shows that caregivers' capacities to provide for their dependents is undermined by detention and incarceration, harming their children in particular in ways that have broader negative intergenerational social outcomes (Hagan and Dinovitzer 1999; Lippke 2007, 48, 178–182; Arditti 2012).

To address the first problem, I develop an argument about the objectives and principles of criminal sanctions, contending against retributive approaches in favor of restorative justice outcomes that aim to reintegrate offenders into their communities whenever possible (Braithwaite 2002; Golash 2005). This marks a departure from the imposition of collateral consequences and "preventive" sanctions that some legal scholars have compared to the colonial sanction of "civil death," by preventing those whom have served their sentence from assuming productive roles in society (Ewald 2002, 1059; Manza and Uggen 2006, 23, 210; Chin 2012; Mayson 2015, 303).[2] Felon disenfranchisement is a key example of "civil death" that denies rehabilitated offenders a chance to participate in their communities (Varsanyi 2012).

By contrast, reintegration involves preparing a former offender to take on more productive roles and responsibilities in society. For parents, the goal is to minimize collateral consequences of punishment by allowing offenders to maintain family relationships in which the parent can provide for his dependents emotionally while incarcerated, with the goal of restoring the offender to his roles as a caregiver and provider upon release (Lippke 2007, 185; Muth 2018, 17–18). A secondary goal is to break the cycle of family dissolutions and distrust in authority among the children of incarcerated

Born Innocent. Michael J. Sullivan, Oxford University Press. © Oxford University Press 2023.
DOI: 10.1093/oso/9780197671238.003.0004

76 BORN INNOCENT

parents that increases the chance that their children will commit criminal offenses (Fassin 2018, 114; Levine and Topalli 2019). Apart from cases where parents pose a danger to their children, the criminal justice and child welfare systems should facilitate family unity wherever possible through visitation, flexible sentencing, and sanctions that aim at reintegration, rather than retribution of offenders (Lippke 2007, 183–188).

The Collateral Consequences of an Inflexible and Retributive Penal System

In the United States, 113 million Americans or 34.4 percent of the population has a family member who has been to jail or prison (Sawyer and Wagner 2020). Estimates regarding the number of children under eighteen with a parent in prison have increased from 945,000 in 1991 to 2.6 million minors in 2012 (Finkeldey and Dennison 2020, 114–115; McLeod 2021, 1). African American children have long been overrepresented in this total. At the peak of the African American parental incarceration crisis, 25 percent of all African American children born in 1990 experienced the incarceration of their parents by age fourteen, compared to 4 percent of white children born that same year (Wildeman 2009, 266). Most of these parents face incarceration for minor crimes like drug possession, property crimes, or immigration violations (Wade-Olson 2019, 111). Mothers have faced a steeper increase in incarceration rates than fathers have over the past generation (Glaze and Maruschak 2010, 2; Sawyer 2018).

The separation of so many Black families through incarceration takes place in the context of a longer history of forced African American family separation dating back to enslavement. Slave owners often separated spouses and children by selling them away from their kin and caregivers, resulting in life-long family separations (Briggs 2020, 17–29). In his *Case for Reparations* (2014), Ta-Nehisi Coates casts Black family separation as part of "the economic foundation for America's experiment in democracy" (Coates 2014, 62–63). This system depended on the ability of slaveholders to sell human beings to turn a profit, where 25 percent of interstate sales of enslaved people "destroyed a first marriage and half of them destroyed a nuclear family" (ibid.). Apart from their economic motivations, slaveholders would often intentionally separate families as a form of punishment (*Nowell v. O'Hara* 1833, 151–152; Sinha 2022, 454). Black families during the Civil Rights era also suffered enforced family separations at the hands of child welfare authorities as a form of collective punishment for their activism (Briggs 2020, 33–44). In this context, family separation served as a technology of social control and community subjugation.

Canada's parental incarceration rate is lower than that of the United States, with an estimated 4.6 percent of Canadian children having experienced parental incarceration by age nineteen (Withers and Folsom 2007). Yet like the United States, parental incarceration rates in Canada are much higher among socioeconomically disadvantaged minority groups. Incarceration rates among Indigenous Canadians rival those of any other ethnic or racial group. Indigenous persons represent 30 percent of the total incarcerated population in Canada in 2020, even as they represent only 5 percent of the Canadian population (Office of the Correctional Investigator 2020). Demands for racial justice in Canada for Indigenous persons victimized by police violence mirror, and at times are merging with demands for racial justice for Black victims of police violence in both Canada and the United States. The coalescence between Indigenous and Black Lives Matter movements protesting carceral violence was evident in June protests in Canada against the beating of Allan Adam, Chief of the Athabascan Chipewyan First Nation, by an Royal Canadian Mounted Police (RCMP) officer in March 2020 (Porter and Bilefsky 2020; SpearChief-Morris 2021).

Indigenous families have a long history of state-mandated separation as a means of undermining the cultural continuity of their tribal polities. Throughout most of the twentieth century, in both Canada and the United States, state officials forced Indigenous parents to surrender their children to attend residential schools far from their tribe. There, they were subject to forced labor, punishment, and abuse, while their teachers and school administrators taught them to reject their language, the values of their tribe and their parents. While the residential schools are now closed, the damage to their culture and family life endures. Now, the criminal justice system is the primary source of Indigenous family separation. Incarcerated Indigenous women, many of whom are mothers, make up 50 percent of the total carceral population in Canada as of May 2022 (White 2022). Despite efforts by the Truth and Reconciliation Commission and the Canadian Supreme Court to address and respond to root causes, the rate of Indigenous incarceration continues to increase (Section 718.2(e), Criminal Code of Canada; *R v. Gladue* 1999, 722; *R v. Ipeelee* 2012, 465–486; Truth and Reconciliation Commission 2015c, 109–111; Arbel 2019, 444–445; Hanington 2020, 38).

78 BORN INNOCENT

The forced separation of Indigenous families through residential schooling and incarceration reinforces fissures in cultural and community bonds resulting from the forced institutionalization of Indigenous children by settler states including Canada, the United States, and Australia (Knudsen 2019, 196–197). Canada's concern with addressing the community consequences of mass incarceration through alternative sanctions has the potential to alleviate the plight of affected communities and families alike by tailoring punishment to an individual's life circumstances (Mégret 2017, 43). Drawing from both settler and traditional Indigenous practices, restorative justice is emerging in Canada as a key mechanism of victim-offender reconciliation and a culturally sensitive alternative to incarceration for Indigenous offenders (*R. v. Gladue* 1999, ¶70–75; Roach 2000, 273–274; Department of Justice 2018; Arbel 2019, 441–443). This approach stands in tension with dominant retributivist theories of punishment, which focus on penalizing the offender for the crime he committed without reference to circumstances that may mitigate his responsibility, or relationships that stand to assist in his rehabilitation (Mégret 2017, 27).

Family members of incarcerated parents suffer a number of collateral consequences from their loved one's incarceration beginning from the time they witness their arrest and prosecution (Levine and Topalli 2019, 55–56). In the criminal justice system, correctional officials manipulate family members of offenders and treat them as potential accessories to their crimes (Goffman 2014, 62–72; Condry 2018, 36). For instance, the Anti-Drug Abuse Act of 1988 authorizes the eviction of entire families from Section 8 public housing if one or more of the occupants engage in drug-related criminal activity (*Department of Housing and Urban Development v. Rucker 2002*; Silva 2015, 789–799; Hoskins 2019, 171). As most incarcerated parents contributed to the well-being of their children prior to incarceration, families suffer a loss of income, emotional support and caregiving services when a parent is imprisoned, in addition to the social stigma of being associated with a prisoner (Arditti and Few 2006; Wade-Olson 2019, 112–116). The task of caring for family members in prison inordinately falls on women as wives, mothers, and intimate partners, adding the cost and time of travelling to distant prisons to their duties as workers and family caregivers (Touraut 2012, 4). These added duties and the anguish of family separation frequently leads to a deterioration of the caregiver's mental and physical health while providing for their incarcerated family member (Touraut 2019, 25). In the immigration detention system, parents regularly face losing custody of their children without a voice in the proceedings while immigration enforcement officials detain them hundreds of miles away (Sullivan 2019, 130). Department of Homeland Security memos justify family separations for their supposed "substantial deterrent effect on those seeking to enter the United States" as asylum-seekers, even though this policy does not deter unauthorized immigration (DHS 2017; Ryo 2019, 547).

Inmates endure the worst of both worlds, separated from their families and community connections while still prone to the ills of the broader society that penetrate the prison walls. Among these challenges is the spread of infectious diseases in crowded jails and prisons. Poor public health conditions in carceral settings place inmates, correctional officials, and their families at risk of acquiring infectious diseases. Jails are congregate settings that hold detained individuals awaiting trial, release on bond, or for short sentences. Those who contract a contagious disease in the close quarters of a jail can readily transmit their infection to the community upon their release. Jails became key vectors for transmitting COVID-19 (Hawks, Woolhandler, and McCormick 2020, E1). During the first wave of the pandemic, jail officials in Texas intentionally released inmates with severe COVID symptoms into the community as part of a cover-up, so the death would not serve as evidence of mismanagement on the part of correctional officials (Sundaram 2020; Deitch et al. 2020, 7). Upon their release, family members of former inmates are also susceptible to this underappreciated collateral consequence of incarceration (Kaufman 2020; Eisler et al. 2020).

Long-term inmates in overcrowded prisons where inmates cannot socially distance or otherwise protect themselves are also more susceptible to the spread of infectious diseases than the general population. In June 2021, while the Delta variant was taking hold in the United States, the U.S. Bureau of Prisons (BOP) reported that 38.5 percent of federal prisoners had tested positive for COVID-19 to that date (U.S. Bureau of Prisons 2021).[3] In Texas prisons, which had the highest number of COVID infections among prisoners and staff in the United States in 2020, COVID contributed to a 79.3 percent increase in prison deaths during the period from April to September 2020 over the same time frame during the preceding five years (Deitch et al. 2020, 8). While deaths among prison staff in Texas decreased with the introduction of the vaccine, mask mandates, and social distancing requirements in early 2021, they rose again as COVID safety precautions were relaxed in July 2021 (McGaughy 2021). Texas's rate of prison staff deaths from COVID-19 rose to three times the national average by February 2022 as the state's correctional system has returned to pre-pandemic operations (Jones, Deitch and Welch 2022, 2, 12). Immigration detainees have also been at heightened risk of contracting COVID. According to U.S. Immigration and Customs Enforcement (ICE), by June 2021, 8.7 percent of all U.S. immigration detainees tested positive for COVID-19 (Immigration and Customs Enforcement 2021).[4] Yet significantly higher numbers have been reported in certain regions of the country, including a 90 percent positive test result at a Corrections Corporation of America facility in Virginia in July 2020. In Texas immigration detention facilities, detainees were fifteen times more likely than the general population of the state to test positive for COVID-19 during the first three months of the pandemic (Schotland 2020, 6). The reality of widespread coronavirus contagion in carceral settings stands at odds with the narrative of control presented by public officials (McCullough 2020). Correctional officials are providing family members of incarcerated individuals with very little information about their loved ones' medical condition as they have succumbed to the disease (Lewis 2020). The coronavirus crisis shows how conditions in carceral settings have broad family and community repercussions that reach beyond prison walls.

Retributivism and Family Separation

By the late 1970s, retribution replaced rehabilitation as the dominant objective for punishment across the Anglophone world (Yankah 2020, 96). Retribution requires that individuals be punished for the crime they committed, without regard for the offender's circumstances or the collateral consequences of punishment for dependents (Hart 1968, 231; Zedner 1994, 229). Retributivists argue that wrongdoers deserve to suffer a penalty that is proportionate to their wrongdoing, and their infraction is all that should be considered in this process (Bülow 2019, 286). In this way, retribution undermines flexible sentencing that would account for an individual's caretaking duties, or the role that family ties and responsibilities may play in rehabilitating offenders, leading to longer family separations (Iskikian 2019, 140–142). The Adoption and Safe Families Act of 1997 has further increased the likelihood of family separations by terminating the parental rights of caregivers when children are in foster care for more than fifteen months (135). In practice, this collateral consequence of incarceration falls more heavily on mothers, who are more likely to be the sole caregiver, than incarcerated fathers who can pass their caregiving responsibilities to another custodial parent (149–150). Regardless of gender, whenever a primary caregiver loses custody of their children for reasons not linked to maltreatment, children suffer a wide range of developmental difficulties that may make them more prone to incarceration later in life (Miller 2006, 477–478).

Critics of retribution see it as an inflexible commitment to punishment as an intrinsic good, which is difficult to differentiate from state-sponsored revenge. Retributivism is only concerned with a person who commits a crime in his role as an offender who needs to be punished for what he has done in the past, setting aside considerations about present remorse and future rehabilitation (Apt 2016, 447). Retributivism shows no regard for the consequences of punishment to the individual, those who depend on him, the victim, or society at large (Flanders 2014, 316). From a utilitarian perspective, the prospect of punishment drift from the offender to his dependents with consequences that include prolonged family separation may be justified for their deterrent value, to make a prospective offender with dependents think twice about committing an offense (Markel, Collins, and Leib 2009, 80; Lippke 2017, 656). On the other hand, retribution militates against the utilitarian impulse to punish an offender's family to deter criminal behavior, given its emphasis on individual responsibility (Hart 1968).

For legal theorists who write from a retributivist perspective, an inquiry into the collateral consequences of punishment for family members is a distraction from the state's pursuit of justice. Some retributivists have justified their approach by arguing that the offender profits unjustly from the rest of society by violating its rules, and he must suffer in proportion to the infraction to restore the balance between benefits and burdens for those who follow the rules (Husak 2008, 86–87). The consequences of retribution are of lesser concern for its theoretical advocates who justify the suffering of the offender for its own sake, even if no good comes of it for the victim, the offender, or society (Flanders 2014, 360). Legal practitioners and criminologists criticize retribution for failing to explain why and what level of punishment is deserved in individual cases (Flanders 2014, 358–359). They also criticize retributivism for failing to address the consequences of criminal behavior for all affected persons, including victims, offenders, and their dependents, and how to make those wronged whole (Barnett 1977, 286; Zedner 1994, 231–232).[5]

From Retributivism to Restorative Justice

Victims' rights advocates have also called into question the state's monopoly over criminal justice, following Nils Christie's trailblazing 1977 article "Conflicts as Property," which urged stakeholders in the criminal justice system to take back conflict resolution from the state (Christie 1977). Restorative approaches to criminal justice have developed in sophistication since this time, providing a forum for mediation between victims and offenders that looks beyond the individual offense toward repairing the harm done to the victim and reintegrating the offender into the community. Care ethics and restorative justice together are more interested in uncovering and attending to the needs of victims, offenders, and those in their circles of care by repairing the relationships that result from wrongdoing between the victim and the offender.

From a civic republican perspective that is interested in protecting civic equality through punishment, "the right to punish and the obligation to reintegrate are complimentary political duties" (Yankah 2020, 75). Elizabeth Cohen rightfully emphasizes that "democratic theory never assumes the current state of a person's character to be permanent," and this requires penal authorities to consider evidence of rehabilitation as an indication "that a person's punishment has been successful and that her rights ought to be restored" (Cohen 2016, 257). Patti Tamara Lenard takes a similar but more qualified stance, allowing that long-term post-sentencing preventive measures like barring a sex offender from living near a school might be justified, but only so long as the person in question is at risk of re-offending (Lenard 2020, 44–45). While Lenard does not state this directly, the preventive restrictions would have to be re-evaluated regularly to ensure that these restrictions do not "deny the capacity of an individual to regain their full and equal status as a citizen" (Lenard 2020, 45). Together, Yankah, Cohen, and Lenard's emphasis on rehabilitation as a requirement of democratic theory and equal citizenship militates against permanent punishments like the death penalty, life in prison without parole or denationalization and banishment. These sentences are unjustified because they preclude the possibility of reintegration into society and rehabilitation.[6] From the perspective of both democratic and civic republican theories, just punishment should be focused on reintegration, rather than retribution (Braithwaite and Pettit 1990, 91). The criminal justice system should supervise the process by which the offender makes amends to the victim in the interests of the broader community.

Advocates of retributive justice emphasize that the community has an interest in ensuring that the criminal justice system equitably penalizes offenders through hard treatment (Markel, Collins, and Leib 2009; Golash 2005, 167). Retributive emotions also provide a way of expressing a community's outrage at the breach of its moral order (Canton and Dominey 2020, 17). However, there are alternative ways of responding to these impulses that may be more beneficial for the victim and the offender alike. Theorists and practitioners of restorative justice respond that the shame that comes from facing up to the consequences of an offense for victims and community members is itself a form of self-denial that can foster moral reform (Braithwaite 1999, 39–45). Judges and other practitioners in the criminal justice system often employ a method of problem-solving adjudication for first time, low-level offenders. This process involves victims and offenders and seeks to resolve the conflict arising from criminal activity, increasing penalties with repeated infractions (Feeley 2020, 127). In more serious offenses against the victim and values of the community, or where the offender is recalcitrant, hybrid approaches are available that start with a traditional retributive punishment followed by a restorative approach centered on rehabilitation (Duff 2003; Brooks 2015, 83–87). These hybrid approaches preserve the expressive principle of punishment for serious crimes: the state and society still have a verdict that deems the offender guilty, but sentencing judges can apply restorative alternatives to incarceration if they serve the interests of victims and other stakeholders (Luzon 2016, 591).

Promoting Rehabilitation by Fostering Caregiving Capacities

Even if one insists upon the retributive maxim that everyone should face equitable hard treatment at the hands of the state to uphold equal accountability to the values of the community, the community still has a competing utilitarian interest in promoting the rehabilitation of offenders who are parents and caregivers wherever possible. Ideally, parents and caregivers serve a key civic role by raising their children as citizens-in-becoming, which should be promoted by the state (Engster 2015, 34). Incarceration undermines the ability for parents to provide financial and emotional support to their children, and increases the burden of caring for children on other family members and state welfare agencies (Withers and Folsom 2007, 13). While the precise mechanisms that lead to intergenerational incarceration are difficult to isolate, studies have shown that the young children of detained parents experience emotional trauma and developmental delays resulting from parental loss that make them more prone to anti-social behavior and incarceration later in life (Roettger and Dennison 2018, 1551–1552). In sum, children with incarcerated parents are more likely to offend as adults, making the community interest in their parents' rehabilitation all the more urgent.

To mitigate these collateral consequences of incarceration for family members and promote the rehabilitation of offenders as caregivers and productive community members, the criminal justice process should account for the offender's social context and the challenges that led him to act in an anti-social manner, with a view toward addressing these root causes (Golash 2005, 153). The crime is temporary, the relationships the offender has with the community are enduring, requiring repair (Canton and Dominey 2020, 29). Wherever possible, the criminal justice system along with social workers should enlist family and community members in the task of rehabilitating the offender as a law-abiding citizen and more capable caregiver. Family and community members understand the offender and may be able to convince him to change in ways that are not accessible to impersonal criminal justice officials (Golash 2005, 167).

Unless an offender has committed a crime that poses a direct and ongoing risk to his or her dependents, there are significant positive potential benefits to allowing offenders to maintain connections with their family members. Visits with family members ease the isolation of incarceration, providing offenders with contacts outside the negative socialization of institutions that often serve as "schools of crime." Continued contact with dependents can provide inmates with a source of hope and motivation to pursue rehabilitation while in prison so they can pursue productive lives in the future as caregivers (Lippke 2007, 180; Bülow 2014, 778). As they look forward to their release from incarceration, law-abiding family members can provide inmates with financial support and social capital to facilitate their reintegration into the community as contributing citizens (Lippke 2007, 181–184; Berg and Huebner 2011, 284–387; Christian 2020, 221–222).

Despite the benefits of ongoing parent-child visitation, in the United States, only a third of all incarcerated parents receive visits from their children, due to factors that corrections scholars link to relationships between the child's caregiver and the incarcerated parent, the isolation of prisons and the distance between the child's home and the parent's prison, and the high cost of travel (Johnston and Sullivan 2016, 110). For children who manage to overcome these barriers, the institutional process of visiting a U.S. prison is often traumatic, overshadowing the joy that comes from a fleeting period of constrained contact. Vannette Thomson's narrative of her childhood experiences visiting an incarcerated father aptly expresses this bittersweet element of the prison visitation experience, wishing that she could spend more time with her father under less constrained conditions:

> After driving eight hours . . . we stand outside the barbed wire fence waiting patiently for everyone to make their way from their car to the first of numerous guard-manned gates we must travel through to get inside the prison. . . . We walk into the main entrance of the Holman State Prison, but before entering the visiting room, we must first be inspected for any contraband or paraphernalia. . . . It won't be long now until I see my Daddy . . . As he proceeds to walk down the steps, my heart races with excitement! Once our arms are locked around one another in a loving hug, our burden is lifted. For a few brief moments we are sharing our lives together face-to-face, not through letters or quick collect phone calls. . . . It is obvious to all who are looking . . . I adore my Daddy. After hours of visiting and pretending we were not actually in a state prison visiting room filled with men who were convicted of murder, the guard quietly comes through the door and shouts out, "Five minutes." How does a little girl who adores her Dad tell him goodbye in 300 seconds? There are no words to adequately end a visit that crushes your heart and leaves your soul weeping like an open wound for weeks to come. Daddy never fails to comfort me, even though he is the one returning to a 5 by 5 foot cell for 23 hours a day. He says, "Don't cry, baby girl. I will be alright. I am so proud of you." (Thomson 2016, 129–131)

Governments and correctional authorities need to facilitate visitation to ease the negative collateral consequences of incarceration for innocent children. This can include providing families with financial support for visitation and travel and providing the children of incarcerated parents with a chaperone in case her caregiver does not want to participate. Facilitating visitation can promote parental rehabilitation and pro-social behavior as parents care for their children's emotional needs.

Restorative justice approaches place rehabilitation, which includes fostering caregiving capacities, in its social context, building upon Nils Christie's original mandate to transfer criminal justice outcomes from institutional actors to community stakeholders (Christie 1977). Restorative justice emphasizes an accountability model of justice where stakeholders in both the victim and the offender's lives, along with community leaders, hold offenders to account and encourage them to take responsibility for the harm they caused. Wherever possible, offenders are encouraged to make amends for their wrongdoing in ways that are acceptable to victims of crime. Restorative justice involves rebuilding relationships as a key focus of preparing offenders for re-entry into productive social roles upon their release (Bazemore 1998, 790). This requires a shift in responsibility from formal sanctions backed by institutional actors like correctional and parole officials to stakeholders that include the offenders' family members, employers, and victims of crime who are willing to participate in this process (Raynor and Robinson 2005, 155). In John Braithwaite's (1989) influential model of reintegrative shaming-based restorative justice, victims testify as to the impact of the offender's crime on their lives and their needs. Victims and offender supporters like family members cooperate to find ways to convince the offender to atone for his crimes, while providing a pathway forward (Raynor and Robinson 2005, 136–141). Where retributive justice sanctions centered on incarceration separate offenders from their dependents and their communities, followed by long-lasting collateral consequences that make it difficult for them to reintegrate into society, restorative justice approaches enlist family members in the rehabilitation process soon after the offender is willing to accept responsibility for his actions (Braithwaite 1999, 17). The anticipated result is one in which the offender informally holds himself accountable for his future actions and desists from future crime (Raynor and Robinson 2005, 29).

One of the aspirations of restorative justice advocates and care ethicists is to overcome the impersonal nature of state justice. While there are reasons for insulating victims from offenders that pose a direct and ongoing threat to them, there are also instances in which offenders are unaware of the victim, and the impact of their offense on others. For instance, the offender who pleads guilty without going to trial may never encounter the victim of a property crime, or know the impact of this crime on the victim. The state serves justice as retribution through incarceration or other state-mandated penalties, without any attempt to ensure that the victim has closure and healing in the process. Care ethics emphasize the importance of maintaining relationships of mutual concern (Schmid 2019, Coverdale 2021, 416). From this perspective, crime can constitute a breach of this relationship between the offender and the community that is in need of repair (Canton and Dominey 2020, 28). The immediate offense may also be symptomatic of the social injustice of a broader breakdown of relationships between those who hold political power over a community and members of groups that are overrepresented as victims of crime and accused offenders. Care and restoration also require that we look beyond simple categorizations of persons as victims and offenders. We must be attentive to the injustice of wrongfully accusing persons of a crime, the victimization of communities that are prone to accusations of criminal activity, and the repair of relationships between these victims and the criminal justice system. The wave of unrest in 2020 against members of the African American communities in the United States in the wake of the murder of George Floyd underscores the ongoing need for more community-sensitive policing, restorative rather than retributive punishments for minor crimes, and racial reconciliation.[7] While people from all walks of life suffer equally when their caregivers are incarcerated, the separation of families by law enforcement is a burden that is borne disproportionately by African Americans and immigrants (Wildeman 2009, 266; Manning 2011, 271; Lee et al. 2015, 275–277; Wakefield and Wildeman 2018).[8]

Restorative justice does not need to involve a call for outright prison abolition, but rather a recentering of the justice system on rehabilitation. This means that even for major crimes, moral reform should play a guiding role in incarceration, rather than simply warehousing offenders who will never be released.

The goal should be to reintegrate offenders into the community as caregivers and citizens upon the completion of their sentence, rather than indefinitely incapacitating serious offenders. The trial, sentencing, and imprisonment of Derek Chauvin for the murder of George Floyd raises some challenging issues that prison abolitionists must grapple with, while addressing visceral community demands for any form of justice available—including imprisonment—in individual cases (Holloway 2021). Abolitionists like Angela Y. Davis in *Freedom is a Constant Struggle* are productively grappling with this tension between the community's demands for accountability through incarceration, and incarceration's failure to address "the sociohistorical conditions that enable these acts," which point to the root causes of violent acts of racism including police violence (Davis 2016, 137). Davis points to the problem of a neoliberal ideology that "drives us to focus on individuals, ourselves, individual victims, individual perpetrators" (ibid.). She asks, "How it is possible to solve the massive problem of racist

88 BORN INNOCENT

state violence by calling on individual police officers to bear the burden of that history and to assume that by prosecuting them, by exacting our revenge on them, we would have somehow made progress in eradicating racism?" (ibid.). Collectively, prison abolitionists are calling for systemic social and political change to address the root causes of crimes committed by disadvantaged individuals. These include a legacy of slavery and segregation in the United States, and settler colonialism in Canada and the United States that is borne out in the disproportionate incarceration of Black and Indigenous people in both countries (Aiken and Silverman 2021, 144). To address root causes of crime that affect all persons in society, abolitionists are calling "for the redistribution of resources to meet humans' needs for adequate health, education, housing, and jobs; while simultaneously rejecting the norms of racial capitalist society" (142).

In sum, Davis and other abolitionists are correct that we need to look beyond the emotions of individual cases to engage in projects that address root causes of abuses of power, which include but are not limited to racism, in law enforcement and other acts of coercive governance. Davis's insights can be extended to cases of systemic and historical injustice where there are no readily identifiable individual perpetrators, or when the perpetrators are deceased and society still has to address the underlying racial injustice that contributed to the act and that poisons community relations to the present day. The intergenerational injustice against the Indigenous communities of settler states through child removals is another apt example of this type of case, which I discuss later in this text.

Still, individual cases with identifiable, living perpetrators, and the emotions and community demands for justice that they engender must be addressed in the moment as we progress toward longer-term solutions. With this in mind, Minnesota Attorney General Keith Ellison spoke for many victims of police brutality when he described Chauvin's 22.5 year sentence as a "moment of real accountability" to the community he wronged, balancing his view "it's difficult to see anyone lose their freedom, but seeing someone lose their life through torture over 9½ minutes is incomparably worse" (Hernandez 2021). Here, Ellison balances his misgivings with the carceral state and the community's continued interest in retribution in discrete cases as a necessary form of justice. The deterrent function of incarceration, or the prospect that a prison sentence for Chauvin may deter other police officers from committing similar offenses, must also be grappled with as part of an effort to satisfy the community's desire for justice in this and other serious offenses (Bagaric, Hunger, and Svilar 2021, 354–355). Ellison also voiced rehabilitative views of justice in the Chauvin verdict, with his hope that "that he takes the time to learn something about the man whose life he took and about the movement that rose up to call for justice in the wake of George Floyd's torture and death" during his years in prison (ibid.).

It is an open question whether a sentence amounting to decades in prison that takes up most of an offender's life is necessary to achieve penitence or atonement. Abolitionists have an insightful critique when they condemn sentencing guidelines that lead to prisoners being warehoused in institutions into old age, long after they have atoned for their crimes and ceased to pose a danger to the community (Davis 2005, 42). Lengthy sentences appeal to penal populist impulses, and they serve incapacitory and retributive functions that satisfy community sentiment, but they are not necessary to bring about penitence and atonement (Mauer and Ellis 2018; Philips and Chagnon 2020, 50–52; *R v. Bissonnette* 2022). Having fulfilled the functions of punishment as rehabilitation and incapacitation, all that remains in a prolonged sentence is a community's demands for retribution, to see a prisoner die in a facility in the distant future, long after his or her initial conviction, without ever having the opportunity to reintegrate and contribute to a community.

The pursuit of remorse and reconciliation is consistent with the goals of the restorative justice movement, but this changed state of mind will not happen by itself while an offender is in prison. For serious offenders, restorative justice processes which foster penitence, atonement, and reflection can form an important part of the rehabilitative process (Garvey 2003, 311–316).[9] The pursuit of penitence is not inconsistent with interaction with family members, or the process of visiting with, and caring for loved ones that prepare offenders for a life of restored caregiving and citizenship in the future. Prison redesign with a focus on rehabilitation and interaction with family, friends, and trusted community members that can aid in this task is to be preferred to a form of prison abolition that would allow an offender to bypass the atonement process, or that would offend the community's sense of justice and the need for accountability.

Caring for the victim, offender, and the community in the context of a criminal offense involves holding people accountable with a view toward restoring their place in the community (Coverdale 2021, 424).

Complementary restorative justice conferences require the offender, the victim, and their circles of care and mediators to discuss the circumstances surrounding the offense and its impact (Grauwiler and Mills 2004, 61). The

90 BORN INNOCENT

aspiration is that a contrite offender will be willing to listen to the testimonies of those whom she indirectly hurt in the process, for instance, the children of those addicted to drugs that she trafficked, or the child who lost a mother in a car accident caused by reckless driving. Care ethicists hope, with some empirical evidence to support their aspirations in actual victim-offender mediation sessions, that victims will allow offenders to work to repair the damage they caused and atone for their misdeeds. They also aspire to bring offenders into lasting, positive relationships as victims make restitution as part of their rehabilitation process. The hope that is this reconciliation process will make the offender a more caring, relational person (Fallinger 2006, 519–524). These are optimistic goals, which are not appropriate to every case, particularly when the victim is unwilling to encounter the offender, or a perpetrator is recalcitrant and refuses to accept responsibility.

Restorative justice approaches to criminal justice reform emphasize alternatives to imprisonment that allow victims, offenders, and other stakeholders including family members of both parties to come together to resolve the conflict arising from wrongdoing. At the community level, the process is partly contingent on bringing the offender to a state of contrition through a process that practitioners describe as "reintegrative shaming." In this context, shaming involves victims discussing harm and community members showing disapproval for the errant action rather than the person (Braithwaite 1989, 100). There is not a labelled offender or an "illegal person," but a person who committed an offense for which atonement is possible. Reintegration follows shaming with treatment and incentives aimed at helping the person who committed a crime to live a pro-social life and to restore his civic standing. One often overlooked facet of rehabilitation is the mental health crisis that exists among incarcerated populations, resulting in part from pre-existing challenges that prison-based mental healthcare often fails to address (MacKay, Comfort, and Lindquist 2016, 5). Social workers, community leaders, and whatever support network the individual has is called upon to help the person who broke the trust of the community to become a better caregiver and a contributing citizen through counselling, values-based education, vocational training, and employment opportunities (Braithwaite 1989, 177–180). Reintegrative shaming works on a model of trusting the first-time offender but following-up and verifying that rehabilitation is taking place. Recidivists are penalized with a pyramid of escalating community-supervised sanctions, with incarceration as a last resort for recalcitrant offenders (Braithwaite 2018, 74). An important objection here is that this approach also needs to recognize that some offenses are serious enough to require immediate escalation even for first-time offenders (i.e., murder), placing retributive and deterrent sanctions before treatment to respond to the overriding need to protect society from past and future extreme acts of violence. However, with all crimes, a rehabilitative element is necessary to recognize that all persons are not simply a function of the crime they committed in the past. Restorative justice and rehabilitative approaches to criminal justice reform aspire to move beyond the hard treatment of retributivism toward a problem-solving approach to crime, helping offenders to become law-abiding contributing members of society.

Crimes against both individuals and communities perpetrated by public officials like the murder of George Floyd by Minneapolis police officer Derek Chauvin on May 25, 2020 raise broader issues of systemic social and racial injustice that extend beyond the discrete crime and the victim and offenders as individuals. Restorative justice theorists and practitioners actively seek to provide a voice to marginalized communities by bringing diverse cultural perspectives about justice into restorative processes, but they have less to say about how to respond to the victimization of communities by systemic state-sponsored racial discrimination (Wood and Suzuki 2020, 7). Here, state officials must respond to the victimized community's sense of injustice before any victim-offender mediation and reconciliation between the police and the community can take place. In this case, the gravity of the offense before the courts (murder) may require carceral officials to apply deterrent sanctions upon conviction, including incarceration, before the victim's representatives can elect to initiate restorative processes. The broader community has an interest in preventing further violations of this magnitude to protect the community's security. Restorative justice can still be relevant to this conversation, as either an alternative or an accompaniment to a state-centered system of policing and incarceration that provides a voice to both victims of crime. Victims of state-centered injustice need the opportunity to transfer conflicts from the criminal justice system, with its racial and social discrimination, to communities marginalized by state-centered justice.[10]

Here, at the intersection of systemic racial injustice and restorative justice, transitional justice between victimized and dominant communities can complement restorative justice at the level of individual victims and offenders. The goal is not retribution or vengeance, but rather to uncover the truth about undisclosed acts of violence, to hold particularly heinous offenders accountable, to make reparations, and to take official actions to ensure nonrecurrence

92　BORN INNOCENT

(Fletcher 2019, 134–136). Accountability does not always need to entail incarceration, allowing for the use of restorative justice practices in individual cases. Post-apartheid South Africa used transitional justice practices to address its legacy of apartheid and violence, which included noncarceral restorative forms of accountability for individual perpetrators (Leebaw 2003, 33–38). Though Canada is not as divided of a society, it has also employed a truth and reconciliation commission to respond to the legacy of discrimination toward Indigenous peoples. The United States, as a country with a deep legacy of state-sanctioned discrimination, coupled with ongoing violence toward its Black and immigrant populations by state officials and a carceral system that victimizes whole families and communities, could benefit from both transitional and restorative remedies (King and Page 2018, 749–751).

Ways to Alleviate Punishment Drift

Collateral consequences of punishment often include civil disabilities that the state intentionally imposes upon offenders beyond the terms of their formal sentence. Since collateral consequences are normatively justified in other contexts to accomplish a desired result, critics of the term argue that framing harm to dependents as "collateral consequences" of their caregiver's incarceration may serve to rationalize the suffering of innocent dependents, by drawing unjustified analogies to military collateral damage (Minson 2020, 35; Condry and Minson 2020, 6). Describing the dependents of incarcerated caregivers using the euphemism of collateral consequences also renders them less visible and obscures their humanity (Minson 2020, 214). The state does not take responsibility for their hardship, as the criminal justice system frames their suffering as incidental and collateral to the perceived overriding social benefit of punishing their parents (Burke 2016, 251). Hence, dependents must suffer the impact of having a caregiver taken from them with minimal emotional, social, and financial support. In one example selected from a compilation of personal accounts of parental incarceration, Natalie Chaidez, the college-aged daughter of an incarcerated mother, describes her decision to "bring my sister," who just started kindergarten, "to live with me in my college apartment" after her mother was sentenced to sixteen months in prison. Adding to the challenge of parental incarceration and being thrust into a surrogate parental role at a young age, Natalie describes how "it was really difficult to work twenty hours a week, attend my college classes, and also take care of my sister" (Chaidez 2016, 90).[11] Here, the underlying systemic problem is the failure of the state to provide support to kinship caregivers of children when their parents are incarcerated, which is an overlooked collateral consequence of incarceration for older children as caregivers. Some family members part ways, but other close dependents, particularly lifelong female partners, experience a parallel sentence, bound to the strictures of visitation rules, and waiting on their partner's release to make long-term plans (Granja 2016, 278; Rodriguez and Turanovic 2018, 192–193).

Legal theorists including William Bülow and Richard Lippke, who otherwise agree that the doctrine of double effect can justify collateral consequences in other contexts disagree that punishing the guilty through incarceration is so valuable to society that it outweighs the harms to families and the children of inmates (Bülow 2014, 784; Lippke 2017, 649–651). Building on this argument, William Bülow and Lars Lindblom contend that parental imprisonment is objectionable from the standpoint of luck egalitarianism. By incarcerating parents away from their children, the state is imposing inequalities on innocent dependents for choices that they are not responsible for. This results in a duty to the children to mitigate this injustice while still ensuring equitable punishment for offenders who happen to be parents (Bülow and Lindblom 2020, 304–305). They argue that there are other ways besides current modes of incarceration to achieve the goods sought through incarceration, such as deterrence and holding offenders accountable. Both urge that we find ways to limit a convicted offender's liberty that allow for more contact with their dependents, ranging from increased family visitation to community sentencing. They argue that as a matter of fairness, officials should design alternatives to detention to make them equal in severity to a custodial sentence. But it is difficult to envision how to design such practices in a way that they would not also harm the dependents of the penalized offender (Bülow and Lindblom 2020, 316–317). The principal contribution of this perspective may be to condemn sentences whereby officials intend to inflict harm on offenders by separating them from their families to serve penal aims including deterrence and retribution (Lippke 2017, 657–658).[12]

Legal theorist Richard Lippke coined the term "punishment drift" to explain, and, later, to condemn state agents for not considering the harm to innocent dependents resulting from punishing their caregivers with incarceration leading to family separation (Lippke 2017, 647). Punishment drift's concern with the impact of state sanctions on nonoffenders aptly describes the individuals whom I am primarily concerned with in this text: the dependents and other family members who suffer when the state punishes their partners and caregivers. To avoid punishment drift, Lippke provides a clear admonition to state officials that they have to design sentences that are shorter and more focused on rehabilitation. He responds to the fairness objection by arguing that society at large would benefit from alternatives to incarceration that are focused on rehabilitation in light of the offender's needs and circumstances, and for this reason, sentencing reforms should not just be limited to caregivers (Lippke 2017, 650, 653–656).

The term "punishment drift" has its own challenges, arising from its tidy distinction between offenders and the innocent. The term "offender" presupposes an essential criminality to a person and a citizen convicted of a crime, who can pass back into innocence through exculpation, exoneration, or the completion of his sentence. Treating people who commit crimes as mere offenders, without regard to their other identities, connections and roles where inmates can still contribute to others, is a disservice to everyone who stands to benefit from the rehabilitation process involved in maintaining relationships outside prison (Brownlee 2020, 180, 191). The term "innocent" presupposes a lack of involvement in a social process that led to the offense in question. There are still problems with punishment for offenders who supposedly deserve it. There are far greater problems with imposing suffering upon those who never committed any offence, and whom the state admits are innocent, simply because they are associated with a convicted caregiver or other family member. Taking all these issues into account, Rachel Condry and Shona Minson (2020) argue that it is best to describe the negative effects of incarcerating caregivers and providers as "symbiotic harms" as a negative feedback loop that undermines relationships of care for prisoners and their families. For instance, while in prison, an incarcerated father cannot provide necessary emotional and disciplinary support for his troubled teenage son, who suffers educationally and turns to street gangs for kinship and protection. News of these developments further undermine the psychological well-being of the incarcerated father, who loses any incentive at rehabilitation while in prison. To this end, carceral officials should provide inmates with as many opportunities as possible to continue to participate in the lives of their dependents to cultivate their capacity for social contributions, unless their dependents' safety is directly at risk. Inmate contributions in these roles while incarcerated can help prepare them for further and more complete social reintegration upon release (Brownlee 2020, 191–192). As it stands, incarcerated individuals report that they have been forced into further isolation from their families during the COVID-19 pandemic, with fewer visitation and paid work opportunities (Maycock 2022, 226).

In spite of these conceptual issues, terms like "punishment drift" or "symbiotic harms" are both valuable as a means of describing and challenging the ways in which the carceral system undermines the well-being of dependents and other family members by incarcerating their caregivers. When immigration enforcement detains noncitizen caregivers for status violations, dependents including citizen-children who are not the targets of immigration enforcement face the emotional, financial, and potential custodial consequences of a loss of a caregiver and provider. Upon deportation of their caregivers, citizen-dependents face constructive removal to their parent's country of origin, where they cannot benefit from their rights and privileges as U.S. citizens, leading to educational, linguistic, and financial disadvantages (Caldwell 2019).

How can we avoid punishment drift, when the process of incarcerating an individual for his violation of the law involves separating him from his dependents, and leaving them without his care and provision? Ideally, we can find ways to sanction offenders without separating them from their dependents. Mothers could care for their infant children while in detention. Correctional officials would detain parents as close to their children's place of residence as possible, or to provide travel assistance to help family members cover the costs of a visit (Bülow 2014, 787). At present, prisons tend to be located in rural areas far from cities where inmates and their families last resided, making it costly and time-consuming for dependents to visit their incarcerated family members (Clark and Duwe 2017, 187). To minimize harm to dependents, the state should facilitate the provision of care by allowing incarcerated parents as providers and caregivers to work for market-level wages while in prison for the purpose of remitting their earnings to dependents, rather than forcing those left behind to rely on social assistance. Rehabilitation would become the primary objective of incarceration. Those incarcerated would learn a trade and skills needed to better care for dependents upon their release. The state also has a duty to affected dependents to avoid applying sanctions that permanently prevent a caregiver from reassuming his duties of provision by making it more difficult for him to obtain employment, housing, or any of the other necessities of life. This can include legislation preventing employers from discriminating

96 BORN INNOCENT

against prospective employees based on their criminal record, as this practice undermines the ability of formerly incarcerated caregivers to be able to provide for their dependents in lieu of the state (Emory et al. 2020).

The alternative to placing incarcerated caregivers on the path to rehabilitation is to place this financial burden on already burdened family members, or to add one more level of charges to taxpayers by adding supporting dependents to the costs of incarcerating offenders (Comfort et al. 2016, 785). Beyond quantifiable financial costs and rewards, care ethicists remind us that the attentiveness of care provided by family members with a long history of experience with their dependents has long-lasting benefits to its recipients (Tronto 2013, 34). Dependents benefit emotionally from the attentive care of family members who "have the potential to provide their members with emotional and material resources, often in a dignified manner that other institutions can rarely match" (Kershaw 2005, 183; Sullivan 2019, 163).

Increased opportunities for family visitations do not free the offender from prison or lessen his sentence; rather, visits are for dependent's benefit, and serve the interest of society in encouraging offender rehabilitation. Denying contact between a fit caregiver who is not guilty of abuse and a dependent is rarely a part of the punishment envisioned in any criminal justice system. Work and skills-building initiatives provided to offenders in prison to pay their child and victim support obligations and rehabilitating inmates so they can be caregivers who are more productive does not lessen the sentence. Rather, it holds offenders to additional obligations for the benefit of dependents, victims, and other criminal justice stakeholders. In short, punishment drift to the dependents of incarcerated caregivers is avoidable even in a retributive criminal justice system that seeks to hold offenders accountable for their violations of the law.

Caveats: When Caregivers Harm Their Partners or Children

The primary objection to allowing incarcerated caregivers to remain in close contact with their dependents is victim centered. In a limited number of cases where child abuse is involved, there is stronger support for state intervention that limits ties between former caregivers and their vulnerable dependents (Manning 2011, 269). From both a care ethics philosophical standpoint and

RESTORING OFFENDERS AS CITIZENS AND CAREGIVERS 97

the best interests of the child legal perspective, children have a right to attentive, responsive, and protective caregivers. Enforcing this right requires a child to be removed from a home in which he is the direct victim of ongoing and irreparable harm by abusive parents and guardians. The best interests of the child standpoint also emphasizes their right to continuity of caregiving within families and communities wherever possible. Child removal is a last resort that should be undertaken when interventions in cases of neglect are unsuccessful.

First, we must distinguish between forms of abuse that give rise to family separations, where civil violations such as "free-range parenting" or a lack of supervision of older children by immigrant parents at work are leading to custody decisions that separate parents from children. Judicial interpretations of the Illegal Immigration Reform and Immigrant Responsibility Act of 1996 have construed these practices as child abuse, leading to the deportation of parents and family separation (Hong and Torrey 2019). While not consistent with middle-class norms of attachment parenting, minimal supervision of older children by parents is not widely construed as abusive on the same level as violence and sexual abuse.

Second, in more severe cases of abuse and violence, restorative justice approaches are available in cases where victims express a strong interest in remaining with their parents or partners, while seeking intervention to end the harmful behavior. Even in the face of widespread penal populism and demands for retribution in cases of abuse, Canadian authorities are using restorative justice approaches to deal with intimate partner violence and child abuse (Cameron 2006, 481). Restorative practices including community-led healing and sentencing circles in which the victim, the offender, family members, and community leaders take part in holding offenders accountable, supervising their reformation and assisting in their reintegration are particularly prevalent in Indigenous communities in Canada (*R v. Moses* 1992; *R v. Gladue* 1999; Cameron 2006, 485). In the Canadian context, Indigenous communities developed healing circles to deal with the legacy of childhood abuse as an underlying cause of other social ills and criminal justice encounters among Indigenous communities (Jaccoud 1999, 87). Indigenous observers are careful to note that these practices are not a panacea: not all native communities share them; external threats undermine the cultural stability and continuity of the underlying traditions; and participants need more than healing (Jaccoud 1999, 95). Their communities need broader social, economic, and political support to help overcome the social problems

98 BORN INNOCENT

that lead to patterns of abuse dating back to the family separations and abuse of the residential schools era.

Some of the main justifications for a restorative approach to family violence and abuse involve the failure of the criminal justice system to expose and address abuse in intimate settings, to confront recidivism, or to address the root causes of the offense (McAlinden 2007). In her argument for applying restorative justice practices to family abuse, Anne McAlinden notes that the criminal justice system has an erroneous view of where abuse occurs (targeting strangers) that is inadequate to expose and treat abuse in families (McAlinden 2007, 4, 189–190, 202). Restorative approaches in cases of abuse remain extremely controversial, with one objection centering on the issue of whether community-based alternatives to punishment can protect victims (Cameron 2006, 497). Practitioners respond by pointing to evidence that restorative justice programs are more effective at exposing abuse within families that are reluctant to involve the criminal justice system, or incidents that state officials cannot readily prosecute (McGlynn, Westmarland, and Godden 2012). Mandatory arrest policies discourage victims from coming forward who do not want their parent or partner arrested, or who do not trust law enforcement or the criminal justice system based on its negative impact on their communities (Morris and Gelsthorpe 2000, 213–214). Based on their community's experience with immigration and law enforcement, victims in minority and immigrant communities have reason to be skeptical that criminal justice officials will respond to their needs or protect them. Removing the threat of incarceration, and requiring the offender to communicate with the victim and his supporters in a mediated setting also removes the incentive to deny, trivialize or lie (Braithwaite 2000, 189; McGlynn, Westmarland, and Godden 2012, 222–228). The exposure of abuse in a context where offenders must confront victims, and families and trusted members of their community hold offenders responsible in a process that emphasizes accountability can protect victims who otherwise would not have come forward.

In the case of family violence, criminal justice approaches that result in punishment for the perpetrator and/or deportation for an immigrant can discourage victims from reporting abuse. Many victims simply want the abuse to stop, without separating the family or creating further trauma (McAlinden 2007, 202; Stubbs 2007, 172). Alternatives to incarceration such as restorative justice can be helpful even in cases of family abuse and violence, but they must respect the victims' needs and interests. Young children need a representative to ensure that their security and care needs are articulated and protected in the process.

Conclusion

The implementation of retributive theories of justice and the attendant widening of the net of mass incarceration to include millions of Americans is a grave social problem for the United States. Systemic racial injustice that led to the disproportionate incarceration of racial minorities and immigrants extends beyond the United States to other countries of immigration and settlement. Mass incarceration is not just a problem for persons convicted of crimes that merit punishment. Rehabilitation has become less of a priority over the past generation, as prisoners serve longer sentences and face barriers to employment and other forms of civic reintegration that prevent them from reestablishing lives as contributing citizens and caregivers. Lost in the political conversation about making offenders pay their just dues is the developmental, social, and financial toll borne by the innocent dependents of incarcerated caregivers, which is also borne by the rest of society.

This chapter uncovers these collateral consequences of punishment for innocent family members and explores alternatives that allow offenders to reconcile with victims, contribute to caregivers, and prepare for reintegration within their communities. Here, I have considered the merits of alternative sanctions that still punish those who threaten the safety of victims and society, with a view of restoring the balance of advantages and disadvantages broken by crime. Incarceration should be used to rehabilitate offenders to be better caregivers and citizens upon their release. In crimes where there is a victim, restorative justice involves allowing victims to take part in the sanctioning process, if they want to be involved, and allowing them to explain the harm that the crime caused them. Restorative justice also involves diverting individuals who commit minor crimes from prison, insofar as they are committed to the process of making amends to victims and society. The goal is to seek accountability and remorse from the person who committed a crime, with a view toward a commitment to changing his future behavior. In all crimes, rehabilitation, rather than retribution or deterrence, should be the main focus of the criminal justice system. Incarceration should not be the default sentence in cases of minor crimes where offenders do not pose an ongoing threat to the community, and victims seek restorative justice as

100 BORN INNOCENT

an alternative to imprisonment. In sentencing, elected officials should give judges the discretion to reserve prison terms for grave crimes that represent an ongoing threat to the community, where the offender absolutely must be incapacitated to protect others. Even in these cases, prison should be a school of caregiving and citizenship, rather than a barrier to future contributions to society. With that in mind, incarcerated individuals should be able to meet with their families with fewer barriers, unless this poses a direct danger to the dependents in question. Prison should be a place where offenders can work for income, learn skills, support dependents, provide compensation to society for their offenses, and to earn funds for re-entering society without resorting to social assistance. Offenders should be eligible for parole when they have demonstrated sufficient rehabilitation and no longer pose a safety risk to the community. Elected officials should pass legislation removing collateral consequences of conviction that prevent offenders from supporting their dependents through employment, facilitating the integration of the former offender into the community. Incarceration should be repurposed with a view toward rehabilitating as many offenders as possible to improve their lives and become better citizens and caregivers.

5

The Collateral Consequences of Banishment

Reintegration should be the goal of punishment for offenders, allowing them to reassume their roles as caregivers, providers, and contributing members of society. The criminal justice system should shield children and other dependents of offenders from the consequences of punishing an offender who is a caregiver and provider wherever possible. In this chapter, I extend this concern beyond the ordinary criminal justice system to anti-state offenses including treason, and terrorism, where liberal democratic states have revived denationalization and banishment as sanctions in recent years as instruments of "preventive justice" (Lavi 2011; Macklin 2014, 18; Tripkovic 2019, 127, 132; Gibney 2020a; Gibney 2020b). Earlier practices of banishment to penal colonies like Australia maintained the state's jurisdiction over the punished individual. Now, liberal democratic states are discarding their citizens and forcing war-torn regimes like the Kurdish authorities in Syria and Iraq to care for them and their children and bring them to justice (Tripkovic 2022). The global war on terror and the fight against the self-styled Islamic State in Iraq and Syria (ISIS) hastened the development of an "enemy criminal law" that dispenses with the protections of citizenship for nationals who are broadly associated with anti-state organizations, including their innocent family members (Roach 2015, 12–13).

ISIS recruited thousands of foreign fighters, settlers and their dependents as part of its terror campaign and nation-building project between 2014 and the caliphate's demise in 2018. As of early 2019, estimates of foreign Islamic state-affiliated persons who remain in detention in Syria range from 44,279 to 52,808 individuals (Cook and Vale 2019, 31). Their countries of origin have prevented their return by denying consular services or passports, and in some cases, stripping them of their citizenship outright rather than allowing them to return to face justice for their anti-state affiliations (Houry 2019, 70–71). Some came willingly as adults and committed war crimes. Many others lie on a scale somewhere between victims and perpetrators. Women and

Born Innocent. Michael J. Sullivan, Oxford University Press. © Oxford University Press 2023.
DOI: 10.1093/oso/9780197671238.003.0005

102 BORN INNOCENT

children came to ISIS territory to join spouses and family members. Though most did not participate in atrocities themselves, they held varying degrees of allegiance and support for their family members' cause.

Minors such as then-fifteen-year-old U.K. citizen Shamima Begum independently left their homes to join ISIS against the will of their families. In Shamima's case, she left in part to escape family tensions brought on by her mother's death and father's remarriage (Khosrokhavar 2021, 245–246). She was compelled to marry upon arriving in ISIS territory at age fifteen and not allowed to leave the country. This raises the defense that she was a victim of online grooming and statutory rape, rather than a willing and fully culpable adult participant in ISIS's atrocities (Masters and Reglime 2020, 353). After the fall of the Islamic State in 2019, Begum's U.K. citizen parents sought permission and assistance for Shamima to return to the United Kingdom with her surviving infant son, Jarrah. Her request was denied by the U.K. home secretary Sajid Javid, and she was denationalized for her affiliation with ISIS and left stranded in a refugee camp in Syria, where her now stateless son died of pneumonia. Before he died, Jarrah Begum was among the estimated 6,173 to 6,577 children who were either born in ISIS-controlled territory or brought there by their parents at a young age (Cook and Vale 2019, 38). Those born in ISIS-controlled territory face statelessness and a life of deprivation in refugee camps, caused by the decision of some Western countries to denationalize their citizens who traveled to Syria, and to deny them and their children citizenship by descent. In addition to the horror of suffering and dying in a war zone, baby Jarrah Begum suffered the modern equivalent of "corruption of blood." He was denied the status and rights of U.K. citizenship that he would otherwise be entitled to by descent because of the status-related punishment meted out to his mother.

As a punishment that aims at retribution by the political community against those who breach their allegiance with their state through their affiliations and actions, denationalization has a long pedigree in legal practice as justified by political theorists (Gibney 2013, 647–648; Krähenmann 2019, 43–44). Today, the purpose of denationalization is defined less as a matter of punishing disloyalty, even when this characterization of terrorist affiliation still carries emotional and symbolic significance in political debates (Duby-Muller 2019; Les Républicains 2020).[1] Denationalization is now justified as a prophylactic measure to prevent individuals who constitute a threat to the security of the state from returning to their country of origin. Denationalizations directed at persons who have committed anti-state

THE COLLATERAL CONSEQUENCES OF BANISHMENT   103

actions linked to their affiliations with terrorist groups are intended to serve the punitive purposes of incapacitation and deterrence. Denationalization is part of a broader risk mitigation strategy on the part of governments that begins with punishing anti-state sympathies and actions such as planning to travel abroad to join a terrorist organization to deter "future treason" and incapacitate potential terrorists (Ashworth and Zedner 2014, 244; Corda 2019, 175). Incapacitation has been justified as a purpose for punishment for pre-inchoate crimes that occur even before the offender has left the country or done anything to actively support a terrorist organization (Corda 2019). But there are other ways to address the risks posed by radicalized citizens, including holding offenders accountable for war crimes in the criminal justice system of their country of origin. Affiliates can be required to undergo rehabilitation and monitored as potential security risks (Kramer 2019). By preventing an individual from re-entering their country of citizenship to pursue a course of deradicalization that would allow them to reintegrate into society, denationalization stands in tension with rehabilitation and restorative justice as objectives of punishment (Pereira 2019). The denationalization of citizens also raises human rights issues, particularly when the individual may face statelessness as a result (Gibney 2013, 651–652).

Across Europe, repatriations of children whose sole affiliation with ISIS resulted from their birth and parentage remain controversial (Baranger, Bonelli, and Pichaud 2017, 253, 259–260). There are concerns about how to respond to the indoctrination of even very young children who were born under ISIS rule, and the risk that they may pose in the country of their parent's citizenship in the future (Pokalova 2020, 211). Concerns about how to balance family unity for children with an accounting for the affiliations and deeds of their foreign fighter parents have proven far more politically controversial (Evans 2021). For instance, the repatriation of children ages five and three to Norway, along with their mother, who faces jail time for her involvement with ISIS, resulted in the breakdown of a coalition government in Norway in January 2020 (Libell 2020).

Some minors arrived in ISIS territory without their full consent as children and younger adolescents accompanying parents, including twelve-year-old British citizen JoJo Dixon, and thirteen-year-old Australian citizen Zaynab Sharrouf (Ananian-Welsh 2019, 176–177; Jackson 2022, 183). Dixon was killed alongside his mother, an ISIS operative, in a U.S. air strike. Though innocent of his mother's crimes, JoJo's death was later justified in the media as collateral damage (Jackson 2022, 184). The British government also justified

104 BORN INNOCENT

JoJo's extrajudicial death as vicarious punishment for his mother's loyalties and crimes (187). Zaynab Sharrouf was compelled by her father to marry ISIS foreign fighters and gave birth to two children in ISIS-controlled territory. Initially, Australia's Prime Minister, Scott Morrison maintained that he would "not put one Australian life at risk to try to extract people from these dangerous situations" since they had "gone and fought against our values and our way of life and peace-loving countries of this world" and "put their children in the middle of it" (Prime Minister of Australia 2019b). Sharrouf also drew individual condemnation for her public statements of support for ISIS. Nevertheless, Morrison later allowed for the repatriation of Zaynab Sharrouf and her children. He justified their rescue on the principle that children "can't be held responsible for the crimes of their parents," and expressing the government's support to ensure "that they can fully integrate into a happy life in Australia" (Prime Minister of Australia 2019a).

Attempts to draw clear lines between the innocence of children and the guilt of their parents and caregivers are illusory, even when we are dealing with adult terrorist suspects who enjoy little popular sympathy. The requirements of due process require that we regard those who are alleged to have committed heinous acts as innocent until proven guilty (Young 2021, 190).[2] The gradients of distinction between Shamima Begum and Zaynab Sharrouf's levels of agency and responsibility in each of their cases begin to point to further mitigating factors in individual cases. Both were adolescents when they traveled to ISIS territory. In the criminal justice system, minors are rarely assigned the same degree of capacity and culpability as adults. Their children had no control over the circumstances of their birth in ISIS territory. When denationalization or the denial of state protection is used as a punishment for anti-state affiliations, its effects extend beyond the offender to innocent parties, including the children of denationalized citizens who were brought to ISIS territory by their parents, and those born in ISIS territory. This can prevent their children from acquiring citizenship and its protections anywhere, leaving the innocent dependents of accused terrorists at the mercy of authorities wherever they are located. The abandonment of citizens in conflict zones for their alleged anti-state affiliations has a similar effect. These actions by states against both parents and their children violate norms of legitimate punishment which rest on the principle of individual responsibility. This harms the blameless young children of alleged terrorists who face statelessness and abandonment in a war zone as a result (Tripkovic 2021, 1052).

THE COLLATERAL CONSEQUENCES OF BANISHMENT   105

In this chapter, I argue that political communities should not deny citizenship and its protections to children based on their parents' allegiances or alleged offenses at the time of their child's birth. To this end, I begin by questioning the use of harsh retributory punishments, including citizenship deprivation and banishment for political crimes such as sympathy for, attempts to join, or affiliations with an anti-state organization (Lenard 2018; Gibney 2020b). I explain the ways in which affiliating with a terrorist organization has been defined as a crime, and a society's purposes for punishing anti-state affiliations through retribution, deterrence, and incapacitation. I argue that distinctions need to be made between beliefs and actions, or rather, suspicions and thoughts of disloyalty, and acting upon these beliefs in a way that causes harm to individuals (Lacey 2016, 152–154). In the context of terrorist group affiliation, this means distinguishing between those who passively affiliate with the organization, and those who commit acts of violence or encourage others to do so.

Second, I will argue that political communities should not be free to decide whether to deny citizenship and its protections to children based on their parents' allegiances or alleged offenses at the time of their child's birth. Citizenship deprivation is an intergenerational punishment when children lose entitlement to citizenship at birth based on their parent's denationalization, as is the case for stateless children born to parents affiliated with anti-state groups (Zedner 2019a, 328). Denationalizations that prevent suspected terrorists from returning to their country of origin deny the state's duty to punish suspected adult terrorists (Tripkovic 2023, 10). These measures are also imposing a multigenerational punishment on their children, who have yet to willfully offend but are now recruitment targets for anti-state groups (Tripkovic 2023, 5). The dependents of suspects and offenders should not lose a *jus sanguinis* or descent-based pathway to citizenship and its rights based on their parents' actions. Further issues that need to be addressed include the care of the dependents of ISIS affiliates, and their integration into society to prevent the radicalization of family members targeted by anti-terrorism legislation and enforcement (Benton and Banulescu-Bogdan 2019; Chulov 2019). For these reasons, I will consider alternative sanctions for anti-state affiliations following repatriation that serve the purposes of rehabilitating the offender as a caregiver and contributing member of society.

Third, in considering denationalization in terms of the purposes of punishment, I will argue that denationalization is a suboptimal form of punishment for anti-state affiliations. While individuals should be held to account

106 BORN INNOCENT

for affiliating with anti-state organizations, denationalization does not adequately serve the purposes of punishment for this offense. Moreover, since denationalization extends to the offender's descendants, it violates the principle "that punishment should not be applied except to an individual who has broken the law" by extending vicarious punishment to the children of accused terrorists for the misdeeds of their parents (Hart 1968, 6, 81).

The Crime of Affiliating with a Terrorist Organization

Historically, the primary use of denationalization as a punishment is for treason, or acts that indicate a breach of allegiance between the individual and his state of origin (Sullivan 2018). The punishment of disowning citizens through expulsion became a source of nonhumanitarian controversy as early as the late nineteenth century, as states asserted their sovereign right to deny entrance and immigration privileges to noncitizens, and refused to accept the risks of accepting potentially dangerous persons expelled from other nations (Gibney 2020b, 296). Then, after the Second World War, human rights considerations led to the decline of denationalization in the late twentieth century as a final, irreversible violation of an individual's state-secured civil and political rights. In 1958, the U.S. Supreme Court ruled in *Trop v. Dulles* that denationalization constitutes "cruel and unusual punishment" in contravention of the Eighth Amendment of the U.S. Constitution. Chief Justice Earl Warren described denationalization as a form of punishment that is "more primitive than torture" because the penalty "strips the citizen of his status in the national and international community," leaving his "very existence at the sufferance of the country in which he finds himself" (*Trop v. Dulles* 1958, 86). Domestic legislation in Australia, Canada, and the United Kingdom followed a similar pattern during the late twentieth century by removing grounds for denaturalization (Gibney 2017, 366). Canada went so far as to refuse to denationalize Nazi war criminals during the 1980s, with government commissions contending that Canada should hold suspected offenders to account in Canadian courts, rather than forcing other countries to accept the burden resulting from the denationalization and deportation of its citizens (Sullivan 2018, 331–332).

Since September 11, 2001, many Western states have increasingly revived denationalization as an instrument of preventive justice, with the goal of incapacitating a potential national security threat by removing citizens suspected of terrorist affiliations from their country of citizenship, or denying them re-entry (Macklin 2018, 164). Their actions have been legitimated by U.N. Security Council Resolution 1373 (2001) and U.N. Security Council Resolution 2178 (2014), which both require member states to respond to the threat posed by foreign terrorist fighters (Zedner 2019b, 102–105). As a matter of political and legal theory, the Global War on Terrorism has brought a revival of the view that citizenship is a conditional and reciprocal bond of allegiance between the individual and the state, rather than a fundamental right (Gibney 2017, 360; Coca-Vila 2020).

The United Kingdom has led the way among Western European countries in using citizenship deprivation as a counterterrorism tool (Zedner 2019b, 104–106). The United Kingdom has cast a widening net in the use of its de-nationalization power as a counterterrorism measure during the first two decades of the twenty-first century. Under the 2006 revision to the British Nationality Act, the Home Secretary could revoke British citizenship whenever he or she is satisfied "that deprivation is conducive to the public good" (Lavi 2010, 411). An active breach of allegiance was no longer required as a condition for the revocation of citizenship, mere risk to the state sufficed. In the 2000s, the U.K. government used this power primarily to strip citizenship from nationals captured on the battlefield by Britain or its allies or those involved in the planning and commission of violent offenses against the state, such as Guantanamo Bay detainee David Hicks (Lavi 2010, 411–412). In this case, denationalization was only justified given Hicks's dual citizenship. Amendments to the British Nationality Act in 2014 deprived persons of British nationality who could theoretically become citizens elsewhere, even if that country refused them citizenship (Zedner 2019a, 325; Jaghai and Van Waas 2020, 160). The U.K. home secretary stripped 120 dual nationals of their British nationality under this provision between 2016 and 2019 (Nyamutata 2020, 252). Moreover, the United Kingdom's denationalization net now encompasses persons who are not participants in violent anti-state activity (Zedner 2019a, 321). Passive affiliation with a terrorist group now constitutes grounds for denationalization for British citizens. This includes adolescent brides not involved in warfare lured to ISIS territory who have since defected from the organization and sought to return to Britain (Baker 2020, 25–26). Under the United Kingdom's Counter-Terrorism and Border Security Act of 2019, humanitarian aid workers face counterterrorism penalties. This includes persons who "traveled to a designated area and engaged in the provision of humanitarian aid for a week, and then spent a further week in the area for any other purpose which is not covered by an exemption" (U.K. Government 2019, §41). This act does not directly provide for denationalization, although the U.K. Home Secretary has stripped U.K. national humanitarian aid workers of their citizenship based on allegations that they provided humanitarian assistance to persons affiliated with terrorist groups in the Syrian conflict zone (Austin 2019; Jaghai and Van Waas 2020, 154).

Since 2015, France has been subject to several violent terrorist attacks resulting in many deaths, while responding to the departure of thousands of its citizens to join ISIS, and their subsequent return after the fall of the caliphate in 2018 (Sheahan 2018, 19). Like the United Kingdom, France has drawn on a long history of responding to terrorism in the courts. In the process, France has denationalized naturalized dual citizens and subjected native-born citizens associated with terrorist organizations to long prison sentences. Even in the face of these national security threats, and overwhelming public support for the denationalization of persons who commit terrorist attacks, the French Senate rejected a 2015 constitutional amendment that would have allowed for the denationalization of native-born French citizens (Le Bot and Phillipe 2017). Still, France has been reluctant to repatriate its citizens who left to join ISIS, holding on to the hope that they can be tried in the conflict zone even though Iraqi Kurdistan lacks the resources to bring perpetrators to justice or to prevent the radicalization and enlistment of their children (Méheut 2020).

Elsewhere in Western Europe, denationalization has been facilitated by liberal dual nationality policies that allow states to claim that they have not violated international norms on statelessness by denationalizing an individual with a theoretical claim to citizenship elsewhere (Gibney 2017, 376; Kapoor and Narkowicz 2019, 46). Western European states, including Norway and Denmark, have accepted dual citizenship for the first time as a mechanism to provide for the denationalization of "disloyal" naturalized citizens without rendering them stateless (Midbøten 2019, 300–303; Shaw 2020, 135). In practice, this claim to dual nationality can be challenged by a state that contends that descendants of citizens born abroad, with another nationality, were never citizens of that state. Even states whose home territory has been less affected by acts of terrorism have followed suit in providing for the denationalization of dual nations, including Canada (between 2014 and 2017) and Australia, under the Allegiance to Australia Act (Sullivan 2018; Irving 2019, 375–376). Both of these cases envision retribution against persons deemed disloyal to their government and the incapacitation of former citizens and their families who are prevented from returning to their countries of origin. While states justify these measures using U.N. Security Council Resolution 2178, in practice, denationalization does not serve the deterrent and incapacitory intent of the U.N. resolution to combat the worldwide impact of foreign fighters (Krähenmann 2019, 55). It simply shifts the risks and costs of former citizens affiliated with terrorist groups to conflict zones like Iraqi Kurdistan and Syria, in camps where ISIS sympathizers are actively recruiting the children of denationalized foreign fighters, and where overburdened local authorities struggle to bear the costs of providing security and humanitarian assistance for former ISIS affiliates and their families (Effendi 2019; OCHA 2020).

A. Naomi Palk (2015) describes detention camps both at home and abroad as the physical embodiment of removal from the larger social and political community, denying detainees the precondition for rights as "enemies, contaminants, and outcasts" (Palk 2015, 219). This is an apt characterization of the camps where denationalized terrorist suspects, and their innocent children now find themselves. By denationalizing these suspected ISIS affiliates and abandoning them abroad, their countries of citizenship are shirking their duties of due process in domestic courts. Countries that denationalize their citizens are also potentially subjecting them to cruel and unusual punishment abroad while shirking their duty to rehabilitate offenders (Seet 2021, 263, 274). Their children suffer the complete rightlessness that comes with abandonment in refugee camps as stateless persons.

Purposes of Punishment: Retribution

There are five primary rationale for punishment: retribution, incapacitation, deterrence, rehabilitation, and reparation (Ashworth and Zedner 2014, 17–19; Cohen 2016, 254; Canton 2017, 40–41). For denationalization to satisfy the demands of retribution, the penalty would have to result from a conviction for a particularly serious offense that was committed with a guilty intent (Hart 1968, 114). A denationalization proceeding arising from a judicial process that finds that a person found guilty of war crimes also deceived immigration authorities in obtaining naturalization satisfies the demands of retributive justice. Current proceedings involving the preventive administrative denaturalization of persons in absentia because of their relationship with terrorists and the potential risk they pose to their societies are less likely to

110 BORN INNOCENT

satisfy the criteria of procedural justice for a grave past intentional offense.[3] Moreover, for terrorist affiliates recruited as minors, or those who seek to leave the organization, assessments of duress, coercion, and capacity upon moral culpability are needed for any retributive punishment to be fair and proportionate to the alleged offense (Drumbl 2012, 180; Nortje and Quénivet 2020, 22).

Among the defenses available to defendants in international criminal law, duress can explain the situation of young people lured into a conflict zone that they are unable to leave, without excusing the broader offense of association with terrorist organizations (Nortje and Quénivet 2020, 22). It is debatable whether adolescents are capable of genuine consent under the circumstances in which they are recruited, which can be analogized—with some direct parallels for female ISIS recruits—to adults unlawfully grooming and enticing minors for sexual acts (93–94). Though duress has not always prevailed as a legal defense for adolescents threatened with psychological rather than imminent physical harm, it still presents a strong moral justification for mitigating their responsibility when threats prevent them from leaving anti-state organizations (52–53, 69, 95).

Throughout the West, retributive attitudes toward juvenile offenders, particularly those who are suspected of serious crimes or terrorist affiliations, have hardened since the 1970s (Drumbl 2012, 128–129). While international legal instruments and children's rights treaties continue to regard minors as passive victims, the context of their offense greatly affects how they are treated as a matter of public opinion and political decision-making. On the one hand, regarding older adolescents who join anti-state groups and commit acts of violence purely as victims denies both their agency and the claims of those who are victimized by juvenile anti-state affiliates and active terrorists (Wessels 2006, 219–220). While young offenders may be able to claim that they acted under duress, their actions still harmed discrete individuals. Those who committed terroristic acts must still answer to those whom they victimized, and ISIS affiliates must answer to their home country, and to those who were harmed by the group they actively supported. On the other hand, Western states that have signed on to protocols that hold recruiters to account for enlisting juveniles have not done enough to recognize that ISIS recruits are partly victims, and not just perpetrators who are deserving of civil death through denationalization and exile (Drumbl 2012, 129; Aptel 2019, 529). Adults in a leadership role in an anti-state organization who enlist juveniles and persuade them to betray their country and take up arms against their compatriots should ultimately be held primarily responsible for the actions of their young recruits.

Vicarious retribution against the family members of an anti-state affiliate or active terrorist is a particular problem as direct victims of a terrorist act and members of the targeted community seek justice. This is a pressing issue when the perpetrator cannot be brought to be justice after having taken his or her own life. States have taken proactive measures to prevent vicarious retribution by the majority against the ethnic and religious communities that anti-state affiliates claim to be a part of by showing that members of minority groups are also victims of terrorism committed in the name of their religion (Pemberton 2010, 164). This disassociation is facilitated by the existence of representatives of a community that can express dissent with the actions of a radical fringe. Vicarious retribution is more of a problem when those associated with the anti-state affiliate or active terrorist cannot defend themselves, as children who are cast under aspersion as future threats because of their parent's actions and influence in their lives. The state itself engages in a form of vicarious retribution when it refuses to acknowledge a child's claim to citizenship by descent because of the deeds of their parent. One example of this is the United Kingdom's abandonment of the child of Shamima Begum, who was born stateless after Shamima's denationalization. Another example comes when a state abandons a child in this situation in a conflict zone to avoid possible risks that might come with their repatriation.

Incapacitation and Deterrence

The strongest case for deterrence is to prevent the commission of an offence that will harm the offender, victims, and society before it even happens. In the case of alienated minors who are susceptible to radicalization and recruitment by anti-state organizations, the ideal response would be for responsible authority figures in a young person's network to intervene at the first sign of radicalization. This could include parents and religious leaders who are not themselves radicalized, or school officials acting *in loco parentis* for inadequately supervised minors. The state should support parental efforts to protect their children from traveling to conflict zones through parental notification requirements for passports, though these measures cannot entirely incapacitate a radicalized young person who might commit terrorist acts in the community.

112　BORN INNOCENT

If an offense has already taken place, John Braithwaite argues in *Restorative Justice and Responsive Regulation* (2002) that communities must act in the case of first-time offenses to take responsibility for the vulnerabilities of their alienated citizens who turn to anti-social behavior. Community leaders should serve as supportive figures who can help first-time offenders to take responsibility for the harm they caused their victims, and then to provide them with the skills, knowledge, and identity-based resources to turn to pro-social behavior (Braithwaite 2002, 134). Deterrence can be used as an escalating response when other advisory and restorative forms of justice fail to curb anti-social behavior and affiliations (Braithwaite 2002, 31–32; Braithwaite 2018, 74). This approach may be challenged on retributive and proportionality grounds: a serious offense deserves a punishment that fully accounts for the harm the offender caused, regardless of whether it is a first-time offense. Braithwaite acknowledges the need for incapacitation in cases of repeated recidivism, but this should include social support to provide the offender with a lifeline if she wants to accept responsibility for her actions (Braithwaite 2018, 108). From this perspective, what is wrong about incapacitory responses to terrorist actions and anti-state group affiliations is that they leave offenders with no incentive to change their behavior or to stop threatening their society of origin from abroad (or from prison, in some cases).

In theory, denationalization can satisfy the criteria of incapacitation and individual deterrence, since the removal of a suspected terrorist affiliate or their prevention from returning makes it less likely that they can commit a future offense in their former country of citizenship. The issue with an incapacitation rationale for denaturalization as an instrument of preventive, risk-reducing justice is that denationalization does not necessarily incapacitate a potential offender, who may continue to pose a danger where she is currently located (Bauböck 2020, 391). If a state is correct in its assessment of her risk profile, the denationalized offender may continue direct attacks toward her state of origin from abroad. If a state is not correct in its assessment of her risk profile, as is the case among young people lured to the conflict zone who did not participate in hostilities and now want to return home, denationalizations may leave nominal terrorist affiliates helpless and prone to further radicalization in pursuit of security (Zedner 2019b, 111–112). Among young people lured to Syria to join ISIS, security experts also warn that "the closed social environments of detention, refugee, and [internally displaced person] camps risk becoming incubators for uninhibited violent radicalization of a transnational cohort of people" (Bosley 2019, 7).

As a matter of general deterrence, homeland security officials may seek to make an example of terrorist affiliates by denationalizing them to dissuade others from following in their footsteps (Ashworth and Zedner 2014, 18). The efficacy of deterrence is predicated in large part on the rationality of persons contemplating committing an offense, and their willingness to engage in cost-benefit analysis when deciding whether to affiliate with a terrorist organization (Canton 2017, 89; Fisher and Dugan 2019, 166–167). This level of rationality may not be present among adolescents who are commonly recruited by terrorist organizations over the internet. This is because their capacity to make informed choices that account for the long-term repercussions of their actions is not as well developed as in mature adults. Denationalization is not likely to deter radicalized citizens who are willing to burn their passports as part of an ISIS initiation ritual, symbolizing their breach of allegiance with their country of origin.

The United States failed to distinguish between adolescent and adult recruits in its war against terror, subjecting a Canadian child soldier captured in Afghanistan at age fifteen, Omar Khadr, to detention as an enemy combatant without regard to juvenile justice standards (Jamison 2008). Similarly, the political narrative in Western Europe surrounding ISIS recruitment does not always differentiate between adolescent and adult recruits, treating all persons who express an inchoate interest in the organization as equally dangerous to their country of origin (Nyamutata 2020, 242; de Rebetz and van den Woude 2020, 16). The criminal justice system acts to incapacitate and deter their perceived threat at an early stage, regardless of whether their beliefs give rise to anti-state actions, or whether their sympathies give rise to travel plans to the conflict zone. It is also in tension with the fact that child soldiers and other adolescent affiliates of anti-state organizations rarely serve as conflict entrepreneurs with a hardened commitment to a group's violent anti-state ideology (Drumbl 2012, 21). All too frequently, those apprehended before leaving are instead subject to sequestered incarceration in prisons that have been known to be centers for radicalizing youth, and those who manage to reach the conflict zone are prevented from returning (Khosrokhavar 2017, 129–131; Micheron 2020; Khosrokhavar 2021, 123–124). The flawed moral premise here is that states can disown responsibility for their alienated adolescent citizens. The flawed empirical premise here is that geographical sequestration will neutralize the threat that a former citizen poses to their homeland, given the ease of internet communication between conflict zone participants and potential

114   BORN INNOCENT

recruits in their country of origin. The denationalization of juvenile terrorist suspects and their abandonment abroad is at odds with ordinary juvenile justice standards in liberal democratic countries or in international human rights treaties, which emphasize the need to rehabilitate and de-radicalize young recruits.

Rehabilitation and Restorative Justice: Toward Alternative Sanctions

The premise of rehabilitation and restorative justice is that the alleged offender can take responsibility for his or her actions and make amends to any direct victims harmed by their behavior, allowing for the offender's reintegration as a law-abiding, contributing citizen. Restorative justice processes aim to contribute to the acknowledgment of responsibility by the offender, his reintegration into the community, and the restoration of interpersonal relations (Maculan and Gil Gil 2020, 143). While restorative justice was originally conceived of as a community-centered response to minor infractions, practitioners and academics alike are now applying restorative principles to more serious offenses, including terrorist activity (Walgrave 2008, 133; Soulou 2018, 349). Both domestic and international criminal law emphasize rehabilitation as an objective of punishment for young people whose personality and moral capacities are still in the process of formation (Canton 2017, 123). When combined with preventive forms of justice like passport cancellation and monitoring, a restorative justice approach applied to young people in the early stages of indoctrination may be used to persuade fellow travelers to understand the impact of terrorist violence on victims that movement leaders dehumanize.

Restorative justice approaches used to address minor crimes may serve a prophylactic role, preventing alienated young immigrants and citizens from becoming vulnerable to recruitment by anti-state organizations like ISIS. Victim-offender mediation and community-based sanctions in place of incarceration may help to break the radicalization process that takes place in prisons, leading perpetrators of minor crimes to commit acts that are more deviant when they are released (Walgrave 2015, 429). Restorative justice can also have a deterrent effect on future crime by first-time offenders before they become hardened criminals as they enter into dialogue with victims to recognize the harm they caused (Braithwaite 2018, 71). Restorative justice serves the aims of deterrence for first-time offenders if they are aware that they will face escalating consequences if they re-offend or refuse to change their behavior (Braithwaite 2018, 81). By permanently severing the relationship between the alleged offender and his or her fellow citizens and state, denationalization stands in sharp contrast to the objectives of rehabilitation and restorative justice (Cohen 2016).

Rehabilitation

Young people who are recruited as ISIS affiliates are akin to child soldiers, in keeping with the broad definition of this role under international law. The European Union, with particularly strong support from France, has advocated denationalizing ISIS affiliates and combatants alike and trying them under special international tribunals in the countries where they fought and now reside (European Union 2017; Bauer 2019). As such, it is worth considering how past international tribunals have addressed the role of child soldiers as juvenile offenders. One prominent recent example is the Special Court for Sierra Leone (SCSL), created by the U.N. under Security Council Resolution 1315 in 2000. The SCSL is an institution of transitional justice emerging from that country's long civil war in which child soldiers played an active part in the hostilities. Article 7(1) of the statute governing the tribunal reads that:

> Should any person who was at the time of the alleged commission of the crime between 15 and 18 years of age come before the Court, he or she shall be treated with dignity and a sense of worth, taking into account his or her young age and the desirability of promoting his or her rehabilitation, re-integration into, and assumption of a constructive role in society, and in accordance with international human rights standards, in particular the rights of the child. (SCSL, Article 7, §1)

Far from contemplating the prospect of exile, as Western countries are contemplating now for ISIS affiliates, the SCSL instead advocated for the re-integration of *ex-combatants* into society and forbade their incapacitation through imprisonment. To promote their rehabilitation, the SCSL authorized the court to order juvenile offenders into educational and community service programs (Drumbl 2012, 122).

116 BORN INNOCENT

Restorative Justice

Beyond the special circumstances of the Sierra Leone civil war, the Paris Principles and Guidelines on Children Associated with Armed Forces or Armed Groups, endorsed by 108 countries as of October 2019 offers pertinent guidance for signatory states confronted with adolescent citizens recruited by ISIS who seek to return to their countries of origin. The Paris Principles resists the categorization of adolescents under the age of eighteen as fully culpable parties, even when they voluntarily traveled to a conflict zone subsequent to their recruitment by adult foreign fighters. Those protected by the Paris Principles include minors who were "used as fighters, cooks, messengers, spies, or for sexual purposes" even if they did not take "a direct part in hostilities" (Paris Principles, §2.1). Rather than denationalizing, abandoning, or otherwise incapacitating these young ISIS recruits, as many Western signatories to the Paris Principles have done with their adolescent citizens, the Paris Principles prioritize their reintegration into their societies of origin (Paris Principles, §2.8, §3.6–3.8).

So far, the U.K. government, which previously endorsed the U.N. Paris Principles and ratified the U.N. Convention on the Rights of the Child, has dealt with adolescent recruits such as the Bethnal Green Trio (Amira Abase, Shamima Begum, and Kadiza Sultana, fifteen- and sixteen-year-old U.K. citizens who traveled to join ISIS) as willing perpetrators. The Paris Principles advise signatories to consider minors in this situation "primarily as victims of offences against international law, not only as perpetrators" (Paris Principles, §3.6). To the extent that they can be implicated in offenses against domestic and international law for their actions in ISIS-controlled territory, "they must be treated in accordance with international law in a framework of restorative justice and social rehabilitation, consistent with international law which offers children special protection" (ibid.).

What would a restorative justice framework entail for youth recruited by ISIS and repatriated by their home countries, tried for their crimes, and enrolled in de-radicalization programs with a view to their eventual reintegration into their societies of origin? Precedents exist on both a societal level (transitional justice) and an individual level (restorative justice) in the aftermath of previous terrorist group violence. In general, a restorative model of justice requires an offender to reflect upon the damage that his or her actions have done to her society of origin, and if applicable, those whom she has directly victimized (Wessells 2006, 222; Levanon 2019, 63). In the

THE COLLATERAL CONSEQUENCES OF BANISHMENT 117

case of involvement with terrorist organizations, where the individual has not directly committed any violent acts, the offender may be asked to meet with, listen to, and respond to the harm to vicarious victims of terrorist actions by the organization with which she was affiliated. In similar victim-offender conferences held in the aftermath of terrorist activity (Basque Country, Northern Ireland, Red Army Faction), affiliates who were not ready to renounce their anti-state allegiances developed empathy for the vicarious victims of terrorism, placing a human face and identity to an impersonal "enemy" (Staiger 2010, 293–297, 316; Zernova 2019, 655).

There are several challenges to applying a restorative justice framework in cases of terrorism, or acts of politically motivated violence in general. Primary victims who immediately suffered from the terrorist group's acts want to see the offenders held accountable in the criminal justice system first, before they enter into victim-offender mediation (Staiger 2010). Second, the political dimension of terrorism complicates efforts at causing offenders to take responsibility for their actions, when offenders and affiliates view themselves as participating in a just cause against a state. From this mindset, individual victims are understood symbolically as everything from collateral damage in an ideological fight for freedom to infidels and potential enemies to the cause. One of the challenges, then, lies in convincing offenders to empathize with the human suffering inflicted upon victims, and to distinguish victims as human beings apart from their place in the ideological narrative constructed by the terrorist organization that is used to justify indiscriminate violence. Another challenge lies in allowing victims to take charge of the restorative process themselves (as first suggested by Nils Christie in "Conflicts as Property"), instead of allowing the process to be directed by the government as is typically the case in the criminal justice system (Christie 1977). A government-led restorative justice initiative delegitimizes the process from the perspective of offenders who may sympathize with their individual victims, while refusing to disassociate themselves with the political objectives they fought for (Zernova 2019, 656). It also allows the government to manipulate the process by requiring offenders to renounce their political allegiances to participate in mediation that is supposed to be for the benefit of individual victims.

De-radicalization is linked primarily to the state's interest in pacifying threats to its collective security. Restorative justice is linked primarily to the victim's interest in recovering from the harm caused by the offender's actions to his or her individual sense of security and well-being. Victims may share

118   BORN INNOCENT

this interest insofar as they fear re-victimization by individuals who share the ideology of those who harmed them. Victims may also be ideologically aligned with the state and its values as guarantors of its security. However, the interests of the victim and offender in pursuing restorative justice, and the state in ideological de-radicalization are not always in complete alignment. De-radicalization and restorative justice may need to be placed on separate tracks to realize competing objectives. Past experience with restorative justice initiatives by persons who committed terrorist acts or affiliated with terrorist organizations in Northern Ireland and the Basque nationalist movement suggest that offender engagement with the process is facilitated by decoupling restorative justice, or the victim-offender mediation element, from de-radicalization initiatives (Zernova 2019, 656). Here, the aim is disengagement from violence, rather than de-radicalization expressed in terms of a change in ideology, affiliation or allegiance (Chapman 2017, 7). This is particularly the case for politically motivated offenders whose participation in terroristic activity stems from a fully informed and ongoing commitment to ideological objectives pursued through violent ends. Depending on the underlying ideology of the anti-state organization, offenders may be convinced to pursue their ideological objectives through peaceful, political means. However, this may preclude the use of restorative justice processes prior to de-radicalization among active affiliates of an anti-state organization like ISIS whose ideology is inexorably linked to violence against outsiders.

While de-radicalization may be a prerequisite for including offenders affiliated with anti-state groups committed to violence as an ideology, this task is not as daunting as it may first appear given varying degrees of commitment to the group's ideology among affiliates, and their reasons for becoming and staying involved with the organization. Not all terrorist affiliates are true believers in its ideology or active participants in its acts of violence. Offenders, particularly affiliates who did not directly participate in terrorist acts or who were recruited as minors, may share the state's interest in de-radicalization if their commitment to a terrorist organization's political objectives and values is superficial. For instance, the individual offender or affiliate may have been motivated to join the organization for reasons that are peripheral to its political objectives, such as a personal desire for a sense of belonging (Bosley 2019, 11). Recruiters may have promised the offender or affiliate material or psychological benefits for affiliating with the organization that were not fulfilled in practice. In the particular case of ISIS, the humanitarian suffering that recruits faced during and after the defeat of the caliphate has neutralized the appeal of the organization's violent ideology for many young recruits who are willing to accept penalties in their nation's criminal justice system if they are allowed to return home (Jaffer 2019). The decision by many Western countries to leave repentant recruits in the conflict zone by denationalizing them or denying them consular services, along with dependents who were born there, or who arrived at a young age and never chose to be a part, may appear to be a means of incapacitating a possible security threat (U.K. Government 2018a, 50). The danger is that these desperate and now stateless families may have no option but to seek protection from anti-state groups that dominate in prison camps in the region, providing them with a new generation of personnel to regroup and retaliate against Western interests (McKernan 2019; Yee 2019).[4]

Denationalization as a Punishment

Denationalization can be categorized as one of the more extreme preventive justice measures that are designed to reduce or eliminate the risk to public safety posed by a suspected or confirmed affiliate of an anti-state organization. States often seek to categorize denationalization as an administrative procedure rather than a punishment, to avoid the safeguards for the accused that come with a criminal trial and to expeditiously remove or prevent persons from re-entering their former country of citizenship (Gibney 2017, 373). Similar considerations are at play in categorizing deportation as an administrative procedure or civil matter rather than a form of punishment (Chiao 2019, 187–189).[5] Conceptual definitions aside, there is very little that distinguishes a harsh preventive justice measure from punishment. Victor Tadros argues that the sole distinction between preventive orders and punishment is that the former aims to prevent the person form harming others in the future, while punishment aims to harm a person for their past offenses (Tadros 2013, 139).

Although denationalization is characterized in the immigration and nationality law of many states as an administrative procedure, as would be the case if citizenship were conferred by mistake and then retracted, legal theorist Shai Lavi argues that the nonvoluntary "revocation of citizenship can only be justified as punishment" (Lavi 2011, 786). For Lavi, the "revocation of citizenship" is best justified as a retributive "punishment for a political crime, tit for tat" (Lavi 2011, 806). The only crimes that would rise to the

120 BORN INNOCENT

level of demanding this particularly brutal condemnation are acts "of public violence against civilians or state officials, performed by the citizen with the intention to fundamentally undermine public government by intimidation or coercion" (Lavi 2011, 802). The maturity of volition required to perform an act with the aim of undermining a political order through coercion would appear to limit this offense to fully consenting adults. Reserving denationalization for citizens who commit harmful acts would rule out this penalty for "thought crimes" such as sympathies with terrorists, or inchoate offenses such as entering into relationships with terrorists through communication, travel, or marriage.

Denationalization has opponents who otherwise seek to broaden the scope of anti-terrorism legislation by reviving the law of treason to denounce and maximally punish anti-state affiliations. For a leading group of British policymakers and legal theorists, existing terrorism laws do not encompass a sufficient range of behaviors that they deem to be disloyal. Their goal is to "modernize" the law of treason to include "entering and remaining in a declared area" of hostilities, as a strict liability offense that does not account for the actor's intent or deeds (Ekins et al. 2018, 29). They argue that more needs to be done to denounce and condemn association with anti-state organizations. But even they stop short of demanding denationalization, following John Finnis in arguing that "states are required to tolerate risks that arise from their own citizens" (Finnis 2007, 422–423; Ekins et al., 2018, 13). This view stems from an assessment of the harms to national security that might result from denationalizing and abandoning terrorist affiliates to regroup elsewhere: "One does not release traitors, for they are and remain members of our political community, members who have done us wrong" (Ekins et al., 2018, 42). Condemning denationalizations that would render citizens stateless, this group of treason law revivalists argues that "a sentence of life imprisonment" would be the punishment that the act of betraying one's country warrants, to incapacitate offenders and "signal clearly that our community condemns betrayal" (Ekins et al., 2018, 41). As part of this planned revival of treason law, equity would be respected by allowing judges to impose lighter sentences if "the circumstances of the offence and the offender would make such an offence manifestly unjust" (42). Flexible, case-by-case sentencing is necessary to distinguish between the degree of responsibility held by leaders of terrorist organizations and innocent or unwilling affiliates born or lured into their network without their ongoing consent.

The Culpability of Affiliation: Victims, Minors, and Infants

Children can become affiliated with terrorist organizations and they can commit atrocities in warfare. The degree of their culpability for these actions is open to contestation. In the case of ISIS, a significant number of foreign affiliates arrived on ISIS territory before the age of eighteen, having either been born to ISIS affiliates, brought by their parents against their will, or recruited over the internet. There, they are at once victims and perpetrators, socialized from early childhood to become contributing members of the caliphate by learning its ideology in schools. At this stage in their development, there is a broad consensus across multiple legal traditions around the principle of *doli incapax*, which holds that children below a minimum age are incapable of understanding the consequences of their actions, and should be held blameless for crimes (Van Bueren 2006, 26–27; Cipriani 2016, 42–43; Nortje and Quénivet 2020, 4).[6]

Children's vulnerability and dependency may also diminish their responsibility for their actions, transferring it to parents or caregivers, if a child has any. In their work on "vulnerability, autonomy, and self-respect," Christine Straehle and Anca Gheaus note and critique the ways in which a child's capacity for choice is diminished by their vulnerability and dependence on adults to help guide their decision-making (Straehle 2016, 38; Gheaus 2018, 63; Gheaus 2021, 7–8). Gheaus's critique of the ways that parents can abuse their monopoly of care can help to delineate a parent's responsibility for neglect and abuse at the hands of their ISIS captors by bringing them to a war zone. We can build on Gheaus's account of vulnerability and parental obligations to justify limited policy interventions to try and prevent parents from bringing children to areas held by regimes that will indoctrinate them as terrorists and train them as child soldiers, permanently impairing their capacity for choice. In the context of families traveling to terrorist-controlled areas, authorities should prevent families from traveling there on child welfare grounds. Here, we are insisting that parents do not place their families in a position where they would be unfree to leave and forced to cede their duty of care to a regime's youth indoctrination system.

Beyond the age of minimum criminal responsibility, most legal systems draw distinctions in sentencing guidelines between adults and adolescents, emphasizing rehabilitation over retribution (Cipriani 2016). To promote rehabilitation, de-radicalization, and moral growth in young offenders, Article 40(3) of the widely ratified U.N. Convention on the Rights of the Child urges

122 BORN INNOCENT

the adoption of "measures for dealing with such children without resorting to judicial proceedings," including restorative justice programs and community supervision (UNCRC 1989; Van Bueren 2006, 27–30). In recent U.S. jurisprudence, the U.S. Supreme Court has ruled that the death penalty and life without imprisonment constitute "cruel and unusual punishment" when they are applied to adolescents (*Roper v. Simmons* 2004; *Miller v. Alabama* 2011). In short, the majority's presumption in both cases was that children are less blameworthy given the state of their neurological development. They are less likely to be deterred given their diminished capacity to make cost-benefit analyses. Adolescents are particularly susceptible to pressure from adults and peers, diminishing their own agency (Report of the Expert of the Secretary General 1996, §38).[7] Finally, the *Roper* and *Miller* court also noted research showing that compared to adults, adolescent identities are more fluid and susceptible to rehabilitation. Critics of fixed aged limits point to the need to distinguish between individuals reflecting unique developmental trajectories and granting full rights and responsibilities to mature adolescents (Yaffe 2018; Berk 2019). This refinement does not erase the rationale for making distinctions based on maturity, coercion, capacity for rehabilitation, and individual consent when we are determining whether and how to punish a person for an act of affiliation or violence associated with terrorism.

As states attempt to hold their citizens accountable for affiliation with ISIS, the circumstances of their recruitment and initiation is relevant in determining their level of culpability for their actions in the conflict zone. Adolescents make up a significant percentage of ISIS foreign recruits. The Islamic State specialized in recruiting disaffected children and teenagers from outside the conflict zone using social media. Adult recruiters would groom boys for violence and girls for forced marriages and sexual abuse. In *Small Arms: Children and Terrorism* (2019), Mia Bloom and John Horgan draw an analogy between terrorists and pedophiles regarding how perpetrators accessed young victims, lured them away from their families into the conflict zone, and secured their loyalty (Bloom and Horgan 2019, 75, 84). Other researchers draw analogies between how street gangs and terrorist organizations including ISIS recruit disaffected teenagers, consolidate loyalty through initiation into criminal activity, and retaliate against defectors (Bovenkerk 2011; Valasik and Phillips 2017). In its long history of responding to terrorism as a criminal infraction, France uses similar legal instruments to respond to organized crime, undocumented immigration and terrorism (Salas 2005, 164–165; De Rebetz and Van den Woude 2020, 2).

The indoctrination and military training that children and youth endured while in ISIS territory is nothing short of child abuse by international human rights standards. Children as young as four or five years of age—a demographic that included persons born to Western foreign fighters in ISIS-controlled territory now languishing in refugee camps—were forced to witness public executions and torture (Nyamutata 2020, 240). ISIS officials initiated boys as young as eight into membership by participating in atrocities, acts designed to foster loyalty and prevent defection. Girls as young as eight were coerced into marrying ISIS fighters and having children to populate and provide intergenerational continuity for an Islamic State (Watkin and Looney 2019, 123). Based on their past ISIS affiliations, adolescent girls are now facing irrevocable punishment in the form of denationalization for acts that involved an element of coercion and deception, including forced marriages, sexual abuse, and captivity. As teenage mothers stranded in a conflict zone, they lack the capacity to provide for their children. Their completely innocent children inherit this intergenerational punishment as they cannot inherit citizenship and its protections from their parent's country of origin by descent. If their children are rescued from their conflict zone, as some Western states are choosing to do for the children of ISIS affiliates, they may gain protection at the cost of care from their mothers. Asylum elsewhere or integration into the local population in their conflict zone is not an option for these denationalized ex-ISIS affiliates. Already, child soldiers and affiliates of terrorist organizations face insurmountable barriers to gaining asylum in any country, even if they disavow its ideology and take the great risks of attempting to escape from its control (Drumbl 2012, 128–133). They may attempt to claim duress as a defense against charges that they committed international crimes (Nortje and Quénivet 2020, 34). However, this defense is of limited utility against deterrent legislation that is designed to keep potential terrorist threats away from their country of origin (Pokalova 2020, 97–98). There are few refuges for a teenager who realizes the errors of their infatuation with anti-state ideology, and the responsibility for their clandestine recruitment is not falling on the organization's leadership as contemplated in international children's rights law and treatises.

Unlike infants born into association with anti-state organizations through no fault of their own, their teenage mothers have an ambiguous dual status as victim and suspected victimizer, with an attenuated responsibility based on their limited capacity for choice. For adolescent affiliates of anti-state organizations above the minimum age of criminal responsibility, the International

Criminal Court's prohibition on the recruitment of adolescents under fifteen as child soldiers can be interpreted to indicate that young adolescents do not have the maturity to make an unforced choice whether to join an armed group (Happold 2005, 158; Drumbl 2012, 135; Fisher 2013, 51–55).[8] As such, primary responsibility for the actions of young adolescent terrorist affiliates should be vested in the organization's leadership and its adult recruiters. Beyond their anti-state thoughts, affiliations, and allegiances, when older adolescents commit crimes that harm discrete individuals, there is a need to provide justice for victims that may be accommodated through restorative justice mechanisms and rehabilitation that recognizes their dual status as victim and victimizer and their capacity for moral learning (Stahn 2019, 316–317).

Conclusion

Political communities are indiscriminately targeting individuals who have any association with an anti-state organization by depriving them of the protection of the state or outright denationalizing them in an attempt to safeguard their domestic security. They are also acting to deter and incapacitate potential terrorists from attacking their country. These are all understandable reactions given the state's responsibility to protect its citizens' security and the harm that terroristic violence causes to direct and indirect victims of attacks. I do not object to a state's desire to hold adults criminally responsible for committing acts of violence or inciting others to do the same, whether as a form of retribution, deterrence, or incapacitation. Nor do I object to a state's objective to deter or incapacitate any individual from committing acts of violence, even if they are minors with diminished capacity to be held individually responsible for an act of violence, as contrasted with their adult recruiters.

That said, this chapter raises several objections to the use of citizenship deprivation or the deprivation of diplomatic protection as a form of punishment for affiliation with a terrorist organization. The first objection applies to all participants, regardless of their age, degree of development of their capacity to make responsible choices, or individual agency. Countries must take responsibility for their citizens, regardless of their actions of affiliations, and bring perpetrators of violent terrorist activities to justice in their legal system, rather than abandoning their citizens and passing this responsibility on to jurisdictions with authority over the territory where they find themselves. In holding individuals criminally responsible, they should distinguish between individuals who merely affiliate with a terrorist organization, and those who commit acts of violence or encourage others to do so. The second objection applies to adolescents who were recruited by a terrorist organization's leadership to travel to the conflict zone and affiliate with the organization. Consistent with international law dealing with the responsibility of child soldiers, and theories of diminished agency as they relate to the choices of adolescents, minors should not be held fully criminally responsible for their misguided decision to affiliate with a terrorist organization. Rather, this responsibility should rest with their adult recruiters. Here, restorative justice mechanisms that require adolescents to face victims of terrorist violence and reconcile with the community hold promise as mechanisms toward holding partially responsible minor offenders accountable for their actions and rehabilitating them as future contributing citizens.

My final objection applies exclusively to the young children of foreign terrorist affiliates who were either born into a conflict zone or who were brought there by their parents. In keeping with objections to vicarious responsibility that pass from perpetrators to innocent family members, these children should not be punished or held accountable in any way for an association with a terrorist organization that was not of their choosing. As such, they should not face barriers to acquiring the citizenship status of their parents by descent, or the protections of their parent's country of origin. At present, denationalization that extends to the offender's descendants violates the principle "that punishment should not be applied except to an individual who has broken the law," by extending vicarious punishment to the children of accused terrorists for the misdeeds of their parents (Hart 1968, 6, 81). Nor should the state take any action to punish these individuals, whether the intent is retributive, deterrent, or to incapacitate. Here, I do not deny the security risk that these children may pose due to their early radicalization in a conflict zone (Pokalova 2020). While these children may have been influenced by their parents or the terrorist organization, the threat posed by their radicalization should be responded to through education and psychological treatment in their parents' country of origin.

6

Collective Intergenerational Responsibilities

In this chapter, I consider the ways in which citizens of Canada and the United States should accept responsibility for past injustices against Indigenous peoples to promote reconciliation. Even though Canada and the United States have pursued independent policies in relation to their Indigenous citizens, the reconciliation processes of the two countries should be linked as they relate to Indigenous peoples whose homelands, communities, and claims to sovereignty extend across settler state boundaries. Throughout Canada and the United States, European settlers forcibly displaced the Indigenous population through a combination of factors including disease, violence, inequitable treaties, and sheer demographic pressure. In the final stages of their dislocation of the Indigenous population, the Canadian and U.S. governments each adopted a policy aimed at "civilizing" their conquered Indigenous subjects by forcing their parents to send their children away to residential boarding schools (Starr and Brilmayer 2003, 234–236; Woolford 2015). In the twenty-first century, policymakers occasionally acknowledge using family separation as a deterrent tool to sanction asylum-seeking parents. On the U.S.–Mexico border, many of the targets of deterrence through family separation are Indigenous peoples from Central America fleeing violent homelands. In the early to mid-twentieth century, authorities were far more open about their deliberate use of family separation as part of a policy to undermine Indigenous culture and autonomy and extinguish treaty rights. In contrast to norms and legal precedents protecting other citizen's parental choice over their children's education (*Pierce v. Society of Sisters* 1925), Indigenous parents could not keep their children close to home or have any say in directing their child's upbringing or formal education.

Here, I argue for three linked responses to the intergenerational legacy of policies that separated Indigenous families and destabilized their communities and political life. The first involves building

Born Innocent. Michael J. Sullivan, Oxford University Press. © Oxford University Press 2023.
DOI: 10.1093/oso/9780197671238.003.0006

Indigenous-immigrant-settler alliances. The second involves the government's responsibility to avoid perpetuating Indigenous family separation and community destabilization through its criminal justice and child welfare policies. The third involves strengthening Indigenous political sovereignty by expanding their self-governance, participation, and free movement rights across their territories divided by settler state borders. This involves reforms to immigration and citizenship policy to address the needs of transnational Indigenous polities.[1]

Collective responsibility for an offense committed by an intergenerational institution as in its capacity as an intergenerational corporate entity persists beyond the generation in which it was committed (Kuo and Means 2021). This does not contradict the presumption of innocence for individuals. In corporations, each of an institution's stakeholders may bear the burdens of an individual's illegal action, even if most individuals within the group are blameless. In the same way, citizens of a democratic nation conceived of as an intergenerational project are collectively morally responsible for its past deeds (Borrows 2014, 499). Corporate entities have a particular obligation to make reparations for their unjust enrichment insofar as they continue to benefit from their legacy, which includes entanglement in exploitation, even if their living members are not individually culpable. At the very least, corporate entities must accept the benefits and burdens of their past. Successful intergenerational institutions like countries, corporations, and universities do not just take passive pride in their legacy. Their connection to the past and longevity is part of their value proposition. Most intergenerational corporations, whether private or public, actively market parts of their legacy. Their members profit from this business practice. To avoid profiting from the legacy of past injustice, corporate entities should market the entirety of their legacy, inviting scrutiny and accepting accountability for their entanglement in historical injustice as part of their commitment to building a more ethical brand for the future. Likewise, nations cannot change the past, but they can take steps to avoid repeating similar injustices, and to ensure that the descendants of those harmed have the capacity to participate as full members of the political community.

The form that accountability for the past ought to take will differ according to the institution and its entanglement in past injustices. In Canada, the process of truth and reconciliation with First Nations began with reparations for survivors of residential schools, followed by criminal justice and child welfare reforms. Some political communities decide to offer citizenship to

128 BORN INNOCENT

the descendants of denationalized former citizens as a form of atonement for the crimes of an earlier regime. Settler states can use immigration and citizenship policy to rectify the damage to sovereign Indigenous communities by granting their members rights to free movement across international borders that divide their territories, citizenship in both states, or by recognizing instruments of tribal sovereignty such as passports. These measures are promising for a variety of reasons. Unlike monetary reparations, no individual is required to provide direct compensation for a wrong in which she did not directly participate. The state as an intergenerational political community is acting on behalf of all citizens by restoring a political status and free movement rights that they would have otherwise inherited from their parents.

By the 1960s, child custody removals began to take the place of residential schools in both Canada and the United States, separating children from their parents and other family caregivers for cultural reasons. The legacy of these actions endures for Indigenous families and children to this day, and the harms inflicted upon them by previous generations of officials remain with our fellow citizens. The generation that first authored these policies of dispossession and profited off the removal of Indigenous peoples from their land are no longer with us, even as their descendants occupy and benefit from land and resources taken from Indigenous peoples. Like the descendants of settlers, later immigrants did not take part in the original acts of Indigenous removal, but by becoming citizens by consent, they choose to accept the burdens and benefits of their country, including its moral responsibility to the victims of its acts of dispossession. In settler states, the ongoing legacy of intergenerational harms against Indigenous communities and families arising from the residential school and child welfare systems speak to the need for truth and reconciliation between the victims and the descendants of settlers.

Citizens and political communities should accept moral responsibility for the crimes of their forebears that were committed in the name of the state as an intergenerational community, even though many of the individuals who perpetrated these offenses are now deceased. Truth and reconciliation processes are often necessary for nations to acknowledge that they have wronged some of their citizens, to restore their dignity, to reincorporate them as members of worth, and for nations to move forward in their commitment to equal citizenship. Hannah Arendt described this process of atonement in terms of vicarious responsibility for things we have not done, this taking upon our-selves the consequences for things we are entirely innocent of, is the price we pay for the fact that we live our lives not by ourselves but among our fellowmen, and that the faculty of action, which, after all, is the political fac-ulty par excellence, can be actualized only in one of the many and manifold forms of human community (Arendt 1987, 50).

Throughout this book, I have spoken out against forms of "vicarious respon-sibility" and punishment drift where innocent dependents and descendants are harmed as a result of their forebears' actions, whether this is intentional or not. Here, it is important that we distinguish between the voluntary pursuit of political redemption by willing citizens seeking to overcome the misdeeds of the past, together, from intergenerational punishments like the corruption of blood that attempt to single out the innocent descendants of perpetrators for revenge.

Intergenerational Harms, Obligations, and the Legacy of Residential Schools

An integral part of the political and economic development of Canada and the United States as settler states of mass immigration involved removing Indigenous peoples from their land and distributing it to new settlers. Both countries imposed an international border across Indigenous homelands and restricted the free movement of Indigenous peoples between the two countries without their consent. By the end of the nineteenth century, both governments sought to make Indigenous people into wards of either Canada or the United States and to restrict their mobility and interactions with kinship groups on the other side of the newly imposed frontier (Rensink 2018, 106–107). Then, during the early twentieth century, governments consolidated their power over Indigenous peoples and sought to extinguish their remaining treaty rights through forced assimilation. This meant for-cibly removing Indigenous children from their parents and communities to far-flung residential schools. There, children were frequently abused, taught to despise their language and heritage, and required to work without pay in preparation for a life of menial labor at the margins of society.

Canadians are only beginning to come to grips with this sordid chapter in their nation's history with revelations in May 2021 of an unmarked mass grave containing the bodies of 215 Indigenous children who died while they were confined at what used to be Canada's largest residential school in Kamloops, British Columbia (Hipolito 2021). More revelations followed in June and July of 2021, with the remains of 751 Indigenous children found at the former Marieval Indian Residential School site located on Cowessess First Nation lands approximately 160 kilometres east of Regina, Saskatchewan and 160 unmarked graves discovered at the Kuper Island Indian Residential School on Penelakut Island, British Columbia, which survivors called "Alcatraz" given the dangers they faced escaping abuse at the facility across a dangerous waterway separating the school from Vancouver Island (Hager and Tait 2021; McKeen 2021). Each of these three residential schools were administered by the Roman Catholic Church, which through its religious orders was the single largest sectarian operator of residential schools in Canada, administering 60 percent of all residential schools in Canada on behalf of the Canadian federal government (MacDonald 2014, 309; Grant 2021a).[2] The search for more unmarked graves continues at other residential school sites.

The Carlisle Model and Its Implementation Across North America

Similar institutions existed throughout the United States, which were as harsh as their Canadian counterparts. In 1879, U.S. Army Captain Richard Henry Pratt founded the Carlisle Indian Industrial School in the Cumberland Valley of Pennsylvania with the stated aim "to kill the Indian in him and save the man" (Pratt 1892, 46). Pratt also served as warden of the military prison at St. Augustine, Florida, where Indigenous Chiricacua Apache families were held as prisoners of war under military governance to promote their forced assimilation (Saito 2021, 39). Pratt's goal for the Carlisle School was to remove Indigenous children from their families and tribes across the United States that "cling to their tribal communistic surroundings," to a central facility. There, children would "work for their support and schooling," the latter designed to "plant treason to the tribe and loyalty to the nation at large" through linguistic and cultural assimilation (Pratt 1892, 57). Pratt saw his role in founding and administering the Carlisle school as a humanitarian enterprise, believing "the Indian youth capable of acquiring the same education and industries our white youth had" when removed from the influence

COLLECTIVE INTERGENERATIONAL RESPONSIBILITIES   131

of their families and tribes, and their work experiences in the community "would make them the equals of our youth" (Pratt 1964, 221).

But Pratt was blind to the emotional toll wrought by separating young children from their families. He ignored the alienation students endured at the school when they were punished for speaking their language and holding on to their identity as members of their tribes, and the abuses they suffered when they were hired out for menial labor as part of the school's vocational mission (Adams 2003, xiv). Even former Carlisle students who later prospered in life, like Lakota Chief Luther Standing Bear nonetheless bitterly recalled the relentless efforts to deprive them of their culture and language at Carlisle. Standing Bear later recalled how "at Carlisle we had been ordered never to speak our own language and I now remembered how hard it had been for us to forego the consolation of speech. I remembered how lonely we used to get and how we longed for the loved ones at home, and the taking away of speech at that time only added to our depression" (Standing Bear [1933] 1978, 242). This sense of alienation and confinement endured for Standing Bear when he returned to his reservation as a ward of the state who could not leave his reservation without the permission of an Indian Agent (Standing Bear [1933] 1978, 238).

Luther Standing Bear was among the more fortunate of the Carlisle survivors. Of the 10,500 students who were brought to Carlisle during its operation from 1879 to 1918, some of whom were sent there as prisoners of war, only 758 graduated (Fear-Seagal and Rose 2016, 2, 5). Most returned to their communities with limited education after serving work terms in the community (ibid.). Pratt and other school officials ordered sick and dying students to be sent back to their communities to lessen the death toll directly linked to the institution amidst criticism of the school's high fatality rate (Fear-Seagal 2016, 155; Vitale 2020, 389–390). At least 232 students perished at the school from causes ranging from disease to suicide (Fear-Seagal 2016, 165; Vitale 2020, 386, 396).

The Carlisle model was emulated in Indigenous boarding schools across the United States and Canada in the late nineteenth and early twentieth centuries (Woolford 2015, 67–68; Hudson and MacDonald 2012, 431). Indian agents forced parents to surrender their children as early as four years of age to attend facilities where they were abused, malnourished, left to suffer untreated from communicable diseases, and forced to perform industrial labor to finance the schools as an integral part of the broader model of settler colonialism in both countries (Coleman 1993, 44; Woolford 2015, 70–71;

132 BORN INNOCENT

Saito 2020, 72; Saito 2021, 39). Prompted by the discovery of mass graves at the Kamloops Indian Residential School in Canada, Deb Haaland, the first Indigenous person to lead the U.S. Secretary of the Interior and the great-granddaughter of a Carlisle Indian Industrial school survivor, launched a U.S. Federal Indian Boarding School investigation in June 2021. This inquiry aims to address the intergenerational impact of facilities that cumulatively held approximately 60,000 Indigenous U.S. residents between the 1870s and 1960s (Woolford 2015, 92–93; Martens 2021; Chen 2021; Department of the Interior 2021). In May 2022, the U.S. Assistant Secretary of Indian Affairs issued a preliminary report identifying 408 facilities administered by the federal government between 1819 and 1969 (Newland 2022, 6). In these institutions, children were forced into industrial labor, disciplined for speaking their native language, and subject to malnutrition and abuse (56, 60–63). As early as 1928, it was acknowledged that the "labor of [Indian] children as carried on in Indian boarding schools would, it is believed, constitute a violation of child labor laws in most states" (Meriam 1928, 378). Fifty-three burial sites for children who died at residential schools have been identified thus far, with the investigation ongoing (Newland 2022, 86). Like Canada, the United States has a legacy of forcibly separating Indigenous families and communities to assimilate them and extinguish their multigenerational land claims. This history is only beginning to come to light in a country where reconciliation with Indigenous peoples has yet to become a national priority.

Residential Schools and the Truth and Reconciliation Commission in Canada

In substandard facilities administered by religious denominations with federal funding, school authorities used harsh discipline to force children to abandon their language and way of life. Abuse was rife. Children often went hungry, as federal funding was limited, and administrations were under pressure to cut costs wherever possible, even by covering up student deaths so the religious orders that administered the schools could continue to receive funding for a student's room, board, and tuition (Rupnik 2021). Mike Cachagee, a survivor of the Moose Factory, Chapleau, and Shingwauk (Sault Ste. Marie) residential schools in the 1950s, recounts that disease and malnourishment was common at the facilities (Cachagee 1991). Cachagee recounts that his classmates who died of starvation and disease at the facilities were buried clandestinely by the clergy that administered the schools in shallow, unmarked graves where he recalls that "in the spring, bears would root about in the cemetery and feed on the student remains" (ibid.). At the Shingwauk residential school that was administered by the Anglican Church near Sault Ste. Marie, Ontario, Bill Fletcher, a former student and survivor recalled in 1981 that during his stay from 1946 to 1955, "a lot of people wouldn't say anything we used to get lard maybe once a day on your bread, lucky if we seen margarine, I just leaving there and that was the time I seen margarine, you got lard on your bread, an orange, an apple, once a week" (Fletcher 1981).[3] He described the school as a "jail" where students had to steal food and pick from the garbage to supplement their meagre rations (ibid.). Fletcher's account is consistent with other survivor testimonies about widespread malnutrition in residential schools across Canada (Truth and Reconciliation Commission 2015b, 70–77; Mosby and Galloway 2017; Talaga 2017, 63).

Teachers and school administrators frequently punished young children for expressing their identity and speaking their Indigenous languages. Children were required to perform industrial labor without wages. Though the purpose of these institutions was to assimilate Indigenous children into mainstream society, the substandard education they received, and the prejudice they faced outside their reserves left them incapable of fully integrating into settler society. Since authorities took them from their parents and deprived them of their community's care and training, they lost the ability to contribute to the perpetuation of their culture in their communities of origin. In both Canada and the United States, government officials threatened to arrest parents and take away their infant children if they tried to keep their older children at home (Truth and Reconciliation Commission of Canada 2012, 17–18; Theobald 2019, 22). The trauma that Indigenous children experienced from being forcibly separated from their parents and abused in the residential school system endured even after the institutions were closed in the late twentieth century. The legacy of the residential school system endures in the challenges residential school victims face finding employment, dealing with lasting mental illness and emotional harm, and parenting without positive role models, resulting in intergenerational harms (Cachagee 1991; Truth and Reconciliation Commission 2015b).[4]

The lasting harms resulting from the residential school experience has contributed to a wide array of social challenges among Indigenous peoples including a high incarceration rate, substance abuse, and a low standard

134 BORN INNOCENT

of living. When survivor Mike Cachagee was interviewed in 1991 at a residential school reunion at the former Shingwauk school in Sault Ste. Marie, Ontario, he described the intergenerational toll of what he described as "residential school syndrome" as the result of a colonial process of "taking people" from their homelands, abusing them, forcing them to deny their identity and language, and leaving them "victims of an assimilation process that have lost their self identity, that have lost their self-esteem" (Cachagee 1991). The victims of the residential school system were then left without the means to integrate into their communities of origin or in settler Canadian society. Over three decades after he left residential school, in his role as a native student counsellor, Cachagee was particularly troubled by the attitudes of "social welfare workers" and religious and educational administrators who were offering half-hearted apologies after the fact. In his view,

> this is what bothered a lot of students more. For them to stand up and say, look, we're sorry we screwed up, we did a lousy mess or whatever else it is and it was a big mistake and it will never happen again, and washing your hands of the whole process, without going back to the communities and without looking at what is happened to a lot of these families of the children that went there, you know, yesterday, today and tomorrow, then, someone's got to give us a hand to clean the mess up. That's basically what we're saying. There was a mess left here and the Native communities themselves do not have the resources or the money required to clean this mess up as a result of someone else's foul up (Cachagee 1991).[5]

Cachagee recovered from years of drug and alcohol abuse resulting from his attempt to self-medicate and cope with the trauma he experienced at the facilities, and at eighty-two years of age, he now occupies a leading role as Chair of the Ontario Residential School Support Services, among other roles of regional prominence (Rupnik 2021; Cachagee 2021). Three decades after his testimony at the Shingwauk reunion, in light of the discovery of mass graves at residential schools across Canada in 2021, Cachagee's sadness turned to anger as he asked:

> Has society especially the media become so insensitive that reporting tragedies against First Nations people on Turtle Island is acceptable and expected, that it is considered normal? How sorry a society we are, to be so colonized and not even recognize it, know it and want to change

COLLECTIVE INTERGENERATIONAL RESPONSIBILITIES   135

it. These children, as young as three years old, never stood a chance, discarded like garbage in a mass grave. This child never felt love, taken from their family, brought to this ominous, huge building and suffered. They were either beaten, raped, tortured, sexually abused, made sick with whatever disease that was prevalent at the school at the time. . . . We don't have access to any of the coroner's reports. The children could have been buried alive! We do know that they were hidden in this mass grave to hide the nefarious acts committed on these children at this Catholic school! (Cachagee 2021).

As a survivor, Cachagee holds "the government of the day, and the Catholic Church responsible for this tragic, horrific discovery," and he is demanding they contribute funding to help Indigenous communities to "recover loved ones" by identifying their remains (Cachagee 2021).

In sum, in the immediate aftermath of the mass grave revelations, settler communities, responsible institutions, and governments need to take a leading role in financing community recovery efforts and uncovering the misdeeds of the past, no matter how embarrassing they may be for the responsible institutions. Ongoing reconciliation efforts must be informed by greater cultural understanding and carefully listening to the lived experiences of survivors to appreciate their trauma. Without this sensitivity to survivor's experiences and a willingness to assume accountability—including financial responsibility for the costs of uncovering the past—settlers who occupy positions of institutional and political power cannot attain true reconciliation with the people their institutions harmed, or their descendants. Self-protective ecclesiastical and governmental leaders are sometimes tempted to pass accountability off onto individual perpetrators (many of whom are now deceased) and affiliated religious orders to escape collective responsibility for their actions (Grant 2021b). This fails as an excuse given the expected degree of oversight of religious orders and denominations over clergy, teachers, and administrators in the residential school system. The abuses that occurred in these institutions were not isolated incidents. They were known to religious leaders, educators, and government officials overseeing the perpetrators in question (Borrows 2014, 499; Daigneault 2018).[6] Reconciliation should never simply amount to an institutional public relations campaign that enables politicians and administrators to offer momentary apologies on behalf of their institutions so they can move on and be absolved of future responsibility. Instead, it must be an active and enduring process of listening and

136 BORN INNOCENT

involving survivors and their descendants to take steps toward remediating the suffering that their institutions created over time.

The residential school tragedy provides an apt example of children, born innocent, penalized by the state for their identity through family separation, inadequate schooling, abuse, and discrimination lasting their entire lives, leaving a legacy of unresolved harms to their children and grandchildren. In Canada, 150,000 children passed through the residential school system, with government officials separating them from their parents as early as four years of age to live for most of the year apart from their families (Woolford and Gacek 2016, 404; Eisenberg 2018, 23). For the children who lived there, the residential schools were carceral institutions of colonial subjugation that were often characterized by corporal punishment for speaking one's native tongue, nutritional deprivation, forced industrial labor, and frequent sexual and physical abuse. Canada's Truth and Reconciliation Commission had estimated that between 4,100 and 6,000 children died while attending these institutions, though this figure is now regarded as an undercount with more recent discoveries of mass graves on residential school sites using ground-penetrating radar technology, coupled with the testimony of residential school survivors (Blum 2021; Rodriguez 2021).

Upon leaving these institutions, Indigenous youth struggled to find a place in society, separated from their communities of origin and without the skills and cultural acceptance they needed to find employment and integration into non-Indigenous Canadian communities. After a hundred years of silence by the federal government and religious denominations regarding abuses in the residential schools, revelations by Assembly of First Nations leader Phil Fontaine about the abuse he faced in these institutions encouraged others to come forward, shining a public spotlight on a long-concealed dark chapter in Canada's history (Nagy 2014, 204; Metatawabin 2014, 276). These revelations and broader issues of Indigenous exploitation by government authorities prompted the Assembly of First Nations to issue a report entitled *Breaking the Silence* (1994) detailing the harms caused by what Indigenous leaders described as a colonization process bent on assimilation and cultural de-struction. Amidst the increasing visibility of Indigenous rights claims in Canada, an increasing number of residential school survivors have publicly testified about the abuses they suffered at the hands of their government, churches, and other authorities responsible for the residential schools policy. Similar testimonies followed by official acknowledgments of the harm caused to Indigenous families by settler authorities have occurred in Australia and

New Zealand, and to a far lesser extent, in the United States (Commonwealth of Australia 1997; Woolford 2015, 276–277).[7]

In the face of growing outcries by Indigenous peoples, Canadian Prime Minister Jean Chrétien's Liberal government issued a limited statement of regret in 1998 with a $350 million "healing fund" (Hudson and MacDonald 2012, 432; Woolford 2015, 278). Then, in 2008, Prime Minister Stephen Harper provided a more comprehensive apology recognizing "that the consequences of the Indian Residential Schools policy were profoundly negative and that this policy has had a lasting and damaging impact on Aboriginal culture, heritage and language" (Harper 2008). In his role as Prime Minister, Harper delivered a vicarious apology on behalf of all Canadians for his nation's contribution to the tragedies of family separation and child abuse, which offered some comfort to survivors even though many of the primary perpetrators escaped prosecution (Cohen 2017, 377). Harper's apology focused on the past, and it did not adequately address the government's current role in perpetuating Indigenous family separation. Only one passage connected the past to the present and future, "recognizing that, in separating children from their families, we undermined the ability of many to adequately parent their own children and sowed the seeds for generations to follow, and we apologize for having done this" (Harper 2008). Bloc Québécois leader Gilles Duceppe went a step further toward illustrating the damage that Canada and Québec perpetrated against Indigenous communities and families by appealing to their empathy. Duceppe asked non-Indigenous Canadians to "picture a small village, a small community. Now picture all of its children, gone. No more children between the ages of seven and sixteen playing in the lanes or the woods, filling the hearts of their elders with their laughter and joy" (Fontaine and Craft 2016, 119–120). In the process, younger and immigrant non-Indigenous Canadians who believe that they were born innocent of the residential school tragedy were being asked to re-think their vision of Canada as a society innocent of colonization, and to sympathize with people who were deprived the hope and freedom they associate with Canada as a place of refuge. Non-Indigenous and Indigenous Canadians alike initially welcomed Harper's apology, but the latter were left disappointed when the government did not follow up with policy interventions that would address "the damaging and lasting impact" noted in the apology (Woolford 2015, 279). By contrast, Australian Prime Minister Kevin Rudd's apology that same year to its "stolen generations" of aboriginals wronged under similar circumstances in residential schools

138   BORN INNOCENT

and by child welfare agencies looked to the future in "resolv[ing] that the injustices of the past must never, never happen again" (Rudd 2008). Rudd's apology promised policy changes leading to "a future where we harness the determination of all Australians, Indigenous and non-Indigenous, to close the gap that lies between us in life expectancy, educational achievement and economic opportunity ... embrac[ing] the possibility of new solutions to enduring problems where old approaches have failed" (ibid.).

These official apologies can only serve as a starting point toward reconciling settler states with Indigenous communities harmed by policies aimed at destroying their identity as self-governing and self-sustaining entities so long as Indigenous people remain disproportionately and systemically victimized across a wide range of interactions with their governments. It is symbolically important but too simple for a government to show contrition for the actions of long-dead officials in previous administrations, when Indigenous people continue to face disproportionate rates of incarceration, child welfare interventions, food insecurity, and negative disparities in health and healthcare (Coulthard 2014, 128; Kirkup 2020). Despite official contrition for past conduct, conflict over resource and environmental issues, land claims, and the treatment of Indigenous children endures into the present in the policies of settler states. This disjunct between apologies for the past and injustice in present was on full display in the year following Harper's apology for his role in family separations and child abuse in residential schools, followed the next September by a statement that Canada had "no history of colonialism" (Ljunggren 2009). Many Indigenous Canadians saw this latter statement as evidence of his government's incomplete contrition and historical amnesia regarding the lasting damage wrought by the subjugation of their communities and families (Assembly of First Nations 2009; Slobodian 2017). The gap between historical remorse and ongoing political injustice was at the heart of the Idle No More movement in Canada that began in 2012 as a protest against the Harper government's introduction of legislation undermining Indigenous authority over resource management and environmental stewardship (Coates 2015). Indigenous communities want more than easy apologies for a sad chapter in their nation's history. They want a transformation in settler-Indigenous relations that will ensure that their families never have to experience similar harms (Woolford 2015, 279). They want the government to act on its promises to mend enduring damage to their communities (Coulthard 2014, 120–126).

Education: Building Immigrant-Settler-Indigenous Alliances

The Restorative Mandate of the Truth and Reconciliation Commission of Canada

The Canadian government has taken an important albeit initially reluctant role in Indigenous-settler reconciliation by convening a Truth and Reconciliation Commission to reveal and atone for its role in the abuses engendered by the residential school program and its aftermath. In 2006, the Government of Canada established the Truth and Reconciliation Commission as part of the Indian Residential Schools Settlement Agreement, which was the largest class-action settlement against the government in Canadian history (Lu 2017, 6). The Commission was one of the few truth and reconciliation commissions that resulted from a change in political outlook, rather than regime change and the end of political violence (Niezen 2017, 42–43). Its goal was to facilitate reconciliation between affected students and families and other Canadians by raising awareness about the abuses they suffered and their enduring legacy for Indigenous communities. Between 2007 and 2015, the Truth and Reconciliation Commission heard from more than 6,500 survivors in communities across Canada (Government of Canada 2020). The commission hosted seven events to educate Canadians about the legacy of the residential school system and its impact on students and families, culminating in the 2015 release of a six-volume report detailing the history of the schools and their adverse impact on generations of students and Indigenous families. The Truth and Reconciliation Commission concluded that the overriding objective of both residential schools and child welfare interventions that separated young children from their parents was to "eliminate Aboriginal people as distinct peoples and to assimilate them into the Canadian mainstream against their will" (Truth and Reconciliation Commission 2015a, 1:4). The task of the commission was to demonstrate this history in detail, moving beyond past efforts to pin abuses on a few perpetrators to uncover what amounts to systemic acts of genocide.

State-sponsored cultural genocide against Indigenous peoples occurred in the assimilatory policies of the residential schools and child welfare removals. Acts of biological genocide lasted even longer, through initiatives in Canada and the United States to sterilize Indigenous women and control their family life throughout the twentieth century that persisted in Canada into

140 BORN INNOCENT

the 2010s (Dubinsky 2010, 83; Theobald 2019, 91–97, 147–172; Shaheen-Hussain 2020, 178; Ryan, Ali, and Shawana 2021; Clarke 2021, 146). The U.N. Committee Against Torture has since condemned the forced sterilization of Indigenous women and girls in Canada as a form of torture in 2018. Canada's Senate detailed the prevalence of anti-Indigenous racism among medical professionals and its connection to their involvement in forced sterilizations in a 2021 report (UNCAT 2018; Atullahjan, Bernard and Hartling 2021, 17–22). Indigenous women are still facing forced sterilizations in Canada according to medical professionals testifying at an April 2022 Senate hearing, prompting many to avoid hospital births altogether (Malhotra 2022).

As a forward-looking enterprise, the Truth and Reconciliation Commission's objective is to educate current and future generations about the ongoing need for reconciliation through cross-cultural understanding and policy changes that will help survivors and their descendants. The forward-looking, peace-building mandate of reconciliation is reliant upon the understanding and support of citizens who came of age and immigrants who arrived after the closure of the last residential schools. In prescribing what should come next, the Truth and Reconciliation's Final Report likened the ongoing task of reconciliation to "dealing with a situation of family violence. It is about coming to terms with events of the past in a manner that overcomes conflict and establishes a respectful and healthy relationship among people going forward" (Truth and Reconciliation Commission 2015a, 6:1). The future of reconciliation requires that immigrants and new generations of citizens have the empathy and will to build new alliances with First Nations peoples. Younger generations and recent immigrants to settler states sometimes claim that they are born innocent of policies of land seizure, forced assimilation and family separation that ended before they came of age or arrived in their country of residence (Miller 2007, 160; Brooks 2004, 188). This is a problematic claim since citizens and immigrants continue to benefit from land title and resources resulting from the dispossession of Indigenous people. For Hannah Arendt, considering the responsibility of later generations of Germans for the crimes of the Nazi regime, political responsibility means "that every generation, by virtue of being born into a continuum, is burdened by the sins of the fathers as it is blessed by the deeds of the ancestors" (Arendt 1963, 297–298). When they come of age or become naturalized citizens of a settler state conceived of as an intergenerational project, they share in the benefits and burdens of this political enterprise that bears the legacy of harms done to First Nations and other exploited peoples (Hough 2020, 162; Borrows 2014, 499). To this end, the Truth and Reconciliation Commission of Canada's recommendation (#94) to add language to Canada's Citizenship Oath "recognizing and affirming the Aboriginal and treaty rights of First Nations, Inuit and Métis peoples" is an important first step toward instructing new Canadian citizens about the importance of Indigenous rights as part of the country they are joining (Bill C-8, 2020).

Some would suggest that reparations are the best way to discharge their responsibility to communities that the state or its agents harmed (Thompson 2009, 77–82; Kuo and Means 2021, 806–819). Reparations are particularly proper as a remedy for past injustices when they were committed by a democratic state that has maintained its identity and character over time. Its citizens are expected to share in the burdens and benefits of the decisions that were made in their state's name by its governing officials (Pasternak 2021, 185, 208–209). However, a further question must be asked about what form these reparations should take to best aid those who have been harmed and their descendants, who will also share indirectly in the costs of providing reparations as citizens of that state. Financial compensation alone is inadequate to help victims and their descendants to overcome the enduring legacy of past abuses. For instance, after receiving compensation beginning in the late 1990s from the religious denominations that administered abusive residential schools, many survivors "recognized money wouldn't heal them," and some testified that "being paid for being abused made them feel ugly, dirty, used by what happened to us—paying cash can reinforce this" (Miller 2018, 99). Beyond one-time monetary payments, forward-looking approaches were needed to consider how Indigenous communities will be affected, and can be better served, in a wide range of initiatives from criminal justice reforms to health care and employment equity policies to help residential school survivors and their descendants. It also means including representatives from Indigenous communities in policy decisions and investing in the future of disadvantaged communities to help them to educate, mentor, and train leaders.

Reparations broadly conceived are only the first forward-looking step in a process of reconciliation. Steps toward solidarity can involve drawing on shared experiences, common interests, and the desire on the part of individual settlers to learn about, and forge grassroots coalitions with Indigenous communities. Reconciliation that draws from the empathy arising from shared experiences may take place between communities

142 BORN INNOCENT

that have a common history of oppression at the hands of their state of origin or current state. North American Indigenous nations have a long history of expressing solidarity with forced migrants. In 1847, shortly after the U.S. government forced them to leave their homelands along a deadly forced migration known as the Trail of Tears, the Cherokee and Choctaw Nations raised funds for the Irish people as they faced their own famine and involuntary migrations in recognition of their shared plight (De Leon 2016, 236; Shrout 2015). Similarly, asylum-seekers arriving in a settler state after facing political violence and dispossession in their homelands have experiences that can help them to empathize with the plight of Indigenous communities, leading to activism based in empathy and solidarity. Some asylum-seekers themselves are from Indigenous communities in other settler states that have experienced many of the same dislocations as their counterparts who are native to Canada. Canada's Truth and Reconciliation Commission has pledged to decolonize naturalization ceremonies by including information about Canada's First Nations in citizenship study guides, testing applicants on this information, and changing the oath of naturalization to include a promise "that I will faithfully observe the laws of Canada including Treaties with Indigenous Peoples" (Truth and Reconciliation Calls to Action 2015d, 93–94; Cohen 2021; Immigration, Refugees, and Citizenship Canada 2023). First Nations and immigrant resettlement organizations are responding to these calls to action by working together to teach immigrants about First Nations' history and their current challenges (Cohen 2021).

Similarly, among multigenerational Canadian residents, Black-Indigenous alliances have developed out of shared experiences of racism and discrimination in settler states, connecting activists in Indigenous movements like #IdleNoMore[8] in Canada with the global Black Lives Matter movement (Maynard 2019). Black and Indigenous people in Canada both face discriminatory policing practices and disproportionate incarceration rates that call for a common front in the movement for criminal justice reform that addresses the root causes of offending and emphasizes rehabilitation over retribution (Reece 2020).[9] Solidarity-based activism can arise from a shared commitment to values that Indigenous people regard as sacred, such as living in harmony with nature, the stewardship of natural resources, and environmental protections. The descendants of settlers and Indigenous peoples can unite around a shared appreciation for conservation and living in harmony with the land in response to our common ecological crisis. In this sense, "reconciliation becomes a task that has significance for this generation, but it is primarily about those who are yet unborn," since the actions that settlers are taking now to revalue Indigenous philosophies of environmental stewardship will be reaped by future citizens (McKay 2008, 104). Each of these settler-Indigenous alliances can serve as a means to build support for Indigenous rights and redress among a diverse community of citizens, pressuring governments to act to address the concerns of what is becoming a broader political movement.

For real change to occur in the way that policymakers treat Indigenous communities, there must be significant growth in understanding and empathy among non-Indigenous settlers and immigrants for the intergenerational plight of Indigenous peoples. The degree of opposition to the modest demands of the #IdleNoMore movement among ordinary Canadians and Conservative Party leaders that were in power during the protests underscores the need for ongoing education and dialogue at the interpersonal and community level. Here, restorative justice approaches have the benefit of being forward-looking and concerned with rebuilding and fostering the growth of positive relationships between previously adversarial parties instead of simply blaming perpetrators and their descendants for past harms (Llewellyn and Philpott 2014, 22). The Truth and Reconciliation Commission of Canada's use of restorative justice in its proceedings set the stage for moving beyond legal and political negotiations between the Crown and Indigenous political communities toward empathetic dialogue between Indigenous and non-Indigenous Canadians (Woolford and Nelund 2019, 71).

In criminal justice proceedings, restorative justice often starts with dialogue between victims and offenders in a dialogue that helps the latter understand and take responsibility for the harms they caused (Sullivan 2017; Woolford and Nelund 2019, 77–79). In the case of residential schools, the passage of time and the death of most of the perpetrators precludes their direct participation in a victim-offender conference. The conventional purposes of individual punishment are moot in most of the cases. There is no prospect for individual deterrence or incapacitation against an elderly former educator or school administrator that abused children and separated them from their families who is not in a position to reoffend. Even when an offender is still alive, most victims are no longer seeking retribution. What is important is to learn from the past to ensure that similar public policy injustices are not repeated.

144 BORN INNOCENT

Instead of seeking justice through traditional punishments, victims and witnesses as participants in truth and reconciliation commissions are seeking a broader role for restorative justice, creating the "conditions of social relationships in which all parties might achieve meaningful, just, and peaceful co-existence" (Llewellyn 2008, 189). This does not require the participation of since-deceased perpetrators, but rather a commitment by their employers involved in the residential school system to rectify the intergenerational legacy of residential schools (Truth and Reconciliation Commission 2015c, 5:116). This can involve offering resources to Indigenous community leaders and educators to help residential school victims and their families. It also involves listening to Indigenous perspectives and being attentive to their expressed needs. The goal must be one of genuine listening and seeking uncomfortable truths with present implications. We must avoid symbolic public relations exercises that allow leaders of institutions that took part in abusive practices to proceed with a clean conscience without confronting their responsibility for past and present injustices. It is important to teach new citizens including children and immigrants about the legacy of settler colonialism. New generations must accept their shared responsibility to decolonize child welfare, criminal justice, and resource allocation policies that harm Indigenous people (Truth and Reconciliation Commission 2015c, 6:135–136). Restorative justice processes should be used to address the ongoing harms that Indigenous persons face in the criminal justice system (Truth and Reconciliation Commission 2015c, 5:239, 255; *R. v. Gladue* 1999, *R. v. Ipeelee* 2012).

In its calls to action for forward-looking solutions to the legacies of settler colonialism, the Truth and Reconciliation Commission of Canada highlighted the lasting harms of family separation and institutionalization of Indigenous young people that endure. After the residential schools were closed beginning in the 1960s, Indigenous children faced new forms of family separation during the "Sixties Scoop," where child welfare agencies declared Indigenous parents unfit for cultural reasons, and sent their children to live with Euro-Canadian foster or adopted parents (Dubinsky 2010, 81; Truth and Reconciliation Commission of Canada, Vol. 2, 181–182; Mussell 2020, 23; Stevenson 2020, 58). Between 1960 and 1985, over 10,000 Canadian Indigenous children were removed from their families and communities and placed with non-Indigenous families, in some cases outside of Canada, making it difficult for them to ever reunite with their birth families (Shaheen-Hussain 2020, 181). The goal of Indigenous child custody removals and adoptions by Euro-Canadian parents was the same as with residential schools. Both policies aimed to separate Indigenous children from their families and communities to extinguish Indigenous tribal polities and the state's pre-existing treaty obligations toward their political communities (Landertinger 2021, 140). Similar developments occurred among Australia and the United States' Indigenous population during the same period (Tilbury 2009, 60–61; Douglas and Walsh 2013, 61–66; Nichols 2017; Goetze 2022, 7).

In the United States, under the auspices of the Indian Adoption Project during the 1960s, child welfare agencies were six times more likely to place Indigenous children in foster care than non-Indigenous children (Government Accountability Office 2005). By the early 1970s, an average of 25 to 35 percent of Indigenous children had been removed from their parents and placed in foster care or Euro-American adoptive homes (Jacobs 2018, 267). Indigenous children were removed from their parents for cultural reasons, such as non-nuclear family childcare, or for perceived inadequacies such as poverty, unemployment, and substandard housing that did not lead to removals among non-Indigenous parents (Indian Child Welfare Program 1974, 3–8, 35–40). Part of the goal of this program was to privatize federal burdens for caring for Indigenous children, and by assimilating a new generation through adoption, eventually ending federal responsibilities toward Indigenous polities (Jacobs 2018, 267). With an understanding of the toll of Indigenous family separation resulting from his upbringing on the Rosebud Sicangu Lakota Oyate reservation, U.S. Senator James Abourezk (D-SD) first introduced and championed legislation in 1974 to address the toll of child welfare interventions in his community (Dubinsky 2010, 85; Jacobs 2014, 138–139). Abourezk highlighted the need for culturally sensitive child welfare responses recognizing the unique role of the extended family and fictive kin in Indigenous childcare (Indian Child Welfare Program 1974, 473). Indigenous leaders blamed the foster care crisis on state "social workers, untutored in the ways of Indian family life or assuming them to be socially irresponsible, [who] consider leaving the child with persons outside the nuclear family as neglect and thus as grounds for terminating parental rights" (Indian Child Welfare Program 1974, 18; Indian Child Welfare Act of 1978). After four years of hearings and debate on revised versions of the legislation, the U.S. Congress enacted the Indian Child Welfare Act (ICWA) of 1978. This act requires tribes to be notified about any child welfare proceeding so they can find a culturally appropriate placement, preferably with extended family, or

146   BORN INNOCENT

a member of the child's birth tribe (25 USC §1903, 1911). Overall, the ICWA promotes the well-being of Indigenous children by keeping them connected with their families, tribes, and cultural heritage. The ICWA's goal is to remediate decades of damage to the political and cultural integrity of tribes caused by state-mandated family separations (25 USC §1901; Mississippi Choctaw Indian Band v. Holyfield 1989, 51–52).

Indigenous leaders supported the act to strengthen tribal sovereignty undermined by decades of family separation that prevented the intergenerational transmission of their tribe's heritage (Indian Child Welfare Act of 1978, 193). They saw the integrity of their community's families as essential to the perpetuation of tribes as sovereign nations (Indian Child Welfare Act of 1978, 193; Mississippi Choctaw Indian Band v. Holyfield 1989, 34). Since its enactment in 1978, the ICWA has been successful in reducing the number of Indigenous child welfare interventions, family separations, and non-Indigenous foster care placements. Historian Margaret Jacobs and legal scholar Lorie Graham regard the hearings leading up the act as an early unofficial truth and reconciliation process, with the ICWA serving as partial reparations for state-mandated Indigenous family separations (Graham 2008, Jacobs 2014, 267). Scholars and policymakers view the ICWA as a model for Indigenous child welfare reform in other settler states, including Australia and Canada (Hahn, Caldwell, and Sinha 2020, 4, 6, 19–20; Zug 2020).

In Canada, Indigenous families are still disproportionately subject to intervention by child welfare agencies as compared to other Canadians. Despite making up only 4.1 percent of the population in Ontario under fifteen, Indigenous children represented approximately 30 percent of foster children in Ontario in 2016 (OHRC 2018, 17). In Canada as a whole, Indigenous children accounted for 52.2 percent of children under fourteen in foster care in 2016, despite representing only 7.7 percent of children overall (Statistics Canada 2018).[10] In the Province of Manitoba, Indigenous children make up 90 percent of the youth in the foster care system (Landertinger 2021, 136). Indigenous children are more likely to be in institutional care away from their parents since the turn of the millennium than during the residential school program that prompted the Truth and Reconciliation Commission's work (Waldock 2020, 113–114). Residential school and foster care victims have been left at the margins of both Indigenous and settler Canadian life. They are scarred by childhood of abuse and neglect. Their ties to their communities have been broken, and many lack an adequate education to succeed on the job market. Some survivors were unable to return to their tribal communities and have fallen prey to a downward spiral into homelessness, substance abuse, and involvement in the criminal justice system.

A generation after the closure of the last residential school in Canada in 1997, inequalities in child welfare and educational outcomes persist among Indigenous youth. There are few secondary schools in remote communities, and so many Indigenous youth have to board in distant facilities to receive a high school education (Talaga 2017, 98–103; Hay 2019, 7–8). There, teenagers as young as fourteen are living without their parents with a minimal support system and often fall prey to alcoholism, racist abuse by Euro-Canadian townspeople, and a criminal justice system that disregards cases that involve missing Indigenous youth. These same young people are at a higher risk of suicide than non-Indigenous teenagers (Talaga 2017, 130–139). Owing to inadequate funding and disputes between levels of government, jurisdictional disputes over responsibility for these and other Indigenous children's welfare and education persist, leading to gaps in the provision of child welfare services. This problem has become the subject a human rights inquest by the Special Rapporteur on the Rights of Indigenous Peoples, calling for increased funding for education, health, and child welfare services for Indigenous peoples to "ensure that the quality of these services is at least equal to that provided to other Canadians" (Anaya 2014, ¶84). Canada has been slow in ensuring that Indigenous peoples enjoy protections set forth in the United Nations Declaration on the Rights of Indigenous Peoples (UNDRIP) (Robinson 2020). The settler states, including Canada, initially rejected the UNDRIP with its statement that "Indigenous children have the right to all levels and forms of education of the state without discrimination" in Article 14 (United Nations 2007, §14). However, that same year, Canada's Parliament enacted Jordan's Principle to resolve jurisdictional disputes involving the care of First Nations children and to ensure they receive timely care, which includes child welfare, health, and educational services (Talaga 2017, 203–205; Forester 2021). Despite this prior commitment, the federal government challenged the scope of its financial responsibility in litigation that is not keeping with its commitment to reconciliation with Indigenous peoples (Forester 2021). After losing its appeal in court, the federal government reached a $40 billion settlement with First Nations groups in December 2021 addressing its role in gaps in child welfare funding that led to Indigenous children being removed from their families (Tait, Kirkup, and Raman-Williams 2022).

148 BORN INNOCENT

To address Indigenous family separation, Canada's Truth and Reconciliation Commission asked the federal government to help First Nations to establish and maintain their own child-welfare agencies, ensuring that placements of Indigenous children are culturally appropriate (Truth and Reconciliation Commission of Canada 2015c). In June 2019, Justin Trudeau's Liberal government enacted legislation drawing on the UNDRIP and the UNCRC to facilitate the development of Indigenous alternatives to government foster care agencies (Bill C-92, 2019). Beginning as early as 1981, with the Spallumcheen First Nation in British Columbia's decision to take over child welfare placements on its reserve, First Nations progressively developed their own child and family welfare programs (Ariss 2021, 117). Bill-C-92 provides greater assistance in this regard, along with greater autonomy given the overreach of provincial child welfare authorities into Indigenous communities that unnecessarily separated children from willing extended family caregivers. With the enactment of this legislation, more Indigenous communities in Canada are developing their own child welfare systems and regulations governing family interventions informed by "traditional practices of raising children and helping each other" (Turner 2021; Eneas 2021). In the Upper Great Lakes region, Anishinabek First Nations are using the funding from their settlement with the Canadian government to create a new child welfare agency and dispute resolution system aimed at keeping children with their extended families whenever possible (Anishinabek Nation Head Office 2022).

Owing to an uneven application of this legislation across the provinces, and a lack of resources for starting Indigenous-led child welfare agencies in some remote Indigenous communities, Indigenous children are still being removed from their communities by social workers in remote communities like the Innu homelands of Northern Labrador (Mullin 2021). Canada's current Indigenous Services Minister, Marc Miller, admits that his government's legislation is only a first step, given the pervasiveness of outside child welfare interventions in Indigenous communities, which have taken more children out of Indigenous communities than the residential school system did while it was in operation (Venn 2021). Nunavut's Member of Parliament, Mumilaaq Qaqqaq, reminded Canadians in June 2021 that the threat to Indigenous family unity is not a thing of the past, with "foster care" resulting from outside social worker interventions serving as the "modern-day residential school system" (Wright 2021).

Similar problems also persist in the United States despite its Indian Child Welfare Act. In the United States, Indigenous children were still overrepresented in foster care at a rate 2.66 times greater than their proportion in the overall population as of 2019 (Puzzanchera and Taylor 2021).

Changing Course: Policies that Protect Indigenous Family Unity

In both Canada and the United States, the challenge that remains for government and Indigenous child welfare agencies is to shift the focus from apprehension to prevention. Provinces and states need to provide more autonomy to Indigenous communities to manage their own culturally sensitive child welfare agencies. More support needs to be given to at-risk parents as caregivers to break the cycle of intergenerational family separation.

Reconciliation through Restorative Justice: Criminal Justice Policy

For Indigenous Canadians struggling with the intergenerational trauma of forced family separation and abuse by their government, prisons have become "the new residential schools," in a system where Indigenous people are ten times more likely to be incarcerated than non-Indigenous people (Macdonald 2016). Similar trends with Indigenous populations are evident in other settler states including the United States, Australia, and New Zealand (Chartrand 2019, 68).

The Final Report of the Truth and Reconciliation Commission highlighted the ways in which "the residential school experience lies at the root of the current overincarceration of Aboriginal people" (Truth and Reconciliation Commission 2015c, 5:7). Many survivors have succumbed to addiction as they attempt to self-medicate for the trauma of early childhood family separation and abuse in residential schools. Their children in turn are at greater risk of fetal alcohol spectrum disorder (FASD), a disability that entails memory impairments, problems with judgment and abstract reasoning, and poor adaptive functioning (ibid.). Young people with FASD are nineteen times more likely to be in prison than youths without FASD, leading to an intergenerational transmission of disadvantage (Popova et al. 2011, 339). In Canada, judges have been required since 1999 under Section 718.2 of the Criminal Code as interpreted by the Supreme Court to "consider all available sanctions other than imprisonment and to pay particular attention to the circumstances of aboriginal offenders" (*R v. Gladue* 1999, ¶93). Despite these guidelines, the Truth and Reconciliation Commission found in 2015 that they remained disproportionately at risk of involvement with the criminal justice system (Truth and Reconciliation Commission 2015c, 5:225, 246, 253). The Office of the Correctional Investigator found that the Indigenous percentage of the incarcerated population steadily increased from 2001 to 2020, rising from 17.59 percent in 2001 to 30.04 percent in 2020 (Office of the Correctional Investigator 2020). Indigenous women with children are also far more likely to be incarcerated than their non-Indigenous counterparts, leading to prolonged family separations with negative impacts on child development (Office of the Correctional Investigator 2021). In short, Indigenous families continue to suffer from an intergenerational legacy of trauma resulting from state intervention and institutionalized separation. The Canadian government acknowledges that this problem is impeding its reconciliation with Indigenous peoples in the 2015 Truth and Reconciliation Commission's Calls to Actions (Truth and Reconciliation Commission 2015d, 30). Subsequent government reports highlighted the need for new approaches that address the root causes of offending by providing more resources for the treatment and rehabilitation of at-risk youth and expanding the use of culturally informed justice practices within Indigenous communities, like restorative justice (Government of Canada 2019). Despite their potential long-term merits, the government has been slow in implementing these approaches, and incarceration and recidivism rates among Indigenous Canadians have continued to rise since the TRC issued its final report (Office of the Correctional Investigator 2020).

Restorative justice is forward-looking and concerned with the reconstruction and maintenance of relationships of equal concern, respect, and dignity (Llewellyn and Philpott 2014, 32). At the societal level, restorative approaches to accountability as part of a truth and reconciliation process involve uncovering the full scope of a historical injustice and the ways that it endures into the present. Accountability does not involve seeking retribution against individuals or vicarious punishment against their descendants for past injustices. In the context of the residential school system, vicarious theories of liability contributed to the perception that punishing a few malign teachers and administrators and their employers was enough to address the injustices of the broader system (Truth and Reconciliation Commission of Canada 2015c, 5:203). The Truth and Reconciliation Commission of Canada rejects this approach, stating that it obscured the systemic nature of the injustice, and the ways in which "residential schools themselves were part of a larger genocidal attack on Aboriginal culture" that extend beyond any given perpetrator (ibid.).

Instead of trying to identify and punish a few scapegoats, the goal of reconciliation is to repair harms to the larger social order by eliciting empathy and support among current citizens for policy changes to address lasting negative outcomes for the victims and their descendants (Truth and Reconciliation Commission of Canada 2015c, 5:286). For the Commission, reconciliation is not about finding guilty parties and punishing them. Rather,

> "reconciliation" is about establishing and maintaining a mutually respectful relationship between Aboriginal and non-Aboriginal peoples in this country. For that to happen, there has to be awareness of the past, acknowledgement of the harm that has been inflicted, atonement for the causes, and action to change behaviour . . . [since] too many Canadians know little or nothing about the deep historical roots of these conflicts. This lack of historical knowledge has serious consequences for First Nations, Inuit, and Métis peoples, and for Canada as a whole. In government circles, it makes for poor public policy decisions. In the public realm, it reinforces racist attitudes and fuels civic distrust between Aboriginal peoples and other Canadians (Truth and Reconciliation Commission 2015c, Vol. 6, 1–3).

The heirs to the institutions, leaders, laypeople and citizens that justified separating young children from their parents and communities to assimilate them and extinguish Indigenous polities first require education to understand what their forebears did. They need to know and appreciate the ways in which their government's policies and prejudice toward Indigenous people that arises out of a misunderstanding of the social challenges their communities are confronting is perpetuating this injustice. Current generations of Canadians are not the perpetrators of the original policies that amounted to cultural genocide against Indigenous families and communities to extinguish Indigenous land claims and culture. In this narrow sense, they are born innocent of their forebears' sins, though they risk repeating the

152 BORN INNOCENT

same mistakes in new forms. However, the descendants of settlers and recent immigrants continue to benefit from the ongoing exploitation of lands and resources unjustly taken from Indigenous peoples (Rice and Snyder 2008, 57). As a result, Indigenous children are born into lives of disadvantage, in which they struggle to overcome the legacy of this dispossession with its impact on their families' and communities' ability to care for them.

Surviving wrongdoers are required to give an account of their crimes, and truth and reconciliation commissions often ask the institutions they represented to provide restitution and to change their internal practices so that they will not repeat similar injustices against other groups in the future. In the Canadian context, the churches that administered residential schools first had to pay financial settlements to their survivors, but then victims asked them to go a step further to commit to honoring the spirituality and culture they once denigrated. Some sanctioned religious denominations that embraced the reconciliation process, such as the United Church of Canada, have already made reconciliation with Indigenous nations part of their doctrine, mandating that future leaders make decisions that will further racial justice (United Church of Canada 2014; Response of the Churches 2015).

The Roman Catholic Church played a leading role in the administration of residential schools on behalf of the Government of Canada. This continues to serve as a source of spiritual and emotional turmoil in the lives of survivors who suffered abuse as children at the hands of its clergy in residential schools (Fontaine 2010, 155; MacDonald 2014, 309; Woolford and Gacek 2016, 10–11; Grant 2021a). One of the Truth and Reconciliation Commission's Calls to Action is for "the Pope to issue an apology," delivered in Canada, "to Survivors, their families, and communities for the Roman Catholic Church's role in the spiritual, cultural, emotional, physical, and sexual abuse of First Nations, Inuit, and Métis children in Catholic-run residential schools" (Truth and Reconciliation Commission 2015d, 58). In the wake of revelations of mass graves on Catholic-administered residential schools, some survivors lashed out against the Catholic Church with acts of violence, arson, and vandalism directed at churches (Malone 2021).

In April 2022, after a year of difficult negotiations, Pope Francis invited Indigenous leaders from Canada to the Vatican. He apologized for his Church's role in separating families and victimizing children "to impose a uniformity based on the notion that progress occurs through ideological colonization, following programmes devised in offices rather than the desire to respect the life of peoples" (Pope Francis 2022b). Francis pledged to resist all remaining forms of "political, ideological, and economic colonization" in the Catholic Church "to reestablish the covenant between grandparents and grandchildren, between the elderly and the young, for this is a fundamental prerequisite for the growth of unity in our human family" (ibid.). Francis also offered to come to Canada to commit the Roman Catholic Church to further acts of reconciliation and restitution in Indigenous communities (ibid.).[11]

Indigenous leaders in Canada see Pope Francis's apology as an important first step. They are cautiously optimistic that Francis's apology will bring diocesan leaders in Canada in line with other religious denominations that already accepted responsibility for the harm they caused Indigenous communities (Goodyear 2022). For the time being, in the wake of the revelations of mass graves at church-administered residential schools in Canada, the U.N. Special Rapporteur has called it "inconceivable that Canada and the Holy See would leave such heinous crimes unaccounted for and without full redress" (United Nations 2021). The U.N. Special Rapporteurs are demanding that "the Catholic Church . . . provide full access to judicial authorities to the archives of the residential schools run by the institution, to conduct prompt and thorough internal and judicial investigations into these allegations, and to publicly disclose the result of those investigations" (ibid.). First Nations leaders are also calling for the Missionary Oblates of Mary Immaculate, the religious order that administered most Roman Catholic residential schools, to release "records on the deaths of Aboriginal children in the care of residential school authorities" pursuant to the Truth and Reconciliation Commission's Call to Action #71, to aid in efforts to locate other grave sites (Wells 2021, Truth and Reconciliation Commission 2015d, 71).

Today, survivors are spiritual leaders in the churches that once administered residential schools. Their message includes one of promoting healing—not just among victims, but also among "perpetrators who are wounded and marked by history" (McKay 2008, 107). Part of the restorative process involves reintegrative shame, the idea that those who have committed a wrong or benefitted from it must first grapple with its consequences, as a step on a pathway toward rehabilitation into a more responsible citizenship (Braithwaite 1989, 4, 97, 178–180). The restorative process does not leave perpetrators to languish in their shame. Those involved in the reconciliation process want to promote forgiveness without forgetting past wrongs, by teaching those involved to treat Indigenous people as spiritual brothers and sisters and co-participants in governance (McKay 2008, 107–108; Castellano 2008, 385, 398).

154 BORN INNOCENT

Reconciliation through Immigration, Tribal Membership, and Citizenship Policy

For Indigenous peoples, the separation of families and disruption of kinship relations by child welfare agencies and religious institutions that operated residential schools was more than a violation of a human right to family integrity. Under the old assimilation regime, government officials used family separation to extinguish the children's birthright to intergenerational tribal membership. That abolished their right to move and live freely across the continent, known to Indigenous people as Turtle Island. These officials aimed to replace Indigenous citizenship in lands that crossed state borders and spanned North America with bounded settler state citizenship. The colonization of kinship disrupted intergenerational spiritual ties between children and their languages, ritual life, and land. Those ties are central to the continuity of Indigenous identity (Stevenson 2020, 57). At the collective level, Indigenous communities are sovereign political entities in their own right. They have the same reasons to object to the removal of their children by welfare agencies as a sovereign nation like Guatemala, which has suspended exploitative international baby trade operations (Fieser 2009; Jacobs 2014, 77). At the individual level, the agency and wishes of Indigenous persons deserve the same respect as those of settler persons. When religious and government adoption agencies pressured young Indigenous women into surrendering their children at the height of the scandal from the 1950s to 1970s, they had the same reason to expect a public outcry as young settler women would, had this been done to them. Instead, their protests were all but ignored (Jacobs 2014, 69–94).[12] Government and religious authorities ignored the pleas of young women and their access to Indigenous caregiving networks which young unmarried mothers traditionally made use of to help them to care for their children, instead deeming them unfit parents as individuals.

Settler states have to do more than just provide monetary reparations. They have to honor their treaty and human rights commitments to Indigenous persons. This includes recognizing the right of Indigenous peoples to cross borders to live and work throughout their traditional territory without restraint (Lu 2017, 267–268). An associated right involves the freedom to trade with other members of the same nation across settler state borders. On June 21, 2021, the United Nations Declaration on the Rights of Indigenous Peoples Act received Royal Assent and came into force as Canadian law (Department of Justice Canada 2021). Article 36 of the UNDRIP states that

Indigenous peoples "have the right to maintain and develop contacts, relations and cooperation, including activities for spiritual, cultural, political, economic and social purposes, with their own members as well as other peoples across borders." Even so, Canada still prevents American members of cross-border Indigenous tribes from crossing the border to live and work in Canada (Imai and Gunn 2018, 241–242). This constitutes a major impediment to Indigenous sovereignty and treaty rights to free movement.

Free Movement and Trade Rights

The United States' Immigration and Nationality Act's clauses pertaining to Indigenous peoples born in Canada is a model for a broader solution to this problem, building upon the Jay Treaty of 1794 between the Crown, the United States, and Indigenous tribes respecting pre-existing rights to free movement (*McCandless v. Diabo* 1928; Act of April 2, 1928; 8 U.S.C. §1359). The United States regards the portion of the Jay Treaty (Article 3) "so far as it relates to the right of Indians to pass across the border" as still in force (U.S. State Department 2020). If Canada ratified the Jay Treaty, this would enable U.S. citizen members of border Indigenous tribes to cross the U.S.–Canada border freely, strengthening tribal unity and sovereignty. Canada's Senate Committee on Aboriginal Peoples views this measure as a potential solution to border crossing disputes (Dyck and Paterson 2016, 7–9; Caron 2017). The Canadian government has yet to act on this recommendation. Similar arrangements exist with a cross-border tribe on the U.S.–Mexico border encompassing members of the Texas Band of Kickapoo Indians residing in Mexico whom Congress granted U.S. citizenship and free passage rights across the U.S.–Mexico border within their ancestral lands in 1983 (Texas Band of Kickapoo Act 1983).

Tribal Membership and Self-Determination

As a starting point, the reciprocal recognition of an Indigenous right to free movement across the U.S.–Canada border based on the U.S. understanding of Indigenous rights in Article 3 of the Jay Treaty would be a helpful starting point for recognizing Indigenous sovereignty that predates and extends across international settler state boundaries. Even so, the U.S. approach to

156 BORN INNOCENT

the Jay Treaty framework has shortcomings from a tribal sovereignty perspective. Further modifications are desirable to recognize Indigenous self-determination over membership rules.

The U.S. government has a strict descent and blood-quantum racial rule for determining who constitutes an "Indian" for the purposes of obtaining free movement rights. An Indigenous person must prove that they have at least 50 percent "Indian blood" to freely enter the United States and obtain many government services there. This ascriptive definition of Indigenous status is inconsistent with the membership allocation practices of many Indigenous tribes. As self-governing political entities, Indigenous nations do not necessarily define their membership based on descent, or have varying rules governing the degree of descent necessary for tribal membership (Sullivan 2022a). The Jay Treaty's blood-based definition of Indigenous membership also runs contrary to decisions by U.S. courts which ruled that membership in Indigenous tribes is a political, rather than a racial classification, reflecting the sovereign will of individual Indigenous polities in relationship with the federal government (*California Valley Miwok Tribe v. United States* 2008, 1263; *Brackeen v. Bernhardt* 2019, 426–430).

The U.S. definition is also inconsistent with the Canadian government's definition of who constitutes a status Indian. In addition to membership by descent, many Indigenous tribes also accord status to new members by adoption, marriage, or consent (Simpson 2014, 188–190; Lee 2019, 790, 815). Indigenous families and tribal polities define their own citizenship policies without relying on external legal orders such as Canadian or U.S. law, allowing for the adoption of children into the polity by consent rather than consanguinity (804, 815).[13] Here, tribal membership can be more like belonging to a civic nation defined politically as an imagined intergenerational community that shares common values, rather than an ethnic nation defined by race or descent (Anderson 1983).

One clear example of this form of community is the Métis nation in Canada, which is not descended from any historic pre-contact tribe but rather from the shared experience of persons of mixed-Indigenous and European descent on the frontier (*R v. Powley* 2003, 210, 214–217; *Daniels v. Canada* 2016, 101–102). *In Métis: Race, Recognition, and the Struggle for Indigenous Peoplehood* (2014), Chris Andersen argues "being Métis (at least politically) is about peoplehood, and thus it is first and foremost about historical and contemporary political self-consciousness and struggles" (Andersen 2014, 199). In doing so, Andersen seeks to part ways with juridical definitions that "infuse courts with a constitutive power they otherwise neither possess nor deserve" (ibid.). To this end, Andersen proposes an alternative definition of the term and political identity of the Métis people that is circumscribed to "refer to the history, events, territories, language, and culture associated with the growth of the buffalo hunting and trading of the northern plains" (Andersen 2014, 24). Only in these places, Andersen, Chartrand, and Giokas argue that the "historical Métis nation of the North West, or 'Riel's people'" was able to "bloom into full political maturity" as "the only group that was able to organize a civil government [and] to defend itself against Canadian intrusion," for a time, if not to the present day (Chartrand and Giokas 2002, 278–279; Andersen 2014, 201). This Métis nation has the additional legitimacy that comes with outside recognition in the Constitution and the terms of the *Manitoba Act, 1870* (Chartrand and Giokas 2002, 279). The issue with this understanding of Métis identity is that "those who self-identify as Métis without a historical connection to the Métis people," may find his explanation "tantamount to a political denial of their indigeneity" (Andersen 2014, 25). This highlights the ways in which questions of belonging to a particular Indigenous polity can be contested among groups that all identify as Métis (Andersen 2014, 25). This internal contestation can force outside institutions like courts to either choose sides or to define their own terms for the purposes of adjudicating who is entitled to the rights that pertain to the identity in question.

In the *Daniels* opinion, the Canadian Supreme Court unequivocally declared that the Métis are included in the aboriginal or "Indian" population under the protection of the federal government as specified in the Canadian Constitution. This decision underlies the Court's previous commitment to recognizing the right of Indigenous polities to define their identity and membership based on shared historical experiences rather than genealogical descent. Since the Métis faced the same historical injustices as other aboriginal groups at the hands of the federal government, they should be equally entitled to the same protections as part of the Truth and Reconciliation process, since "reconciliation with all of Canada's Aboriginal peoples is Parliament's goal" (*Daniels v. Canada* 2016, ¶37). This argument follows similar logic as Rogers M. Smith's idea for redressing state actions that coercively constitute identities given that "persons have had their identities extensively constituted by coercively enforced state policies concerning permissible forms of family structures, educational curricula, religious and cultural practices, political action, economic pursuits, and much more" (Smith 2015, 222). Smith goes beyond the *Daniels* court's protection of constitutional

158 BORN INNOCENT

rights to membership, to require that "governments extend citizenship to most, if not all persons born and raised on their territories" (ibid.). In the case of the Indigenous peoples of the Americas, whose ancestral lands extend across boundaries imposed by settler states on their territories, more than one government may have a duty to grant citizenship to members of Indigenous polities born and raised in a binational territory.

Like any other set of political membership rules, Indigenous membership is subject to a boundary problem that rises to a problem of political justice when persons who are affiliated with and affected by a tribe, and desire membership therein, are denied this right (Gover 2014). This boundary problem is exacerbated by the fact that Indigenous status is not simply determined by the tribe or First Nation in question, but also by the settler state government, which has its own interests in determining who is granted this status, and its attendant rights and exemptions (Simpson 2014, 178–180; 188–190). As citizens of their Indigenous polity and the settler states that now claim sovereignty over their ancestral lands, Indigenous individuals should have recourse to the same rights and privileges as other citizens of both their tribe and nation-state, including protection against gender-based discrimination by their tribal leaders and laws (*Lovelace v. Canada* 1979). This can mean allowing individuals to challenge discriminatory Indigenous membership rules imposed by settler state authorities in the past, such as blood and marriage boundary rules, by drawing from both internal matrilineal Indigenous traditions and gender equality norms taken from the laws of modern settler states. In this way, Indigenous women have successfully challenged their exclusion from membership, land ownership and governance in their tribal polities (Gover 2014, 215–216). In Canada, Indigenous women have also regained a partial right to pass their status and attendant rights to their descendants (*McIvor v. Canada* 2009 BCCA 153; Gender Equity in Indian Registration Act 2010).

Within First Nations communities, the revival of Indigenous approaches granting membership based on kinship, adoption, and relationships of care have the potential to resolve multiple challenges identified in this chapter. This includes determining who is a status member of an intergenerational Indigenous community with its internal and external status rights, restoring intergenerational kinship ties broken by government mandated family separation, and ensuring that children in disadvantaged homes have access to stable relationships of care without resorting to outside government intervention. Like all children, Indigenous youth have the right to be born innocent, with a new chance at a life without the encumbrances of the status-based suffering of past generations.[14] They also require the protection of families and communities with the capacity to safeguard their rights and interests and to provide them with a sense of belonging. These families and communities offer the strengths of a connection to an intergenerational polity that precedes the existence of the settler states in which they are also citizens. Yet these same families are also vulnerable to ongoing mistreatment by citizens and government officials that endures to the present day, despite efforts at reconciliation. Part of that vulnerability in the Americas lies in settler states' imposition of boundary lines across their territory that limit their right to work, live, and trade throughout their ancestral lands. To protect tribal unity and sovereignty, and their right to influence political decisions that affect them, First Nations need both a right to membership in their tribe and citizenship in each of the settler states with sovereignty over their homelands (Sullivan 2022a).

Citizenship

Since settler state authorities imposed "medicine lines" across their traditional homelands, Indigenous peoples living along the borders of North America like the Cree and Métis on the Canada–U.S. border and the Yaqui along the U.S.–Mexico border have moved across the line for many reasons. Most of the time they have simply sought to pursue their livelihoods and maintain ties with family members on both sides. At times groups like the Cree and the Yaqui moved to seek refuge, and at times formal recognition as citizens, on the other side (Rensink 2018, 82–93; 180–181). They are now being joined by Indigenous peoples of the Americas from further afield, like the Maya and Tlaxcala of Central America in their pursuit of asylum in the United States (Reed-Sandoval 2020, 543–544). Their nations have been coercively constituted by the settler state governments that colonized their homelands and/or undermined their sovereignty. They want refuge, and the protection that comes with U.S. citizenship, without giving up the right to travel back and forth within their traditional homelands and inter-American migratory routes (Reed-Sandoval 2020, 556–559; Riley and Carpenter 2021, 65–70, 116–117).

Beyond free movement rights, Indigenous tribes along the U.S.–Mexico border, led by the Tohono O'Odham people, have sought a Congressional

160 BORN INNOCENT

grant of U.S. citizenship to their members living in Mexico as a way of securing their ancestral free movement rights. Such a measure would build upon precedents like the Texas Band of Kickapoo Act in a manner that furthers U.S. recognition of Indigenous land and sovereignty claims that exist prior to the implementation of the nations in question. Beyond the logic of existing precedents, citizenship grants can serve as a further form of rectification for past treatment that coercively constituted the identities of the affected tribes, providing assurance that those compensated will have a political voice to contest future decisions that might affect their community. The construction of a border wall through their territory and through their ancestral burial grounds is an example of a political decision affecting the Tohono O'Odham people on both sides of the U.S.–Mexico border that they can contest as U.S. citizens and voters (Imai and Gunn 2018, 243–244; Norris 2020).

From a republican perspective, it is important that the state rectify past crimes against Indigenous persons and provide assurances that these crimes of dispossession will not be perpetuated again (Pettit 1997, 72, 77). There is little danger of dominating the offender through excessive punishment since most of the officials responsible for first taking Indigenous land and dividing tribes with borders are deceased. The state assumes responsibility for their actions, and for restoring the free movement rights of Indigenous persons. Granting the members of border tribal polities citizenship in every settler state that claims sovereignty over their territory is a practical way to resolve their border crossing issues, promoting cultural exchange and reuniting families. It also fulfills a moral duty to Indigenous polities to rectify the policies of settler states that divided the ancestral homelands of First Nations without their consent.[15]

Citizenship as redress is a prominent feature of reconciliation processes in which earlier regimes dislocated established communities from their native lands. Several states including Germany and Austria with a history of forcibly exiling long-established communities are atoning for their misdeeds by granting the descendants of exiles a claim to citizenship by descent (Harpaz 2019; Republic of Austria 2021). These citizenship grants allow the descendants of exiles to return to live, work, and participate in the political processes of their ancestral homelands. The history of the relationship between the settler states of the Americas and their Indigenous peoples differs from that of other states that have offered citizenship as redress only in the form that exile took there. The Indigenous peoples of the Americas have been dispossessed of their land, their traditional territories bisected by boundaries not of their making, which have separated them from their traditional territory and fellow members of their polities. The countries that divided them will not give them back their land or dissolve their boundary lines. And so they must allow them to cross freely to live, work, and participate in the governance of the countries that now rule over them with the right of citizenship there, if they want this status.

In the context of Indigenous-settler state relations in the Americas, settler states must be careful to distinguish any offers of citizenship as redress from past assimilatory efforts to avoid undermining antecedent Indigenous identities, sovereignty, and treaty rights. To this end, any offer of citizenship must be consensual, respecting the rights of individuals to accept or reject this status, and plural, respecting Indigenous peoples' antecedent membership claims in a polity that can transcend national borders. For instance, during Québec's independence referendum of 1995, leaders of the Cree Nation sought self-determination to continue to associate with Canada on their own terms, with a greater respect for their land and resource rights (Grand Council of the Crees 1998, 95–96). The Cree Nation refused to be incorporated into an independent Québec without their consent. With the further consent of all settler states that claim international legal sovereignty (Krasner 1999) over an Indigenous nation's territory, a grant of citizenship as redress can also serve to recognize the dual sovereignties of Indigenous ancestral polities and the multiple settler states that have constituted the identities of an Indigenous people.

Many Indigenous individuals and polities continue to object to the way that Canada and the United States forced their citizenship status upon Indigenous peoples as another instrument of assimilation and a violation of the sovereignty of First Nations (Simpson 2014, 22; Maynard 2019, 141). Together, residential schools, non-Indigenous child welfare and adoption policies, and the unilateral imposition of citizenship have all been part of the assimilatory technologies of settler states aimed at extinguishing intergenerational tribal land claims, sovereignty, and identity at the individual, family, and community levels. Resistance to unilateral settler state citizenship grants, and an alternative insistence on pre-existing rights to free movement has been expressed in an institutional form since the 1920s, with the foundation of the Indian Defense League of America and its subsequent successful defense of Jay Treaty free movement rights in the U.S. courts (Brunyeel 2004, 41; Simpson 2014, 136; Maynard 2019, 141). Here, the context of resistance

162 BORN INNOCENT

to past citizenship grants is also important. Indigenous nations whose lands are divided by the U.S.–Canada border, including the Six Nations of the Haudenosaunee Confederacy, were particularly resistant to the unilateral grant of U.S. citizenship in 1924. One problem was that it occurred in the broader context of border enforcement and immigration restrictions that divided Indigenous territory and people from one another (Brunyeel 2004, 37–42). The unilateral grant of U.S. citizenship served as a settler-nation building project at the expense of Haudenosaunee sovereignty and treaty rights. The ideal way to overcome similar objections as part of a citizenship as redress program is to ensure that it has the consent of all affected parties and recognizes each of their claims to self-determination. At the very least, individual persons must be free to accept or reject a grant of citizenship as redress.[16] Settler states should also be clear that they are offering citizenship as redress to affirm and protect pre-existing aboriginal and treaty rights to travel, live, and work on lands that span international legal borders.

Conclusion

The ethical individualist proposition that current generations should not be held responsible for the sins of their forebears has its merits, but it obscures the ways that past injustices endure into the present and need to be accounted for today. The cases of family separation and abuse of Indigenous children in residential schools and in the child welfare system have lasting impacts for current Indigenous communities. These enduring harms present an obstacle to the goal of protecting the equal rights of all citizens in a liberal democratic country when some citizens continue to suffer disproportionate rates of incarceration at the hands of the state. They also perpetuate the cycle of family separation that undermines the well-being of Indigenous persons, families, and communities.

Indigenous children today are continuing to suffer as the result of the injustices committed against their families and their political communities by earlier generations. The Government of Canada has taken some important initial steps to reckon with the damage inflicted on a significant minority of its population through its truth and reconciliation process. Yet many of its citizens are still resistant to accepting responsibility in ways that will impose costs on current citizens, believing themselves to be innocent of the injustice of their forebears. They need to recognize that their fellow citizens who are Indigenous were also born innocent and undeserving of the treatment that was inflicted upon them in the name of a multigenerational state whose benefits and burdens are distributed to all citizens to this day. Most of their fellow citizens are not directly responsible for the abusive policies of their forebears. However, as descendants of settlers and recent immigrants, they continue to benefit from access to property and resources resulting from attempts to undermine Indigenous polities, status, and land claims by separating families in residential schools and in the child welfare system.

There are pathways forward. Solidarity at the individual level is one of them. Immigrants and their descendants who fled from atrocities in their homeland can draw from resources of empathy to join their Indigenous neighbors in their struggle for redress, to better understand their adopted nation and share in the benefits and burdens of living together as fellow citizens. Reconciliation is necessary at the societal level, which requires states to take steps to rectify the enduring injustices of past policies. Here, in the context of the aftermath of the residential school system in Indigenous communities, reforms to child welfare and criminal justice policy are needed to break the cycle of state-sponsored family separation that undermines the life chances of Indigenous children. Indigenous communities should be allowed to administer their own child welfare reforms to attend to the needs of their families in a culturally sensitive manner. Criminal justice reforms should account for past trauma and abuse in sentencing and emphasize rehabilitation for minor offenses. Initiatives that draw from Indigenous legal traditions, including restorative justice and healing circles, are also promising avenues for rehabilitating and reintegrating offenders in ways that are sensitive to the needs and experiences of members of Indigenous communities. These reforms would also be of benefit to other communities that have experienced similar legacies of intergenerational state-sponsored family separation and abuse.

7

Conclusion

Addressing State-Mandated Family Separation in the 2020s

There are many new and enduring threats in the 2020s to the well-being of children and the integrity of their families arising from immigration controls, incarceration, anti-terrorism operations, and the legacy of the internal colonization of Indigenous peoples. For instance, border closures in many countries separated caregivers and dependents in mixed citizenship status families at the height of the COVID-19 pandemic (Hurst 2020; Wood and Butler 2020; Quiggin 2020; Gooch 2021; Taylor 2021). Health authorities in China continued to separate children from their parents in quarantine facilities in 2022 (Kanthor 2022). A common theme throughout this book is the use of family separation to penalize caregivers and weaken communities. In the United States, when President Biden took office in January 2021, he vowed to end the use of family separation as a form of deterrence at the border, and to respect the claims of children of undocumented immigrants to citizenship at birth. Despite this commitment, 1,512 of these immigrant children remained separated from their parents as of March 2022 (DHS 2022b, 10). The Biden administration introduced immigration reform legislation designed to regularize undocumented immigrants and protect caregivers from deportation and separation from their citizen-children (U.S. Citizenship Act of 2021). Unfortunately, this, like earlier comprehensive immigration reform bills, failed to pass the Senate and did not become law (Song and Bloemraad 2022). Some victories have been achieved, however, like the pause in the construction of the border wall dividing Indigenous homelands that destroyed sacred burial grounds on the way.

Immigration detentions and deportations have continued during the pandemic, separating families and exposing immigration detainees to COVID-19 in detention facilities (Arbel and Joeck 2021; Paperny 2021; McGillivray 2021). While there, all prisoners suffer the common vulnerability of COVID-19 infection and death in congregate settings with inadequate public health

Born Innocent. Michael J. Sullivan, Oxford University Press. © Oxford University Press 2023.
DOI: 10.1093/oso/9780197671238.003.0007

CONCLUSION 165

precautions. In the United States, the COVID-19 case rate for prisoners was 5.5 times higher than the U.S. population case rate during the first wave of the pandemic in 2020 (Saloner, Parish, and Ward 2020, 602). By the third wave of the pandemic in Canada during January 2021, 5.6 percent of all prisoners tested positive for COVID-19, compared to 2 percent of the overall population (Correctional Service Canada 2021). Failing to protect detained and incarcerated persons from a higher risk of contracting COVID-19 in carceral settings can constitute an undeserved collateral consequence of immigration detention or incarceration.

A common thread ties together the disparate injustices of the legacy of the incarceration of asylum-seekers discussed in Chapter 2, the division of mixed-citizenship status families in Chapter 3, the overincarceration of African Americans discussed in Chapter 4, the plight of the children of terrorists in Chapter 5, and Native American subjugation in Chapter 6. The tie that binds is the forcible division and destruction of family ties by authorities, leaving vulnerable individuals exposed for oppression and undermining intergenerational community ties. During the Trump administration, authorities singled out Central American migrants at the U.S. border for family separation as a deterrent aimed at preventing them from exercising their human right to seek asylum. Inclusive citizenship policies coupled with exclusive immigration laws that do not allow children to sponsor their non-citizen parents or caregivers to stay with them are leading to the separation of mixed-citizenship status families.

The history of Black people in America is one of family destruction from their initial capture in Africa and enslavement, rape by their captors, and sale of their spouses and children. The legacy of this injustice continues with the overpolicing, murder, and mass imprisonment of their descendants that continues today. Countries that denationalize terrorists are punishing innocent children with statelessness for their parent's crimes, leaving them to languish in displaced people's camps. Some countries are repatriating the children but abandoning their parents to be their country of captivity's problem, while others are denying the protection of citizenship and repatriation to entire families, even when the children are stateless and innocent of any crimes. Indigenous families continue to suffer the legacy of the fissure of cycles of care beginning with state-mandated residential schooling, continuing through child welfare interventions that endure to the present day, along with disproportionate incarceration rates separating caregivers from their children. The ties that bind these cases are state policies that indirectly

166 BORN INNOCENT

or directly mandate family separation, undermining children's human rights to family unity (Starr and Brilmayer 2003, 219, 234, 242; Woolford 2015, 290). State actions taken for a variety of reasons—to deter asylum claims, to prevent undocumented immigration, out of retribution for criminal activity, or to assimilate minorities—disrupt cycles of caregiving and cultural transmission across generations. They sever links between child and parent, community, territory, or nation, amounting to cultural genocide (Woolford 2015, 290). These policies target parents for their actions or affiliations, but the lasting harm falls on innocent children who end up withstanding the worst of the suffering that comes with growing up without the care of their parents and extended families.

Epilogue: What Remains to be Done?

On the whole, this book addresses measures to prevent family separations resulting from immigration detention, incarceration, denationalization, and the removal of Indigenous children from their families as an assimilatory strategy.

Deterrence Is Punishment: Stop Separating Asylum-Seeking Families

Chapter 2 dealt with the meaning of punishment, and the use of family separation and other vicarious punishments that harm innocent dependents and family members of targeted persons as a form of punishment meant to deter, incapacitate, and as retribution. When we speak of vicarious punishment, we mean harming innocent persons while penalizing guilty offenders. As persons that are not yet morally responsible for their actions and completely dependent on their parents and guardians, actions that lead to the vicarious punishment of young children are especially unjust from the perspective that individuals should be solely accountable for their violations of the law. State actors ordinarily do not intend to punish the dependents and relatives of persons who violate the law, yet they sometimes threaten those close to a prospective offender to deter him, to reach someone they cannot apprehend, or to augment the offender's suffering.

We can identify punishment by the intentions of state actors as they impose hard treatment on individuals. For instance, the separations of mixed-citizenship status families that are occurring as countries close their borders to combat the COVID-19 epidemic are a grave hardship to spouses and children who temporarily cannot be with one another. Countries should find ways to mitigate this hardship while protecting their residents from the further spread of the disease. However, states are not directing these emergency measures at individuals for their conduct. Nor do they mark those prevented from crossing borders as criminal, unless they subsequently attempt to evade the law. The family separations that result from temporary COVID border closures and mobility restrictions within countries are regrettable, and they cause considerable hardship to families, but re-entry and exit controls directed at ordinary travelers are not punishments, though willful violations will result in punitive actions. Governments cross the line between prevention and punishment as deterrence and condemnation if they intentionally separate families. Instead, authorities should provide these families with a safe means of reuniting that follows public health orders.[1]

By contrast, the family separations of asylum-seekers at the U.S.–Mexico border were expressly justified by the Trump administration as punitive measures, with punishment defined in terms of its deterrent, incapacitory, and communicative functions. The goal of the family separation policy was to inflict emotional harm and incapacitate persons who had a legal right in U.S. and international law to seek asylum in the United States. In so doing, Trump administration officials communicated that it intended to harm prospective asylum-seekers and their families by separating them, deterring others from arriving and signaling the state's condemnation of persons seeking asylum at the southern border of the United States. On March 20, 2020, the Trump administration directed the Department of Health and Human Services (HHS) to issue an emergency regulation under Section 265 of U.S. Code Title 42 barring certain individuals from entering the United States by land in response to the coronavirus crisis (Department of Health and Human Services 2020; U.S. Customs and Border Protection 2020). This regulation came despite objections by then-CDC director Robert Redfield and other public health officials claiming that the order was medically unnecessary (Dearen and Burke 2020). Beginning the next day, Customs and Border Protection began to use this rule to expel asylum-seeking migrants. While the order applies to the U.S. land borders with both Canada and

168 BORN INNOCENT

Mexico, the vast majority of COVID-19 pandemic-related Title 42 expulsions since March 2020 have occurred at the U.S.–Mexico border. There have been 2,308,533 expulsions at the southern border compared to 9,603 expulsions at the U.S.–Canada border as of the end of Fiscal Year 2021 (September 30, 2021) (U.S. Customs and Border Protection 2020; U.S. Customs and Border Protection 2021a; U.S. Customs and Border Protection 2021b).

Soon after taking office, the Biden administration promised to accept more asylum-seeking migrants into the United States to await their eligibility hearings, and in February 2021, the Biden administration announced the formation of a task force to reunite families separated at the U.S.–Mexico border (Biden 2021a). The Biden administration also revised the Title 42 expulsion order to exempt unaccompanied children in February 2021. This change prompted many asylum-seeking families to decide to self-separate, to provide their children with a chance of protection in the United States (Herrera 2021). By March 25, 2021, during his first news conference, President Biden was asked, "How are you choosing which families can stay and which can go, given the fact that even though, with Title 42, there are some families that are staying?" He responded that "they should all be going back, all be going back," and the only reason "why are not—some not going back? Because Mexico is refusing to take them back" (Biden 2021b). The Department of Homeland Security escalated the pace of Title 42 expulsions in 2021 as a deterrence measure amid a rise in the number of migrants seeking asylum at the U.S.-Mexico border.[2] In short, to dissuade prospective asylum-seekers from entering the United States, President Biden made it clear that the government's focus on expeditiously removing them had not shifted with the change in administrations.

In August 2021, the Department of Homeland Security argued in court that ending its authority to expel "families would exacerbate overcrowding at DHS facilities and create significant public health risks" given the spike of Delta variant cases over the summer in Texas (Shahoulian 2021, ¶3). This is consistent with the COVID-control narrative that Texas governor Greg Abbott cited in ordering state troopers to interdict vehicles carrying migrants, even as public health officials in the affected border regions traced most new cases to domestic community transmission (Abbott 2021; Solis and Morris 2021). In September 2021 alone, amidst an influx of asylum-seeking Haitian migrants along the U.S.–Mexico border, the United States expelled nearly 8,000 asylum-seeking migrants to Haiti without a credible fear hearing as part of a deterrence maneuver condemned by USCIS asylum officers and their union (Rosenberg and Cooke 2021; Sánchez 2021). These expulsions occurred despite advice by public health officials that asylum-seekers can be safely processed, tested, vaccinated and quarantined first before they are released without adding to the transmission of COVID-19 in the United States (Backster et al. 2021). Anthony Fauci underscored this message in an October 3, 2021 interview stating that "focusing on immigrants, expelling them or what have you, is not the solution to an outbreak" arising primarily by community spread among unvaccinated U.S. residents (Fauci 2021).

The U.S. Centers for Disease Control and Prevention (CDC) issued a directive on April 1, 2022 terminating Title 42 powers to turn away migrants and asylum-seekers at the border (CDC 2022). Twenty-four states challenged the end to Title 42 in court, led by administrations that oppose other COVID-19 safety measures. On May 20, 2022, the Fifth Circuit Court granted a preliminary injunction blocking the administration from lifting Title 42, setting the stage for further appeals (García 2022). While the DHS continued at that point to enforce the order "to protect against the spread of communicable disease," its supporters value Title 42 primarily as a deterrent measure to block asylum-seekers from the United States (Office of the Texas Governor 2022; DHS 2022a). The CDC and DHS have other tools at their disposal to address the COVID-19 risk posed by entering migrants, including mandatory vaccinations and quarantines for those who test positive upon entry into the United States. Critics of the CDC's decision like Texas Governor Greg Abbott, who opposes other COVID-19 public health mandates, have responded with unilateral enforcement measures to deter "the anticipated surge of illegal immigrants" (Office of the Texas Governor 2022). Abbott's enforcement notice does not refer to public health at all.

Even as official assessments of the severity of the COVID-19 pandemic diminished (for now), the U.S. Title 42 policy is still in place that has resulted in the separation of asylum-seeking families at the U.S.-Mexico border (*Arizona et al. v. Alejandro Mayorkas* 2022; Jervis 2023). The U.S. Supreme Court's December 27, 2022 ruling means that Title 42 may persist until at least May 11, 2023, the date when President Biden's latest plan to end the COVID-19 national emergency is scheduled to take effect (Executive Office of the President 2023). This policy remains in force even though governors who have supported Title 42 measures in court have long since lifted pandemic-related public health measures like masking, vaccination mandates, and social distancing in their own states (Harper 2023). As officials discard public health measures in their own communities, their stated justification for using

170   BORN INNOCENT

the pandemic to separate asylum seeking families at the border is becoming even less defensible.

The United States' asylum challenge on its southern border is augmented by longstanding interventions in Central American countries from which many asylum-seekers are fleeing. They are what David Miller describes as particularity claimants, coming from nearby countries where the United States has created "situations in which the state to which the asylum-seeker applies is at least in part responsible for making her into a refugee" (Miller 2016, 90; Miller 2021, 106–107). As refugees from the Russian invasion of Ukraine are being welcomed into the United States, those fleeing for their lives from political persecution and war from Central America should be welcomed on the same terms. As of April 21, 2022, the United States instituted the Uniting for Ukraine program allowing U.S. residents with sufficient financial resources the ability to sponsor a Ukrainian refugee beneficiary to temporarily come to the United States (DHS 2022c). Canada has made it even easier for Ukrainian refugees to enter under its Canada-Ukraine Authorization for Emergency Travel (Immigration, Refugees, and Citizenship Canada 2022). This program grants Ukrainian refugees open work permits and settlement assistance (ibid.). Ideally, similar programs should be extended to all refugees and asylum-seekers fleeing violence and persecution in their homelands.

Protecting Family Unity by Allowing Birthright Citizens to Sponsor Their Immigrant Parents

Chapter 3 addressed the ways in which states are penalizing unauthorized and temporary resident parents through proposals to deny their children citizenship where they were born. It also dealt with efforts to penalize parents for living abroad by denying their children citizenship by descent. In *Of Love and Papers* (2020), Laura Enriquez discusses the idea of "multigenerational punishment," in which "the sanctions intended for a specific population spill over to harm individuals who are not targeted by the law" (Enriquez 2020, 7). Her understanding of punishment highlights "how immigration policies produce family-level inequalities that endure into the next generation as dependent social ties and daily interactions place citizen children in a de facto undocumented status" (136). Already, in Canada and the United States, where *jus soli* birthright citizenship status is still entrenched in law, citizen-children of undocumented parents suffer the consequences of their parents' status and the ever-present danger of enforcement, detention, and deportation. Being dependent on deportable parents limits their opportunities for upward mobility and endangers their prospects to remain in their communities with their caregivers.

When the irregular immigrant parents of citizen-children are in immigration detention, the children face the same challenges as citizens with incarcerated caregivers. They risk permanent separation from their caregivers when family courts take custody away from their parents, judging their parents as unfit parents for being detained and undocumented (Sullivan 2019, 130; Enriquez 2020, 5). Multigenerational punishment is already a problem for the citizen-children of undocumented parents even with a nearly unrestricted right to *jus soli* birthright citizenship for native-born children. The political campaign to curtail birthright citizenship for the children of irregular immigrants and visitors penalizes children for the actions and status of their parents. This campaign has been successful in Britain, Australia, New Zealand, and Ireland, leading to the deportation of life-long resident children and driving others into the shadows. If the long-term resident children of undocumented parents in Canada and the United States lose this right to citizenship where they are born, because of their parents' immigration status, they will have fewer chances to break out of an intergenerational cycle of poverty and disadvantage.

The way forward is threefold. First, birthright citizenship requires constitutional protection to safeguard this right from legislative encroachment by political majorities that aim to deny this right and status to the children of irregular migrants, asylum-seekers, and visitors, harming children to attack their parents because their actions and status are politically suspect. In Canada, where it is merely a statutory right, it should be entrenched in the Charter of Rights and Freedoms, as it is in the Fourteenth Amendment to the United States Constitution, to prevent political majorities from stripping *jus soli* citizenship from politically unpopular children of irregular migrants, including asylum claimants. Second, children who are life-long residents should be able to sponsor their undocumented parents to become legal residents, to ensure the continuity of care in the communities where they reside. This also builds upon my recommendation in *Earned Citizenship* (2019) that the caregiving work of guardians is a civic contribution and investment in the well-being of future citizens that merits an earned pathway to legalization. Third, birthright citizenship in Canada and the United States recognizes the claims of Indigenous persons born in the United States to citizenship

172   BORN INNOCENT

there, but not the members of border tribes who were born in Canada or Mexico. This has the effect of dividing Indigenous families and communities across borders that are not of their making, undermining the sovereignty of transnational Indigenous tribes. The solution is to offer birthright citizenship to all native-born members of Indigenous tribes that have territory and are recognized in that country, ensuring their right to live, work, and maintain ties throughout their ancestral territory.

Beyond Retribution: Include Families in Efforts to Rehabilitate Offenders as Caregivers

In Chapter 4, I addressed the ongoing problem of family separation as a collateral consequence of incarceration, and the vicarious punishment that children experience when their parents are incarcerated or detained. Dependents of incarcerated caregivers are harmed when their parents, guardians, or other primary caregivers are imprisoned. The state and society have an obligation to lessen the burden on the innocent children of incarcerated parents and guardians for the deprivation of support resulting from the state's decision to incarcerate their caregivers. At the very minimum, the state owes a duty of care that begins with financial support and supplemental social assistance for children of incarcerated parents. Since the state cannot replace the attentive, personal care that a parent provides for a child, it should do whatever is necessary to allow incarcerated parents to maintain a relationship with their children within the strictures of their sentence. An exception to this rule is warranted when the parent has abused the child and poses a clear and present danger of reoffending and harming the dependent.

Here, I argue that retributive criminal justice theories and policies aimed at giving offenders their "just deserts" through inflexible custodial sentences overlook the social causes of offending, victims' interests, and the interests of dependents left behind without their primary caregivers. Inflexible policies governing sentencing, visitation, and child custody for incarcerated persons also ignore society's interests in rehabilitating offenders to become better caregivers and citizens. Restorative justice approaches that seek victim-offender reconciliation and aim to rehabilitate persons convicted of a crime are preferable to "preventive" sanctions as means of reintegrating offenders into their communities and breaking the intergenerational cycle of offending in at-risk communities (Braithwaite 2002, Golash 2005). For instance, there

CONCLUSION 173

is overlap between restorative justice and traditional Indigenous forms of justice including healing circles in at-risk Indigenous communities. In Canada, the Supreme Court has mandated judges to consider Indigenous offenders' past trauma, and to consider restorative approaches in sentencing (*R v. Gladue* 1999; *R v. Ippelee* 2012). Studies have shown that the implementation of healing circles in Indigenous communities decreases recidivism rates, increases victim satisfaction, and breaks the cycle of sexual offending within families and communities (Sawatsky 2009). Unless they pose a clear and present danger of reoffending, it is preferable to keep offenders within their communities where they can continue to serve as caregivers, and where their families and other community leaders can participate in the process of their rehabilitation. Where their crimes are sufficiently severe as to mandate a custodial sentence, flexible visitation and child custody policies help to minimize the collateral consequences of a parent or guardian's offense for their dependent children. Carceral officials should allow inmates to provide emotionally and financially for their dependents during their sentence through visitation, flexible sentencing, and training leading to paid employment. Incarceration and parole should be rehabilitative, with the goal of helping all offenders to become better caregivers and citizens upon their release.

Prevent the Radicalization of a New Generation: Repatriate the Children of Suspected Terrorists

Chapter 5 reveals how the war on terror is harming the innocent children of suspected terrorists by denying them citizenship by descent, repatriation, or the care of their parents. This is not just a moral failing on the part of states that denationalize and refuse to repatriate their citizens, but also a tactical error for the future of the war on terror, as ISIS holdouts recruit and radicalize stateless children in displaced persons camps. The failure of many European states to repatriate their citizens who are terrorist suspects also passes the problem on to beleaguered authorities in conflict zones like the Kurdish-occupied areas of Syria and Iraq without the resources, institutions, or human rights protections of suspected terrorists' countries of origin.

For the innocent young children of terrorism suspects who are still being held abroad in war zones, 2022 opened with the prospect of suffering through another winter in dire conditions, with little change or hope for their innocent dependents to be brought to their parents' countries of

174   BORN INNOCENT

origin. The camps in which these children are held are incubators for ISIS ideology, resulting in the radicalization of the stranded children of foreign terrorist affiliates in the absence of repatriation efforts (Brzozowski 2020; Mironova 2020; Doherty 2020). In camps like Al-Hol in Syria, 70 percent of the 56,000 residents are children under eighteen, many of whom were born stateless and serve as potential recruits for ISIS's revitalization in the absence of other options (Yacoubian 2022). At these facilities, former ISIS affiliates and their children abandoned by their countries of origin are subject to reprisals for straying from the terrorist organization's ideology and rules (Sheikho 2021). Given the danger of radicalization of a new generation, Iraq has called for Western nations to repatriate citizens suspected of terrorism and their families (Yacoubian 2022). But instead of holding suspected terrorist affiliates accountable in their country's justice system, their home countries are passing the problem of holding their former citizens on to other countries by denationalizing them and refusing to repatriate them and their children. Their young children who did nothing to deserve their plight have no pathway for integration into any country without the right to citizenship by descent. The danger is that these children without a country, born and raised in a war zone, will become the next generation of terrorist recruits (Loyd 2020).

Given the risk of radicalization among the children of former foreign ISIS affiliates if they remain in the conflict zone, the U.N. counterterrorism center has urged countries of origin to repatriate the estimated 27,000 former ISIS affiliates and their children remaining in Syria in 2021 (Lederer 2021). Many European countries are reluctant to do so. They also have limited means to incapacitate terrorist affiliates or to prevent them from reoffending in the region or returning to their countries of origin without authorization to commit further atrocities. The pathway to justice, deradicalization, and protecting the rights of the innocent children of terrorist affiliates is to repatriate terrorist affiliates and their children. Countries of origin should repatriate their citizens, and adults who willingly affiliated with ISIS should face charges in their country's criminal justice system. Those who are found guilty should be punished for their crimes. Many offenders who are now in displaced persons camps after they were recruited by ISIS as teenagers regret their affiliation with the organization as adults. They should be encouraged to participate in deradicalization courses as part of their sentence, preparing the way for their reintegration into society. Consistent with the lessons of community and family-based rehabilitation discussed in previous chapters, family members and spiritual advisers not affiliated with terrorist organizations should be given a prominent role in the deradicalization of their family member. Given the importance of maintaining continuity of caregiving relationships in the rehabilitative process, parents at low risk of recidivism should be allowed the opportunity to visit with, and maintain custody over, and relationships with their children (Mironova 2020).

End the Intergenerational Cycle of State-Mandated Indigenous Family Separation

Chapter 6 uncovers the ongoing legacy of the state mandated family separation of Indigenous communities and the need for redress by settler states that strengthens Indigenous families and tribal polities. Even in the immediate aftermath of revelations of mass graves at residential schools across Canada in the Summer of 2021, the Canadian federal government contested decisions by the Canadian Human Rights Tribunal (CHRT) providing compensation, service, and supports to Indigenous children to make up for the government's inadequate funding for child and family services (Kirkup 2021). The gap between the current government's symbolic statements of support for reconciliation and practice is emblematic of the ways in which "Canada is often cited as a paradox in the international arena of Indigenous rights and emancipation" (Dhillon 2017, 51). Canada is at once the subject of "global admiration" for "exploring models for living together that balance a universal humanity with a commitment to personal autonomy and cultural rights" while the country is criticized "for failing to match theoretical ideals with changes in the material conditions facing Indigenous peoples" (ibid.).

For the victims of state-mandated separation of Indigenous families in Canada, truth and reconciliation initiatives are ongoing, with many areas that still need to be addressed. Eighteen of the Truth and Reconciliation Calls for Action address criminal justice reforms, including sentencing that accounts for the life circumstances of Indigenous offenders (Government of Canada 2019; Bailey 2021). Only two of these calls for action have been fully implemented, with a Statistics Canada homicide report that now includes analysis of homicides of Indigenous women and girls (#39), and a missing and murdered Indigenous women and girls inquiry (#41) (CBC 2020). So far, government responses to these Calls for Action have failed to slow increases

176 BORN INNOCENT

in the Indigenous incarceration rate in Canada (Office of the Correctional Investigator 2020).

Despite sharing a similar history of settler colonialism, the United States has yet to convene the equivalent of Canada's Truth and Reconciliation Commission for its Indigenous citizens. Official inquiries addressing the intergenerational legacy of a similar policy of family separation, dispossession, and forced assimilation through boarding schools are just beginning. In June 2021, the revelation of mass graves at residential schools in Canada prompted U.S. Interior Secretary Deb Haaland, a member of the Pueblo Laguna nation and descendant of boarding school survivors, to "address the intergenerational impact of Indian boarding schools" in the United States (Haaland 2021; Child 2021). Haaland's leadership role as the first Indigenous secretary of the U.S. Interior Department is groundbreaking, as she seeks to rectify the abuses inflicted on her people at the helm of a key agency responsible for the administration of Indigenous boarding schools in the United States (Chalcraft 2004, xi–xii, 205). For the Indigenous communities that suffered over generations as their children were taken away and forced to deny their heritage, a more extensive U.S. Truth and Reconciliation process is long overdue, as part of the broader U.S. conversation about racial justice and reconciliation.

Today, COVID-19 has emerged as a racial justice issue in its own right in the United States and Canada, as racialized minorities suffer higher death and hospitalization rates than the broader population (Artiga, Hill, and Haldar 2021; Tam 2021). COVID-19 has also greatly affected Indigenous communities in Canada and the United States, many of which are isolated and located at great distances from full service medical facilities. Many Indigenous communities in North America have asserted their sovereignty by closing their territorial borders to nonresidents to protect their communities (White 2021; Pringle et al. 2021, 5–6; Vanderklippe 2022). In Canada, the rate of reported cases of COVID-19 in First Nations reservations was 4.2 times the respective rate in the general Canadian population as of October 12, 2021 (Indigenous Services Canada 2021). However, the COVID-19 death rate on First Nations reserves was less than that of the general Canadian population, with an on-reserve fatality rate that was 59 percent of the case fatality rate of the Canadian population (Indigenous Services Canada 2021).

In the United States, the overall death rate per capita from COVID-19 was 2.82 times higher than in Canada (John Hopkins Coronavirus Resource

CONCLUSION 177

Center 2022). Within the United States, there has also been a disproportionately higher death rate from COVID-19 among Indigenous U.S. citizens as compared to other U.S. residents. Nationwide, in the United States, as of May 4, 2022, 1 out of 220 Indigenous residents had died of COVID-19, compared to 1 out of 306 white U.S. residents and 1 out of 291 Black U.S. residents (APM Research Lab 2022). Indigenous peoples are keenly aware of the historic impact of pandemics on their population, leading many Indigenous nations to take early proactive measures to shelter their communities from COVID-19 (United Nations 2020, 15). Despite efforts by some U.S. Indigenous reserves to protect their communities by closing their territorial borders, U.S. Indigenous communities and their elders are facing much higher COVID infection and death rates than non-Indigenous citizens, and this has further undermined the intergenerational transfer of cultural and linguistic knowledge already imperiled by decades of forced family separations (Healy 2021).

To overcome the intergenerational legacy of state-mandated family separations beginning with the residential and boarding school policies of settler states, governments must give Indigenous communities more autonomy to manage their own child welfare policies. In Canada, the first call to action of the Truth and Reconciliation Commission was to reduce the number of Indigenous children taken into custody by child welfare agencies (Government of Canada 2019). Legislation allowing for the development of Indigenous alternatives to child welfare agencies is an important first step. A second encouraging development involves the end of the practice of "birth alerts" in most Canadian provinces that allowed hospitals and social services to flag expectant mothers deemed to be high-risk, to seize their babies upon delivery. The most common factors resulting in birth alerts include substance abuse, interpersonal violence, housing instability, intellectual limitations, and a parent's childhood involvement in the child welfare system (Choate et al. 2020, 288). The birth alert practice is objectionable as it takes the place of programs designed to help at-risk mothers to care for their children, punishing them for substance abuse challenges instead of financing rehabilitation initiatives. The prospect of "child alerts" and hospital baby seizures are devastating for any new mother. Conscious of the prospect that their baby might be taken from them, at-risk women avoid prenatal care or social programs that might otherwise improve their pregnancy and birth outcomes (Douglas and Walsh 2015, 498; Taplin 2017, 74).

Non-Indigenous social welfare agencies continue to disproportionately target Indigenous pregnant women for "birth interventions," furthering the

178 BORN INNOCENT

cycle and legacy of state-mandated Indigenous family separation (Turnbull 2019, 249; Choate et al. 2020, 289). Ending birth alerts was a top priority in Canada's National Inquiry into Missing and Murdered Indigenous Women and Girls (National Inquiry 2019, 364–368). The report detailed how Indigenous women are more likely to have their babies seized by child welfare authorities under the birth alert system simply because they were once in the child welfare system themselves, regardless of the subsequent course of their lives (365–366). The assumption is that a woman who was once a foster child may not be able to care for her own children, perpetuating the cycle of family separation in Indigenous communities (ibid.). The Canadian government's Act Respecting First Nations, Inuit and Métis Children, Youth and Families enacted in 2019 contains a clause requiring agencies to prioritize the provision of prenatal services for at-risk mothers over post-birth social service interventions (Bill C-92, 2019, §14). Some of the Canadian provinces have complied with this directive. Manitoba, which has the highest provincial per capita rate of children in child welfare custody in Canada, and among the highest rates in the world at 3 percent of the total population, ended the alert and seizure program in January 2020 (Wall-Wieler et al. 2018, 2; Bergen 2020). This occurred after a government review found that there was no evidence that the practice improved the safety of children in any way (Government of Manitoba 2020; Funk and Brohman 2020). Before the end of the birth alert practice in Manitoba, 15 percent of children in the child welfare system were taken from their mothers at birth (Wall-Wieler et al. 2018, 1). Ontario and British Columbia followed suit by ending the practice of child alerts later in 2020. Prince Edward Island, Saskatchewan, Newfoundland and Labrador, New Brunswick, and Nova Scotia ended the practice of birth alerts and baby seizures by December 2021 (Allen 2021; Abbott 2021; Government of New Brunswick 2021; Nova Scotia 2021). Each of these provinces acted to end child welfare removals at birth as part of their commitment to the truth and reconciliation process with Indigenous communities (Favaro, St. Philip, and Jones 2021).

Within Canada, Québec is a holdout in its ongoing use of birth alerts without any immediate plans to end the practice. One region (Abitibi-Témiscamingue) reports that 30 percent of interventions in the past two years involved Indigenous families, who make up only 4 percent of the region's population (Ambroise 2021). There, the *Femmes Autochtones du Québec* advocacy group is leading a pressure campaign to end the practice as a continuation of a colonial system of oppression that renders all aboriginal women afraid to go to the hospital, especially for preventive care during their pregnancies (Duchaine 2021; Petiquay Barthold 2021). Québec's child welfare authorities also face broader allegations of racism and ableism for targeting parents with disabilities and ethnic minorities with child custody removals at birth (Elkouri 2021; Serebrin 2021). Elsewhere in Canada, birth alerts persist at the local level despite provincial commitments to end this practice. Indigenous babies continue to be separated from their mothers in First Nations communities, according to an April 2022 report by the Matawa Chiefs Council of Thunder Bay, Ontario (Audet 2022). Similar incidents have been reported elsewhere in other Northern Ontario communities (Radio-Canada 2022). Provinces must follow through with their commitments to end birth alerts. Mothers targeted because of their poverty, experiences of domestic violence, or past involvement in the child welfare system are victims themselves who need support from social workers. Indigenous communities need more resources to provide support to their members and to protect mothers and children from abusive situations.

Similar child welfare interventions target disadvantaged minority women in other jurisdictions, including the United States, where Black women are the main target for birth removals. There, Black mothers face child custody removals at rates up to ten times those of white mothers, for many of the same reasons that lead to birth alerts among Indigenous Canadian women, including poverty, addiction, and insecure housing (Harp and Bunting 2020, 261). Black mothers often face custody removals because of their precarious economic circumstances, creating a set of conditions that make it difficult for them to ever attain the degree of self-sufficiency required by child welfare authorities to regain custody of their children (Woodward 2021, 441–442).

Birth alerts are another example of a preventive justice action that penalizes and condemns women for seeking help for situations and behaviors they cannot always control on their own. Their at-risk situation is not an individual character failing that merits condemnation and enforcement, but a medical condition or structural issue best addressed through treatment and social support. While the end to birth alerts in some Canadian jurisdictions is an encouraging first step, what is needed—across all jurisdictions—are child welfare policies that emphasize support and rehabilitation for mothers to be and their families, rather than policies that punish disadvantaged mothers for challenges they cannot overcome on their own. Mothers experience birth alerts and baby seizures as punishment, harming their infants at a crucial stage in their development by depriving them of their mother's

180 BORN INNOCENT

care, nursing, and bonding. When birth alerts are issued in response to an expecting mother's addiction, they do nothing to prevent fetal alcohol spectrum disorder (FASD) after her baby is already born. Instead of issuing birth alerts resulting in baby seizures, child welfare agencies should reach out to at-risk expecting mothers with help to treat addictions, provide support, and find housing before and after they give birth. Culturally sensitive social services workers should address the root causes of child welfare risks as part of a broader program of rehabilitation. Expecting mothers need to know that social service agencies will not punish them with child removal at birth when they reach out to seek addiction treatment and other forms of social assistance.

Conclusion

Overall, children in a wide range of circumstances are suffering from vicarious punishment directed at their parents and communities. In the Indigenous case, they are suffering as members of vulnerable communities, with high incarceration rates linked to a legacy of state-sponsored family separation and abuse. Their parents who are in the criminal justice system can be better equipped to serve as caregivers and to break the cycle of incarceration and family separation if governments take more efforts to rehabilitate and reintegrate them into society. In the case of anti-terrorism prosecutions, this means repatriating suspects, rather than allowing them and their children to languish in camps where radical ideologies fester alongside disease, starvation, and early death. Where immigration and citizenship status separates families, the solution is to allow families to live together in the country where they currently reside with the opportunity to become citizens there.

In *Earned Citizenship* (2019), I argued that parenting has an important civic value, and polities should allow immigrant parents the chance to earn legalization and a pathway to citizenship based on the contribution of their parenting to the well-being of their citizen-children (Sullivan 2019, 167). Here, I build on that argument, by pointing to the ways that caregiving serves as a means of rehabilitation and reintegration into society. I argue that criminal justice policies should facilitate the preservation of caregiving relationships wherever possible through sentencing, visitation, rehabilitation and deradicalization programs that are in the interests of parents and their innocent children. For persons without children, other caregiving relationships may serve a similar purpose, albeit not for the benefit of a developing and dependent citizen-in-becoming. In the context of Indigenous communities, rehabilitation through traditional practices including restorative justice and healing circles promotes reintegration that strengthens the bonds between members of tribal communities and repairs the cycle of intergenerational care. In each of these cases, state agencies have a responsibility to re-examine their practices to find ways to promote the revitalization and maintenance of intergenerational caregiving relationships within family and cultural communities wherever possible.

Acknowledgments

Born Innocent was conceived during the first COVID-19 lockdown of 2020, written in draft form during the second shutdown, and revised in large part during the Delta and Omicron variant states of emergency in Ontario. These unique circumstances informed my work and shaped my research and writing process in unexpected ways. I would like to thank Anne Beaupré at Algoma University's Wishart Library in Sault Ste. Marie, and Carolyn Sullivan at the University of Ottawa Library for their help finding resources while library access was limited.

I discussed some of the material in the text with my students in my seminars in Religion, Identity and Global Politics, Border Security, Citizenship and Global Inequality, and Research and Writing. The students in these classes asked great questions with insights that shaped my ideas in this book. I am particularly thankful to my research assistants at St. Mary's University who read parts of this book and offered their feedback including Samantha Skory, Laura Cruz, Karol Diepenhorst, and Polina Protozanova. Finally, I would like to thank St. Mary's University and both my chair and dean for a sabbatical during the 2020–2021 school year, which helped immeasurably with the initial research and writing process.

My family has been incredibly understanding during this unique research and writing process. I would like to thank my wife Laura for her patience and close reading of my manuscript drafts. Our son Michael is now old enough to offer his own comments on the manuscript, and our daughter Catherine has plenty of questions about my book as we combine work, family life and school in new ways. Laura and I eagerly await the arrival of our third child shortly after this book is released. We hope for a brighter future in a more just society for Clara or John as they grow and learn about the social justice issues in *Born Innocent*.

The project took shape in a very challenging period amidst the pandemic, the Black Lives Matter protests of 2020 and the revelations of unmarked graves at Indigenous residential schools across Canada in 2021. I would like to thank Madison Bifano for her assistance accessing the archival resources at the Shingwauk Residential Schools Centre in Sault Ste. Marie, Ontario

184 ACKNOWLEDGMENTS

during the lockdowns and reopening process. These resources added immeasurably to my understanding of the challenges of reconciliation and the courage of the Anishinaabe people as they continue to respond to the legacy of residential schooling and child welfare removals in their upper Great Lakes homelands. I presented earlier versions of parts of this book at Annual Meetings of the American Political Science Association and the Canadian Political Science Association. The references that follow at the end of the text list many people whose ideas shaped the development of this book.

At Oxford University Press, I am thankful to Angela Chnapko for believing in this project and guiding it through the review process, and Alexcee Bechthold for her assistance as I prepared the manuscript for submission. I appreciate Elizabeth Cohen and Patti Tamara Lenard's close read of *Born Innocent* and their comments for the cover. I would like to thank Anne Sanow and the staff at NEWGEN for their proofreading and final touches, and whatever errors remain are my own. The reviewers who anonymously read and commented on this book for Oxford University Press refined its focus and helpfully shared new suggestions for its development, for which I am very grateful.

Notes

Chapter 1

1. By contrast, Black people account for 7.2 percent of federal offenders in Canada during 2019 while comprising 3.5 percent of Canada's population. 2019 was the last year for which statistics on Black federal offenders were available as of early 2022 (Public Safety Canada 2020, 55; Owasu-Bempah et al. 2021, 4).
2. As a brief note on case selection, Canada stands out as a case study given the extent of its government's more recent efforts to make redress for the legacy of state-mandated Indigenous family separation, which other governments including the United States could learn from (Jacobs 2014, xxviii; Woolford 2015, 277–278).
3. Australia is also included among the settler states that define themselves as countries of immigration, which have used immigrants, the narrative of a country of immigration, and the fiction of an empty country devoid of pre-existing land claims to justify assimilatory policies resulting in the separation of Indigenous families to undermine their cultures, polities, and sovereignty claims (Jacobs 2014, xxviii; Vickers and Isaac 2012, 103–104; Hamlin 2021, 33, 47). New Zealand is also studied as an English common law settler state alongside Australia, Canada, and the United States for the purposes of comparing law and policy on Indigenous-settler state treaties (Gover 2015, 356). The government of Australia's Indigenous policies have had some commonalities with those of Canada and the United States. Yet in terms of lived experience, the Indigenous peoples of Canada and the United States are often the same, inhabiting common histories, shared geographical territory, and political space distinct from those of aboriginal Australians, whose experiences with state-mandated family separation would require a separate narrative.
4. The critical element of both *Born Innocent* and my previous project, *Earned Citizenship*, needs to be underscored here. My conception of "earned citizenship" was by no means a celebration of "neoliberal nationalism," as Christian Joppke (2021) mentioned in passing connecting the theme of the book to what I also regard as unfortunate developments in some states that require immigrants to pay increasing sums or to make future sacrifices to merit naturalization (Sullivan 2018; Joppke 2021, 183). In a nonideal political system—focusing in on the United States in particular—where military personnel, veterans, and caregivers are being deported and denaturalized despite their service, *Earned Citizenship* had a strong critical element. There, I condemned the United States for refusing to fairly compensate past immigrant service, or rejecting their presence altogether (Sullivan 2019, 80–81, 111–115). I argued that those who had already undertaken costly sacrifices on behalf of the state should be rewarded with citizenship, instead of facing deportation

186 NOTES

and denationalization. In *Earned Citizenship*, I specifically stated that immigrants should not be required to serve in the military to become citizens (33). Those who were already connected to the polity from early childhood, like the Deferred Action for Childhood Arrivals recipients in the United States, should not be asked to do anything more to become citizens (212–213). Far from ignoring the exploitative sacrifices that immigrant caregivers make for unconnected affluent citizens, as Joppke (2021, 183) claims, I highlighted the contributions of nannies and other nonkinship caregivers make for well-off citizens and characterized this as a form of exploitation whereby those who are exploited deserve proper recompense from the state and its citizens (Sullivan 2019, 153–156). What Joppke (2021, 183) calls the "capacious" or overencompassing element of *Earned Citizenship* is instead a move to normatively redefine the potential of earned citizenship. Earned citizenship is an open-ended concept, which does not need to be bounded by the neoliberal conception of what is and is not valuable and meritorious. It can value forms of service that are undervalued by the neoliberal state, like parenting, or that challenge its foundations, like union organizing and dissent, which are covered both in *Earned Citizenship* (2019, 40–41, 184–186), and in more detail in a follow-up work, "Labor Citizenship for the Twenty-First Century" (2021). Earned citizenship is compatible with a further gratitude-based argument for conferring permanent residence to unauthorized immigrants who risked their health to provide essential services to their adopted country, like frontline workers during the COVID-19 crisis, even *if* the country did not consent to their presence in the first place (Sullivan 2019, 18–19; Gerver 2022, 96). The pandemic underscored the need to accord marginalized persons in society—like immigrant low-wage essential workers—standing and rewards for their civic works (Brown 2020, 411–412). *Born Innocent* sharpens my earlier argument in *Earned Citizenship* for conceiving caregiving as a civic service. Here, I revalue the caregiving potential of parents and caregivers who face condemnation by the state as individuals (undocumented immigrants, prisoners, and terrorism suspects) or as members of previously disfavored communities (Indigenous people and racialized minorities). *Born Innocent* seeks ways to protect family unity and the parenting capacity of parents and caregivers that have been cast outside the community of value, for their benefit, and that of their innocent children.

Chapter 2

1. There is also a distinction to be made between intentional punishment and other state actions, which limit an individual or corporation's liberty but are not expressly punitive in that they are not directly intended to cause harm, including jury duty, military conscription, taxation, and eminent domain, among others (Boonin 2008, 15, 62).
2. See, for instance, Canada's Quarantine Act, which imposes restrictions on the entry of persons and goods into Canada during an emergency, including the COVID-19 crisis. Under the terms of the act, "the Government of Canada will use its authority

NOTES 187

under the Quarantine Act to ensure compliance with the order. Failure to comply with this Order is an offense under the Quarantine Act. Maximum penalties include a fine of up to $750,000 and/or imprisonment for six months" (Public Health Agency of Canada 2020).

3. The link between quarantine and immigration detention extends further when we consider that the first immigration control initiatives in Australia and North America were designed as infectious disease control measures. These measures disproportionately affected poor and minority immigrants who were inspected and held offshore, sometimes indefinitely. So-called enemy aliens suffered the same treatment in internment camps, which were punitive (incapacitory, expressing social condemnation) in effect, if not in their legal characterization (Bashford and Strange 2002, 515–522). This characterization of immigration detention as quarantine is itself disturbing, when we consider the long history of racialized fears of contagion by foreigners as a justification for the detention of immigrants throughout the nineteenth and early twentieth century (Longazel et al. 2016, 991; Witt 2020, 30–33).

4. Here, the operative meaning of the term "banishment" is "denationalization and exclusion from membership in a nation-state." In other jurisdictions, banishment describes less encompassing sanctions involving the expulsion of an individual from an Indigenous nation (R v. Williams 1997, British Columbia, Canada), or "precluding a person from being present in a certain community" as part of a temporary probation order (R v. Klein 2011, Saskatchewan, Canada). In the Indigenous context, banishment was historically recognized as "the ultimate form of punishment, since to be banished meant you no longer existed, and without the support system of shared community resources, banishment meant likely death" (Hand, Hanks, and House 2012, 460). Today, Indigenous banishment in many North American Indigenous nations means casting a person out of the community and its dispute resolution mechanisms into "the western retributive judicial system," which harms those cut off from their identity, family, and formative ties. It also marks the community's disheartening acknowledgment of the failure of its alternative forms of conflict resolution, including restorative justice.

5. High infection rates in Canadian immigration detention centers during the first wave of COVID-19 in Canada resulted in a public outcry that led to the release of most immigration detainees by November 2020 (Bureau 2020a).

6. Similar enforcement panics accompanied the arrival of ships carrying asylum-seekers in other countries, including the Golden Venture, arriving in New York with 286 Chinese asylum-seekers in 1993, at the same time as Haitian and Cuban migrants were arriving en masse by boat in South Florida, and the MV Tampa in Australia in 2001 (carrying 433 Afghani asylum-seekers). These cases precipitated the development of new interception and detention as deterrence initiatives, which marked a lasting departure from international norms governing the protection of asylum-seekers by receiving states (Mountz and Hiemstra 2012).

7. The Committee urges the State party to bring its immigration and asylum laws into full conformity with the Convention and other relevant international standards. In doing so, the State party is urged to consider the Committee's general comment No.

188 NOTES

6 (2005) on. In addition, the Committee urges the State party to: "(a) Reconsider its policy of detaining children who are asylum-seeking, refugees and/or irregular migrants; and ensure that detention is only used in exceptional circumstances, in keeping with the best interests of the child, and subject to judicial review" (U.N. Committee on the Rights of the Child 2012, ¶74).

8. The Canadian government has also been complicit in the security-related deportation of its citizens by third parties, including a high-profile case where the Royal Canadian Mounted Police (RCMP) provided intelligence to U.S. authorities that was used to justify the detention and deportation of Canadian citizen Maher Arar to Syria, where he faced torture (Commission of Inquiry 2006).

9. Legal commentators comparing Canada's record on prolonged immigration detention and rendition to torture to the United States throughout the period following increased enforcement after the September 11, 2001 terrorist attacks note that Canada's humanitarian self-image as a model in protecting the rights of noncitizens in general, and refugees in particular is not entirely deserved (Okafor 2020, 244–245).

10. The Canadian practice of supervised release for noncitizens under similar circumstances is even more restrictive, leaving noncitizens in the program without work authorization, and forcing them to perform unpaid work in what amounts to an indefinite sentence of community service (Benslimane and Moffette 2019, 53–57).

11. From a retributivist perspective that views legitimate punishment as "institutionalized moral blame for wrongful conduct," the state may also be at fault for sanctioning people for wrongs they did not commit (Lippke 2008, 388–389). However, legislators and prosecutors could easily respond to this philosophical critique by moving the goalpost and saying that being in the wrong place at the wrong time or viewing incriminating information is now the wrong they are seeking to prohibit. A stronger position would be to argue that legitimate punishment constitutes official censure for acting to intentionally harm others, resulting in punishment that is proportional to the harm that the offender caused, rather than the uncertain risk of potential harm that an offender might cause in the future. This position respects a liberal society's regard for the moral autonomy and free will of individuals to consider an action, and then to choose, or refrain from acting after assessing the resulting consequences to themselves, and harm to others (Walen 2008).

12. This case was narrowly decided, not because the concept of guilt by association was in dispute, but because the dissenters (Warren, Douglas, Brennan, and Frankfurter) were far more forthright (consistent with the broader principles set forth in this volume about the presumption of innocence and the belief-action distinction) that prosecuting a person for their beliefs, sympathies, or even membership in an organization advocating revolution was at odds with the nation's founding principles and violated their first amendment rights.

13. Apart from the moral illegitimacy of preventive detention, the Northern Ireland case showed how it can be counterproductive by engendering more sympathy among the targeted population for anti-state forces (Donohue 2008, 38).

Chapter 3

1. The United States already bars pregnant visitors from entering the country if they cannot prove that they have sufficient medical coverage or resources to pay for their child's birth in the United States (U.S. Customs and Border Protection 2022).
2. On the symbolic functions of punishment for a society to include/exclude—see for instance Carvalho and Chamberlen (2018).
3. Though the scope of this chapter is largely limited to current Canadian and U.S. citizenship policy, it is worth noting that the practice of *jus soli* citizenship is derived from a common English precedent, *Calvin's Case* (1608), 77 ER 377, (1608) Co Rep 1a, which once shaped citizenship policies across the British commonwealth.
4. The Bahamas, Colombia, the Dominican Republic, Haiti, and Surinam are exceptions to this rule (Vonk 2015, 11). The political motivation behind the Dominican Republic's departure from *jus soli* was to exclude Dominican-born persons of Haitian descent, who had already faced ethno-racial discrimination in Dominican society, linking racism and more exclusionary *jus sanguinis* citizenship laws (Shaw 2020, 108–109).
5. Variations of territorial birthright citizenship exist in the nationality laws of many countries outside the Western Hemisphere, including unconditional acquisition of nationality at birth by the third generation (the practice of "double *jus soli*" in France), acquisition based on birth and extended residence, and unconditional acquisition by foundlings as infants or young children of unknown parentage (Weil 2001, 29).
6. Early in the nineteenth century, Africans brought illegally to the United States were arguably "unauthorized migrants," while later in the nineteenth century at the time that *Wong Kim Ark* was decided, those subject to the Chinese exclusion laws filled this category (Chin and Finkelman 2021, 2218, 2257; *Wong Kim Ark* 1898).
7. Regrettably, the majority in that case chose to prefer the colonial and exclusionary *Insular Cases* over the inclusive and anti-racist *Wong Kim Ark* framework for understanding the potential U.S. citizenship claims of persons born in American Samoa (*Fitisemanu v. United States* 2021, 13). The ruling also suggests that it would be wrong to impose birthright citizenship, and American citizenship more generally, on American Samoa against the will of its people, which raises important issues about imposing citizenship on an Indigenous people without its consent that I touch on in Chapter 6 when I deal with citizenship as redress. There is value in "defer[ring] to the preferences of Indigenous peoples, so that they may chart their own course," if they are doing so in a way that is consensual and democratic. Writing for the majority, Judge Carlos Lucero re-interprets the exclusionary *Insular Cases* as a means of providing this deference (16). However, Judge Lucero's ruling also acknowledges that he has "little evidence" that most of the American Samoan people are currently opposed to this grant of citizenship, or the added rights that this would grant them both in their territory, and in the mainland United States (8). Moreover, it is not desirable to base the citizenship claims of individuals on the interests of hereditary elites in their community, or to shield illiberal inheritance practices from constitutional scrutiny, as justified by the majority in the *Fitisemanu* ruling (7–9). This is especially true when

190 NOTES

individuals, like the Plaintiffs in the *Fitisemanu* case now residing in Utah, are appealing to the courts to protect their citizenship claims outside of their community.

8. Symbolic efforts to foster and preserve national unity have played an important role in citizenship law debates in Canada, as shown in the 1994 report commissioned by Liberal MP Sergio Marchi, Minister of Citizenship and Immigration, to "identify ways in which the symbolic nature of citizenship can be enhanced" (Bethel 1994, 1). The then-opposition Bloc Québécois attributed this project to "an identity crisis that Canada is undergoing" as sovereigntists anticipated a referendum on Quebec's independence (Bethel 1994, 51).

9. This poll came during a period from March 21, 2020 to July 4, 2021, in which entry to Canada by noncitizens was restricted due to COVID-19 public health measures, preventing many noncitizens from entering on a tourist visa to have children, without barring access to noncitizens already present on student or work visas (Griffith 2021; Keung 2021). One study attempts to link COVID-19 related restrictions on travel to a decline in birth tourism. It indicates that births to "nonresident self-pay" persons, an imprecise designation that includes all individuals ineligible for provincial health benefits (including nonresident Canadian citizens whom no one identifies as birth tourists), declined by 57 percent while entry restrictions were in place from the previous year (Griffith 2021). The same restrictions also divided families and prevented women in mixed-citizenship status couples with strong ties to Canada from entering Canada to give birth, in a year when overall birth rates also declined (Bureau 2020b; Macklin 2020, 6; Statistics Canada 2021).

10. *Wong Kim Ark v. United States*, 169 U.S. 649, 693 (1898). The Wong Kim Ark decision also referred to "the children of members of Indian tribes owing direct allegiance to their several tribes," but the U.S. Congress rendered this exception obsolete with the Indian Citizenship Act of 1924 granting U.S. citizenship to members of Indigenous tribes born the United States.

11. DACA was also upheld by the U.S. Supreme Court for separate reasons, namely that the U.S. Department of Homeland Security's actions to rescind DACA were arbitrary and capricious under the U.S. Administrative Procedure Act, on June 18, 2020 in a 5–4 ruling (*Trump v. NAACP*, No. 18-588).

12. This is a pressing issue for children stranded in Syria after the collapse of ISIS, as European nations have refused to repatriate the Syrian-born children of their citizens who left to affiliate with the terrorist organization (Mustassari 2020, 22).

13. At 47 percent of all unauthorized immigrants in the United States, Mexican citizens are still a much larger percentage of all unauthorized immigrants than those from other countries of origin (Lopez, Passel, and Cohn 2021).

Chapter 4

1. On the state of the research on this issue, see Bülow 2014: "Though research on collateral consequences is an established subdiscipline in criminology, research on the

NOTES 191

harms beyond the criminal offender are scant. According to Murray (2005), the effect on prisoners' families and children is an almost entirely neglected topic in academic research, prison statistics, public policy, and media coverage. Comfort (2007) points out that the studies that exist are rather scant. Still, the studies have pointed out several consequences of imprisonment for families and children of inmates. These consequences include (1) decreased psychological and mental wellbeing, (2) financial costs and loss of economic opportunities, and (3) intrusions and control of private life" (Bülow 2014, 1776).

2. Ewald (2002) notes that disenfranchisement is just one dimension of "civil death," and that the practice was originally one that cast an individual out of society, and applied intergenerationally to the offender as well as his descendants (Ewald 2002, 1059).

3. As of June 12, 2021, there were 44,315 positive COVID-19 tests out of 115,153 completed tests administered to incarcerated inmates in U.S. Bureau of Prisons managed institutions.

4. As of June 11, 2021, 17,377 out of 198,866 U.S. immigration detainees who received a coronavirus test tested positive (8.7 percent) (Immigration and Customs Enforcement 2021). In Canada, Canada Border Services Agency officials have recognized the risk to detainees arising from COVID outbreaks in crowded prisons where they are being held, and have ordered the release, subject to electronic monitoring, of detainees who were previously deemed "too risky" for community supervision (Arbel and Joeck 2021).

5. Randy Barnett's libertarian vision of restorative justice is outside the mainstream of the restorative movement, which is centered on restoring community relations through conferencing, rather than privatizing the criminal justice system by moving toward payment as restitution for crime (Cohen 2019, 912–914).

6. Consistent with the conviction "that every individual is capable of repenting and re-entering society" as part of a just and humane penal system, the Canadian Supreme Court recently overturned the section of the Criminal Code that effectively permitted life without parole. In his ruling for the Court in *R v. Bissonnette* (2022), Chief Justice Richard Wagner rightly denounced such sentences as "degrading in nature in that it presupposes at the time of its imposition that the offender is beyond redemption and lacks the moral autonomy needed for rehabilitation." Such a sentence adds little deterrent value and deprives offenders "of any incentive to reform" while languishing in perpetual "isolation from their loved ones and from the outside world."

7. Accusations of a nonviolent nature (in this case, Floyd was alleged to have spent a counterfeit banknote at a deli) could receive a summons and be released on their own recognizance. The offender could benefit from a thorough investigation of his alleged crime, and if convicted, the business owner and offender would undergo a victim-offender mediation session to determine the appropriate restitution.

8. Sara Wakefield and Christopher Wildeman (2018) note that 44 percent of Black women and 32 percent of Black men in the United States report having a family member incarcerated, compared to 12 percent of white women and 6 percent of White men.

192 NOTES

9. It is important to differentiate the ideal of penitence in community that I am advocating here from the extreme reliance on isolation that characterized an earlier era of penitential reforms in the criminal justice system in nineteenth-century prisons with their adverse impact on prisoners' mental health and their capacity for community reintegration (Schmid 2003).

10. Advocates of restorative justice continue to debate whether retribution and vengeance—which is involved in placing heinous offenders in prison for most of their lives to pay for their offenses—is consistent with the decarceral, rehabilitative focus of the restorative justice movement focused on victim and community-directed rehabilitation after the offender accepts full responsibility for his crimes.

11. The authors of the compilation, Megan Sullivan, the adult daughter of an incarcerated father who died in prison, and Denise Johnston, who was incarcerated as a mother, situate this story in the context of a wide range of narratives of children coping with their parent's incarceration, some of whom were not as fortunate as Chaidez, with their own experiences of incarceration as parents repeating the same cycle into the next generation (Johnston and Sullivan 2016, i, xxi, 85–103).

12. As a practical example, consider, for instance, immigration enforcement measures including family separation that have been justified by the Trump administration as deterrent measures designed to prevent parents from entering the United States without authorization to claim asylum (DHS 2017).

Chapter 5

1. To take just one example, the centre-right *Les Républicains* political party in France adopted a platform in 2020 that aimed to follow the United Kingdom's example, denationalizing citizens affiliated with ISIS, and allowing for their extraterritorial judgment. The justification that the party offers for this sanction is to punish treason and betrayal: "Ils ont trahi la France, ils n'ont plus leur place en France" (Les Républicains 2020). Even more ominously, the United States still makes treason punishable by death as the ultimate act of retribution for anti-state allegiances, even though this penalty has fallen into disuse (18 U.S.C §2381).

2. In his book *Forever Prisoners: How the United States Made the World's Largest Immigrant Detention System*, Elliot Young makes a broader point about the problems with "distinctions reflexively made between alleged criminals and terrorists, on the one hand, and innocent migrants, on the other" that is also helpful for understanding the link between different case studies in this book (Young 2021, 190). Many readers will have greater sympathy for innocent children than their parents suspected of terrorism (Chapter 5), or who respond to past victimization by becoming involved in the criminal justice system as adults (Chapter 6). But even in the case of the adults, there is a past and potential for innocence that must be respected. Suspects must be presumed innocent until proven guilty. The lives of convicted offenders are about

more than just their offenses. Their capacity for future rehabilitation and redemption must be respected.

3. The same can be said of asylum proceedings that deny former child soldiers and terrorist affiliates the right to protection given their role as victims and unwitting victimizers (Nortje and Quénivet 2020, 33–34).

4. "Child soldiers generally come from similar backgrounds: the first to be recruited into armed groups are generally the most vulnerable and disadvantaged children—those without traditional families to protect them, those with little or no education, and those from marginalized sectors of society. The vast majority of child soldiers come from poor, conflict ridden areas and know nothing but war" (McQueen 2018, 101).

5. Historically in the United States, Elizabeth Cohen points to the "lack of provision for punishments that could be applied to people who didn't have documentation" as the undoing of U.S. immigration enforcement from its inception (Cohen 2020, 94). More to the point, the level of discretion in the system and the absence of equitably applied penalties signaled that immigration law violations were not a serious matter if they served a purpose for powerful stakeholders like agribusiness operators that depended on low-wage undocumented immigrant labor (96; Song and Bloemraad 2022). Expanding access to cancellation of removal, following a clearer set of guidelines that follow the principles of regularity and publicity would bring immigration justice more into line with key rule of law principles (Song and Bloemraad 2022, 13).

6. To provide some determinacy to this age of minimum responsibility, Article 38 of the United Nations Convention on the Rights of the Child sets the age for voluntary recruitment at fifteen, while the Optional Protocol on the Involvement of Children in Armed Conflicts sets the age of voluntary recruitment at eighteen (Vandiwiele 2006, 7–9). When evaluating responsibility for the conduct of child soldiers and terrorist affiliates, armed group/military leadership and recruiters are ultimately liable for illegal solicitation (44).

7. "In addition to being forcibly recruited, youth also present themselves for service. It is misleading, however, to consider this voluntary. While young people may appear to choose military service, the choice is not exercised freely. They may be driven by any of several forces, including cultural, social, economic or political pressures" (Report of the Expert of the Secretary General 1996, §38).

8. The United Kingdom and the United States have legislation providing for universal jurisdiction over persons who committed the crime of recruiting child soldiers (Child Soldier Accountability Act of 2008, U.S. Public Law 110–340; International Criminal Court Act, United Kingdom (2001), section 51(2)).

Chapter 6

1. For the binational Indigenous polities along the southern border of the United States, Mexico should be included in this project, which could conceivably be extended across the Americas.

194 NOTES

2. Among the 60 percent of Canadian residential schools operated under Roman Catholic auspices, the majority of the schools were operated by the Missionary Oblates of Mary Immaculate. The Anglican Church of Canada administered 30 percent of the residential schools in Canada, with the remaining 10 percent distributed among other Protestant denominations (Presbyterian, Methodist, and United Church of Canada) and nonsectarian entities (MacDonald 2014, 309).

3. Fletcher's testimony came during a reunion in 1981 organized by the Anglican Diocese of Algoma, which administered the school, and Algoma University in Sault Ste. Marie, which now occupies the site of the former Shingwauk Residential School. Other attendees shared a mix of gratitude and regret for the experience, recounting happier childhood experiences amidst the work regimen, punishment for speaking Indigenous languages, and dislocation that came from the experience.

4. In Australia, intergenerational family victimization originated in official eugenics policies. Beginning in the 1930s, the Australian government used child welfare agencies, residential schools, and "vocational training" as instruments of a pernicious policy of "managed miscegenation" in which half-caste aboriginal girls were taken from their mothers at a young age, and hired out as vocational workers (Commonwealth of Australia 1997, 94–98; McGregor 2011, 2–14). While the original government policy envisioned that biological assimilation would come through arranged marriages, in practice, later inquiries revealed that most pregnancies resulted from the rape of mixed-race foster children and household servants at the hands of their white male employers (Commonwealth of Australia 1997, 101–102, 143, 161, 195; Haebich 2000, 273–279). Child welfare authorities in turn forced them to surrender their children as part of a deliberate intergenerational strategy to "whiten" the aboriginal population (Commonwealth of Australia 1997, 99–102). Owing to this cycle of victimization, survivors and their descendants continue to face overwhelming disadvantages in their adult life, including difficulties parenting given their fears that authorities may take their own children, and their lack of positive role models (Cunneen and Grix 2004, 5–6).

5. While some victims prefer confidentiality, Cachagee has been outspoken in the media about his desire to publicize records of his abuse at residential schools. He called government efforts to have evidence of his Truth and Reconciliation hearings, and the materials of 38,000 other survivors destroyed "in an effort to protect their privacy" as a means of "protecting, in essence, the perpetrators. They don't want the public to see the devastation and ugliness of what happened, under the guise of protecting my innocence" (Alamenciak 2014).

6. Moreover, as small children, survivors experienced Catholic residential schools in terms of that faith's theological claims during their religious education there. They find it disingenuous for the Roman Catholic Church to later deny or minimize its responsibility by pointing to the doctrine of subsidiarity and the administrative division of authority between the papacy and the church's many religious orders (Grant 2021b). These are bureaucratic subtleties that do not conform to survivors' lived experience of the institution as children, the content of the religious teachings that they

were proselytized with, or its clergy's colonial denial of the value of their own religion and culture in favor of Roman Catholic Christianity and Euro-Canadian ideas of civilization (Daigneault 2018). One survivor described her experiences in these terms: "First of all, I am a residential school survivor of the Île-à-la-Crosse residential school (1962–64). While there, I endured not only cultural, personal and physical abuse at the hands of the nuns but also sexual violence of the worst sort by a priest who would quote scripture as he was performing his mortifying acts. . . . It is a shameful disgrace that the Catholic church has been so reluctant to participate in and contribute toward compensation efforts by the Canadian government and other churches to residential school survivors who are recognized. It is even difficult if not impossible to take the Catholic church to court because, as a church, you have avoided status as a legal entity that can be held accountable in court just like any other corporate body in Canada. So not only is the Catholic church avoiding taking responsibility for the genocidal nature of residential schools but now you as the patriarchal head of the Catholic church are refusing to apologize" (Daigenault 2018).

7. Central government authorities in Russia, China, Vietnam, and parts of Africa have also taken away children from their parents to attend residential schools with similar integrative purposes and culturally disruptive dysfunctions (Bloch 2004, xiv; Firpo and Jacobs 2018). In Xinjiang, the Chinese state is engaged in a more extensive project of cultural genocide using twenty-first century surveillance technology and re-education facilities operating on the same principles as twentieth-century North American and Australian residential schools. In Xinjiang, state officials separate adults and children alike from their families, hold them in indoctrination camps, and subject them to forced sterilizations and abortions aimed at lowering the Uyghur Muslim birthrate in proportion to the Han (Finley 2020, 16; Haitiwaji and Morgat 2021). In Russia's 2022 invasion of Ukraine, survivors testify that "Russian soldiers told them they would rape them to the point where they wouldn't want sexual contact with any man, to prevent them from having Ukrainian children" (Berger 2022). In each instance, governments are actively destroying the physical and cultural reproductive capacities of vulnerable families from subaltern communities for political ends.

8. Idle No More is a Canadian Indigenous social movement that started in November 2012 as a protest against changes by Stephen Harper's Conservative government to the Indian Act and Environmental Assessment Act (among other acts). The movement escalated in 2013 to encompass rallies, marches, teach-ins and even blockades with supporters across North America, drawing many non-Indigenous participants concerned about environmental issues and Indigenous rights (Coates 2015). The movement persists to the present day, bringing non-Indigenous and Indigenous people together to fight for human rights, social justice and environmental protection (Palmater 2020).

9. In 2020, Black Canadians made up 3 percent of the Canadian population, and 10 percent of the federal prison population in Canada. Indigenous Canadians represented 5 percent of the Canadian population, and 30.4 percent of the Canadian federal prison population (Reece 2020).

196 NOTES

10. According to Statistics Canada, the 2016 census recorded that 14,970 children with an "aboriginal identity" between the ages of 0 and 14 were in foster care, out of 28,665 Canadian children in the same age group in foster care. The same census recorded that 448,865 children between ages 0 and 14 have an "aboriginal identity," out of 5,817,050 Canadians in the same age group (Statistics Canada 2018).

11. As this book went into publication, Pope Francis issued an apology at Maskwacis, Alberta, Canada on July 25, 2022. There, he asked for "forgiveness, in particular, for the ways in which many members of the Church and of religious communities cooperated, not least through their indifference, in projects of cultural destruction and forced assimilation promoted by the governments of that time, which culminated in the system of residential schools" (Pope Francis 2022a). On his return flight to the Vatican, Francis described the residential school system and its impact on survivors as genocide (Vatican News 2022). Indigenous leaders in Canada responded to the Pontiff's apology with mixed emotions (Paperny 2022). The Assembly of First Nations and other representatives of Indigenous nations in Canada want Pope Francis to go further, by formally repealing the Doctrine of Discovery in Pope Alexander VI's 1493 Papal Bull *Inter caetera divinai* (Assembly of First Nations 2022). This doctrine laid the foundation for the dispossession of the Indigenous people from their lands throughout the Americas (Miller 2012, 12). The Assembly of First Nations also continues to demand the return of diocesan land back to First Nations and returning sacred items currently being held both in storage and on public display at the Vatican "as essential steps for advancing reconciliation" (Assembly of First Nations 2022).

12. The denial of agency to young Indigenous women who would have rather kept their children or raised them in their communities has some similarities to the Magdalene Laundries scandal of church-run adoption facilities in Ireland where church authorities abused young single women and their children with the complicity of the state (Garrett 2017, 364–366).

13. In the context of the Anishinaabe First Nation (with communities across the upper Great Lakes region), sociologist Damien Lee writes that "families use adoption to regulate citizenship by *intentionally* bringing new citizens into the nation while also deciding who does not belong. Anishinaabe citizenship law is vested in families as actors that make political decisions within the nation" (Lee 2019, 815). An individual's subsequent behavior can also determine if the community continues to regard an adoptee as a member, pointing to a provisional character of membership by adoption (816).

14. Justice to Indigenous children may require a duty of remediation by the parties responsible for undermining their family's condition to ensure that they will have the same life chances as non-Indigenous children.

15. Conceivably, the principle of citizenship as redress could be extended further by requiring a citizenship grant as redress from every settler state that coercively constituted an Indigenous nation, driving the forced migration of people from U.S.-influenced Indigenous polities beyond its borders to the United States. Many Mexican and Central American individuals are of Indigenous descent, and identify with Indigenous political entities (i.e., Maya, Tlaxcala) in their homelands (Hall 2003, 92). Conflicts that marginalized the Indigenous populations of their homelands—of

which the United States was involved—helped to push immigrants and asylum-seekers northward. In Harvest of Empire, Juan Gonzalez argues that "U.S. economic and political domination over Latin America has always been—and continues to be—the underlying reason for the massive Latino presence here, and our vast Latino population is the unintended harvest of the U.S. empire" (Gonzalez 2011). We may sharpen his argument by disaggregating Latinx immigration and highlighting the particular claims of the Indigenous peoples of Mexico and Central America that are now coming to the United States as asylum-seekers, both in relation to their countries of origin and U.S. involvement in the political conflicts that heightened their desperation and led them to the United States. The proportion of Indigenous migrants who are entering the United States over its Southern border has increased each year in the 2010s and early 2020s with the influx of Central American asylum-seekers from predominantly Indigenous areas of Guatemala, Honduras, and El Salvador (Riley and Carpenter 2021). In the United States and Canada, Indigenous peoples whose lands also divided by borders have expressed solidarity with Indigenous asylum-seekers, recognizing their common plight given the many violations of their sovereignty in their homelands.

16. In practice, I recognize the difficulty of simultaneously securing the consent of multiple nation-states to grant citizenship as redress, where separate countries are at divergent stages of their truth and reconciliation processes. Even so, settler states that already recognize or tolerate dual citizenship (including Canada, the United States, and Mexico) have no practical reason to object to another state granting citizenship as redress to some of their members.

Chapter 7

1. Civil liberties organizations have joined plaintiffs alleging that Canada crossed this line between prevention and punishment by imposing a mandatory hotel stay on returning citizens while condemning their actions and seeking to deter others from traveling between February 22 and July 4, 2021 (Humphreys 2021). On June 18, 2021, in *Spencer v. Canada,* the Federal Court of Canada ruled against plaintiffs making these arguments, determining that the hotel quarantine policy did not constitute a punishment under Article 12 of the Canadian Charter of Rights and Freedoms barring cruel and unusual punishment, and that the measure was proportionate to the risk posed by returning travelers who might spread a more contagious COVID variant acquired abroad (*Spencer v. Canada* 2021, ¶202–205, 257, 289). In the process, Chief Justice Paul Crampton framed civic duty during a pandemic as follows: "Like times of war and other crises, pandemics call for sacrifices to save lives and avoid broad based suffering. If some are unwilling to make such sacrifices, and engage in behaviour that poses a demonstrated risk to the health and safety of others, the principles of fundamental justice will not prevent the state from performing its essential function of protecting its citizens from that risk" (¶311).

2. During President Biden's first eight months in office, the number of Title 42 expulsions at the U.S.–Mexico border of individuals in a family unit (FMUA) increased from 9,478 removals in February 2021 to 17,599 removals in September 2021, with an average of 13,888 removals of individuals in a family unit during this period (U.S. Customs and Border Protection 2021a). This marks a 472 percent increase over the average monthly rate (2,429) of Title 42 removals of individuals in a family unit from April 2020 to January 2021 while President Trump was in office (ibid.).

References

Abbott, Greg. 2021. Executive Order GA-37 by the Governor of Texas Relating to the Transportation of Migrants During the COVID-19 Disaster. July 28. https://gov.texas.gov/uploads/files/press/EO-GA-37_transportation_of_migrants_during_COVID_IMAGE_07-28-2021.pdf

Abbott, John G. 2021. Provincial Government Discontinues Birth Alerts to Hospitals in Newfoundland and Labrador. June 30. https://www.gov.nl.ca/releases/2021/cssd/0630n03/

Abji, Salina, and Lindsay Larios. 2021. "Migrant Justice as Reproductive Justice: Birthright Citizenship and the Politics of Immigration Detention for Pregnant Women in Canada." *Citizenship Studies* 25(2): 253–272.

Abourezk, James. 1974. Indian Child Welfare Program. Hearings Before the Subcommittee on Indian Affairs, Committee on Indian and Insular Affairs, United States Senate, 93rd Congress, 2nd Session, April 9, pp. 446–474.

AbouZahr, Carla, Martin W Bratschi, Emily Cercone, Anushka Mangharam, Don de Savigny, Irina Dincu, Anette Bayer Forsingdal, Olga Joos, Montasser Kamal, Doris Ma Fat, Gloria Mathenge, Fatima Marinho, Raj Gautam Mitra, Jeff Montgomery, William Muhwava, Remy Mwamba, James Mwanza, Alvin Onaka, Tanja Brøndsted Sejersen, Maletela Tuoane-Nkhasi, Lynn Sferrazza, Philip Setel. 2021. "The COVID-19 Pandemic: Effects on Civil Registration of Births and Deaths and on Availability and Utility of Vital Events Data." *American Journal of Public Health* 111(6): 1123–1131.

Abrams, Kerry. 2018. "'No More Blood' in 'Bloodlines and Belonging: Time to Abandon Ius Sanguinis?'" In *Debating Transformations of National Citizenship*, edited by Rainer Bauböck, 121–125. Cham, Switzerland: Springer Publishing.

Acosta v. Gaffney. 558 F.2d 1153 (3rd Cir. 1977).

Act of April 2, 1928. "Chapter 308: An Act to Exempt American Indians Born in Canada from the Operation of the Immigration Act of 1924." P.L. 234. 70th Congress, April 2.

Adams, David Wallace. 2003. "Foreword to the Paperback Edition." In *Battlefield and Classroom: An Autobiography by Richard Henry Pratt*, edited by Robert M. Utley, xi–xvi. Norman: University of Oklahoma Press.

Adams, Tim. 2022. "The UK Government's Hypocrisy is Keeping Jack Letts and His Mother in Purgatory." *The Guardian,* March 12. https://www.theguardian.com/commentisfree/2022/mar/12/uk-government-hypocrisy-keeping-jack-letts-and-mother-in-purgatory

Aiken, Sharry, and Stephanie J. Silverman. 2021. "Decarceral Futures: Bridging Immigration and Prison Justice towards an Abolitionist Future." *Citizenship Studies* 25(2): 141–161.

Alamenciak, Tim. 2014. "Survivors of Residential Schools Push Back Against Document Destruction." *Toronto Star,* June 20. https://www.thestar.com/news/gta/2014/06/20/survivors_of_residential_schools_push_back_against_document_destruction.html

200 REFERENCES

Al Faour, Nadia, Kim Hjelmgaard, Trevor Hughes, and Deirdre Shesgreen. 2019. "The Making of an American Terrorist: Hoda Muthana Joined ISIS. Now She Can't Come Back." *USA Today*, April 7. https://www.usatoday.com/story/news/world/2019/04/06/hoda-muthana-married-isis-fighters-so-trump-wont-let-her-back-usa/3350233002/

Aliverti, Ana. 2017. "The Wrongs of Unlawful Immigration." *Criminal Law and Philosophy* 11: 375–391.

Allen, Bonnie. 2021. "Mothers Call for Support, not Threats, as Sask. and P.E.I. End Birth Alerts." *CBC News*, February 1. https://www.cbc.ca/news/canada/saskatchewan/mothers-call-for-support-not-threats-as-sask-and-p-e-i-end-birth-alerts-1.5894014

Allen, Scott, and Josiah Rich. 2022. "Boosters, Other Measures Needed to Protect Workers, Immigrants and the Public From COVID-19 in Immigration Detention Settings." *Government Accountability Project*, January 26. https://whistleblower.org/wp-content/uploads/2022/01/012622-LETTER-TO-MAYORKAS-FROM-DRS-RE-COVID-IN-IMM-DETENTION.pdf

Ambroise, Sylvie. 2021. "Signalements à la Naissance en Abitibi: « Je crois qu'il y a un Profilage Racial »." *APTN*, March 18. https://www.aptnnews.ca/reportages/signalements-de-la-naissance-en-labitibi-quebec/

America's CHILDREN Act. 2021. S.2753, 117th Congress, 1st Sess. September 15.

Amir, Noureddine. 2019. *Letter from the Committee on the Elimination of Racial Discrimination to the Government of Canada, CERD/100th session/FU/MJA/ks.* December 13. Geneva: UN Office of the High Commissioner on Human Rights.

Amrami, Yosef, and Rafael Art. Javier. 2020. "Termination of Parental Rights: Psychological Impact on the Children of Immigrants." In *Assessing Trauma in Forensic Contexts*, edited by Rafael Art. Javier, Elizabeth A. Owen, and Jemour A. Maddux, 247–269. Cham: Springer Publishing.

An Act Granting Citizenship to Certain Indians. 1919. H.R. 5007, 66th Congress, 1st Sess. November 6.

Ananian-Welsh, Rebecca. 2019. "Crimmigration-Counterterrorism in the War on Foreign Terrorist Fighters." In *Crimmigration in Australia: Law, Politics and Society*, edited by Peter Billings, 173–196. Cham, Switzerland: Springer Publishing.

Anaya, James. 2014. *Report of the Special Rapporteur on the Rights of Indigenous Peoples: The Situation of Indigenous Peoples in Canada.* United Nations Human Rights Council, Twenty Seventh Session, Agenda Item 3, July 4. https://undocs.org/A/HRC/27/52/Add.2

Andersen, Chris. 2014. *Métis: Race, Recognition, and the Struggle for Indigenous Peoplehood.* Vancouver: University of British Columbia Press.

Anderson, Amy, Dallas K. Miller, and Dwight Newman. 2018. "Canada's Residential Schools and the Right to Integrity." *Dalhousie Law Review* 41(2): 301–338.

Anderson, Benedict. 1983. *Imagined Communities.* New York: Verso Publishing.

Anishinabek Nation Head Office. 2022. "Withdrawal of Judicial Review of CHRT Ruling a Relief for Anishinabek Nation Communities Rebuilding and Reclaiming Their Role in Child and Youth Well-Being." *Anishinabek News*, January 28. https://anishinabeknews.ca/2022/01/28/withdrawal-of-judicial-review-of-chrt-ruling-a-relief-for-anishinabek-nation-communities-rebuilding-and-reclaiming-their-role-in-child-and-youth-well-being/

Anstis, Siena, and Molly Joeck. 2020. "Detaining the Uncooperative Migrant." *Journal of Law and Social Policy* 33(1): 38–64.

REFERENCES 201

APM Research Lab. 2022. *The Color of Coronavirus: COVID-19 Deaths by Race and Ethnicity in the U.S.* American Public Media, May 4. https://www.apmresearchlab.org/covid/deaths-by-race#counts-over-time

Apt, Benjamin L. 2016. "Do We Know How to Punish." *New Criminal Law Review* 19(3): 437–472.

Aptel, Cécile. 2019. "The Protection of Children in Armed Conflicts." In *International Human Rights of Children*, edited by Ursula Kikelly and Ton Liefaard, 515–536. Singapore: Springer Nature.

Arbel, Efrat. 2015. "Between Protection and Punishment: The Irregular Arrival Regime in Canadian Refugee Law." In *Extreme Punishment: Comparative Studies in Detention, Incarceration and Solitary Confinement*, edited by Keramet Reiter and Alexa Koenig, 197–219. London: Palgrave Macmillan.

Arbel, Efrat. 2019. "Rethinking the Crisis of Indigenous Mass Imprisonment." *Canadian Journal of Law and Society* 34(3): 437–456.

Arbel, Efrat, and Molly Joeck. 2021. "Immigration Detention in the Age of COVID-19." In *Research Handbook on the Law and Politics of Migration*, edited by Catherine Dauvergne, 260–276. Cheltenham: Edward Elgar Press.

Arditti, Joyce A. 2012. *Parental Incarceration and the Family*. New York: NYU Press.

Arditti, Joyce A. 2018. "Parental Incarceration and Family Inequality in the United States." In *Prisons, Punishment, and the Family: Towards a New Sociology of Punishment?*, edited by Rachel Condry and Peter Scharff, 41–57. Oxford: Oxford University Press.

Arditti, Joyce A., and April L. Few. 2006. "Mothers' Reentry into Family Life Following Incarceration." *Criminal Justice Policy Review* 17(1): 103–123.

Arendt, Hannah. 1963. *Eichmann in Jerusalem: A Report on the Banality of Evil*. New York: Viking University Press.

Arendt, Hannah. 1987. "Collective Responsibility." In *Amor Mundi: Explorations in the Faith and Thought of Hannah Arendt*, edited by J. James W. Bernauer, 43–50. Boston: Martinus Nijhoff.

Ariss, Rachel. 2021. "Bearing Witness: Creating the Conditions of Justice for First Nations Children." *Canadian Journal of Law and Society* 36(1): 113–133.

Arizona et al. v. Alejandro Mayorkas, 598 U.S. _____ (2022).

Artiga, Samantha, Latoya Hill, and Sweta Haldar. 2021. *COVID-19 Cases and Deaths by Race/Ethnicity: Current Data and Changes Over Time*. Kaiser Family Foundation, October 8. https://www.kff.org/racial-equity-and-health-policy/issue-brief/covid-19-cases-and-deaths-by-race-ethnicity-current-data-and-changes-over-time/

Ashworth, Andrew. 2013. *Positive Obligations in Criminal Law*. London: Bloomsbury Publishing.

Ashworth, Andrew, and Lucia Zedner. 2014. *Preventive Justice*. Oxford: Oxford University Press.

Ashworth, Andrew, and Lucia Zedner. 2019. "The Rise and Restraint of the Preventive State." *Annual Review of Criminology* 2: 429–450.

Assembly of First Nations. 2009. "AFN National Chief Responds to Prime Minister's Statements on Colonialism." *Newswire*, October 1. https://www.newswire.ca/news-releases/afn-national-chief-responds-to-prime-ministers-statements-on-colonialism-538635682.html

Assembly of First Nations. 2022. *AFN National Chief Archibald and AFN Regional Chief Antoine Reflect on Papal Visit to Canada*. August 2. https://www.afn.ca/afn-national-chief-archibald-and-afn-regional-chief-antoine-reflect-on-papal-visit-to-canada/

202 REFERENCES

Atak, Idil. 2019. "The Criminalization of Migration in Canada and Its Unintended Consequnces." In *The Oxford Handbook of Migration Consequences*, edited by Cecelia Menjívar and Marie Ruiz, 467–484. New York: Oxford University Press.

Atullahjan, Salma, Wanda Elaine Thomas Bernard, and Nancy J. Hartling. 2021. *Forced and Coerced Sterilization of Persons in Canada*. Ottawa: Standing Senate Committee on Human Rights, June 3. https://sencanada.ca/content/sen/committee/432/RIDR/repo rts/2021-06-03_ForcedSterilization_E.pdf

Audet, Carol. 2022. "Matawa Chiefs Council Express Concerns About Ongoing Birth Alerts." *Matawa Chiefs Council*, April 1. http://www.matawa.on.ca/matawa-chiefs-council-express-concerns-about-ongoing-birth-alerts-on-indigenous-newborns-in-thunderbay-despite-government-directives-to-discontinue-the-practice/

Austin, Rod. 2019. "Aid Worker Stranded in Syria After British Citizenship Revoked." *The Guardian*, March 4. https://www.theguardian.com/global-development/2019/mar/04/aid-worker-stranded-in-syria-after-british-citizenship-revoked

Australian Government. 2021. "Frequently Asked Questions: Declared Area Offence." July 29. https://www.nationalsecurity.gov.au/what-australia-is-doing/places-you-cant-go

Aziz, Sahar F. 2014. "Policing Terrorists in the Community." *Harvard National Security Journal* 5(1): 147–224.

Backster, Anika, Jennifer Balkus, Jacqueline Bhabha, Ietza Bojorquez, Baltica Cabieses, Megan Coffee, Joanne Csete, Kacey C. Ernst, Paul J. Fleming, Linda P. Fried, Lynn R. Goldman, M. Claire Greene, Anjum Hajat, Michele Heisler, Cesar Infante Xibille, S. Patrick Kachur, Michel Khoury, Ling San Lau, William Lopez, Joseph B. McCormick, Ayman El-Mohandes, Rachel T. Moresky, Kathleen Page, Kathleen A. Parker, Anne R. Pebley, Amanda Phipps, Paulina Rebolledo, Les Roberts, Leonard Rubenstein, Wafaa El-Sadr, Goleen Samari, John Santelli, Craig Spencer, Paul B. Spiegel, Steffanie A. Strathdee, Parmi Suchdev, Patrick Vinck, Ronald Waldman, Monette Zard, and Amy Zeidan. 2021. *Letter to CDC Director Walensky, HHS Secretary Becerra, and DHS Secretary Mayorkas on the August 2021 Title 42 Order*. September 1. https://www.publi chealth.columbia.edu/sites/default/files/sept_1_2021_title_42_letter.pdf

Bagaric, Mirko, Dan Hunger, and Jennifer Svilar. 2021. "Prison Abolition: From Naïve Idealism to Technological Pragmatism." *Journal of Criminal Law and Criminology* 111(2): 351–406.

Bailey, Ian. 2021. "Avoid Seeking Jail Time for Indigenous Offenders, B.C. Prosecutors Told." *Globe and Mail*, January 15. https://www.theglobeandmail.com/canada/brit ish-columbia/article-avoid-seeking-jail-time-for-indigenous-offenders-bc-prosecut ors-told/

Baker, Dennis J. 2020. "Treason Versus Outraging Public Decency: Over-Criminalization and Terrorism Panics." *Journal of Criminal Law* 84(1): 19–36.

Baranger, Thierry, Laurent Bonelli, and Frédéric Pichaud. 2017. "La Justice des Mineurs et les Affaires de Terrorisme." *Les Cahiers de Justice* 2017(2): 253–264.

Barnett, Randy. 1977. "Restitution: A New Paradigm for Criminal Justice." *Ethics* 87(4): 279–301.

Barrett, Lindsey. 2017. "Reasonably Suspicious Algorithms: Predictive Policing At The United States Border." *NYU Review of Law and Social Change* 41(3): 327–363.

Bashford, Alison, and Carolyn Strange. 2002. "Asylum Seekers and National Histories of Detention." *Australian Journal of Politics and History* 48(4): 509–527.

Bauböck, Rainer. 2009. "The Rights and Duties of External Citizenship." *Citizenship Studies* 13(5): 475–499.

Bauböck, Rainer. 2018. *Debating Transformations of National Citizenship*. Cham, Switzerland: Springer Publishing.

Bauböck, Rainer. 2020. "A Free Movement Paradox: Denationalization and Deportation in Mobile Societies." *Citizenship Studies* 24(3): 389–403.

Bauböck, Rainer, and Vesco Paskalev. 2015. *Citizenship Deprivation: A Normative Analysis*. CEPS Papers in Liberty and Security in Europe, no. 82. Brussels: Centre for European Policy Studies.

Bauer, Nicolas. 2019. "La France a-t-elle d'autres choix que de juger elle-même ses djihadistes?" *Le Figaro*, October 16. https://www.lefigaro.fr/vox/politique/la-france-a-t-elle-d-autres-choix-que-de-juger-elle-meme-ses-djihadistes-20191016

Bayer, Ronald, Lawrence O. Gostin, Bruce Jennings, and Bonnie Steinbock. 2007. *Public Health Ethics: Theory, Policy and Practice*. Oxford: Oxford University Press.

Baylis, Elena A. 2022. "White Supremacy, Police Brutality, and Family Separation: Preventing Crimes Against Humanity Within the United States." *University of Illinois Law Review* 2022(4): 1475–1538.

Bazemore, Gordon. 1998. "Restorative Justice and Earned Redemption: Communities, Victims, and Offender Reintegration." *American Behavioral Scientist* 41(6): 768–813.

Beccaria, Cesar. (1764) 1995. *On Crimes and Punishments and Other Writings*. Translated by Richard Bellamy. Cambridge: Cambridge University Press.

Beck, Elizabeth, Sarah Britto, and Arlene Andrews. 2007. *In the Shadow of Death: Restorative Justice and Death Row Families*. Oxford: Oxford University Press.

Becklumb, Penny. 2014. *Bill C-37: An Act to Amend the Citizenship Act*. Ottawa: Library of Parliament.

Bell, Abraham. 2010. "A Critique of the Goldstone Report and Its Treatment of International Humanitarian Law." *Proceedings of the Annual Meeting of the American Society of International Law* 104: 79–86.

Belton, Kristy. 2017. "Heeding the Clarion Call in the Americas: The Quest to End Statelessness." *Ethics and International Affairs* 31(1): 17–29.

Bensadoun, Emerald. 2019. "How Immigration Detention Centres Work in Canada." *CTV News*, July 7. https://www.ctvnews.ca/canada/how-immigration-detention-cent res-work-in-canada-1.4497688

Benslimane, Souheil, and David Moffette, 2019. "The Double Punishment of Criminal Inadmissibility for Migrants." *Journal of Prisoners on Prisons* 28(1): 44–65.

Benton, Meghan, and Natalia Banulescu-Bogdan. 2019. "Foreign Fighters: Will Revoking Citizenship Mitigate the Threat?" *Migration Policy Institute*, April 3, https://www.migr ationpolicy.org/article/foreign-fighters-will-revoking-citizenship-mitigate-threat.

Berg, Mark, and Beth Huebner. 2011. "Reentry and the Ties that Bind: An Examination of Social Ties, Employment, and Recidivism." *Justice Quarterly* 28(2): 382–410.

Bergen, Rachel. 2020. "Manitoba to End Birth Alerts System That Sometimes Leads to Babies Being Taken." *CBC News*, January 31. https://www.cbc.ca/news/canada/manit oba/birth-alerts-ending-1.5447296

Berger, Miriam. 2022. "Ukraine Has Accused Russian Troops of Rape, A Tough Crime to Prosecute." *Washington Post*, May 5. https://www.washingtonpost.com/world/2022/ 05/05/ukraine-russia-rape-war-crime/

Berk, Christopher. 2019. "Children, Development, and the Troubled Foundations of Miller v. Alabama." *Law and Social Inquiry* 44(3): 752–770.

Bethel, Judy. 1994. *Standing Committee on Citizenship and Immigration, Canadian Citizenship: A Sense of Belonging*. June. Ottawa: Citizenship and Immigration Canada.

Biden, Joseph. 2021a. *Executive Order on the Establishment of Interagency Task Force on the Reunification of Families*. February 2. https://www.whitehouse.gov/briefing-room/presidential-actions/2021/02/02/executive-order-on-the-establishment-of-interagency-task-force-on-the-reunification-of-families/.

Biden, Joseph. 2021b. *Remarks by President Biden in Press Conference*. March 25. https://www.whitehouse.gov/briefing-room/speeches-remarks/2021/03/25/remarks-by-president-biden-in-press-conference/.

Bill C-8 (Canada). 2020. An Act to Amend the Citizenship Act (Truth and Reconciliation Commission of Canada's Call to Action Number 94). October 22. https://parl.ca/DocumentViewer/en/43-2/bill/C-8/first-reading

Bill C-92 (Canada). 2019. An Act Respecting First Nations, Inuit and Métis Children, Youth and Families. June 21. https://laws-lois.justice.gc.ca/eng/annualstatutes/2019_24/page-1.html

Bindra, Tanya. 2020. Los Niños Migrantes en México ya no Estarán Encerrados en los Centro de Acogida." *UN News*, November 12. https://news.un.org/es/story/2020/11/1483972

Birthright Citizenship Act of 2021. "Rep. Brian Babin (TX-36) Introduces H.R.140, Birthright Citizenship Act." *NumbersUSA*, January 7. https://www.numbersusa.com/news/rep-brian-babin-tx-36-introduces-hr140-clarify-those-classes-individuals-born-united-states-who

Blackwell, Tom. 2021. "Britain Won't Take Alleged Ex-ISIL Member Jack Letts Back so His Last Hope is Canada." *National Post*, December 7. https://nationalpost.com/news/canada/parents-of-english-canadian-convert-and-ex-isil-member-push-for-his-transfer-from-syria

Blake, Michael. 2003. "Moral Equality and Birthright Citizenship." In *Nomos XLIV: Child, Family and State*, edited by Steven Macedo and Iris Marion Young, 398–410. New York: NYU Press.

Bloch, Alexia. 2004. *Red Ties and Residential Schools: Indigenous Siberians in a Post-Soviet State*. Philadelphia: University of Pennsylvania Press.

Bloemraad, Irene, and Alicia Sheares. 2017. "Understanding Membership in a World of Global Migration: How Does Citizenship Matter." *International Migration Review* 51(4): 823–867.

Bloom, Mia, and John Horgan. 2019. *Small Arms: Children and Terrorism*. Ithaca, NY: Cornell University Press.

Blum, Benjamin. 2021. "Canadians Should be Prepared for More Discoveries like Kamloops, Murray Sinclair Says." *CBC News*, June 1. https://www.cbc.ca/news/canada/sinclair-kamloops-residential-remains-1.6049525

Boonin, David. 2008. *The Problem of Punishment*. New York: Cambridge University Press.

Borrows, John. 2014. "Residential Schools, Respect, and Responsibilities for Past Harms." *University of Toronto Law Journal* 64(4): 486–504.

Bosley, Chris. 2019. "Injecting Humanity: Community Focused Responses for People Exiting Violent Extremist Conflict." *United States Institute of Peace* 452: 1–19.

Bosniak, Linda. 2008. *The Citizen and the Alien: Dilemmas of Contemporary Membership*. Princeton, NJ: Princeton University Press.

Bosworth, Mary. 2019. "Immigration Detention, Punishment, and the Transformation of Justice." *Social and Legal Studies* 28(1): 81–99.

Bosworth, Mary, Katja Franko, and Sharon Pickering. 2018. "Punishment, Globalization and Migration Control: 'Get Them the Hell out of Here.'" *Punishment and Society* 20(1): 34–53.

REFERENCES 205

Bovenverk, Frank. 2011. "On Leaving Criminal Organizations." *Crime, Law and Social Change* 55(4): 261–276.

Bowling, Ben. 2013. "Epilogue: The Borders of Punishment." In *The Borders of Punishment: Migration, Citizenship, and Social Exclusion*, edited by Katja Franko Aas and Mary Bosworth, 291–306. Oxford: Oxford University Press.

Brackeen v. Bernhardt. 937 F.3d 406 (5th Cir. 2019).

Braithwaite, John. 1989. *Crime, Shame, and Reintegration*. Cambridge: Cambridge University Press.

Braithwaite, John. 1999. "Restorative Justice: Assessing Optimistic and Pessimistic Accounts." *Crime and Justice* 25: 1–127.

Braithwaite, John. 2000. "Restorative Justice and Social Justice." *Saskatchewan Law Review* 63(1): 185–194.

Braithwaite, John. 2002. *Restorative Justice and Responsive Regulation*. Oxford: Oxford University Press.

Braithwaite, John. 2018. "Minimally Sufficient Deterrence." *Crime and Justice: A Review of Research* 47(1): 69–118.

Braithwaite, John, and Philip Pettit. 1990. *Not Just Deserts: A Republican Theory of Criminal Justice*. Oxford: Clarendon Press.

Brennan, Mariette, and Miriam Cohen. 2018. "Citizenship by Descent: How Canada's One Generation Rule Fails to Comply with International Legal Norms." *International Journal of Human Rights* 22(10): 1302–1317.

Brief of Citizenship Scholars as Amici Curiae in Support of Plaintiffs-Appellees and Affirmance. 2021. *Fitisemanu v. United States of America*, May 31, https://www.supremecourt.gov/DocketPDF/21/21-1394/226610/20220531125853185_Amicus%20Brief.pdf.

Briggs, Laura. 2020. *Taking Children: A History of American Terror*. Berkeley: University of California Press.

Brighouse, Harry, and Adam Swift. 2014. *Family Values: The Ethics of Parent-Child Relationships*. Princeton, NJ: Princeton University Press.

Brock, Gillian. 2020. *Justice for People on the Move: Migration in Challenging Times*. Cambridge: Cambridge University Press.

Brooks, Roy. 2004. *Atonement and Forgiveness: A New Model for Black Reparations*. Berkeley: University of California Press.

Brooks, Thom. 2015. "Punitive Restoration: Rehabilitating Restorative Justice." *Raisons Politiques* 59(3): 73–89.

Brooks, Thom. 2021. "Retribution." In *The Routledge Handbook of the Philosophy and Science of Punishment*, edited by Farah Focquaert, Elizabeth Shaw, and Bruce N. Waller, 18–25. New York: Routledge.

Brouwer, Jelmer. 2020. "Bordered Penality in the Netherlands: The Experiences of Foreign National Prisoners and Prison Officers in a Crimmigration Prison." *Punishment and Society* 22(5): 703–722.

Brown, Brookes. 2020. "Reciprocity Without Compliance." *Philosophy and Public Affairs* 48(4): 382–421.

Brownlee, Kimberley. 2020. *Being Sure of Each Other: An Essay on Social Rights and Freedoms*. New York: Oxford University Press.

Brunton-Smith, Ian, and Daniel McCarthy. 2017. "The Effects of Prisoner Attachment to Family on Re-entry Outcomes: A Longitudinal Assessment." *British Journal of Criminology* 57(2): 463–482.

206 REFERENCES

Brunyeel, Kevin. 2004. "Challenging American Boundaries: Indigenous People and the "Gift" of U.S. Citizenship." *Studies in American Political Development* 18(1): 30–43.

Brzozowski, Alexandra. 2020. "Foreign IS Fighters in Northeast Syrian Camps: A Ticking Time Bomb for Europe." *EURACTIV Network,* December 14. https://www.euractiv.com/section/defence-and-security/news/foreign-is-fighters-in-northeast-syrian-camps-a-ticking-time-bomb/

Buhler, Sarah. 2002. "Babies as Bargaining Chips: In Defence of Birthright Citizenship in Canada." *Journal of Law and Social Policy* 17(1): 87–114.

Budlakoti v. Canada (Citizenship and Immigration). 2015 FCA 139 (Federal Court of Appeal, Canada).

Bülow, William. 2014. "The Harms Beyond Imprisonment: Do We Have Special Moral Obligations Towards the Families and Children of Prisoners." *Ethical Theory and Moral Practice* 17(4): 1775–1789.

Bülow, William. 2019. "Retributivism and the Use of Imprisonment as the Ultimate Back-up Sanction." *Canadian Journal of Law and Jurisprudence* 32(2): 285–303.

Bülow, William, and Lars Lindblom. 2020. "The Social Injustice of Parental Imprisonment." *Moral Philosophy and Politics* 7(2): 299–320.

Bureau, Brigitte. 2020a. "Immigration Detention Centres Emptied over Fear of Possible COVID-19 Outbreaks." *CBC News,* November 10. https://www.cbc.ca/news/canada/montreal/immigration-detainees-released-covid-1.5795659

Bureau, Brigitte. 2020b. "Turned Away at Border: Pregnant Couple Stranded in New York's Coronavirus War Zone." *CBC News,* May 7. https://www.cbc.ca/news/canada/ottawa/turned-away-at-border-pregnant-couple-1.5538669 https://www.cbc.ca/news/canada/ottawa/turned-away-at-border-pregnant-couple-1.5538669

U.S. Bureau of Prisons. 2021. "COVID-19: Coronavirus Update." June 12. https://www.bop.gov/coronavirus/

U.S. Bureau of Prisons. 2022. "Inmate Race." May 14. https://www.bop.gov/about/statistics/statistics_inmate_race.jsp

Burke, Lol. 2016. "Children and Families: The Collateral Consequences of Punishment." *Probation Journal* 63(3): 251–255.

Byler, William. 1974. "Statement of William Byler, Executive Director, Association on American Indian Affairs," Indian Child Welfare Program. Hearings Before the Subcommittee on Indian Affairs, Committee on Indian and Insular Affairs, United States Senate, 93rd Congress, 2nd Session, April 8.

Cachagee, Mike. 1991. *Shingwauk Reunion: Oral Recording Transcription,* Shingwauk Fonds, Algoma University, Sault Ste. Marie, Ontario.

Cachagee, Mike. 2021. "LETTER: Indigenous Community 'Grief Stricken, Enraged' Following Kamloops Indian Residential School Discovery." *SooToday,* May 31. https://www.sootoday.com/local-news/letter-indigenous-community-grief-stricken-enraged-following-kamloops-indian-residential-school-discovery-3826060

Caldwell, Beth. 2019. *Deported Americans: Life After Deportation to Mexico.* Durham, NC: Duke University Press.

California Valley Miwok Tribe v. United States, 515 F.3d 1262 (D.C. Cir. 2008).

Cameron, Angela. 2006. "Sentencing Circles and Intimate Violence: A Canadian Feminist Perspective." *Canadian Journal of Women and the Law* 18(2): 479–512.

Campesi, Guiseppe. 2020. "Genealogies of Immigration Detention: Migration Control and the Shifting Boundaries Between the Penal and Preventive State." *Social and Legal Studies* 29(4): 527–548.

REFERENCES 207

Canada (Attorney General) v. First Nations Child and Family Caring Society of Canada. 2021 FC 969 (Federal Court of Appeal, Canada, September 29).

Canada Citizenship Act. 2021. November 23, https://laws-lois.justice.gc.ca/PDF/ C-29.pdf.

Canada Council for Refugees. 2019. *Immigration Detention and Children: Rights Still Ignored, Two Years Later.* Montreal: Canada Council for Refugees (November).

Canada Revenue Agency. 2022. "Canada Child Benefit: Who Can Apply." February 15. https://www.canada.ca/en/revenue-agency/services/child-family-benefits/canada-child-benefit-overview/canada-child-benefit-before-you-apply.html

Canadian Broadcasting Corporation (CBC) 2020. "Beyond 94: Truth and Reconciliation Commission." December 14, https://newsinteractives.cbc.ca/longform-single/beyond-94

Canton, Rob. 2017. *Why Punish: An Introduction to the Philosophy of Punishment.* Bastingstroke, U.K.: Palgrave Macmillan.

Canton, Rob, and Jane Dominey. 2020. "Punishment and Care Reappraised." In *Spaces of Care*, edited by Loraine Gelsthorpe, Perveez Mody, and Brian Sloan, 15–38. Oxford: Hart Publishing.

Capps, Randy, Michael Fix, and Jie Zong. 2016. A Profile of U.S. Children with Irregular Immigrant Parents. Washington, DC: Migration Policy Institute. https:// www.migr ationpolicy.org%2Fsites%2Fdefault%2Ffiles%2Fpublications%2FChildrenofIrregular-FactSheet-FINAL.pdf&usg=AOvVaw3y4tTQIcJc2N60Uv-S4Y1c

Carens, Joseph. 2016. "In Defense of Birthright Citizenship." In *Migration in Political Theory*, edited by Sarah Fine and Lea Ypi, 205–224. Oxford: Oxford University Press.

Caron, Fred. 2017. *Report on First Nation Border Crossing Issues.* Ottawa: Indigenous and Northern Affairs Canada, August 31. https://www.aadnc-aandc.gc.ca/eng/1506622719 017/1506622893512

Caruso, Gregg D., and Derk Pereboom. 2021. "A Non-Punitive Alternative to Retributive Punishment." In *The Routledge Handbook of the Philosophy and Science of Punishment*, edited by Farah Focquaert, Elizabeth Shaw, and Bruce N. Waller, 355–365. New York: Routledge.

Carvalho, Henrique, and Anastasia Chamberlen. 2018. "Why Punishment Pleases: Punitive Feelings in a World of Hostile Solidarity." *Punishment and Society* 20(2): 217–234.

Castellano, Marlene Brant. 2008. "A Holistic Approach to Reconciliation: Insights from Research of the Aboriginal Healing Foundation." In *From Truth to Reconciliation: Transforming the Legacy of Residential Schools*, edited by Marlene Brant Castellano, Linda Archibald, and Mike DeGagné, 383–402. Ottawa: Aboriginal Healing Foundation.

Centers for Disease Control 2022. *CDC Public Health Determination and Termination of Title 42 Order.* U.S. Centers for Disease Control and Prevention, April 1. https://www.cdc.gov/media/releases/2022/s0401-title-42.html

Chaidez, Natalie. 2016. "My Mother's Incarceration." In *Parental Incarceration: Personal Accounts and Developmental Impact*, edited by Denise Johnston and Megan Sullivan, 88–90. New York: Routledge.

Chalcraft, Edwin L. 2004. *Assimilation's Agent: My Life as a Superintendent in the Indian Boarding School System.* Edited by Cary C. Collins. Lincoln: University of Nebraska Press.

Chapman, Tim. 2017. *The Reintegration of Prisoners Engaged in Violent Extremism through Restorative Justice: Findings and Lessons from Northern Ireland.* Paris: European Forum for Urban Security.

208 REFERENCES

Charkaoui v. Canada (Citizenship and Immigration), 1 SCR 350 (Supreme Court of Canada, 2007).

Chartrand, Paul L. A. H., and John Giokas. 2002 "Defining 'The Métis People,' The Hard Case of Canadian Aboriginal Law." In *Who Are Canada's Aboriginal Peoples?*, edited by Paul L. A. H. Chartrand, 268–304. Saskatoon, SK: Purich Publishing Limited.

Chartrand, Vicki. 2019. "Unsettled Times: Indigenous Incarceration and the Links between Colonialism and the Penitentiary in Canada." *Canadian Journal of Criminology and Criminal Justice* 61(3): 67–89.

Chavez, Leo. 2017. *Anchor Babies and the Challenge of Birthright Citizenship*. Stanford, CA: Stanford University Press.

Chen, Ming Hsu. 2020. *Pursuing Citizenship in the Enforcement Era*. Stanford, CA: Stanford University Press.

Chen, Nancy. 2021. "Indigenous Americans Call for Justice Over Residential Schools." *CBS News*, July 10. https://www.cbsnews.com/news/indigenous-american-residential-schools/

Cherney, Adrian, and Kristina Murphy. 2016. "Being a 'Suspect Community' in a Post 9/11 World: The Impact of the War on Terror on Muslim communities in Australia." *Australian and New Zealand Journal of Criminology* 49(6): 480–496.

Chiao, Vincent. 2019. *Criminal Law in the Age of the Administrative State*. New York: Oxford University Press.

Chiarelli v. Canada, 1 SCR 711 (Supreme Court of Canada, 1992).

Child, Brenda J. 2021. "U.S. Boarding Schools for Indians Had a Hidden Agenda: Stealing Land." *Washington Post*, August 27. https://www.washingtonpost.com/outlook/2021/08/27/indian-boarding-schools-united-states/

Childress, James F., Ruth R. Faden, Ruth D. Gaare, Lawrence O. Gostin, Jeffrey Kahn, Richard J. Bonnie, Nancy E. Kass, Anna C. Mastroianni, Jonathan D. Moreno, and Phillip Nieburg. 2002. "Public Health Ethics: Mapping the Terrain." *Journal of Law, Medicine and Ethics* 30(2): 170–178.

Chin, Gabriel. 2012. "The New Civil Death: Rethinking Punishment in the Era of Mass Conviction." *University of Pennsylvania Law Review* 160(6): 1789–1833.

Chin, Gabriel, and Paul Finkelman. 2021. "Birthright Citizenship, Slave Trade, Legislation, and the Origins of Federal Immigration Regulation." *University of California Davis Law Review* 54(4): 2215–2265.

Choate, Peter W., Christina Tortorelli, Danielle Aalen, Jina Baek, Jessica McCarthy, Carolina Moreno, and Oomila Santhuru. 2020. "Parents With Fetal Alcohol Spectrum Disorder Within Canada's Child Protection Trials." *Canadian Family Law Quarterly* 39(3): 283–307.

Chow, Olivia. 2009. "Citizenship and Identity." 40th Parliament, 2nd Session, February 11 (15:02), p. 678.

Choy, Olivia. 2021. "Biosocial Risk Factors for Future Offending." In *The Routledge Handbook of the Philosophy and Science of Punishment*, edited by Farah Focquaert, Elizabeth Shaw, and Bruce N. Waller, 215–230. New York: Routledge.

Christian, Johanna. 2020. "Formerly Incarcerated Men's Negotiation of Family Support." In *Beyond Recidivism: New Approaches to Prisoner Reentry and Reintegration*, edited by Andrea Leverentz, Elsa Y. Chen, and Johnna Christian, 219–234. New York: NYU Press.

Christie, Nils. 1977. "Conflicts as Property." *The British Journal of Criminology* 17(1): 1–26.

Chulov, Martin. 2019. "Up to 3,000 ISIS Children Living in Extremely Dire Conditions." *The Guardian*, March 13.

REFERENCES 209

Cipriani, Don. 2016. *Children's Rights and the Minimum Age of Criminal Responsibility: A Global Perspective*. New York: Routledge.

Citizenship and Immigration v. Vavilov (Supreme Court of Canada), 2019 SCC 65.

Clark, Valerie, and Grant Duwe. 2017. "Distance Matters: Examining the Factors that Impact Prisoner Visitation in Minnesota." *Criminal Justice and Behavior* 44(2): 184–204.

Clarke, Erin. 2021. "Indigenous Women and the Risk of Reproductive Healthcare: Sterilization, Genocide, and Contemporary Population Control." *Journal of Human Rights and Social Work* 6: 144–147.

Cloud, David, Cyrus Ahalt, Dallas Augustine, David Sears, and Brie Williams. 2020. "Medical Isolation and Solitary Confinement: Balancing Health and Humanity in US Jails and Prisons During COVID-19." *Journal of General Internal Medicine* 35(9): 2738–2742.

Coates, Ken. 2015. *#Idle No More and the Remaking of Canada*. Regina: University of Regina Press.

Coates, Ta-Nehisi. 2014. "A Case for Reparations." *The Atlantic* 313(5): 54–71.

Coca-Vila, Ivó. 2020. "Our Barbarians at the Gate: On the Undercriminalized Citizenship Deprivation as a Counterterrorism Tool." *Criminal Law and Philosophy* 14(2): 149–167.

Cohen, Amy. 2019. "Moral Restorative Justice: A Political Genealogy of Activism and Neoliberalism in the United States." *Minnesota Law Review* 104(2): 889–953.

Cohen, Andrew. 2017. "Vicarious Apologies as Moral Repair." *Ratio* 30(3): 359–377.

Cohen, Daniela. 2021. "A Decolonized Citizenship Ceremony Is a Step Towards Reconciliation." *SooToday*, August 7. https://www.sootoday.com/local-news/a-deco lonized-citizenship-ceremony-is-a-step-towards-reconciliation-4199885

Cohen, Elizabeth. 2016. "When Democracies Denationalize: The Epistemological Case Against Revoking Citizenship." *Ethics and International Affairs* 30(2): 253–259.

Cohen, Elizabeth. 2018. *The Political Value of Time*. New York: Cambridge University Press.

Cohen, Elizabeth. 2020. *Illegal: How America's Lawless Immigration Regime Threatens Us All*. New York: Basic Books.

Cole, David. 1999. "Hanging With the Wrong Crowd: Of Gangs, Terrorists, and the Right to Freedom of Association." *The Supreme Court Review* 1999: 203–252.

Cole, David. 2003. "The New McCarthyism: Repeating History in the War on Terrorism." *Harvard Civil Rights—Civil Liberties Review* 38(1): 1–30.

Cole, David. 2009. "Out of the Shadows: Preventive Detention, Suspected Terrorists, and War." *California Law Review* 97(3): 693–750.

Cole, David. 2015. "The Difference Prevention Makes: Regulating Preventive Justice." *Criminal Law and Philosophy* 9(3): 501–519.

Coleman, Michael C. 1993. *American Indian Children at School, 1850–1930*. Jackson: University Press of Mississippi.

Comfort, Megan. 2007. "Punishment Beyond the Legal Offender." *Annual Review of Law and Social Sciences* 3: 271–296.

Comfort, Megan, Tasseli McKay, Justin Landwehr, Erin Kennedy, Anupa Bir, and Christine Lindquist. 2016. "The Costs of Incarceration for the Families of Prisoners." *International Journal of the Red Cross* 98(3): 783–798.

Commission of Inquiry. 2006. *Report of the Events Related to Maher Arar: Analysis and Recommendations*. Ottawa: Government of Canada.

Commonwealth of Australia. 1997. *Bringing them Home: National Inquiry into the Separation of Aboriginal and Torres Strait Islander Children from their Families*. Canberra: Commonwealth of Australia.

210 REFERENCES

Condry, Rachel. 2018. "Prisoners' Families and the Problem of Social Justice." In *Prisons, Punishment, and the Family: Towards a New Sociology of Punishment?*, edited by Rachel Condry and Peter Scharff Smith, 27–40. Oxford: Oxford University Press.

Condry, Rachel, and Shona Minson. 2020. "Conceptualizing the Effects of Imprisonment on Families: Collateral Consequences or Symbiotic Harms?" *Theoretical Criminology* 25(4): 540–558.

Cook, Joana, and Gina Vale. 2019. "From Daesh to 'Diaspora' II: The Challenges Posed by Women and Minors After the Fall of the Caliphate." *Combating Terrorism Center Sentinel* 12(6): 30–45.

Corda, Alessandro. 2019. "Dealing with Potential Terrorists within a Censure-Based Model of Sentencing." In *Penal Censure: Engagements Within and Beyond Desert Theory*, edited by Antje du Bois-Pedain and Anthony E. Bottoms, 161–183. Oxford: Hart Publishing.

Cortright, David. 2022. "Defections are Crucial to Ending Putin's War—Russian Soldiers Looking For a Way Out Need Support." *Waging Nonviolence*, April 22. https://waging nonviolence.org/2022/04/defections-russian-soldiers-crucial-to-end-putins-war-ukraine/

Correctional Service Canada. 2021. "Testing of Inmates in Federal Correctional Institutions for COVID-19." January 22. https://www.csc-scc.gc.ca/001/006/001 006-1014-en.shtml

Cosh, Colby. 2019. "Vancouver's Birth Tourism Issue Could Soon Become Ottawa's Problem." May 17. https://vancouversun.com/opinion/colby-cosh-vancouvers-birth-tourism-issue-could-soon-become-ottawas-problem/wcm/d98841f7-a124-4636-9c5c-ec0f7deeb705

Coulthard, Glen Sean. 2014. *Red Skin, White Masks: Rejecting the Colonial Politics of Recognition*. Minneapolis: University of Minnesota Press.

Coverdale, Helen Brown. 2021. "Caring and the Prison in Philosophy, Policy and Practice: Under Lock and Key." *Journal of Applied Philosophy* 38(3) (July): 415–430.

Creating Law Enforcement Accountability & Responsibility (CLEAR) Project. 2013. *Mapping Muslims: NYPD Spying and Its Impact on American Muslims*. New York City: CUNY School of Law.

Cunneen, Chris, and Julia Grix. 2004. *The Limitations of Litigation in Stolen Generations Cases*. Canberra: Australian Institute of Aboriginal and Torres Islander Studies.

Curry, Bill, and Andrea Woo. 2021. "Trudeau Says Sorry to B.C. First Nation for Tofino Beach Vacation." *Globe and Mail*, October 3. https://www.theglobeandmail.com/polit ics/article-trudeau-apologizes-to-bc-first-nation-after-travelling-to-tofino-beach/

Daigneault, Bernice. 2018. "Residential School Survivor Pens Open Letter to Pope After Pontiff's Decision not to Apologize." *CBC News*, April 17. https://www.cbc.ca/news/ canada/saskatchewan/open-letter-pope-francis-residential-school-survivor-apology-1.4621962

Daniels v. Canada (Indian Affairs and Northern Development). [2016] 1 SCR 99 (Supreme Court of Canada).

Darcy, Shane. 2007. *Collective Responsibility and Accountability under International Law*. Leiden: Brill.

Dauvergne, Catherine. 2016. *The New Politics of Immigration and End of Settler Societies*. New York: Cambridge University Press.

Davis, Angela Y. 2005. *Abolition Democracy: Beyond Prisons, Empire and Torture*. New York: Seven Stories Press.

REFERENCES   211

Davis, Angela Y. 2016. *Freedom is a Constant Struggle*. Chicago: Haymarket Books.

Dearen, Jason, and Garance Burke. 2020. "Pence Ordered Borders Closed After CDC Experts Refused." *AP News*, October 3. https://apnews.com/article/virus-outbreak-pandemics-public-health-new-york-health-4ef0c6c5263815a26f8aa17f6ea490ae

De Coensel, Stéphanie. 2020. "Incitement to Terrorism: The Nexus Between Causality and Intent and the Question of Legitimacy—A Case Study of the European Union, Belgium and the United Kingdom." In *Human Dignity and Human Security in Times of Terrorism*, edited by Christophe Paulussen and Martin Scheinin, 269–298. The Hague: T.M.C. Asser Press.

De Leon, Justin. 2016. "Lakota Experiences of Security: Self and Social." Phd diss., University of Delaware.

De Massol de Rebetz, Roxane and Maartje van den Woude. 2020. "Marianne's Liberty in Jeopardy? A French Analysis on Recent Counterterrorism Legal Developments." *Critical Studies on Terrorism* 13(1): 1–23.

Deitch, Michele, Alycia Welch, William Bucknall, and Destiny Moreno. 2020. *COVID and Corrections: A Profile of COVID Deaths in Custody in Texas*. November. Austin, TX: Lyndon B. Johnson School of Public Affairs.

Dellinger, Walter. 1995. "Societal and Legal Issues Surrounding Children Born in the United States to Illegal Alien Parents." Joint Hearing before the Subcommittee on Immigration and Claims and the Subcommittee on the Constitution of the Committee on the Judiciary. House of Representatives, 104th Congress, 1st Session (December 13), pp. 77–82.

Demleitner, Nora V. 2014. "Types of Punishment." In *The Oxford Handbook of Criminal Law*, edited by Markus Dubber and Tatjana Hornle, 941–963. New York: Oxford University Press.

Department of Health and Human Services (United States). 2020. "Order Suspending Introduction of Persons From a Country Where a Communicable Disease Exists." March 20, *Federal Register* 85(57): 16567.

Department of Housing and Urban Development v. Rucker, 535 U.S. 125 (2002).

Department of the Interior (United States). 2021. *Secretary Haaland Announces Federal Indian Boarding School Initiative*. June 22. https://www.doi.gov/pressreleases/secret ary-haaland-announces-federal-indian-boarding-school-initiative

Department of Justice (Canada). 2018. *Spotlight on Gladue: Challenges, Experiences, and Possibilities in Canada's Criminal Justice System*. Ottawa: Department of Justice, Research and Statistics Division. https://www.justice.gc.ca/eng/rp-pr/jr/gladue/p3.html

Department of Justice (Canada). 2021. *News Release: Government of Canada advances implementation of the United Nations Declaration on the Rights of Indigenous Peoples Act*. December 10. https://www.canada.ca/en/department-justice/news/2021/12/governm ent-of-canada-advances-implementation-of-the-united-nations-declaration-on-the-rights-of-indigenous-peoples-act.html

Department of Justice and Equality (Ireland). 2019. Citizenship Based on a Great-Grandparent Born in Ireland. http://www.inis.gov.ie/en/INIS/Pages/citizenship-great grandparent-born-Ireland-b

Dhillon, Jaskiran. 2017. *Prairie Rising: Indigenous Youth, Decolonization, and the Politics of Intervention*. Toronto: University of Toronto Press.

Dickerson, Caitlin. 2020. "Parents of 545 Children Separated at the Border Can't Be Found." *New York Times*, October 21. https://www.nytimes.com/2020/10/21/us/migr ant-children-separated.html

212 REFERENCES

Dickson, Janice. 2018. "Scheer Defends Birthright Policy, Says Ending 'Birth Tourism' is Objective." *Toronto Star*, August 27. https://www.thestar.com/news/canada/2018/08/27/scheer-defends-birthright-policy-says-ending-birth-tourism-is-objective.html

Diplock, William. 1972. *Commission on Legal Procedures to Deal with Terrorist Activities in Northern Ireland*. London: Her Majesty's Stationery Office.

Doherty, Ben. 2020. "Australian Mother of Five Stripped of Citizenship, Leaving Two Children Potentially Stateless." *The Guardian*, January 17. https://www.theguardian.com/world/2020/jan/18/australian-mother-of-five-stripped-of-citizenship-leaving-two-children-potentially-stateless

Donohue, Laura K. 2008. *The Cost of Counterterrorism: Power, Politics and Liberty*. New York: Cambridge University Press.

Douglas, Heather, and Tamara Walsh. 2013. "Continuing the Stolen Generations: Child Protection Interventions and Indigenous People." *International Journal of Children's Rights* 21(1): 59–87.

Douglas, Heather, and Tamara Walsh. 2015. "Mandatory Reporting of Child Abuse and Marginalised Families." In *Mandatory Reporting Laws and the Identification of Severe Child Abuse and Neglect*, edited by Ben Matthews and Douglas C. Bross, 491–512. New York: Springer Publishing.

Drumbl, Mark A. 2012. *Reimagining Child Soldiers in International Law and Policy*. New York: Oxford University Press.

Duby-Muller, Virginie. 2019. "Proposition de Loi: Visant à Supprimer la Protection Consulaire Française pour les Dijhadistes de Nationalité Française." *Assemblé Nationale*, No. 2518, December 17. http://www.assemblee-nationale.fr/dyn/15/textes/l15b2518_proposition-loi.pdf.

Dubinsky, Karen. 2010. *Babies Without Borders: Adoption and Migration Across the Americas*. Toronto: University of Toronto Press.

Duchaine, Gabrielle. 2021. "Accoucher la Peur au Ventre." *La Presse*, May 15. https://www.lapresse.ca/actualites/2021-05-15/les-deux-solitudes/accoucher-la-peur-au-ventre.php

Duff, Antony. 2003. "Restoration and Retribution." In *Restorative Justice and Criminal Justice: Competing or Reconcilable Paradigms?*, edited by Andrew von Hirsch, Julian V. Roberts, and Anthony E. Bottoms, 43–60. Oxford: Hart Publishing.

Duff, R. A. 2018. *The Realm of Criminal Law*. Oxford: Oxford University Press.

Dumbrava, Costica. 2018. "Bloodlines and Belonging: Time to Abandon Ius Sanguinis?" In *Debating Transformations of National Citizenship*, edited by Rainer Bauböck, 73–81. Cham, Switzerland: Springer Publishing.

Dwyer, Dialynn. 2020. "Harvard Epidemiologist Warns That Stigma Around COVID-19 Breaks Down Public Health Efforts." *Boston.com*, November 13. https://www.boston.com/news/coronavirus/2020/11/13/julia-marcus-coronavirus-stigma

Dyck, Lillian Eva, and Dennis Glen Paterson. 2016. *Border Crossing Issues and the Jay Treaty*. Ottawa: Standing Senate Committee on Aboriginal Peoples.

Edelman, Adam. 2018. "Trump Vows to End Birthright Citizenship with an Executive Order. Speaker Ryan Says No Way." *NBC News*, October 30. https://www.nbcnews.com/politics/immigration/trump-wants-end-birthright-citizenship-executive-order-n926081

Edkins, Vanessa A. 2019. "Collateral Consequences and Disenfranchisement." In *A System of Pleas: Social Science's Contributions to the Real Legal System*, edited by Vanessa A. Edkins and Allison D. Redlich, 168–186. New York: Oxford University Press.

REFERENCES   213

Effendi, Rena. 2019. "Almost 10,000 Children of Islamic State Live in Perilous Limbo in Syrian Camps." *Wall Street Journal*, December 31. https://www.wsj.com/articles/alm ost-10-000-children-of-islamic-state-live-in-perilous-limbo-in-syrian-camps-1157 7735072

Eisenberg, Avigail. 2018. "The Challenges of Structural Injustice to Reconciliation: Truth and Reconciliation in Canada." *Ethics and Global Politics* 11(1): 22–30.

Eisler, Peter, Linda So, Ned Parker, and Brad Heath. 2020. "Death Sentence: The Hidden Coronavirus Toll in U.S. Jails and Prisons." *National Post*, May 18. https://nationalpost. com/pmn/health-pmn/death-sentence-the-hidden-coronavirus-toll-in-u-s-jails-and-prisons

Ekins, Richard, Patrick Hennessey, Khalid Mahmood, and Tom Tugendhat. 2018. *Aiding the Enemy: How and Why to Restore the Law of Treason*. London: Policy Exchange.

Elk v. Wilkins. (112 U.S. 94), 1884 (U.S. Supreme Court).

Elkouri, Rima. 2021. "Une « Alerte Bébé » Injuste." *La Presse*, May 21. https://www.lapre sse.ca/actualites/chroniques/2021-05-21/une-alerte-bebe-injuste.php

Emory, Allison Dwyer, Lenna Nepomnyaschy, Maureen R. Waller, Daniel P. Miller, and Alexandra Haralampoudis. 2020. "Providing After Prison: Nonresident Fathers' Formal and Informal Contributions to Children." *Russell Sage Foundation Journal of the Social Sciences* 6(1): 84–112.

Eneas, Bryan. 2021. "Muskeg Lake Cree Nation Moves Forward With Plan to Take Control of Community's Child and Family Services." *CBC News*, February 14. https://www.cbc. ca/news/canada/saskatchewan/muskeg-lake-cree-nation-self-managed-child-family-services-1.5913632

Engster, Daniel. 2015. *Justice, Care and the Welfare State*. Oxford: Oxford University Press.

Enriquez, Laura. 2020. *Of Love and Papers: How Immigration Policy Affects Romance and Family*. Berkeley: University of California Press.

Erfani, Parsa, Nishant Uppal, Caroline H. Lee, Ranit Mishori, and Katherine R. Peeler. 2021. "COVID-19 Testing and Cases in Immigration Detention Centers, April-August 2020." *Journal of the American Medical Association* 325(2): 182–184.

Escudero, Rafael. 2014. "Road to Impunity: The Absence of Transitional Justice Programs in Spain." *Human Rights Quarterly* 36(1): 123–146.

Espindola, Juan. 2021. "Compensatory Justice and the Wrongs of Deportation." *Critical Review of International Social and Political Philosophy*, May 4. https://doi.org/10.1080/ 13698230.2021.1922852

European Union. 2017. "Directive (EU) 2017/541 of the European Parliament and of the council of 15 March 2017 on Combating Terrorism." March 15. https://eur-lex.europa. eu/legal-content/EN/TXT/PDF/?uri=CELEX:32017L0541&from=EN

Evans, Margaret. 2021. "Canadian Mothers in ISIS Detention Camp Fear Their Children Are Being Judged on the Actions Of Their Parents." *CBC News*, March 18. https://www. cbc.ca/news/world/syria-detention-camps-canadian-women-children-1.5953524

Ewald, Alec C. 2002. "Civil Death: The Ideological Paradox of the Criminal Disenfranchisement Law in the United States." *Wisconsin Law Review* 2002(5): 1045–1132.

Executive Office of the Presidency. 2023. *Statement of Administration Policy*. January 30. https:// www.whitehouse.gov/wp-content/uploads/2023/01/SAP-H.R.-382-H.J.-Res.-7.pdf.

Fabricant, M. Chris. 2011. "War Crimes and Misdemeanors: Understanding Zero Tolerance Policing as a Form of Collective Punishment and Human Rights Violation." *Drexel Law Review* 3(2): 373–414.

214 REFERENCES

Fallinger, Marie. 2006. "Lessons Unlearned: Women Offenders, the Ethics of Care, and the Promise of Restorative Justice." *Fordham Urban Law Journal* 33(2): 487–526.

Fassin, Didier. 2018. *The Will to Punish*. New York: Oxford University Press.

Favaro, Avis, Elizabeth St. Philip, and Alexandra Mae Jones. 2021. "Indigenous Families Disproportionately Affected by 'Birth Alerts'; B.C. lawsuit Seeks Damages." *CTV News*, October 31. https://www.ctvnews.ca/canada/indigenous-families-disproportionately-affected-by-birth-alerts-b-c-lawsuit-seeks-damages-1.5646384

Fauci, Anthony. 2021. "Interview with Dana Bash." *CNN State of the Union Transcript*, October 3. https://transcripts.cnn.com/show/sotu/date/2021-10-03/segment/01

Fear-Seagal, Jacqueline. 2016. "The History and Reclamation of a Sacred Space: The Indian School Cemetery." In *Carlisle Indian Industrial School: Indigenous Histories, Memories and Reclamations*, edited by Jacqueline Fear-Seagal and Susan D. Rose, 152–184. Lincoln: University of Nebraska Press.

Fear-Seagal, Jacqueline, and Susan D. Rose. 2016. *Carlisle Indian Industrial School: Indigenous Histories, Memories and Reclamations*. Lincoln: University of Nebraska Press.

Feeley, Malcolm M. 2020. "Criminal Justice as Regulation." *New Criminal Law Review* 23(1): 113–138.

Feinberg, Joel. 1968. "Collective Responsibility." *Journal of Philosophy* 65(12): 674–688.

Feinberg, Joel. 1970. *Doing and Deserving*. Princeton, NJ: Princeton University Press.

Ferracioli, Luara. 2022. *Liberal Self-Determination in a World of Migration*. Oxford: Oxford University Press.

Ferguson, Andrew G. 2017. "Policing Predictive Policing." *Washington University Law Review* 94(5): 1109–1189.

Fieser, Ezra K. 2009. "Guatemala Confronts One of Its Largest Businesses: Adoptions." *Institute of Current World Affairs Letters* (November).

Finkeldey, Jessica G., and Christopher R. Dennison. 2020. "Multilevel Effects of Parental Incarceration on Adult Children's Neighborhood Disadvantage." *Social Problems* 67(1): 113–130.

Finley, Joanne Smith. 2021. "Why Scholars and Activists Increasingly Fear a Uyghur Genocide in Xinjiang." *Journal of Genocide Research* 23(3): 348–370.

Finnis, John. 2007. "Nationality, Alienage, and Constitutional Principle." *Law Quarterly Review* 123(3): 417–445.

Firpo, Christina, and Margaret Jacobs. 2018. "Taking Children, Ruling Colonies: Child Removal and Subjugation in Australia, Canada, French Indochina, and the United States, 1870–1950s." *Journal of World History* 29(4): 529–562.

First Nations Child and Family Caring Society of Canada. 2021. *Our Statement on Canada's Decision to Appeal the Compensation Decision (2019 CHRT 39)*. October 29. https://fncaringsociety.com/sites/default/files/oct_29_2021_appeal_statement.pdf

Fisher, Daren, and Laura Dugan. 2019. "Sociological and Criminological Explanations of Terrorism." In *Oxford Handbook on Terrorism*, edited by Erica Chenoweth, Richard English, Andreas Gofas, and Stathis N. Kalyvas, 163–176. New York: Oxford University Press.

Fisher, Kirsten. 2013. *Moral Accountability and International Criminal Law: Holding Agents of Atrocity Accountable to the World*. New York: Routledge.

Fitisemanu v. United States. 2021. U.S. Tenth Circuit Court of Appeals (June 15).

Fitzgerald, David. 2008. *A Nation of Emigrants*. Berkeley: University of California Press.

REFERENCES 215

Flanders, Chad. 2014. "Can Retributivism Be Saved." *Brigham Young University Law Review* 2014(2): 309–362.

Fleming, Sean. 2020. *Leviathan on a Leash: A Theory of State Responsibility*. Princeton, NJ: Princeton University Press.

Fletcher, Bill. 1981. *Shingwauk Reunion: Oral Recording Transcription*, Shingwauk Fonds, Algoma University, Sault Ste. Marie, Ontario, July 4. 16:18–23:50.

Fletcher, George P. 2004. "Collective Guilt and Collective Punishment." *Theoretical Inquiries in Law* 5: 163–178.

Fletcher, George P. 2020. *The Grammar of the Criminal Law*. Oxford: Oxford University Press.

Fletcher, Laurel E. 2019. "What International Transitional Justice Can Offer U.S. Social Justice Movements." *Northern Kentucky Law Review* 46(2): 132–142.

Fong Yue Ting v. United States. 1893 (149 U.S. 698).

Fontaine, Philip. 2010. *Broken Circle: The Dark Legacy of Indian Residential Schools: A Memoir*. Surrey, BC: Heritage House Publishing.

Fontaine, Philip, and Aimée Craft. 2016. *A Knock on the Door: The Essential History of Residential Schools from the Truth and Reconciliation Commission of Canada*. Winnipeg, MB: University of Manitoba Press.

Forester, Brett. 2021. "Ottawa Claims It Has 'No Duty to Compensate' Thousands of First Nations Families Who Were Denied Essential Services: Court Documents." *APTN News*, June 4. https://www.aptnnews.ca/national-news/ottawa-claims-no-duty-to-compensate-first-nations-families-class-action/

Frank v. Canada (Attorney General), Supreme Court of Canada, (2019 SCC 1).

Franko, Katja. 2019. *The Crimmigrant Other: Migration and Penal Power*. New York: Routledge.

Freckelton, Alan. 2022. "Could Canada Abolish Birthright Citizenship?" *Journal of International Migration and Integration* 23(2): 701–732.

Funk, Cory, and Erin Brohman. 2020. "Review Finds No Evidence Birth Alerts Improve Child Safety." *CBC News*, January 30. https://www.cbc.ca/news/canada/manitoba/birth-alerts-manitoba-child-welfare-1.5446706.

Gailberger, Jade. 2020. "Spy Agency Wants Terror Laws Extended." *The Australian*, September 23. https://www.theaustralian.com.au/breaking-news/spy-agency-wants-terror-laws-extended/news-story/cd83bc9574642bf7a6be61693eacf7cf

García Hernández, César Cuauhtémoc. 2014. "Immigration Detention as Punishment." *UCLA Law Review* 61(5): 1347–1414.

García Hernández, César Cuauhtémoc. 2017. "Abolishing Immigration Prisons." *Boston University Law Review* 97(1): 245–300.

García, Uriel J. 2022. "Judge Blocks Biden Administration from Lifting Public Health Order used to Quickly Expel Migrants." *Texas Tribune*, May 20. https://www.texastrib une.org/2022/05/20/title-42-border-judge-ruling-migrants/

Garrett, Paul Michael. 2017. "Excavating the Past: Mother and Baby Homes in the Republic of Ireland." *British Journal of Social Work* 47(2): 358–374.

Garvey, Stephen. 2003. "Restorative Justice, Punishment and Atonement." *Utah Law Review* 2003(1): 303–317.

Garza v. Hagan. 2017. 874 F.3d. 735. (U.S. Court of Appeals for the District of Columbia).

Gaucher, Megan, and Lindsay Larios. 2020. "Birth Tourism and the Demonizing of Pregnant Migrant Women." *Policy Options*, January 17. https://policyoptions.irpp.

216 REFERENCES

org/magazines/january-2020/birth-tourism-and-the-demonizing-of-pregnant-migr
ant-women/

Gaynes, Elizabeth, and Tanya Krupat, 2018. "Minimizing the Impact of Parental Incarceration."
In *Decarcerating America*, edited by Ernest M. Drucker, 179–199. New York: New Press.

Gender Equity in Indian Registration Act. 2010. Statutes of Canada, Third Session,
Fortieth Parliament, 59 Elizabeth II 2010. December 15. https://laws-lois.justice.gc.ca/
PDF/2010_18.pdf.

Gerson, Pedro. 2022. "Embracing Crimmigration to Curtail Immigration Detention." *UC
Irvine Law Review* 12(4): 1209–1240.

Gerver, Mollie. 2022. "The Case for Permanent Residency for Frontline Workers."
American Political Science Review 116(1): 87–100.

Gheaus, Anca. 2018. "Children's Vulnerability and Legitimate Authority Over Children."
Journal of Applied Philosophy 35(S1): 60–75.

Gheaus. Anca. 2021. "Childhood: Value and Duties." *Philosophy Compass*, October
8. https//doi.org/10.1111/phc3.12793

Gibney, Matthew. 2013. "Should Citizenship Be Conditional? The Ethics of
Denationalization." *Journal of Politics* 75(3): 646–658.

Gibney, Matthew. 2017. "Denationalization." In *The Oxford Handbook of Citizenship*, edited by Ayelet Shachar, 358–382. Oxford: Oxford University Press.

Gibney, Matthew. 2020a. "Denationalisation and Discrimination." *Journal of Ethnic and
Migration Studies* 46(12): 2551–2568.

Gibney, Matthew. 2020b. "Banishment and the Pre-History of Legitimate Expulsion
Power." *Citizenship Studies* 46(3): 277–300.

Gilmore, Ruth Wilson. 2007. *Golden Gulag: Prisons, Surplus, Crisis, and Opposition in
Globalizing California*. Berkeley: University of California Press.

Glaze, Lauren E., and Laura M. Maruschak. 2010. *Parents in Prison and their Minor
Children*. Washington, DC: Bureau of Justice Statistics.

Goetze, Catherine. 2022. "When the State Shatters Families. The US Family Separation
Policy of 2018, Cruelty and Patrimonial Sovereignty." *Global Studies Quarterly* 2(2): 1–10.

Goffman, Alice. 2014. *On the Run*. Princeton, NJ: Princeton University Press.

Golash, Deidre. 2005. *The Case Against Punishment*. New York: NYU Press.

Gonzalez, Juan. 2011. *Harvest of Empire*, 2nd ed. New York: Penguin Books.

Gooch, Carly. 2021. "Covid Immigration Changes has Mother Wondering When She'll
Be with Her Family Again." *Stuff.co.nz*, January 25. https://www.stuff.co.nz/national/
124006320/covid-immigration-changes-has-mother-wondering-when-shell-be-
with-her-family-again

Goodyear, Sheena. 2022. "Pope's Apology Must be Followed by Concrete Action, Says
Anishinaabe Advocate." *CBC Radio*, April 4. https://www.cbc.ca/radio/asithappens/
as-it-happens-friday-edition-1.6405332/pope-s-apology-must-be-followed-by-concr
ete-action-says-anishinaabe-advocate-1.6405619

Gover, Kirsty. 2014. "When Tribalism Meets Liberalism: Human Rights and Indigenous
Boundary Problems in Canada." *University of Toronto Law Journal* 64(2): 206–242.

Gover, Kristy. 2015. "Settler–State Political Theory, 'CANZUS' and the UN Declaration
on the Rights of Indigenous Peoples." *European Journal of International Law*
26(2): 345–373.

Government Accountability Office. 2005. *Indian Child Welfare Act: Existing Information
on Implementation Issues Could Be Used to Target Guidance and Assistance to States*.
April. Washington, DC: U.S. Government Accountability Office.

REFERENCES   217

Government of Canada. 2019. Delivering on Truth and Reconciliation Commission Calls to Action. 2019. *Justice—Call to Action #30*. Ottawa: Crown-Indigenous Relations and Northern Affairs Canada. September 5. https://www.rcaanc-cirnac.gc.ca/eng/152450 2695174/1557513515931

Government of Canada. 2020. *Truth and Reconciliation Commission of Canada*. Ottawa: Crown and Indigenous Relations and Northern Affairs Canada.

Government of Canada. 2022. *Quarantine or Isolation*. March 8. https://travel.gc.ca/tra vel-covid/travel-restrictions/isolation

Government of Manitoba. 2020. *Manitoba to End The Use of Birth Alerts*. January 31. https://news.gov.mb.ca/news/index.html?item=46808&posted=2020-01-31

Government of New Brunswick. 2021. *New Brunswick Ends Birth Alert Practice in Support of Reconciliation*. October 29. https://www2.gnb.ca/content/gnb/en/news/news_rele ase.2021.10.0762.html

Graham, Lorie. 2008. "Reparations, Self-Determination, and the Seventh Generation." *Harvard Human Rights Law Journal* 21(1): 47–103.

Grand Council of the Crees. 1998. *Never Without Consent: James Bay Crees' Stand Against Forcible Inclusion Into an Independent Quebec*. Nemaska, Quebec: Grand Council of the Crees/Eeyou Istchee.

Granja, Rafaela. 2016. "Beyond Prison Walls: The Experiences of Prisoners' Relatives and Meanings Associated with Imprisonment." *Probation Journal* 63(3): 273–292.

Grant, Tavia. 2021a. "Catholic Church Ran Most of Canada's Residential Schools, Yet Remains Largely Silent About Their Devastating Legacy." *Globe and Mail*, June 5. https://www.theglobeandmail.com/canada/article-catholic-church-ran-most-of-canadas-residential-schools-yet-remains/

Grant, Tavia. 2021b. "Archbishop Won't Commit to Asking Pope for Residential School Apology." *Globe and Mail*, June 30. https://www.theglobeandmail.com/canada/article-archbishop-wont-commit-to-asking-pope-for-residential-school-apology/

Grauwiler, Peggy, and Linda Mills. 2004. "Moving Beyond the Criminal Justice Paradigm: A Radical Restorative Justice Approach to Intimate Abuse." *Journal of Sociology and Social Welfare* 31(1): 49–69.

Griffith, Andrew. 2018. "Hospital Stats Show Birth Tourism Rising in Major Cities." *Policy Options*, November 22. https://policyoptions.irpp.org/magazines/november-2018/hospital-stats-show-birth-tourism-rising-in-major-cities/

Griffith, Andrew. 2021. "Birth Tourism in Canada Dropped Sharply Once the Pandemic Began." *Policy Options*, December 16. https://policyoptions.irpp.org/magazines/december-2021/birth-tourism-in-canada-dropped-sharply-once-the-pande mic-began/

Gros, Hanna. 2017. *Invisible Citizens*. Toronto: University of Toronto Faculty of Law.

Gros, Hanna, and Yolanda Song. 2016. *No Life for a Child: A Roadmap to End Immigration Detention of Children and Family Separation*. Toronto: University of Toronto Faculty of Law, 2016.

Guru, Surinder. 2012. "Under Siege: Families of Counter-Terrorism." *British Journal of Social Work* 42(6): 1151–1173.

H.C. 7015/02, *Ajuri v. IDF Commander in West Bank*, 3 Sept. 2002. http://versa.cardozo. yu.edu/sites/default/files/upload/opinions/Ajuri%20v.%20IDF%20Commander%20 in%20West%20Bank_0.pdf

Haaland, Debra. 2021. *Memorandum: Federal Indian Boarding School Initiative*. June 22. Washington, DC: U.S. Department of the Interior, https://www.doi.gov/sites/doi.gov/

files/secint-memo-esb46-01914-federal-indian-boarding-school-truth-initiative-2021-06-22-final508-1.pdf.

Hacker, Daphna. 2017. *Legalized Families in the Era of Bordered Globalization.* Cambridge: Cambridge University Press.

Haebich, Anna. 2000. *Broken Circles: Fragmenting Indigenous Families 1800–2000.* North Freemantle, Western Australia: Freemantle Press.

Hagan, John, and Ronit Dinovitzer. 1999. "Collateral Consequences of Imprisonment for Children, Communities and Prisoners." *Crime and Justice* 26: 121–162.

Hager, Mike, and Carrie Tait. 2021. "Cowessess First Nation Discovers Hundreds of Unmarked Graves at Former Residential School Site." *Globe and Mail,* June 23. https://www.theglobeandmail.com/canada/british-columbia/article-saskatchewan-first-nation-discovers-hundreds-of-unmarked-graves-at/

Hahn, Hayley, Johanna Caldwell, and Vandha Sinha. 2020. "Applying Lessons from the U.S. Indian Child Welfare Act to Recently Passed Federal Child Protection Legislation in Canada." *International Indigenous Policy Journal* 11(3): 1–30.

Haitiwaji, Gulbahar, and Rozenn Morgat. 2021. "'Our Souls Are Dead': How I Survived a Chinese 'Re-Education' Camp for Uighurs." *The Guardian,* January 12. https://www.theguardian.com/world/2021/jan/12/uighur-xinjiang-re-education-camp-china-gulbahar-haitiwaji

Hall, Anthony J. 2003. *The American Empire and the Fourth World.* Montreal: McGill-Queen's University Press.

Hallevy, Gabriel. 2013. *The Right to be Punished.* New York: Springer.

Hamlin, Rebecca. 2021. *Crossing: How We Label and React to People on the Move.* Stanford, CA: Stanford University Press.

Hand, Carol, Judith Hankes, and Toni House. 2012. "Restorative Justice: The Indigenous Justice System." *Contemporary Justice Review* 15(4): 449–467.

Handoll, John. 2006. "Ireland." In *Acquisition and Loss of Nationality, Volume 2: Country Analyses,* edited by Rainer Baubock, Eva Ersbøll, Kees Groenendijk, and Harald Waldrauch, 289–328. Amsterdam: Amsterdam University Press.

Hanington, Deni. 2020. "From the Inside Out: Effects of Parental Incarceration on Children." *Canadian Journal of Family and Youth* 12(2): 36–47.

Haney López, Ian. 2006. *White by Law,* 10th Anniversary ed. New York: NYU Press.

Happold, Matthew. 2005. *Child Soldiers in International Law.* Manchester, UK: Manchester University Press.

Harp, Kathi L.H., and Amanda M. Bunting. 2020. "The Racialized Nature of Child Welfare Policies and the Social Control of Black Bodies." *Social Politics* 27(2): 258–281.

Harpaz, Yossi. 2013. "Rooted Cosmopolitans: Israelis with a European Passport: History, Property, Identity." *International Migration Review* 47(1): 166–206.

Harpaz, Yossi. 2019. *Citizenship 2.0.: Dual Nationality as a Global Asset.* Princeton, NJ: Princeton University Press.

Harper, Stephen. 2008. *Prime Minister Harper offers Full Apology on Behalf of Canadians for the Indian Residential Schools System.* Ottawa: Government of Canada, June 11.

Harper, Karen Brooks. 2023. "Gov. Greg Abbott Says He Won't Give Up COVID-Era Power Until Texas Lawmakers Ban Vaccine Mandates, Strengthen Border." *Texas Tribune,* January 26. https://www.texastribune.org/2023/01/26/texas-abbott-covid-mandates-immigration/.

Hart, H. L. A. 1968. *Punishment and Responsibility.* Oxford: Oxford University Press.

REFERENCES 219

Hatz, Sophia. 2020. "Selective or Collective? Palestinian Perceptions of Targeting in House Demolition." *Conflict Management and Peace Science* 37(5): 515–535.

Hawks, Laura, Steffie Woolhandler, and Danny McCormick. 2020. "COVID-19 in Prisons and Jails in the United States." *JAMA Internal Medicine*, April 28, E1–E2. https://jama network.com/journals/jamainternalmedicine/fullarticle/2765271

Hay, Travis. 2019. "Foreclosing Accountability: The Limited Scope of the Seven Youth Inquest in Thunder Bay, Ontario." *Canadian Review of Social Policy* 78: 1–24.

Healy, Jack. 2021. "Tribal Elders Are Dying From the Pandemic, Causing a Cultural Crisis for American Indians." *New York Times*, January 12. https://www.nytimes.com/2021/ 01/12/us/tribal-elders-native-americans-coronavirus.html

Heffernan, William C. 2019. *Rights and Wrongs: Rethinking the Foundations of Criminal Justice.* Cham, Switzerland: Palgrave Macmillan.

Heidbrink, Lauren. 2019. "Youth Navigate Deportation." In *Illegal Encounters: The Effect of Detention and Deportation on Young People*, edited by Deborah A. Boehm and Susan J. Terrio, 135–146. New York: NYU Press.

Hernandez, Joe. 2021. "Minnesota AG Keith Ellison Calls Chauvin Sentence a Moment Of Real Accountability." *NPR News*, June 25. https://www.npr.org/sections/trial-over-killing-of-george-floyd/2021/06/25/1010419654/keith-ellison-derek-chauvin-sente nce-accountability-george-floyd

Herrera, Jack. 2021. "Biden Brings Back Family Separation—This Time in Mexico." *Politico*, March 20. https://www.politico.com/news/magazine/2021/03/20/border-fam ily-separation-mexico-biden-477309

Hester, Torrie. 2015. "Deportability and the Carceral State." *Journal of American History* 102(1): 141–151.

Hill, Max. 2017. *UK Building Bridges Programme: Community Roundtables: A Report on the Aftermath of the Terrorist Attacks in London and Manchester.* London: Forward Thinking.

Hill, Peter D. 2010. *Marine Migrants: Program Strategy for the Next Arrival.* Ottawa: Canada Border Services Agency. https://web.archive.org/web/20190509182945/https://ccr web.ca/sites/ccrweb.ca/files/atip-cbsa-sun-sea-strategy-next-arrival.pdf

Hipolito, Chad. 2021. "The Kamloops Residential School's Unmarked Graves: What We Know About the Children's Remains, and Canada's Reaction So Far." *Globe and Mail*, May 31. https://www.theglobeandmail.com/canada/british-columbia/article-kamlo ops-residential-school-mass-graves-215-children-explainer/

Hirsch, Bertram. 1974. "Statement of Bertram Hirsch, Staff Attorney, Association of American Indian Affairs." Indian Child Welfare Program. Hearings Before the Subcommittee on Indian Affairs, Committee on Indian and Insular Affairs, United States Senate, 93rd Congress, 2nd Session, April 8.

Hofman, Michiel. 2019. "I'm a Humanitarian. Don't Prosecute Me for Doing My Job." *The New Humanitarian*, November 12. https://www.thenewhumanitarian.org/opinion/ 2019/11/12/humanitarian-aid-Dutch-counter-terror-law

Holder v. Humanitarian Law Project, 561 U.S. 1 (2010).

Holloway, Kari. 2021. "I'm for Abolition. And Yet I Want the Capitol Rioters in Prison." *The Nation*, February 4. https://www.thenation.com/article/society/prison-abolition-capitol-riot/

Hong, Kari E. and Philip L. Torrey. 2019. "What Matter of Soram Got Wrong: 'Child Abuse' Crimes that May Trigger Deportation Are Constantly Evolving and Even Target Good Parents." *Harvard Civil Rights-Civil Liberties Law Review Amicus Blog.* https://

harvardcrcl.org/what-matter-of-soram-got-wrong-child-abuse-crimes-that-may-trigger-deportation-are-constantly-evolving-and-even-target-good-parents/

Honohan, Iseult. 2018. "Limiting the Transmission of Family Advantage: Ius Sanguinis With an Expiration Date." In *Debating Transformations of National Citizenship*, edited by Rainer Bauböck, 131–135. Cham, Switzerland: Springer Publishing.

Hooks, Gregory, and Bob Libal. 2020. *Hotbeds of Infection: How ICE Detention Contributed to the Spread of COVID-19 in the United States*. Washington, DC: Detention Watch Network.

Hopper, Simon. 2020. "The Parents Treated as Terrorists for Trying to Save Their Son." *Middle East Eye*, February 14. https://www.middleeasteye.net/news/islamic-state-syria-saving-jack-letts-parents-terrorists-british-police

Horton, Sarah. 2016. *They Leave Their Kidneys in the Fields: Illness, Injury, and Illegality Among U.S. Farmworkers*. Berkeley: University of California Press.

Hoskins, Zachary. 2019. *Beyond Punishment: A Normative Account of the Collateral Consequences of Conviction*. New York: Oxford University Press.

Hough, Maegan. 2019. "The Harms Caused: A Narrative of Intergenerational Responsibility." *Alberta Law Review* 56(3): 841–880.

Hough, Maegan. 2020. "Taking Responsibility for Intergenerational Harms: Indian Residential Schools Reparations in Canada." *Northern Review* 50: 137–178. https://doi.org/10.22584/nr50.2020.006.

Houle, France, and Karine Mac Allister. 2022. "Human Smuggling Under Canadian Refugee Law: Protecting a System, Not Persons." In *Law and Migration in a Changing World*, edited by Marie-Claire Foblets and Jean-Yves Carlier, 181–207. Cham: Springer Nature Switzerland AG.

Houry, Nadim. 2019. "The 'Unreturned': Dealing with the Foreign Fighters and Their Families who Remain in Syria and Iraq." In *Militant Jihadism: Today and Tomorrow*, edited by Serafettin Pektas and Johan Leman, 59–82. Leuven: Leuven University Press.

Hudson, Graham. 2018. "The Mis-Uses of Analogy: Constructing and Challenging Crimmigration in Canada." In *The Criminalization of Migration: Context and Consequences*, edited by Idil Atak and James C. Simeon, 37–70. Montreal: McGill-Queens's University Press.

Hudson, Graham, and David MacDonald. 2012. "The Genocide Question and Residential Schools in Canada." *Canadian Journal of Political Science* 45(2): 427–449.

Hughes, Sara. 2021. "Flint, Michigan, and the Politics of Safe Drinking Water in the United States." *Perspectives on Politics* 19(4): 1219–1232.

Human Rights Watch. 2021. *"I Didn't Feel Like a Human in There" Immigration Detention in Canada and its Impact on Mental Health* (June). Washington, DC: Human Rights Watch.

Humphreys, Adrian. 2021. "Quarantine Hotels on Trial as Federal Court Hears Constitutional Challenge of COVID Restrictions." *National Post*, June 1. https://nationalpost.com/news/canada/quarantine-hotels-on-trial-as-federal-court-hears-constitutional-challenge-of-covid-restrictions

Hunt, Greg. 2022. "Australia's Biosecurity Emergency Pandemic Measures to End." *Australia Department of Health*, March 25. https://www.health.gov.au/ministers/the-hon-greg-hunt-mp/media/australias-biosecurity-emergency-pandemic-measures-to-end

REFERENCES 221

Hurst, Allison. 2020. "Loophole Allows Cross-Border Families to Continue to Meet at Peace Arch Park." *CTV News*, June 29. https://bc.ctvnews.ca/loophole-allows-cross-border-families-to-continue-to-meet-at-peace-arch-park-1.5005030

Husak, Douglas. 2008. *Overcriminalization: The Limits of the Criminal Law.* Oxford: Oxford University Press.

Husak, Douglas. 2010. "Lifting the Cloak: Preventive Detention as Punishment." *San Diego Law Review* 48(4): 1173–1204.

Imai, Shin, and Kathryn Gunn. 2018. "Group Identity, Self-Determination, and Relations with States, Indigenous Belonging: Membership and Identity in the UNDRIP: Articles 9, 33, 35, and 36." In *The UN Declaration on the Rights of Indigenous Peoples: A Commentary*, edited by Jessie Hohmann and Marc Weller, 213–246. New York: Oxford University Press.

Immigration and Customs Enforcement (United States). 2021. "COVID ICE Detainee Statistics by Facility." June 11. https://www.ice.gov/coronavirus

Immigration, Refugees and Citizenship Canada. 2019. *Citizenship Grants: Statelessness.* https://www.canada.ca/en/immigration-refugees-citizenship/corporate/publicati ons-manuals/operational-bulletins-manuals/canadian-citizenship/grant/statelessn ess.html

Immigration, Refugees, and Citizenship Canada. 2021. *Guide 5772—Application to Sponsor Parents and Grandparents.* https://www.canada.ca/en/immigration-refugees-citizenship/services/application/application-forms-guides/guide-5772-application-sponsor-parents-grandparents.html

Immigration, Refugees, and Citizenship Canada. 2022. *Canada-Ukraine Authorization for Emergency Travel.* March 22. https://www.canada.ca/en/immigration-refugees-citi zenship/news/2022/03/canada-ukraine-authorization-for-emergency-travel.html.

Immigration, Refugees, and Citizenship Canada. 2023. *The Oath of Citizenship/Le Serment de Citoyenneté.* January 30. https://www.canada.ca/en/immigration-refugees-citizenship/corporate/publications-manuals/discover-canada/read-online/oath-citi zenship.html.

In Re Gault, 387 U.S. 1, 1967.

In re Interest of Angelica L. and Daniel L. 767 N.W.2d 74 (Supreme Court of Nebraska, June 26, 2009)

In re the Adoption of C.M.B.R., a Minor. No. SC91141 (Supreme Court of Missouri, January 25, 2011). https://www.aclu-mo.org/sites/default/files/field_documents/ opinion012511.pdf

Indigenous Services Canada. 2021. "Confirmed Cases of COVID-19." October 22. https:// www.sac-isc.gc.ca/eng/1598625105013/1598625167707

INS v. Lopez-Mendoza, 468 U.S. 1032, 1984.

Isaac, Calvin. 1978. Indian Child Welfare Act of 1978. Hearings Before the Subcommittee on Indian Affairs, Committee on Indian Affairs and Public Lands, United States House of Representatives, 95th Congress, 2nd Session, February 9, pp. 190–198.

Iskikian, Anna. 2019. "The Sentencing Judge's Role in Safeguarding the Parental Rights of Incarcerated Individuals." *Columbia Journal of Law and Social Problems* 53(1): 133–166.

Irving, Helen. 2019. "The Concept of Allegiance in Citizenship Law and Revocation." *Citizenship Studies* 23(4): 372–387.

Jaccoud, Mylène. 1999. "Les Cercles de Guérison et les Cercles de Sentence Autochtones au Canada." *Criminologie* 32(1): 79–104.

222 REFERENCES

Jackson, Leonie B. 2022. *The Monstrous and the Vulnerable*. Oxford: Oxford University Press.

Jacobs, Margaret. 2014. *A Generation Removed: The Fostering and Adopting of Indigenous Children in the Postwar World*. Lincoln: University of Nebraska Press.

Jacobs, Margaret D. 2018. "Seeing Like a Settler Colonial State." *Modern American History* 1(2): 257–270.

Jaffer, Nabeelah. 2019. "Teenage Terrorists Aren't Lost Forever." *Foreign Policy*, February 28. https://foreignpolicy.com/2019/02/28/teenage-terrorists-arent-lost-forever/#

Jaghai, Sangita, and Laura Van Waas. 2020. "Stripped of Citizenship, Stripped of Dignity? A Critical Exploration of Nationality Deprivation as a Counter-Terrorism Measure." In *Human Dignity and Human Security in Times of Terrorism*, edited by Christophe Paulussen and Martin Scheinin, 153–180. The Hague: T.M.C. Asser Press.

James, Michael. 2022. "Spanish Citizenship and Responsibility for the Past: The Case of the Sephardim, Moriscos, and Saharawis." *Politics, Groups and Identities* 10(4): 536–557.

Jamison, Melissa A. 2008. "The Sins of the Father: Punishing Children in the War on Terror." *University of La Verne Law Review* 29: 88–151.

Jervis, Rick. 2023. "Grandmothers, Grandchildren Separated at the Border, Despite Move to Reunite Migrant Families." *USA Today*, January 30. https://www.usatoday.com/story/news/nation/2023/01/23/us-immigration-migrant-children-grandparents-separated/11088510002/.

Jiménez, Marina. 2006. "For Muslims, Guilt by Association." *Globe and Mail*, September 8. https://www.theglobeandmail.com/news/national/for-muslims-guilt-by-associat ion/article18172921/

John Hopkins Coronavirus Resource Center. 2022. *Cases and Mortality by Country*. June 13. https://coronavirus.jhu.edu/data/mortality

Johnson, Daniel. 2019. *Majority Staff Report: Court-Mandated "Catch and Release" of Apprehended Families Incentivizes Illegal Immigration*. Washington, DC: U.S. Senate Committee on Homeland Security and Governmental Affairs. January 10. https://www.hsgac.senate.gov/media/majority-media/majority-staff-report-court-manda ted-catch-and-release-of-apprehended-families-incentivizes-illegal-immigration

Johnston, Denise, and Megan Sullivan. 2016. *Parental Incarceration: Personal Accounts and Developmental Impact*. New York: Routledge.

Jones, Alexi, Michele Deitch, and Alycia Welch. 2022. *Canary in the Coal Mine: A Profile of Staff COVID Deaths in the Texas Prison System*. Austin, TX: Lyndon B. Johnson School of Public Affairs.

Jones, Martha S. 2018. *Birthright Citizens: A History of Race and Rights in Antebellum America*. New York: Cambridge University Press.

Joppke, Christian. 2010. *Citizenship and Immigration*. Malden, MA: Polity Press.

Joppke, Christian. 2021. *Neoliberal Nationalism*. New York: Cambridge University Press.

Jordán Wallace, Sophia, and Chris Zepeda-Millán. 2020. *Walls, Cages, and Family Separation*. New York: Cambridge University Press.

Kanno-Youngs, Zolan. 2020. "Trump Moves to Block Visas for Pregnant Women on 'Birth Tourism.'" *New York Times*, January 23. https://www.nytimes.com/2020/01/23/us/politics/trump-travel-ban-pregnant-women.html

Kanno-Youngs, Zolan. 2021. "Mexican Law Halts U.S. From Turning Back Some Migrant Families." *New York Times*, February 4. https://www.nytimes.com/2021/02/04/us/polit ics/mexico-united-states-border-immigration.html

Kansas v. Hendricks, 521 U.S. 346 (1997)

Kanstroom, Daniel. 2000. "Deportation, Social Control, and Punishment: Some Thoughts About Why Hard Laws Make Bad Cases." *Harvard Law Review* 113(8): 1890–1935.

Kanthor, Rebecca. 2022. "'My Daughter Was Alone in the Hospital for 5 Days.' Chinese Parents Protest Child Separation for COVID-19." *Time*, April 12. https://time.com/6166032/shanghai-covid-child-separation/

Kapoor, Nisha, and Kasia Narkowicz. 2019. "Unmaking Citizens: Passport Removals, Preemptive Policing and the Reimagining of Colonial Governmentalities." *Ethnic and Racial Studies* 42(16): 45–62.

Kaufman, Emma. 2015. *Punish and Expel. Border Control, Nationalism, and the New Purpose of the Prison*. Oxford: Oxford University Press.

Kaufman, Emma. 2019. "Segregation by Citizenship." *Harvard Law Review* 132(5): 1380–1444.

Kaufman, Kelsey. 2020. "Why Jails Are Key to Flattening the Curve of Coronavirus." *The Appeal*, March 13. https://theappeal.org/jails-coronavirus-covid-19-pandemic-flattening-curve/

Kennedy v. Mendoza-Martinez, 372 U.S. 144 (1963).

Kennedy-Pipe, Caroline. 2004. *The Origins of the Present Troubles in Northern Ireland.* London: Routledge.

Kenney, Jason. 2012. "Protecting Canada's Immigration System Act, Bill C-31, Second Reading." March 6, 15:30.

Keon, Wilbert J. 2008. "Citizenship Act—Bill to Amend—Second Reading," 39th Parliament, 2nd Session. *Debates of the Senate (Hansard)* 144(38): 1519–1531.

Kershaw, Paul. 2005. *Carefair: Rethinking the Rights and Responsibilities of Citizenship.* Vancouver: University of British Columbia Press.

Kerwin, Donald, Daniela Alulema, Michael Nicholson, and Robert Warren. 2020. "Statelessness in the United States: A Study to Estimate and Profile the US Stateless Population." *Journal of Migration and Human Security* 8(2): 150–213.

Keung, Nicholas. 2021. "Its Critics Call it 'Birth Tourism.' But is the Practice Real? COVID-19 Is Providing Clues." *Toronto Star*, December 16. https://www.thestar.com/news/canada/2021/12/16/its-critics-call-it-birth-tourism-but-is-the-practice-real-covid-19-is-providing-clues.html

Khosrokhavar, Farhad. 2017. *Radicalization: Why Some People Choose the Path of Violence.* New York: New Press.

Khosrokhavar, Farhad. 2021. *Jihadism in Europe.* Oxford: Oxford University Press.

Kindy, Kimberly, Miroff, Nick, and Maria Sacchetti. 2019. "Trump Says Ending Family Separation Practice Was a 'Disaster' That Led to Surge in Border Crossings." *Washington Post*, April 28. https://www.washingtonpost.com/politics/trump-says-ending-family-separation-practice-was-a-disaster-that-led-to-surge-in-border-crossings/2019/04/28/73e9da14-69c8-11e9-a66d-a82d3f3d96d5_story.html

King, Desmond, and Jennifer Page. 2018. "Towards Transitional Justice: Black Reparations and the End of Mass Incarceration." *Ethnic and Racial Studies* 41(4): 739–758.

Kingston, Lindsey. 2019. *Fully Human: Personhood, Citizenship and Rights.* Oxford: Oxford University Press.

Kirkup, Kristy. 2020. "Truth and Reconciliation Commissioners Call for Governments, Canadians to Renew Commitments Five Years On." *Globe and Mail*, December 15. https://www.theglobeandmail.com/politics/article-truth-and-reconciliation-commissioners-call-for-governments-canadians/

Kirkup, Kristy. 2021. "Human Rights Tribunal Findings on Indigenous Children Unreasonable: Government Lawyer." *Globe and Mail*, June 14. https://www.theglobe

andmail.com/politics/article-human-rights-tribunal-findings-on-indigenous-child ren-unreasonable/

Kleinig, John. 2012. *Punishment and Desert*. The Hague: Martinus Nijhoff.

Klocker, Cornelia. 2020. *Collective Punishment and Human Rights Law: Addressing Gaps in International Law*. New York: Routledge.

Knopf, Alison. 2018. "Children of Incarcerated Citizens: Change System to Reduce Trauma." Brown University Child and Adolescent Behavior Letter (November): 3–4.

Knudsen, Else Marie. 2019. "La Curieuse Invisibilité des Enfants de Détenus dans la Politique Canadienne de Justice Pénale." *Criminologie* 52(1): 177–202.

Kordan, Bohdan, and Craig Steven Mahovsky. 2004. *A Bare and Impolitic Right: Internment and Ukrainian-Canadian Redress*. Montreal: McGill-Queen's University Press.

Korematsu v. United States 1944, 323 U.S. 214.

Krähenmann, Sandra. 2019. "Challenges Posed by Foreign Fighters." In *How International Law Works in Times of Crisis*, edited by George Ulrich and Ineta Ziemele, 40–58. New York: Oxford University Press.

Kramer, Andrew E. 2019. "Kazazhstan Welcomes Women Back from the Islamic State, Warily," *New York Times*, August 10, http://www.nytimes.com/2019/08/10/world/eur ope/kazazhstan-women-islamic-state-deradicalization.html.

Kramer, Matthew H. 2011. *The Ethics of Capital Punishment: A Philosophical Investigation of Evil and Its Consequences*. New York: Oxford University Press.

Krasner, Stephen. 1999. *Sovereignty: Organized Hypocrisy*. Princeton, NJ: Princeton University Press.

Kronick, Rachel, and Cécile Rousseau. 2015. "A Critical Discourse Analysis of the Parliamentary Debates on the Mandatory Detention of Migrant Children in Canada." *Journal of Refugee Studies* 28(4): 1–26.

Kukathas, Chandran. 2021. *Immigration and Freedom*. Princeton, NJ: Princeton University Press.

Kuo, Susan S., and Benjamin Means. 2021. "A Corporate Law Rationale for Reparations." *Boston College Law Review* 62(3): 799–850.

Labman, Shauna. 2019. *Crossing Law's Border: Canada's Refugee Resettlement Program*. Vancouver: UBC Press.

Lacey, Nicola. 2016. *In Search of Criminal Responsibility*. New York: Oxford University Press.

Lakhani, Nina. 2021. "Indigenous Americans dying from Covid at twice the rate of white Americans." *The Guardian*, February 4.

Lamond, Grant. 2000. "The Coerciveness of Law." *Oxford Journal of Legal Studies* 20(1): 39–62.

Landertinger, Laura. 2021. "Settler Colonialism and the Canadian Child Welfare System." In *Routledge Companion to Sexuality and Colonialism*, edited by Chelsea Schields and Dagmar Herzog, 136–144. London: Routledge.

Laufer, William S., and Hughes, Robert. 2021. "Justice Undone." *American Criminal Law Review* 58(1): 155–204.

Lavi, Shai. 2010. "Punishment and the Revocation of Citizenship in the United Kingdom, United States, and Israel." *New Criminal Law Review* 13(2): 404–426.

Lavi, Shai. 2011. "Citizenship Revocation as Punishment: On the Modern Duties of Citizens and their Criminal Breach." *University of Toronto Law Journal* 61(4): 783–810.

Layton-Henry, Zig, and Czarina Wilpert. 2003. *Challenging Racism in Britain and Germany*. Basingstoke, U.K.: Palgrave Macmillan.

REFERENCES 225

Le Bot, Olivier, Xavier Phillipe. 2017. "Les Réponses Juridiques aux Attentats Terroristes du 13 novembre 2015 à Paris: de la Déclaration de l'État d'Urgence à la Révision Constitutionnelle Abandonnée." *Annuaire International de Justice Constitutionnelle* 32: 43–57.

Leach, Brittney R. 2022. "At the Borders of the Body Politic: Fetal Citizens, Pregnant Migrants, and Reproductive Injustices in Immigration Detention." *American Political Science Review* 116(1): 116–130.

Lederer, Edith. 2021. "UN Urges Countries to Repatriate 27,000 Children from Syria." *The Independent*, January 30. https://www.independent.co.uk/news/world/syria-refugee-children-repatriation-b1795120.html

Lee, Damien. 2019. "Adoption Constitutionalism: Anishinaabe Citizenship Law at Fort William First Nation." *Alberta Law Review* 56(3): 785–816.

Lee, Hedwig, Tyler McCormick, Margaret Hicken, and Christopher Wildeman. 2015. "Racial Inequalities in Connectedness to Imprisoned Individuals in the United States." *Du Bois Review* 12(2): 269–282.

Leebaw, Bronwyn. 2003. "Legitimation or Judgment: South Africa's Restorative Approach to Transitional Justice." *Polity* 36(1): 23–51.

Lenard, Patti Tamara. 2018. "Democratic Citizenship and Denationalization," *American Political Science Review* 112(1): 99–111.

Lenard, Patti Tamara. 2020. *How Should Democracies Fight Terrorism?* Cambridge: Polity Press.

Lenard, Patti Tamara. 2021. "The Ethics of Sanctuary Policies in Liberal Democratic States." In *The Political Philosophy of Refuge*, edited by David Miller and Christine Strahele, 231–250. Oxford: Oxford University Press.

Les Républicains. 2020. "Lutte Contre l'Islamisme." https://republicains.fr/nos-propositions/lutte-contre-islamisme/

Levanon, Liat. 2019. "Reflective Censure: Punishment and Human Development." In *Penal Censure: Engagements Within and Beyond Desert Theory*, edited by Antje du Bois-Pedain and Anthony E. Bottoms, 41–68. Oxford: Hart Publishing.

Levine, Kay, and Volkan Topalli. 2019. "Process as Intergenerational Punishment." In *The Legal Process and the Promise of Justice*, edited by Rosan Greenspan, Hadar Aviram, and Jonathan Simon, 55–71. New York: Cambridge University Press.

Levinson, Daryl. 2003. "Collective Sanctions." *Stanford Law Review* 56(2): 345–428.

Lewis, Nicole. 2020. "They Don't Care: Families of the Incarcerated Fear the Worst as Coronavirus Spreads." *The Marshall Project*, March 26. https://www.themarshallproject.org/2020/03/26/they-don-t-care-families-of-the-incarcerated-fear-the-worst-as-coronavirus-spreads

Li, Enshen. 2021. "In the Name of Prevention? Policing 'Social Dangerousness' Through Arrest in China." *Social and Legal Studies* 30(4): 581–604.

Libell, Henrik Pryser. 2020. "ISIS Wife's Return to Norway Divides Government." *New York Times*, January 20. https://nyti.ms/2NJI10B

Lindskoog, Carl. 2018. *Detain and Punish*. Gainesville: University of Florida.

Lippke, Richard. 2007. *Rethinking Imprisonment*. Oxford: Oxford University Press.

Lippke, Richard. 2008. "No Easy Way Out: Dangerous Offenders and Preventive Detention." *Law and Philosophy* 27(4): 383–414.

Lippke, Richard. 2017. "Punishment Drift: The Spread of Penal Harm and What We Should Do About It." *Criminal Law and Philosophy* 11(4): 645–659.

Ljunggren, David. 2009. "Every G20 Nation Wants to be Canada, Insists PM." *Reuters*, September 25. https://www.reuters.com/article/columns-us-g20-canada-advantages-idUSTRE58P05Z20090926

226 REFERENCES

Llewellyn, Jennifer. 2008 "Bridging the Gap between Truth and Reconciliation: Restorative Justice and the Indian Residential Schools Truth and Reconciliation Commission." In *From Truth to Reconciliation: Transforming the Legacy of Residential Schools*, edited by Marlene Brant Castellano, Linda Archibald, and Mike DeGagné, 185–201. Ottawa: Aboriginal Healing Foundation.

Llewellyn, Jennifer, and Daniel Philpott. 2014. *Restorative Justice, Reconciliation and Peacebuilding*. New York: Oxford University Press.

Longazel, Jamie, Jake Berman, and Benjamin Fleury-Steiner. 2016. "The Pains of Immigrant Imprisonment." *Sociology Compass* (2016): 989–998.

Lopez, Mark Hugo, Jeffrey S. Passel, and D'Vera Cohn. 2021. *Key Facts About the Changing U.S. Unauthorized Immigrant Population*. Washington, DC: Pew Research Center, April 13. https://www.pewresearch.org/fact-tank/2021/04/13/key-facts-about-the-changing-u-s-unauthorized-immigrant-population/

Lopez, Sarah. 2019. "From Penal to 'Civil': A Legacy of Private Prison Policy in a Landscape of Migrant Detention." *American Quarterly* 71(1): 105–134.

Lovelace v. Canada, Comm. 24/1977, U.N. Doc. CCPR/C/OP/1, at 10 (HRC 1979), August 14. http://www.worldcourts.com/hrc/eng/decisions/1979.08.14_Lovelace_v_Canada.htm

Lowry, David. 1976. "Internment: Detention Without Trial in Northern Ireland." *Human Rights* 5(3): 261–331.

Loyd, Anthony. 2020. "'Europe's Guantanamo' Breeds New Generation of ISIS Militants in Syria." *The Guardian*, November 25. https://www.thetimes.co.uk/article/al-hawl-camp-europes-guantanamo-breeds-new-generation-of-isis-militants-s90rs7rjz

Lu, Catherine. 2017. *Justice and Reconciliation in World Politics*. New York: Cambridge University Press.

Lucas, J. R. 1993. *Responsibility*. Oxford: Clarendon Press.

Luibhéid, Eithne. 2013. *Pregnant on Arrival: Making the Illegal Immigrant*. Minneapolis: University of Minnesota Press.

Luzon, Golan. 2016. "Challenges Shared by Restorative Justice and Strict Liability in the Absence of Mens Rea." *New Criminal Law Review* 19(4): 577–591.

Lyons, Patrick J. 2019. "Trump Wants to Abolish Birthright Citizenship, Can He Do That?" *New York Times*, August 22. https://www.nytimes.com/2019/08/22/us/birthright-citizenship-14th-amendment-trump.html

Mabie, Nora. 2021. "Montana Tribal Members, Fearing Water Contamination, Relieved as Keystone XL Pipeline Blocked." *USA Today*, January 21. https://www.usatoday.com/story/news/nation/2021/01/21/montana-tribes-react-president-biden-blocks-keystone-xl-pipeline/6659608002/

MacDonald, David. 2014. "Genocide in the Residential Schools." In *Colonial Genocide in Indigenous North America*, edited by Alexander Laban Hinton, Andrew Woolford, and Jeff Benvenuto, 306–324. Durham, NC: Duke University Press.

Macdonald, Nancy. 2016. "Canada's Prisons are the 'New Residential Schools.'" *Macleans*, February 18. https://www.macleans.ca/news/canada/canadas-prisons-are-the-new-residential-schools/

MacIntyre, Alasdair. 1984. *After Virtue*. Notre Dame, IN: University of Notre Dame Press.

MacKay, Tasseli, Megan Comfort, and Christine Lindquist. 2016. "If Family Matters: Supporting Family Relationships during Incarceration and Reentry." *Criminology and Public Policy* 15(2): 1–14.

Macklin, Audrey. 2014. "Citizenship Revocation, the Privilege to have Rights and the Production of the Alien." *Queen's Law Journal* 40(1): 1–54.

REFERENCES 227

Macklin, Audrey. 2017. "From Settler Society to Warrior Nation and Back Again." In *Citizenship in Transnational Perspective: Australia, Canada, and New Zealand*, edited by Jatinder Mann, 285–313. Cham, Switzerland: Palgrave Macmillan.

Macklin, Audrey. 2018. "The Return of Banishment: Do the New Denationalization Policies Weaken Citizenship." In *Debating Transformations of National Citizenship*, edited by Rainer Bauböck, 163–172. Cham, Switzerland: Springer Publishing.

Macklin, Audrey. 2020. "(In)Essential Bordering: Canada, COVID, and Mobility." *Frontiers in Human Dynamics* 2. https://doi.org/10.3389/fhumd.2020.609694

Macklin, Audrey, and François Crépeau. 2010. *Multiple Citizenship, Identity and Entitlement in Canada*. Montreal: Institute for Research on Public Policy.

Maculan, Elena, and Alicia Gil Gil. 2020. "The Rationale and Purposes of Criminal Law and Punishment in Transnational Contexts." *Oxford Journal of Legal Studies* 40(1): 132–157.

Major, Darren. 2021. "Residential School Survivors Call for an End to Arson Attacks on Churches." *CBC News*, July 5. https://www.cbc.ca/news/politics/residential-school-survivors-end-church-arson-1.6090511

Malakieh, Jamal. 2020. *Adult and Youth Correctional Statistics in Canada, 2018–2019*. Ottawa: Statistics Canada, December 21. https://www150.statcan.gc.ca/n1/pub/85-002-x/2020001/article/00016-eng.htm#n16-refa

Malhotra, Unjali. 2022. *The Senate Standing Committee on Human Rights: Evidence*. April 25, 17:45. https://sencanada.ca/Content/SEN/Committee/441/RIDR/55473-e.htm

Malone, Kelly Geraldine. 2021. "Politicians, Indigenous Leaders say Burning Churches not the Way to Get Justice." *CBC News*, July 1. https://www.cbc.ca/news/canada/edmonton/burning-churches-unmarked-graves-1.6087602

Manning, Rita. 2011. "Punishing the Innocent: Children of Incarcerated and Detained Parents." *Criminal Justice Ethics* 30(3): 767–787.

Manza, Jeff, and Christopher Uggen. 2006. *Locked Out: Felon Disenfranchisement and American Democracy*. New York: Oxford University Press.

Markel, Dan, Jennifer M. Collins, and Ethan J. Leib. 2009. *Privilege or Punish: Criminal Justice and the Challenge of Family Ties*. Oxford: Oxford University Press.

Martens, Kathleen. 2021. "U.S. Announces Investigation into Boarding Schools Set Up To Assimilate Native Americans." *APTN News*, June 25. https://www.aptnnews.ca/national-news/u-s-announces-investigation-into-boarding-schools-set-up-to-assimilate-native-americans/

Martin, Tara E., and Scott Wolfe. 2020. "Lead Exposure, Concentrated Disadvantage, and Violent Crime Rates." *Justice Quarterly* 37(1): 1–24.

Martín-Pérez, Alberto, and Francisco Javier Moreno-Fuentes. 2012. "Migration and Citizenship Law in Spain: Path-Dependency and Policy Change in a Recent Country of Immigration." *International Migration Review* 46(3): 625–655.

Masters, Mercedes, and Salvador Santino F. Reglime Jr. 2020. "Human Rights and British Citizenship: The Case of Shamima Begum as Citizen to Homo Sacer." *Journal of Human Rights Practice* 12(2): 341–363.

Mateos, Pablo. 2019. "The Mestizo Nation Unbound: Dual Citizenship of Euro-Mexicans and U.S.-Mexicans." *Journal of Ethnic and Migration Studies* 45(6): 917–938.

Matlow, Ryan, and Daryn Reicherter. 2019. "Reducing Protections for Noncitizen Children—Exacerbating Harm and Trauma." *New England Journal of Medicine* 380(1): 5–7.

228 REFERENCES

Matos, Yalidy. 2021. "The 'American DREAM': Understanding White Americans' Support for the DREAM Act and Punitive Immigration Policies." *Perspectives on Politics* 19(2): 422–441.

Mauer, Marc, and Ashley Ellis. 2018. *The Meaning of Life: The Case for Abolishing Life Sentences.* New York: New Press.

May, Larry. 1992. *Sharing Responsibility.* Chicago: University of Chicago Press.

Maycock, Matthew. 2022. "'Covid-19 Has Caused a Dramatic Change to Prison Life'. Analysing the Impacts of the Covid-19 Pandemic on the Pains of Imprisonment in the Scottish Prison Estate." *British Journal of Criminology* 62(1): 218–233.

Maynard, Robyn. 2019. "Black Life and Death across the U.S.- Canada Border." *Critical Ethnic Studies* 5(1–2): 124–151.

Mayson, Sandra. 2015. "Collateral Consequences and the Preventative State." *Notre Dame Law Review* 91(1): 301–362.

McAlinden, Anne Marie. 2007. *The Shaming of Sexual Offenders: Risk, Retribution and Reintegration.* Oxford: Hart Publishing.

McCandless, Commissioner of Immigration v. United States ex rel. Diabo, 25 F. 2d 71 (March 9, 1928). Third Circuit Court of Appeals, United States.

McCulloch, Daniel. 2019. "Terror Expert Wants Travel Bans Scrapped," *The Canberra Times,* July 10. https://www.canberratimes.com.au/story/6267198/terror-expert-wants-travel-bans-scrapped/?cs=14264

McCulloch, Jude, and Dean Wilson. 2015. *Pre-Crime: Pre-emption, Precaution and the Future.* New York: Routledge.

McCulloch, Jude, and Sharon Pickering. 2009. "Pre-Crime and Counterterrorism: Imagining Future Crime in the 'War on Terror.'" *British Journal of Criminology* 49(5): 628–645.

McCullough, Jolie. 2020. "Inmates Report Dangerous Practices inside the Texas Prison with the Most Coronavirus Deaths." *Texas Tribune,* June 8. https://www.texastribune.org/2020/06/08/texas-prison-coronavirus-deaths/

McGaughy, Lauren. 2021. "Prison Staff Death Toll Spikes After State Relaxes Coronavirus Precautions Behind Bars." *Dallas Morning News,* October 7. https://www.dallasnews.com/news/investigations/2021/10/07/prison-staff-death-toll-spikes-after-state-relaxes-coronavirus-precautions-behind-bars/

McGillivray, Kate. 2021. "Family Facing Deportation from Canada Says Return to Portugal 'Puts Their Lives at Risk.'" *CBC News Toronto,* February 7. https://www.cbc.ca/news/canada/toronto/family-facing-deportation-from-canada-says-return-to-portugal-puts-their-lives-at-risk-1.5902716

McGlynn, Clare, Nicole Westmarland, and Nikki Godden. 2012. "I Just Wanted Him to Hear Me: Sexual Violence and the Possibilities of Restorative Justice." *Journal of Law and Society* 39(2): 213–240.

McGregor, Russell. 2011. *Indifferent Inclusion: Aboriginal People and the Australian Nation.* Canberra: Aboriginal Studies Press.

McIvor v. Canada (Registrar of Indian and Northern Affairs), 2009 BCCA 153 (Court of Appeal for British Columbia).

McKay, Stan. 2008. "Expanding the Dialogue on Truth and Reconciliation—In A Good Way." In *From Truth to Reconciliation: Transforming the Legacy of Residential Schools,* edited by Marlene Brant Castellano, Linda Archibald, and Mike DeGagné, 101–115. Ottawa: Aboriginal Healing Foundation.

McKeen, Alex. 2021. "Drowning of Two Sisters Among Haunting Stories of B.C. Island Residential School where First Nation has Found 160 Unmarked Graves." *Toronto Star,*

July 13. https://www.thestar.com/news/canada/2021/07/13/drowning-of-two-sist ers-among-haunting-stories-of-bc-island-residential-school-where-first-nation-has-found-160-unmarked-graves.html

McKernan, Bethan. 2019. "Inside al-Hawl Camp, the Incubator for Islamic State's Resurgence." *The Guardian,* August 31. https://www.theguardian.com/world/2019/ aug/31/inside-al-hawl-camp-the-incubator-for-islamic-states-resurgence

McLeod, B.A. 2021. "The Effect of Multiple Forms of Father-Child Contact During Imprisonment on Fathers' Reports of Relationship Quality." *Corrections.* https://doi. org/10.1080/23774657.2021.1874846

McQueen, Ally. 2018. "Falling Through the Gap: The Culpability of Child Soldiers Under International Law." *Notre Dame Law Review* 94(2): 91–118.

Meadows, William C. 2017. "Native American "Warriors" in the U.S. Armed Forces." In *Inclusion in the American Military: A Force for Diversity,* edited by David E. Rohall, Morten G. Ender, and Michael D. Matthews, 83–108. Lanham, MD: Lexington Books.

Mégret, Frédéric. 2017. "Pénalité et Familles: A Propos des Victimes Collatérales de la Peine." Unpublished Paper, posted November 21. https://papers.ssrn.com/sol3/papers. cfm?abstract_id=3070297

Mégret, Frédéric. 2018. "Punir Les Coupables, Punir Leurs Familles? Le Point de Vue Canadien." *Les Cahiers de la Justice* 2018(3): 523–538.

Méheut, Constant. 2020. "France Judges Dead Jihadists but Refuses to Repatriate the Living." *New York Times,* January 26. https://www.nytimes.com/2020/01/26/world/eur ope/france-ghost-trials-isis.html.

Mendlow, Gabriel S. 2019. "The Elusive Object of Punishment." *Legal Theory* 25(2): 105–131.

Meriam, Lewis. 1928. *The Problem of Indian Administration.* Baltimore, MD: Johns Hopkins University Press.

Metatawabin, Edmund. 2014. *Up Ghost River: A Chief's Journey through the Turbulent Waters of Native History.* Toronto: Knopf Canada.

Miceli, Thomas J. 2014. "Collective Responsibility." *University of Connecticut Department of Economics Working Paper Series,* Working Paper 2013–23 (January).

Miceli, Thomas J., and Kathleen Segerson. 2007. "Punishing the Innocent Along With the Guilty: The Economics of Individual Versus Group Punishment." *Journal of Legal Studies* 36(1): 81–106.

Micheron, Hugo. 2020. " «La prison, c'est l'ENA du djihad», analyse le chercheur Hugo Micheron." *Europe 1,* January 11. https://www.europe1.fr/societe/un-etat-des-lieux-du-djihadisme-francais-la-prison-cest-lena-du-djihad-3942461

Midbøten, Arnfinn. 2019. "Dual Citizenship in an Age of Securitization: The Case of Denmark." *Nordic Journal of Migration Research* 9(3): 293–309.

Miller v. Alabama, 567 U.S 460 (2012).

Miller, David. 2007. *National Responsibility and Global Justice.* Oxford: Oxford University Press.

Miller, David. 2016. *Strangers in Our Midst.* Oxford: Oxford University Press.

Miller, David. 2021. "Selecting Refugees." In *The Political Philosophy of Refuge,* edited by David Miller and Christine Straehle, 97–113. Cambridge: Cambridge University Press.

Miller, James Rodger. 2018. *Residential Schools and Reconciliation: Canada Confronts Its History.* Toronto: University of Toronto Press.

Miller, Keva M. 2006. "The Impact of Parental Incarceration on Children: An Emerging Need for Effective Interventions." *Children and Adolescent Social Work* 23(4): 472–486.

230 REFERENCES

Miller, Robert J. 2012. "The Doctrine of Discovery." In *Discovering Indigenous Lands: The Doctrine of Discovery in the English Colonies*, edited by Robert J. Miller, Jacinta Ruru, Larissa Behrendt, and Tracey Lindberg, 1–25. Oxford: Oxford University Press.

Minson, Shona. 2020. *Maternal Sentencing and the Rights of the Child.* Cham, Switzerland: Palgrave Macmillan.

Mironova, Vera. 2020. "What to Do About the Children of the Islamic State." *Foreign Policy*, November 25. https://foreignpolicy.com/2020/11/25/islamic-state-isis-repatriation-child-victims/

Mississippi Choctaw Indian Band v. Holyfield, 490 U.S. 30 (1989).

Morin, Rebecca. 2019. "Trump Says He Directed Pompeo Not to Let ISIS Bride Back in U.S." *Politico*, February 20. https://www.politico.com/story/2019/02/20/trump-hoda-muthana-isis-1176678

Morris, Allison, and Lorraine Gelsthorpe. 2000. "Revisioning Men's Violence Against Female Partners." *The Howard Journal* 39(4): 412–428.

Mosby, Ian, and Tracey Galloway. 2017. "'Hunger Was Never Absent': How Residential School Diets Shaped Current Patterns of Diabetes Among Indigenous Peoples in Canada." *Canadian Medical Association Journal* 189(32): E1043–E1045.

Mountz, Alison, and Nancy Hiemstra. 2012. "Spatial Strategies for Rebordering Human Migration at Sea." In *A Companion to Border Studies, First Edition*, edited by Thomas Wilson and Hastings Donnan, 455–472. New York: Blackwell Publishing.

Mullin, Malone. 2021. "N.L.'s Indigenous Kids are Still Being Taken Away. But the Foster-Care System is Slowly Changing." *CBC News*, June 8. https://www.cbc.ca/news/canada/newfoundland-labrador/indigenous-child-welfare-1.6052140

Murray, Joseph. 2005. "The Effects of Imprisonment on Families and Children of Prisoners." In *The Effects of Imprisonment*, edited by Allison Liebling and Shadd Maruna, 442–462. Willan, Cullompton.

Murray, Joseph, and David P. Farrington. 2008. "The Effects of Parental Incarceration on Children." *Crime and Justice* 37(1): 133–206.

Mussell, Linda. 2020. "Intergenerational Imprisonment: Resistance and Resilience in Indigenous Communities." *Journal of Law and Social Policy* 33(1–2): 15–37.

Mustassari, Sanna. 2020. "Finnish Children or 'Cubs of the Caliphate'? *Oslo Law Review* 7(1): 22–45.

Muth, William. 2018. *Fathers, Prisons, and Family Reentry: Presencing as a Framework and Method.* Lanham, MD: Lexington Books.

Muthana v. Pompeo. 2021. U.S. District Court of Appeals for the District of Columbia.

NAACP v. Claiborne Hardware, 458 U.S. 886 (1982).

Nagy, Rosemary. 2014. "The Truth and Reconciliation Commission of Canada: Genesis and Design." *Canadian Journal of Law and Society* 29(2): 199–217.

National Inquiry into Missing and Murdered Indigenous Girls. 2019. *Reclaiming Power and Place: The Final Report of the National Inquiry into Missing and Murdered Indigenous Women and Girls.* Ottawa: Government of Canada.

Newland, Brian. 2022. *Federal Indian Boarding School Initiative: Investigative Report.* Washington, DC: United States Department of the Interior.

Nichols, Roger L. 2017. "From the Sixties Scoop to Baby Veronica: Transracial Adoption of Indigenous Children in the USA and Canada." In *International Adoption in North American Literature and Culture*, edited by Mark Shackleton, 3–26. Bastingstroke: Palgrave Macmillan.

REFERENCES   231

Niezen, Ronald. 2017. *Truth and Indignation: Canada's Truth and Reconciliation Commission on Indian Residential Schools,* 2nd ed. Toronto: University of Toronto Press.

Norris, Jesse. 2019. "Explaining the Emergence of Entrapment in Post-9/11 Terrorism Investigations." *Critical Criminology* 27(3): 467–483.

Norris, Ned. 2020. "Stop the Destruction of Tohono O'odham Lands." *High Country News,* October 30. https://www.hcn.org/issues/52.12/indigenous-affairs-borderlands-stop-the-destruction-of-tohono-oodham-lands

Nortje, Windell, and Noëlle Quénivet. 2020. *Child Soldiers and the Defence of Duress under International Criminal Law.* Cham, Switzerland: Palgrave Macmillan.

Notice of Appeal. 2021. *Canada (Attorney General) v. First Nations Child and Family Caring Society of Canada.* October 29. https://fncaringsociety.com/sites/default/files/cfn_tbd_-_agc_v_fncfcs_et_al_-_notice_of_appeal_october_29_2021.pdf

Nottebohm Case (second phase), Judgment of April 6th: I.C.J. Reports 1955, 4–65.

Nova Scotia. 2021. *Province Ending Birth Alerts.* November 30. https://novascotia.ca/news/release/?id=20211130001

Nowell v. O'Hara. 19 S.C.L. 150 (Court of Appeal of Law and Equity, South Carolina, 1833).

Nyamutata, Conrad. 2020. "Young Terrorists or Child Soldiers? ISIS Children, International Law, and Victimhood." *Journal of Conflict and Security Law* 25(2): 237–261.

Office of the Correctional Investigator (Canada). 2020. *Indigenous People in Federal Custody Surpasses 30%: Correctional Investigator Issues Statement and Challenge.* Ottawa: Government of Canada, January 21. https://www.oci-bec.gc.ca/cnt/comm/press/press20200121-eng.aspx

Office of the Correctional Investigator (Canada). 2021. *Proportion of Indigenous Women in Federal Custody Nears 50%: Correctional Investigator Issues Statement.* Ottawa: Government of Canada, December 17. https://www.oci-bec.gc.ca/cnt/comm/press/press20211217-eng.aspx

Office of the Inspector General (United States). 2021. *Review of the Department of Justice's Planning and Implementation of Its Zero Tolerance Policy and Its Coordination with the Departments of Homeland Security and Health and Human Services.* Washington, DC, Department of Justice, January 14.

Office of the Press Secretary (United States) 2014. *FACT SHEET: Immigration Accountability Executive Action.* Washington, DC: The White House. https://obamawhitehouse.archives.gov/the-press-office/2014/11/20/fact-sheet-immigration-accountability-executive-action

Office of the Texas Governor. 2022. *Governor Abbott Takes Aggressive Action To Secure The Border As President Biden Ends Title 42 Expulsions.* April 6. https://gov.texas.gov/news/post/governor-abbott-takes-aggressive-action-to-secure-the-border-as-president-biden-ends-title-42-expulsions

Oforji v. Ashcroft. 354 F.3d 609 (7th Cir. 2003).

Okafor, Obiora Chinedu. 2020. *Refugee Law After 9/11: Sanctuary and Security in Canada and the United States.* Vancouver: University of British Columbia Press.

Ontario Human Rights Commission (OHRC). 2018. *Interrupted Childhoods: Overrepresentation of Indigenous and Black Children in Ontario Child Welfare.* Toronto: Ontario Human Rights Commission.

Organick, Aliza G. 2009. "Holding Back the Tide: The Existing Indian Family Doctrine and Its Continued Denial of the Right to Culture for Indigenous Children." In *Facing*

232 REFERENCES

the Future: The Indian Child Welfare Act at 30, edited by Matthew L.M. Fletcher, Wenona T. Singel, and Kathryn E. Fort, 221–234. East Lansing: Michigan State Press.

Overmyer-Velázquez, Mark. 2018. "Out of the Fires: Peruvian Migrants in Post-Pinochet Chile." In *Global Latin(o) Americanos*, edited by Mark Overmyer-Velázquez and Enrique Sepúlveda III, 17–42. New York: Oxford University Press.

Owasu-Bempah, Akwasi, Maria Jung, Firdaous Sbaï, Andrew S. Wilton, and Fiona Kouyoumdjian. 2021. "Race and Incarceration: The Representation and Characteristics of Black People in Provincial Correctional Facilities in Ontario, Canada." *Race and Justice*. http://doi:10.1177/21533687211006461

Padilla, Alex. 2021. "Padilla, Paul, Introduce Bipartisan Bill to Protect Thousands of 'Documented Dreamers.'" *Alex Padilla, U.S. Senator For California*, September 15. https://www.padilla.senate.gov/newsroom/press-releases/padilla-paul-introduce-bip artisan-bill-to-protect-thousands-of-documented-dreamers/

Padilla v. Kentucky, 559 U.S. 356 (2011).

Palk, A. Naomi. 2015. *Rightlessness: Testimony and Redress in U.S. Prison Camps Since World War II*. Chapel Hill: University of North Carolina Press.

Palmater, Pam. 2020. "What We're Seeing in 2020 Is Idle No More 2.0." *Macleans*, September 15. https://www.macleans.ca/opinion/what-were-see ing-in-2020-is-idle-no-more-2-0/

Paperny, Anna Mehler. 2021. "Exclusive: Canada Deporting Thousands Even As Pandemic Rages." *Reuters*, January 22. https://www.reuters.com/article/us-health-coro navirus-canada-deportation/exclusive-canada-deporting-thousands-even-as-pande mic-rages-idUSKBN29R1EL

Paperny, Anna Mehler. 2022. "Pope's Apology in Canada Falls Short for Some Indigenous Survivors." *Reuters*, July 27. https://www.reuters.com/world/americas/popes-apology-canada-falls-short-some-indigenous-survivors-2022-07-27/

Paris Principles. 2007. *Principles and Guidelines on Children Associated With Armed Forces or Groups*, February: https://childrenandarmedconflict.un.org/publications/Par isPrinciples_EN.pdf.

Passel, Jeffrey, D'Vera Cohn, and John Gramlich. 2018. "Number of U.S.-Born Babies with Unauthorized Immigrant Parents Has Fallen Since 2007." *Pew Research Center*, November 1. https://www.pewresearch.org/fact-tank/2018/11/01/the-number-of-u-s-born-babies-with-unauthorized-immigrant-parents-has-fallen-since-2007/

Pasternak, Avia. 2021. *Responsible Citizens: Irresponsible States*. Oxford: Oxford University Press.

Patel, Priti. 2022. *Response from Rt Hon Priti Patel to Matthew Rycroft: Migration and Economic Development Partnership*. April 13. https://www.gov.uk/government/publi cations/migration-and-economic-development-partnership-ministerial-direction/response-from-rt-hon-priti-patel-to-matthew-rycroft-accessible

Patler, Caitlin, and Gabriela Gonzalez. 2021. "Compounded Vulnerability: The Consequences of Immigration Detention for Institutional Attachment and System Avoidance in Mixed-Immigration-Status Families." *Social Problems*. https://doi.org/10.1093/socpro/spaa069

Patler, Caitlin, and Nicholas Branic. 2017. "Patterns of Family Visitation During Immigration Detention." *Russell Sage Foundation Journal of the Social Sciences* 3(4): 18–36.

REFERENCES 233

Pemberton, Antony. 2010. "Psycho-Social Assistance." In *Assisting Victims of Terrorism: Towards a European Standard of Justice*, edited by Rianne Letschert, Ines Staiger, and Antony Pemberton, 143–170. New York: Springer.

Pereboom, Derk. 2014. *Free Will, Agency, and Meaning in Life*. Oxford: Oxford University Press.

Pereira, Ana. 2019. "Imagining a Restorative Approach to Individual Reintegration in the Context of (de)Radicalization." In *Restorative Approach and Social Innovation: From Theoretical Grounds to Sustainable Practices*, edited by Giovanni Grandi and Simone Grigoletto, 61–82. Padova: University of Padova Press.

Petiquay Barthold, Doreen. 2021. Préjugés et Discrimination Envers les Femmes Autochtones Dans les Systèmes de Santé et Services Sociaux: le Système Colonial qui se Perpétue." *Femmes Autochtones du Québec*, May 18. https://www.faq-qnw.org/wp-cont ent/uploads/2021/05/FAQ-Communiqu%C3%A9-Le-syst%C3%A8me-colonial-qui-se-perp%C3%A9tue.pdf

Pettit, Philip. 1997. "Republican Theory and Criminal Punishment." *Utilitas* 9(1): 59–79.

Pettit, Philip. 2012a. "Legitimacy and Justice in Republican Perspective." *Current Legal Problems* 65(1): 59–82.

Pettit, Philip. 2012b. *On the People's Terms: A Republican Theory and Model of Democracy*. Cambridge: Cambridge University Press.

Philips, Nickie D., and Nicholas Chagnon. 2020. "Six Months is a Joke: Carceral Feminism and Penal Populism in the Wake of the Stanford Sexual Assault Case." *Feminist Criminology* 15(1): 47–69.

Philpott, Daniel. 2006. *The Politics of Past Evil*. Notre Dame: University of Notre Dame Press.

Pierce v. Society of Sisters, 268 U.S. 510 (1925).

Plyler v. Doe, 457 U.S. 202 (1982).

Pokalova, Elena. 2020. *Returning Foreign Fighters: Threats and Challenges to the West*. Cham, Switzerland: Palgrave Macmillan.

Policy Options. 2017. "Policy Options to Respond to Border Surge of Illegal Immigration." *Department of Homeland Security*, December. https://assets.documentcloud.org/documents/5688664/Merkleydocs2.pdf

Pope Francis 2022a. *Meeting with Indigenous Peoples: First Nations, Métis and Inuit: Address of His Holiness*. Maskwacis, Alberta, July 25. https://www.vatican.va/cont ent/francesco/en/speeches/2022/july/documents/20220725-popolazioniindigene-can ada.pdf

Pope Francis. 2022b. *Meeting with Representatives of Indigenous Peoples in Canada: Address of His Holiness Pope Francis*. Vatican City: Libreria Editrice Vaticana, April 1. https:// www.vatican.va/content/francesco/en/speeches/2022/april/documents/20220401-popoli-indigeni-canada.html

Popova, Svetlana, Shannon Lange, Dennis Bekmuradov, Alanna Mihic, and Jürgen Rehm. 2011. "Fetal Alcohol Spectrum Disorder Prevalence Estimates in Correctional Systems: A Systematic Literature Review." *Canadian Journal of Public Health* 102(5): 336–340.

Porter, Catherine, and Dan Bilefsky. 2020. "Video of Arrest of Indigenous Leader Shocks Canada." *New York Times*, June 13. https://www.nytimes.com/2020/06/12/world/can ada/Allan-Adam-athabasca-police.html

234 REFERENCES

Pratt, Richard Henry. 1892. "The Advantages of Mingling Indians with Whites." In *Proceedings of the National Conference of Charities and Correction*, edited by Isabel C. Barrows, 45–59. Boston: Press of George H. Ellis.

Pratt, Richard Henry. 1964. *Battlefield and Classroom*. Edited by Robert M. Utley. New Haven, CT: Yale University Press.

Preston, Julia. 2014. "Detention Center Presented as Deterrent to Border Crossers." *New York Times*, December 15.

Price, Polly. 2017. "Jus Soli and Statelessness: A Comparative Perspective from the Americas." In *Citizenship in Question: Evidentary Birthright and Statelessness*, edited by Benjamin Lawrence and Jacqueline Stevens, 27–42. Durham, NC: Duke University Press.

Prime Minister of Australia. 2019a. "Doorstop, Perth WA, June 24." https://web.archive. org/web/20190624084552/https://www.pm.gov.au/media/doorstop-perth-wa-0

Prime Minister of Australia. 2019b. "Doorstop with the Minister for Health, Assistant Minister for Treasury and Finance, April 1." https://web.archive.org/web/20190603033 646/https://www.pm.gov.au/media/doorstop-minister-health-assistant-minister-treas ury-and-finance

Pringle, Angela Mashford, Christine Skura, Sterling Stutz, and Thilaxcy Yohathasan. 2021. *What We Heard: Indigenous Peoples and COVID-19*. Ottawa: Public Health Agency of Canada.

Public Health Agency of Canada. 2020. *New Order Makes Self-Isolation Mandatory for Individuals Entering Canada*. Ottawa: Government of Canada, https://www.canada.ca/ en/public-health/news/2020/03/new-order-makes-self-isolation-mandatory-for-indi viduals-entering-canada.html

Public Safety Canada. 2020. *Corrections and Conditional Release: Statistical Overview*. Ottawa: Government of Canada.

Puzzanchera, C., and Taylor, M. 2021. *Disproportionality Rates for Children of Color in Foster Care Dashboard*. National Council of Juvenile and Family Court Judges. https:// www.ncjj.org/AFCARS/Disproportionality_Dashboard.aspx

Quan, Douglas. 2021. "COVID-19 Scrutiny has stopped some Women Headed to Canada to Give Birth, Documents Allege." *Toronto Star*, January 27. https://www.thestar.com/ news/canada/2021/01/27/covid-19-scrutiny-has-stopped-more-women-headed-to-canada-to-give-birth-documents-allege.html

Quiggin, John. 2020. "After the Pandemic, Let's Not Keep Families Separated by Borders." *Canberra Times*, December 31. https://www.canberratimes.com.au/story/7070879/ after-the-pandemic-lets-not-keep-families-separated-by-borders/?cs=14246

R v. Bissonnette [2022], 2022 SCC 23.

R v. Ipeelee [2012], 1 SCR 433.

R v. Gladue [1999], 1 SCR 688.

R v. Powley [2003], 2 SCR 207.

R. v. Moses [1992], 71 CCC (3d) 347 (Yukon Territorial Court).

Radio-Canada. 2022. "Les Alertes à la Naissance Continuent à Thunder Bay, dit le Chef d'une Première Nation." *Radio-Canada*, April 5. https://ici.radio-canada.ca/nouvelle/ 1874132/naissance-protection-enfance-nord-ontario

Rawls, John. 1955. "Two Conceptions of Rules." *Philosophical Review* 64(1): 3–32.

Raynor, Peter, and Gwen Robinson. 2005. *Rehabilitation, Crime and Justice*. Bastingstoke, U.K.: Palgrave Macmillan.

REFERENCES   235

Reece, Rai. 2020. *Carceral Redlining: White Supremacy is a Weapon of Mass Incarceration for Indigenous and Black Peoples in Canada.* June 24. Toronto: Yellowhead Institute. https://yellowheadinstitute.org/wp-content/uploads/2020/06/carceral-redlining-yellowhead-institute-infographics.pdf

Reed-Sandoval, Amy. 2020. "Settler-State Borders and the Question of Indigenous Immigrant Identity." *Journal of Applied Philosophy* 37(4): 543–561.

Rensink, Brendan W. 2018. *Native But Foreign: Indigenous Immigrants and Refugees in the North American Borderlands.* College Station: Texas A&M University Press.

Report of the Expert of the Secretary General. 1996. *Impact of Armed Conflict on Children.* U.N. Doc. A/51/306 §38, August 26. https://www.un.org/ga/search/view_doc.asp?symbol=A/51/306

Republic of Austria (European and International Affairs). 2021. *One Year Citizenship for Descendants of Victims of the National Socialist Regime—A First Review.* August 29. https://www.bmeia.gv.at/en/the-ministry/press/news/2021/08/one-year-citizenship-for-descendants-of-victims-of-the-national-socialist-regime-a-first-review/

Response of the Churches. 2015. *Response of the Churches to the Truth and Reconciliation Commission of Canada.* June 2. https://united-church.ca/sites/default/files/trc-churches-respond.pdf

Rice, Bryan, and Anna Snyder. 2008. "Reconciliation in the Context of a Settler Society: Healing the Legacy of Colonialism in Canada." In *From Truth to Reconciliation: Transforming the Legacy of Residential Schools*, edited by Marlene Brant Castellano, Linda Archibald, and Mike DeGagné, 43–61. Ottawa: Aboriginal Healing Foundation.

Riley, Angela, and Kristen A. Carpenter. 2021. "Decolonizing Indigenous Migration." *California Law Review* 109(1): 63–139.

R.I. L-R v. Jeh Johnson et al. 80 F.Supp. 3d 164 (D.D.C. 2015).

Roach, Kent. 2000. "Changing Punishment at the Turn of the Century: Restorative Justice on the Rise." *Canadian Journal of Criminology* 42 (July): 249–280.

Roach, Kent. 2011. *The 9/11 Effect: Comparative Counter-Terrorism.* Cambridge: Cambridge University Press.

Roach, Kent. 2015. *Comparative Counter-Terrorism Law.* Cambridge: Cambridge University Press.

Robinson, Andrew. 2020. "Governments Must Not wait on Courts to Implement UNDRIP Rights Concerning Indigenous Sacred Sites: Lessons from Canada and Ktunaxa Nation v. British Columbia." *International Journal of Human Rights* 24(10): 1642–1665.

Robinson, Oliver. 2012. *Collateral Convicts: Children of Incarcerated Parents.* New York: Quaker United Nations Office.

Rodriguez, Jeremiah. 2021. "What We Know About How Many Children Died at Canada's Residential Schools." *CTV News,* May 31. https://www.ctvnews.ca/canada/what-we-know-about-how-many-children-died-at-canada-s-residential-schools-1.5450277

Rodriguez, Nancy, and Jillian J. Turanovic. 2018. "Impact of Incarceration on Families and Communities." In *Oxford Handbook of Prisons and Imprisonment*, edited by John Wooldredge and Paula Smith, 189–207. New York: Oxford University Press.

Roettger, Michael, and Susan Dennison. 2018. "Interrupting Intergenerational Offending in the Context of America's Social Disaster of Mass Imprisonment." *American Behavioral Scientist* 62(11): 1545–1561.

236 REFERENCES

Rollings, Willard Hughes. 2004. "Citizenship and Suffrage: The Native American Struggle for Civil Rights in the American West: 1830–1965." *Nevada Law Journal* 5(1): 126–140.

Roper v. Simmons, 543 U.S. 551 (2004).

Rosenberg, Mica, and Kristina Cooke. 2021. "For Asylum Advocates, Border Expulsions Strain Faith in Biden." *Reuters,* September 22. https://www.reuters.com/world/ameri cas/asylum-advocates-border-expulsions-strain-faith-biden-2021-09-22/

Rosenberg Rubins, Rottem. 2022. "Crimmigration and the Paradox of Exclusion." *Oxford Journal of Legal Studies* 42(1): 266–297.

Rosenbloom, Rachel. 2017. "From the Outside Looking In: U.S. Passports in the Borderlands." In *Citizenship in Question: Evidentiary Birthright and Statelessness,* edited by Benjamin Lawrence and Jacqueline Stevens, 132–146. Durham, NC: Duke University Press.

Rosenbloom, Rachel. 2020. "There's No Question About Harris's Citizenship. So Why Is Trump Questioning It?" *Washington Post,* August 16. https://www.washingtonpost. com/outlook/2020/08/16/theres-no-question-about-harriss-citizenship-so-why-is-trump-questioning-it/

Rudd, Kevin. 2008. *Apology to Australia's Indigenous Peoples.* Canberra: Government of Australia, February 13.

Rupnik, Frank. 2021. "'You Can't Go Back and Redact the Parts of History You Don't Like,' Says Residential School Survivor." *Soo Today,* June 22. https://www.sootoday.com/ following-up/you-cant-go-back-and-redact-the-parts-of-history-you-dont-like-says-residential-school-survivor-3880863

Ryan, Chanessa, Abrar Ali, and Christine Shawana. 2021. "Forced or Coerced Sterilization in Canada: An Overview of Recommendations for Moving Forward." *International Journal of Indigenous Health* 16(1): 275–290. https://doi.org/10.32799/ijih.v16i1.33369

Ryo, Emily. 2019. "Detention as Deterrence." *Stanford Law Review* 71 (March): 237–250.

Ryo, Emily, and Ian Peacock. 2020. "Denying Citizenship: Immigration Enforcement and Citizenship Rights in the United States." *Studies in Law, Politics and Society* 84: 43–67.

Sacchetti, Maria. 2022. "COVID Infections Surge in Immigration Detention Facilities." *Washington Post,* February 1.

Saito, Natsu Taylor. 2020. *Settler Colonialism, Race, and the Law.* New York: NYU Press.

Saito, Natsu Taylor. 2021. "Indefinite Detention, Colonialism, and Settler Prerogative in the United States." *Social and Legal Studies* 30(1): 32–65.

Salas, Denis. 2005. *La Volonté de Punir: Essai sur le Populisme Pénal.* Paris: Hachette.

Saloner, Brendan, Kalind Parish, and Julie A. Ward. 2020. "COVID-19 Cases and Deaths in Federal and State Prisons." *Journal of the American Medical Association* 324(6): 602–603.

Salyer, Lucy. 1995. *Laws as Harsh as Tigers: Chinese Immigrants and the Shaping of Modern Immigration Law.* Chapel Hill: University of North Carolina Press.

Sánchez, Sofía. 2021. "7,000+ Migrants Turned Away by the US Have Been Victims of Violent Attacks Since Biden Took Office." *Texas Public Radio,* October 22. https://www. tpr.org/border-immigration/2021-10-22/7-000-migrants-turned-away-by-the-us-have-been-victims-of-violent-attacks-since-biden-took-office

Saunders, Harry David. 1970. "Civil Death: A New Look at an Ancient Doctrine." *William and Mary Law Review* 11(4): 988–1003.

Sawatsky, Jarem. 2009. *The Ethic of Traditional Communities and the Spirit of Healing Justice.* Philadelphia: Jessica Kingsley Publishers.

REFERENCES   237

Sawyer, Wendy. 2018. "The Gender Divide: Tracking Women's State Prison Growth." *Prison Policy Initiative*, January 9. https://www.prisonpolicy.org/reports/women_overt ime.html

Sawyer, Wendy, and Peter Wagner. 2020. *Mass Incarceration: The Whole Pie 2020*. Northampton, MA: Prison Policy Initative. https://www.prisonpolicy.org/reports/pie2 020.html

Scales v. United States, 367 U.S. 203 (1961).

Schiro, Dora. 2010. "Improving Conditions of Confinement for Criminal Inmates and Immigrant Detainees." *American Criminal Law Review* 47(4): 1441–1452.

Schmid, Muriel. 2003. "The Eye of God: Religious Beliefs and Punishment in Early Nineteenth Century Prison Reform." *Theology Today* 59(4): 546–558.

Schmid, Sophia. 2019. "Taking Care of the Other: Visions of a Caring Integration in Female Refugee Support Work." *Social Inclusion* 7(2): 118–127.

Schotland, Sara. 2020. "A Plea to Apply Principles of Quarantine Ethics to Prisoners and Immigration Detainees During the COVID-19 Crisis." *Journal of Law and the Biosciences* 7(1): 1–11.

Schrag, Philip G. 2020. *Baby Jails: The Fight to End the Incarceration of Refugee Children in America*. Berkeley: University of California Press.

Schuck, Peter. 2017. *One Nation Undecided: Clear Thinking About Five Hard Issues That Divide Us*. Princeton, NJ: Princeton University Press.

Schuck, Peter, and Rogers M. Smith. 1985. *Citizenship Without Consent*. New Haven, CT: Yale University Press.

Schuck, Peter, and Rogers M. Smith. 2018. "The Question of Birthright Citizenship." *National Affairs* 36 (Summer): 50–67.

Seet, Matthew. 2021. "'Cosmopolitan Citizenship', Territorial Borders, and Bringing Denationalized Terrorists to Justice." *Journal of International Criminal Justice* 19(2): 247–274.

Sentas, Victoria. 2014. *Traces of Terror: Counter-Terrorism Law, Policing and Race*. Oxford: Oxford University Press.

Sentencing Project. 2021. *Trends in U.S. Corrections*. July. https://www.sentencingproject. org/wp-content/uploads/2021/07/Trends-in-US-Corrections.pdf

Serebrin, Jacob. 2021. "Quebec Father Blames Anti-Muslim Prejudice, Language Barrier After Baby Taken Away." *Montreal Gazette*, June 25. https://montrealgazette.com/pmn/ news-pmn/canada-news-pmn/quebec-father-blames-anti-muslim-prejudice-langu age-barriers-after-baby-taken-away/wcm/a14eab34-ce47-4f22-9d7c-d7dcf4c0be6c

Serota, Michael. 2020. "How Criminal Law Lost Its Mind." *Boston Review*, October 27. http://bostonreview.net/law-justice/michael-serota-how-criminal-law-lost-its-mind

Sessions, Jeff. 2018. "Attorney General Sessions Delivers Remarks Discussing the Immigration Enforcement Actions of the Trump Administration." May 7. https://www. justice.gov/opa/speech/attorney-general-sessions-delivers-remarks-discussing-immi gration-enforcement-actions

Shachar, Ayelet. 2009. *The Birthright Lottery*. Cambridge, MA: Harvard University Press.

Shaheen-Hussain, Samir. 2020. *Fighting for a Hand to Hold: Confronting Medical Colonialism Against Indigenous Children in Canada*. Montreal: McGill-Queens's University Press.

Shahoulian, David. 2021. *Declaration of David Shahoulian, Assistant Secretary for Border and Immigration Policy for the U.S. Department for Homeland Security in Huisha*

238 REFERENCES

Huisha v. Mayorkas. (U.S. District Court for the District of Columbia). August 7. http://cdn.cnn.com/cnn/2021/images/08/02/dhs.declaration.pdf

Shaw, Jo. 2020. *The People in Question: Citizens and Constitutions in Uncertain Times.* Bristol, U.K.: Bristol University Press.

Shaw, Jo. 2021. "Citizenship and COVID-19: Syndemic Effects." *German Law Review* 22(8): 1635–1660.

Sheahan, Frances. 2018. *Children, the Justice System, Violent Extremism, and Terrorism: An Overview of Law, Policy and Practice in Six European Countries.* Brussels: International Juvenile Justice Observatory.

Shear, Michael D., and Zolan Kanno-Youngs. 2019. "Migrant Families Would Face Indefinite Detention Under New Trump Rule." *New York Times,* August 21. https://www.nytimes.com/2019/08/21/us/politics/flores-migrant-family-detention.html

Sheikho, Kamal. 2021. "UN Calls Upon Kurdish Authorities to Ensure Safety of Al-Hol Residents, Relief Workers." *Asharq Al-Awsat,* January 23. https://english.aawsat.com/home/article/2759756/iraqi-pm-vows-baghdads-security-breach-%E2%80%98wont-be-repeated%E2%80%99

Shrout, Anelise Hanson. 2015. "A "Voice of Benevolence from the Western Wilderness": The Politics of Native Philanthropy in the Trans-Mississippi West." *Journal of the Early Republic* 35(4): 553–578.

Silva, Lahny R. 2015. "Collateral Damage: A Policy Housing Consequence of the War on Drugs." *UC Irvine Law Review* 5(4): 783–812.

Simlansky, Saul. 1994. "The Time to Punish." *Analysis* 54(1): 50–53.

Simpson, Audra. 2014. *Mohawk Interruptus: Political Life Across the Borders of Settler States.* Durham, NC: Duke University Press.

Sinha, Anita. 2022. "A Lineage of Family Separation." *Brooklyn Law Review* 87(2): 445–500.

Siskay, Bill. 2010. "Citizenship Act," House of Commons Debates, 40th Parliament, 3rd Session. 28 September (17:17). *House of Commons Debates* 145(72): 4521–4525.

Sivakumaran, Sandesh. 2010. "War Crimes Before the Special Court for Sierra Leone." *Journal of International Criminal Justice* 8(4): 1009–1034.

Slobodian, Mayana C. 2017. "Official Apology, Official Denial: Making Sense of Canada's Truth Commission." *C4eJournal: Perspectives on Ethics*: 12.

Smith, Emma. 2021. "Calls to ban birth alerts grow louder as other provinces end controversial practice," *CBC News,* February 8, https://www.cbc.ca/news/canada/nova-scotia/birth-alerts-mothers-babies-child-welfare-indigenous-women-1.5904676

Smith, Joy. 2012. "Protecting Canada's Immigration System Act, Bill C-31, Second Reading." 41st Parliament, 1st Session, March 15, 16:05.

Smith, Nicky, and Michelle Forster. 2020. "Protests in Top 25 Virus Hot Spots Ignite Fears of Contagion." *Associated Press,* June 2. https://www.usnews.com/news/us/articles/2020-06-02/protests-in-top-25-virus-hot-spots-ignite-fears-of-contagion

Smith, Rogers M. 2009. "Birthright Citizenship and the Fourteenth Amendment in 1868 and 2008." *University of Pennsylvania Journal of Constitutional Law* 11(5): 1329–1335.

Smith, Rogers M. 2015. *Political Peoplehood: The Roles of Values, Interests, and Identities.* Chicago: University of Chicago Press.

Solis, Dianne, and Allie Morris. 2021. "Are Migrants Fueling the COVID-19 Surge? 'No, This is the Pandemic of the Unvaccinated.'" *Dallas Morning News,* August 9. https://www.dallasnews.com/news/2021/08/09/pandemic-of-the-migrants-no-this-is-the-pandemic-of-the-unvaccinated/

Song, Sarah. 2018. *Immigration and Democracy.* New York: Oxford University Press.

REFERENCES 239

Song, Sarah, and Irene Bloemraad. 2022. "Immigrant Legalization: A Dilemma Between Justice and the Rule of Law." *Migration Letters*. https://doi.org/10.1093/migration/mnac014

Soulou, Katerina. 2018. "L'approche Restaurative de la Criminalité et son Application aux cas de Terrorisme." *Cahiers de la Justice* 2018 (2): 341–359.

SpearChief-Morris, Joy. 2021. "Indigenous and Black Communities Have a Shared Past of Injustice. They Deserve a Shared Future of Justice." *Globe and Mail*, May 29. https://www.theglobeandmail.com/opinion/article-indigenous-and-black-communities-have-a-shared-past-of-injustice-they/

Speckhard, Anne, and Molly Ellenberg. 2020. *PERSPECTIVE: Can We Repatriate the ISIS Children?* Washington, DC: Homeland Security Today, July 7. https://www.hstoday.us/subject-matter-areas/counterterrorism/perspective-can-we-repatriate-the-isis-children/

Spencer v. Canada (Health) 2021 FC 621, June 18. (Federal Court of Canada).

Stahn, Carsten. 2019. *A Critical Introduction to International Criminal Law*. Cambridge: Cambridge University Press.

Staiger, Ines. 2010. "Restorative Justice and Victims of Terrorism." In *Assisting Victims of Terrorism: Towards a European Standard of Justice*, edited by Rianne Letschert, Ines Staiger, and Antony Pemberton, 267–337. New York: Springer.

Standing Bear, Luther. (1933) 1978. *Land of the Spotted Eagle*. Lincoln: University of Nebraska Press.

Standing Committee on Citizenship and Immigration Canada (CIMM). 2020. "Birth on Soil." March 12. https://webcache.googleusercontent.com/search?q=cache:UVzCl ql7wtIJ:https://www.canada.ca/en/immigration-refugees-citizenship/corporate/trans parency/cimm-binders/march-12-2020/birth-on-soil.html+&cd=11&hl=en&ct= clnk&gl=ca&client=firefox-b-d

Starr, Sonja, and Lea Brilmayer. 2003. "Family Separation as a Violation of International Law." *Berkeley Journal of International Law* 21(2): 213–287.

Statistics Canada. 2018. "Data Tables, 2016 Census, Family Characteristics of Children Including Aboriginal Identity (9)." March 28. https://www12.statcan.gc.ca/census-rece nsement/2016/dp-pd/dt-td/Rp-eng.cfm?LANG=E&APATH=3&DETAIL=0&DIM= 0&FL=A&FREE=0&GC=0&GID=0&GK=0&GRP=1&PID=112124&PRID= 10&PTYPE=109445&S=0&SHOWALL=0&SUB=0&Temporal=2017&THEME= 122&VID=0&VNAMEE=&VNAMEF=

Statistics Canada. 2021. *Births 2020*. September 28. https://www150.statcan.gc.ca/n1/daily-quotidien/210928/dq210928d-eng.htm

Stevens, Jacqueline. 2010. *States Without Nations*. New York: Columbia University Press.

Stevenson, Allyson. 2020. *Intimate Integration: A History of the Sixties Scoop and the Colonization of Indigenous Kinship*. Toronto: University of Toronto Press.

Stibbe, Matthew. 2019. *Civilian Internment During the First World War*. London: Palgrave Macmillan.

Stier, Max. 1992. "Corruption of Blood and Equal Protection: Why the Sins of the Parents Should Not Matter." *Stanford Law Review* 44(3): 727–757.

Stinneford, John F. 2020. "Is Solitary Confinement a Punishment." *Northwestern University Law Review* 115(9): 9–44.

Straehle, Christine. 2016. "Vulnerability, Autonomy, and Self-Respect." In *Vulnerability, Autonomy and Applied Ethics*, edited by Christine Straehle, 33–48. New York: Routledge.

240 REFERENCES

Stubbs, Julie. 2007. "Beyond Apology: Domestic Violence and Critical Questions for Restorative Justice." *Criminology and Criminal Justice* 7(2): 169–187.

Stumpf, Juliet. 2020a. "Justifying Family Separation," *Wake Forest Law Review* 55(5): 1037–1086.

Stumpf, Juliet. 2020b. "The Terrorism of Everyday Crime." In *Crimmigrant Nations: Resurgent Nationalism and the Closing of Borders*, edited by Robert Koulish and Maartje van der Woude, 89–115. New York: Fordham University Press.

Suliman, Adela. 2022. "Alabama Woman Who Became 'ISIS Bride' Will Continue Legal Fight to Return to U.S., Lawyers Say." *Washington Post,* January 13. https://www.washingtonpost.com/nation/2022/01/13/hoda-muthana-islamic-state-alabama-supreme-court/

Sullivan, Michael. 2016. "Legalizing Parents and Other Caregivers: A Family Immigration Policy Guided by a Public Ethic of Care." *Social Politics* 23(2): 263–283.

Sullivan, Michael. 2017. "A Restorative Justice Approach to Legalising Unauthorised Immigrants." *Restorative Justice* 5(1): 70–92.

Sullivan, Michael. 2018. "Beyond Allegiance: Toward A Right to Canadian Citizenship Status." *Canadian Review of American Studies* 48(3): 327–343.

Sullivan, Michael. 2019. *Earned Citizenship*. New York: Oxford University Press.

Sullivan, Michael. 2021. "Labor Citizenship for the Twenty-First Century." *Seattle Journal of Social Justice* 19(3): 809–840.

Sullivan, Michael. 2022a. "The Border Crossed Us: Enhancing Indigenous International Mobility Rights." *Journal of Borderlands Studies*, July 18 .https://doi.org/10.1080/08865655.2022.2101140

Sullivan, Michael. 2022b. "Protecting Minorities From De Facto Statelessness: Birthright Citizenship in the United States." *Statelessness and Citizenship Review* 4(1): 66–87.

Sullivan, Michael. 2022c. "A Limited Defence of Public Health Exit Restrictions." *International Migration*, December 13. https://doi.org/10.1111/imig.13103

Sullivan, Michael, and Roger Enriquez. 2016. "The Impact of Interior Immigration Enforcement on Mixed-Citizenship Families." *Boston College Journal of Law and Social Justice* 36(1): 33–57.

Sundaram, Arya. 2020. "How Texas Jails Avoid Investigations of Inmate Deaths." *Texas Observer*, October 29. https://www.texasobserver.org/how-texas-jails-avoid-investigations-of-inmate-deaths/

Tadros, Victor. 2013. "Controlling Risk." In *Prevention and the Limits of the Criminal Law*, edited by Andrew Ashworth, Lucia Zedner, and Patrick Tomlin, 133–155. Oxford: Oxford University Press.

Tait, Carrie, Kristy Kirkup, and Menaka Raman-Wilms. 2022. "Ottawa Reaches $40 Billion Deal With First Nations Over Child Welfare." *Globe and Mail*, January 3. https://www.theglobeandmail.com/canada/article-ottawa-reaches-40-billion-deal-with-first-nations-over-child-welfare/

Talaga, Tanya. 2017. *Seven Fallen Feathers: Racism, Death, and Hard Truths in a Northern City*. Toronto: House of Anansi Press.

Tam, Theresa. 2021. *CPHO Sunday Edition: The Impact of COVID-19 on Racialized Communities*. Ottawa: Public Health Agency of Canada, February 21. https://www.canada.ca/en/public-health/news/2021/02/cpho-sunday-edition-the-impact-of-covid-19-on-racialized-communities.html

Tanasoca, Ana. 2018. *The Ethics of Multiple Citizenship*. Cambridge: Cambridge University Press.

REFERENCES   241

Taplin, Stephanie. 2017. "Prenatal Reporting to Child Protection: Characteristics and Service Responses in one Australian Jurisdiction." *Child Abuse and Neglect* 65 (March): 68–76.

Taylor, Darren. 2021. "Border Closure Taking an Emotional Toll on Local Married Couple." *Soo Today*, January 2. https://www.sootoday.com/coronavirus-covid-19-sault-ste-marie-news/border-closer-taking-an-emotional-toll-on-local-married-cou ple-3228947

Ten, Chin Liew. 1987. *Crime, Guilt and Punishment*. Oxford: Clarendon Books.

Terrorism Act 2000, United Kingdom (UK Public General Acts, 2000, Chapter 11). July 20.

Texas Band of Kickapoo Act, Public Law 97-429, January 8, 1983.

Theobald, Brianna. 2019. *Reproduction on the Reservation: Pregnancy, Childbirth, and Colonialism in the Long Twentieth Century*. Chapel Hill: University of North Carolina Press.

Thompson, Janna. 2009. *Intergenerational Justice: Rights and Responsibilities in an Intergenerational Polity*. New York: Routledge.

Thomson, Vannette. 2016. "Visiting Day." In *Parental Incarceration: Personal Accounts and Developmental Impact*, edited by Denise Johnston and Megan Sullivan, 129–131. New York: Routledge.

Tilbury, Clare. 2009. "The Over-Representation of Indigenous Children in the Australian Child Welfare System." *International Journal of Social Welfare* 18(1): 57–64.

Titshaw, Scott. 2018. "Family Matters: Modernize, Don't Abandon Ius Sanguinis." In *Debating Transformations of National Citizenship*, edited by Rainer Bauböck, 97–102. Cham, Switzerland: Springer Publishing.

Tonry, Michael. 2020a. *Doing Justice, Preventing Crime*. Oxford: Oxford University Press.

Tonry, Michael. 2020b. *Of One-Eyed and Toothless Miscreants: Making the Punishment Fit the Crime?* Oxford: Oxford University Press.

Touraut, Caroline. 2012. *La Famille à l'Épreuve de la Prison*. Paris: Presses Universitaires de la France.

Touraut, Caroline. 2019. "L'Expérience Carcérale Élargie: Une Peine Sociale Invisible." *Criminologie* 52(1): 19–36.

Towes, Vic. 2012. "Protecting Canada's Immigration System Act, Bill C-31, Second Reading." 41st Parliament, 1st Session, March 15.

Tripkovic, Milena. 2019. *Punishment and Citizenship: A Theory of Criminal Disenfranchisement*. New York: Oxford University Press.

Tripkovic, Milena. 2021. "Transcending the Boundaries of Punishment: On the Nature of Citizenship Deprivation." *British Journal of Criminology* 61(4): 1044–1065.

Tripkovic, Milena. 2022. "Renouncing Criminal Citizens: Patterns of Denationalization and Citizenship Theory." *Punishment and Society*, February 21. https://journals.sage pub.com/doi/pdf/10.1177/14624745221080705.

Tripkovic, Milena. 2023. "No Country For 'Bad' Men: Volatile Citizenship and the Emerging Features Of Global Neo-colonial Penality." *British Journal of Criminology*, January 24. https://doi.org/10.1093/bjc/azac103

Tronto, Joan. 2013. *Caring Democracy*. New York: NYU Press.

Trop v. Dulles, 356 U.S. 86 (1958).

Trump, Donald. 2017. *President Donald J. Trump's Letter to House and Senate Leaders & Immigration Principles and Policies*. October 8. Washington, DC: Office of the White House.

242 REFERENCES

Trump, Donald. 2018. *Remarks by President Trump on the Illegal Immigration Crisis and Border Security*. November 1. Washington, DC: Office of the White House.

Truth and Reconciliation Commission. 2012. *They Came for the Children: Canada, Aboriginal Peoples, and Residential Schools*. Winnipeg: University of Manitoba Press.

Truth and Reconciliation Commission. 2015a. *Canada's Residential Schools: The Final Report of the Truth and Reconciliation Commission of Canada*. Montreal: McGill-Queen's University Press.

Truth and Reconciliation Commission. 2015b. *The Survivors Speak*. Ottawa: Government of Canada.

Truth and Reconciliation Commission of Canada. 2015c. *What We Have Learned: Principles of Truth and Reconciliation*. Ottawa: Truth and Reconciliation Commission of Canada.

Truth and Reconciliation Commission of Canada. 2015d. *Calls for Action*. Ottawa: Truth and Reconciliation Commission of Canada.

Turnbull, Lorna A. 2019. "Matricentric Policy Research: Making Room for Mothers in an Inclusive Research Partnership." *Journal of the Motherhood Initiative* 10(1–2): 245–256.

Turner, Logan. 2021. "Wabaseemoong Independent Nations will have Anishinaabe law on child Welfare Start in New Year." *CBC News*, January 1. https://www.cbc.ca/news/canada/thunder-bay/wabaseemoong-child-welfare-law-1.5854482

U.K. Crown Prosecution Service. 2019. *Sally Lane and John Letts Sentenced for Sending Money to Daesh Supporting Son*. June 21. https://www.cps.gov.uk/cps/news/sally-lane-and-john-letts-sentenced-sending-money-daesh-supporting-son

U.K. Government. 2018a. *CONTEST: The United Kingdom's Strategy for Countering Terrorism*. London: United Kingdom Government Home Office. https://assets.publish ing.service.gov.uk/government/uploads/system/uploads/attachment_data/file/716 907/140618_CCS207_CCS0218929798-1_CONTEST_3.0_WEB.pdf

U.K. Government. 2018b. *Impact Assessment: Counter-Terrorism and Border Security Bill*. London: United Kingdom Government Home Office. (August 30), https://assets.pub lishing.service.gov.uk/government/uploads/system/uploads/attachment_data/file/740981/CTBS_Bill_Impact_Assessment_Lords_Introduction.pdf

U.K. Government. 2019. *Circular 004/2019: Counter-Terrorism and Border Security Act 2019*. London: United Kingdom Government Home Office. https://www.gov.uk/government/publications/circular-0042019-counter-terrorism-and-border-secur ity-act-2019/0042019-counter-terrorism-and-border-security-act-2019-accessible-version

United Church of Canada. 2014. *Statement to the Truth and Reconciliation Commission of Canada*. Edmonton, Alberta, March 28. https://united-church.ca/sites/default/files/trc-statement-2014.pdf

United Nations. 2007. *United Nations Declaration on the Right of Indigenous Peoples (UNDRIP)*. New York: United Nations General Assembly, September 13.

United Nations. 2020. *Report of the Special Rapporteur on the Rights of Indigenous Peoples, José Francisco Calí Tzay*. New York: United Nations General Assembly, July 20. https://documents-dds-ny.un.org/doc/UNDOC/GEN/N20/188/47/PDF/N2018847.pdf

United Nations. 2021. *UN Experts Call on Canada, Holy See to Investigate Mass Grave at Indigenous School*. Geneva: United Nations Office of the High Commissioner, June 4. https://www.ohchr.org/EN/NewsEvents/Pages/DisplayNews.aspx?NewsID=27141&LangID=E

REFERENCES   243

United Nations Committee Against Torture (UNCAT). 2018. *Concluding Observations on the Seventh Periodic Report of Canada*. December 5. https://tbinternet.ohchr.org/Treat ies/CAT/Shared%20Documents/CAN/CAT_C_CAN_CO_7_33163_E.pdf

United Nations Committee on the Rights of the Child. 2012. *Concluding Observations on the Combined Third and Fourth Periodic Report of Canada*. December 6. https://docume nts-dds-ny.un.org/doc/UNDOC/GEN/G12/484/87/PDF/G1248487.pdf?OpenElement

United Nations Convention on the Rights of the Child (UNCRC). 1989. Treaty Series 1577 (November): 3.

United Nations Office for the Coordination of Humanitarian Affairs (OCHA). 2020. "Syrian Arab Republic: Northeast Syria, Al Hol Camp." January 13. https://www. humanitarianresponse.info/sites/www.humanitarianresponse.info/files/documents/ files/al-hol-snapshot-sitrip-130120.pdf

United Nations Security Council Resolution 1315 (Special Court for Sierra Leone), August 14.

U.S. Census Bureau. 2022. "Quick Facts: U.S. Census Bureau." https://www.census.gov/ quickfacts/fact/table/US/IPE120219.

U.S. Citizenship and Immigration Services. 2023. *Children Born in the United States to Accredited Diplomats*. February 2. https://www.uscis.gov/policy-manual/volume-7- part-o-chapter-3.

U.S. Customs and Border Protection. 2020. *FY 2020 Nationwide Enforcement Encounters: Title 8 Enforcement Actions and Title 42 Expulsions*. November 20. https:// www.cbp.gov/newsroom/stats/cbp-enforcement-statistics/title-8-and-title-42-statist ics-fy2020.

U.S. Customs and Border Protection. 2021a. *Southwest Land Border Encounters*. October 22. https://www.cbp.gov/newsroom/stats/southwest-land-border-encounters

U.S. Customs and Border Protection. 2021b. *U.S. Border Patrol Monthly Enforcement Encounters 2021: Title 42 Expulsions and Title 8 Apprehensions*. December 2. https:// www.cbp.gov/newsroom/stats/cbp-enforcement-statistics/title-8-and-title-42-statist ics-fy2021.

U.S. Customs and Border Protection. 2022. Can I Visit the U.S. While Pregnant? May 11. https://help.cbp.gov/s/article/Article1838?language=en_US

U.S. Department of Homeland Security (DHS). 2017. "Policy Options to Respond to Border Surge of Illegal Immigration." December. https://www.documentcloud.org/ documents/5688664-Merkleydocs2.html

U.S. Department of Homeland Security (DHS). 2022a. *DHS Statement on District Court Ruling on Title 42*. May 20. https://www.dhs.gov/news/2022/05/20/dhs-statement- district-court-ruling-title-42

U.S. Department of Homeland Security (DHS). 2022b. *Interim Progress Report: Interagency Task Force on the Reunification of Families*. March 31. https://www.dhs.gov/sites/defa ult/files/2022-04/22_0420_frtf-interim-progress-report-march-2022.pdf

U.S. Department of Homeland Security (DHS). 2022c. *Uniting for Ukraine,* May 27, https://www.dhs.gov/ukraine

U.S. State Department. 2018. *Foreign Affairs Manual: U.S. Citizenship and Nationality, Vol. 8, §301.1-1.*

U.S. State Department. 2020. *Treaties in Force: A List of Treaties and Other International Agreements of the United States in Force on January 1, 2020*. https://www.state.gov/wp- content/uploads/2020/08/TIF-2020-Full-website-view.pdf

REFERENCES

United States v. Salerno, 481 U.S. 739, 1987.

Valasik, Matthew, and Matthew Phillips. 2017. "Understanding Modern Terror and Insurgency Through the Lens of Street Gangs: ISIS as a Case Study." *Journal of Criminological Research, Policy and Practice* 3(3): 192–207.

Van Bueren, Geraldine. 2006. *Article 40: Child Criminal Justice*. Leiden: Martinus Nijhoff Publishers.

Vanderklippe, Nathan. 2022. "Indigenous Groups in U.S. Have Been Leaders in Pandemic. Why Are Reservations Still Among Deadliest Places to Get Sick with COVID-19?" *Globe and Mail,* January 16. https://www.theglobeandmail.com/world/article-us-ind igenous-communities-struggle-with-rising-covid-19-cases-deaths/

Vandiwiele, Tiny. 2006. *Optional Protocol: The Involvement of Children in Armed Conflicts*. Leiden: Martinus Nijhoff Publishers.

Van Green, Ted. 2021. "Americans Overwhelmingly Say Marijuana Should be Legal for Recreational or Medical Use." *Pew Research Center,* April 16. https://www.pewresea rch.org/fact-tank/2021/04/16/americans-overwhelmingly-say-marijuana-should-be-legal-for-recreational-or-medical-use/.

Varsanyi, Monica. 2012. "Fighting for the Vote." In *Beyond Walls and Cages*, edited by Jenna M. Loyd, Matt Mitchelson, and Andrew Burridge, 266–276. Athens: University of Georgia Press.

Vatican News. 2022. "Pope Francis: It Was a Genocide Against Indigenous Peoples." July 30. https://www.vaticannews.va/en/pope/news/2022-07/pope-francis-apostolic-jour ney-inflight-press-conference-canada.html

Vavilov v. Canada. 2017. (2017 Federal Court of Appeal, Canada 132), June 21.

Venn, David. 2021. "Colonization Is a 'Book,' Not a 'Chapter' in Indigenous History, Says Nunavut MP." *Turtle Island News,* June 8. https://theturtleislandnews.com/index.php/ 2021/06/08/colonization-is-a-book-not-a-chapter-in-indigenous-history-says-nuna vut-mp/

Vickers, Jill, and Annette Isaac. 2012. *The Politics of Race: Canada, the United States and Australia*, 2nd ed. Toronto: University of Toronto Press.

Vitale, Frank. 2020. "Counting Carlisle's Casualties: Defining Student Death at the Carlisle Indian Industrial School, 1879–1918." *American Indian Quarterly* 44(4): 383–414.

Vonk, Olivier. 2015. *Nationality Law in the Western Hemisphere: A Study of Grounds for Acquisition and Loss*. Leiden: Martinus Nijhoff.

Wade-Olson, Jeremiah. 2019. *Punishing the Vulnerable: Discrimination in American Prisons*. Denver, CO: ABC-CLIO, 2019.

Wakefield, Sara, and Christopher Wildeman. 2018. "How Parental Incarceration Harms Children and What to Do About It." *National Council of Family Relations* 3(1): 1–2.

Waldinger, Roger. 2015. *The Cross-Border Connection: Immigrants, Emigrants and their Homelands*. Cambridge, MA: Harvard University Press.

Waldock, Thomas. 2020. "Child Welfare and the Status of Children Requiring Support and Care." In *A Question of Commitment: The Status of Children in Canada*, 2nd ed., edited by Thomas Waldock, 107–130. Waterloo: Wilfrid Laurier University Press.

Walen, Alec. 2008. "Crossing a Moral Line: Long-Term Preventive Detention in the War on Terror." *Philosophy and Public Policy Quarterly* 28(3/4): 15–21.

Walgrave, Lode. 2008. *Restorative Justice, Self-Interest and Responsible Citizenship*. New York: Routledge.

Walgrave, Lode. 2015. "Le Terrorisme Intérieur: Un Défi Pour La Justice Restaurative." *Les Cahiers de la Justice* 2015(3): 423–438.

REFERENCES 245

Walker, Clive. 2014. *Blackstone's Guide to the Anti-Terrorism Legislation*. Oxford: Oxford University Press.

Wall-Wieler, Elizabeth, Leslie L. Roos, Marni Brownell, Nathan C. Nickel, and Dan Chateau. 2018. "Predictors of Having a First Child Taken Into Care at Birth: A Population-Based Retrospective Cohort Study." *Child Abuse and Neglect* 76 (February): 1–9.

Walters, William. 2002. "Deportation, Expulsion, and the International Police of Aliens." *Citizenship Studies* 6(3): 265–292.

Watkin, Amy-Louise, and Seán Looney. 2019. "'The Lions of Tomorrow': A News Value Analysis of Child Images in Jihadi Magazines." *Studies in Conflict and Terrorism* 42(1–2): 120–140.

Weil, Patrick. 2001. "Access to Citizenship: A Comparison of Twenty-Five Nationality Laws." In *Citizenship Today: Global Perspectives and Practices*, edited by T. Alexander Aleinikoff and Douglas Klusmeyer, 17–35. Washington, DC: Carnegie Endowment for International Peace.

Weiss, Dov. 2017. "Sins of the Parents in Rabbinic and Early Christian Literature." *Journal of Religion* 97(1): 1–25.

Wellman, Christopher. 2017. *Rights Forfeiture and Punishment*. New York: Oxford University Press.

Wells, Paul. 2021. "No Co-Operation, No Comment: Missionary Oblates who ran Kamloops School Won't Release Records." *National Post*, June 3. https://nationalpost.com/news/canada/identifying-childrens-remains-at-b-c-residential-school-stalled-by-lack-of-records

Wessels, Michael. 2006. *Child Soldiers: From Violence to Protection*. Cambridge, MA: Harvard University Press.

White, Erik. 2021. "Some Northern Ontario First Nations Going Back into Lockdown, While Others Have Kept Borders Closed." *CBC News*, January 18. https://www.cbc.ca/news/canada/sudbury/first-nations-northeastern-ontario-covid-second-wave-1.5871291

White, Patrick. 2022. "Shocking and Shameful: For the First Time, Indigenous Women Make Up Half the Female Population in Canada's Federal Prisons." *Globe and Mail*, May 5. https://www.theglobeandmail.com/canada/article-half-of-all-women-inmates-are-indigenous/

Wildeman, Christopher. 2009. "Parental Imprisonment, the Prison Boom and the Concentration of Childhood Disadvantage." *Demography* 46(2): 265–280.

Wilder, LeRoy. 1978. *Indian Child Welfare Act of 1978*. Hearings Before the Subcommittee on Indian Affairs, Committee on Indian Affairs and Public Lands, United States House of Representatives, 95th Congress, 2nd Session, February 9, pp. 62–74.

Withers, Lloyd, and Jean Folsom. 2007. "Incarcerated Fathers: A Descriptive Analysis." *Correctional Service of Canada*, May. https://www.csc-scc.gc.ca/research/r186-eng.shtml

Witt, John Fabian. 2020. *American Contagions and the Law from Smallpox to COVID-19*. New Haven, CT: Yale University Press.

Witte, John. 2009. *Sins of the Fathers*. New York: Cambridge University Press.

Wong Kim Ark v. United States, 169 U.S. 649 (1898).

Wood, Patrick, and Jordyn Butler. 2020. "Ongoing Coronavirus Border Closures Take Their Toll as Families Separated for Months." *Australian Broadcasting Corporation*, August 22. https://www.abc.net.au/news/2020-08-23/coronavirus-border-closures-take-toll-as-families-separated/12564488

246 REFERENCES

Wood, William R., and Masahiro Suzuki. 2020. "Are Conflicts Property? Re-Examining the Ownership of Conflict in Restorative Justice." *Social and Legal Studies* 29(6): 903–924.

Woodward, Kerry C. 2021. "Race, Gender, and Poverty Governance: The Case of the U.S. Child Welfare System." *Social Politics* 28(2): 428–450.

Woolford, Andrew. 2015. *This Benevolent Experiment*. Lincoln: University of Nebraska Press.

Woolford, Andrew, and James Gacek. 2016. "Genocidal Carcerality and Indian Residential Schools in Canada." *Punishment and Society* 18(4): 400–419.

Woolford, Andrew, and Amanda Nelund. 2019. *The Politics of Restorative Justice*, 2nd ed. Boulder, CO: Lynne Rienner Publishing.

Wright, Pauline. 2020. *Opening Statement: PJCIS Review Into the 'Declared Area' Provisions*. Canberra: Law Council of Australia.

Wright, Teresa. 2021. "Foster Care is Modern-Day Residential School System: Inuk MP Mumilaaq Qaqqaq." *CBC News*, June 4. https://www.cbc.ca/news/politics/foster-care-is-modern-day-residential-school-1.6054223

Yacoubian, Mona. 2022. *Al-Hol: Displacement Crisis is a Tinderbox that Could Ignite ISIS 2*. Washington, DC: U.S. Institute of Peace. https://www.usip.org/publications/2022/05/al-hol-displacement-crisis-tinderbox-could-ignite-isis-20

Yaffe, Gideon. 2018. *The Age of Culpability: Children and the Nature of Criminal Responsibility*. New York: Oxford University Press.

Yankah, Ekow N. 2020. "The Right to Reintegration." *New Criminal Law Review* 23(1): 74–112.

Yeates, Neil. 2014. "SECRET: Citizenship Reform Proposal #19: Birth on Soil." Ottawa: Citizenship and Immigration Canada.

Yee, Vivian. 2019. "Guns, Filth, and ISIS: Syrian Camp is 'Disaster in the Making.'" *New York Times*, September 3. https://www.nytimes.com/2019/09/03/world/middleeast/isis-alhol-camp-syria.html

Young, Margaret. 1997. *Canadian Citizenship Act and Current Issues*. Ottawa: Law and Government Commission of Canada.

Young, Elliot. 2021. *Forever Prisoners: How the United States Made the World's Largest Immigrant Detention System*. New York: Oxford University Press.

Yousaf, Humza. 2022. Twitter Post, April 14, 3:46 a.m. https://twitter.com/HumzaYousaf/status/1514510417120354304

Zayas, Luis, and M.H. Bradlee. 2014. "Exiling Children, Creating Orphans: When Immigration Policies Hurt Citizens." *Social Work* 59(2): 167–175.

Zadvydas v. Davis 533 U.S. 678 (2001).

Zappalà, Gianni and Stephen Castles. 1999. "Citizenship and Immigration in Australia." *Georgetown Immigration Law Journal* 13(2): 273–316.

Zedner, Lucia. 1994. "Reparation and Retribution: Are They Mutually Irreconcilable." *Modern Law Review* 57(2): 228–250.

Zedner, Lucia. 2007. "Pre-Crime and Post-Criminology." *Theoretical Criminology* 11(2): 261–281.

Zedner, Lucia. 2013. "Is the Criminal Law Only for Citizens?" In *The Borders of Punishment: Migration, Citizenship, and Social Exclusion*, edited by Katja Franko Aas and Mary Bosworth, 40–57. Oxford: Oxford University Press.

Zedner, Lucia. 2015. "Penal Subversions: When is a Punishment Not Punishment, Who Decides and on What Grounds?" *Theoretical Criminology* 20(1): 3–20.

Zedner, Lucia. 2019a. "The Hostile Border: Crimmigration, Counterterrorism, or Crossing the Line on Rights." *New Criminal Law Review* 22(3): 318–343.

Zedner, Lucia. 2019b. "Curtailing Citizenship Rights as Counterterrorism." In *Security and Human Rights* 2nd ed., edited by Benjamin J. Goold and Liora Lazarus, 99–124. Oxford: Hart Publishing.

Zedner, Lucia. 2021. "Countering Terrorism or Criminalizing Curiosity? The Troubled History of UK Responses to Right-Wing and Other Extremism." *Common Law World Review* 50(1): 57–75.

Zedner, Lucia, and Andrew Ashworth 2019. "The Rise and Restraint of the Preventive State." *Annual Review of Criminology* 2: 429–450.

Zernova, Margarita. 2019. "Restorative Justice in the Aftermath of Politically Motivated Violence: The Basque Experience." *Critical Studies on Terrorism* 12(4): 649–672.

Zug, Marcia. 2020. "ICWA Downunder: Exploring the Costs and Benefits of Enacting an Australian Version of the United States' Indian Child Welfare Act." *Canadian Journal of Family Law* 33(1): 161–249.

Index

For the benefit of digital users, indexed terms that span two pages (e.g., 52–53) may, on occasion, appear on only one of those pages.

Abbott, Greg, 168–69
abolitionism, 87–88, 89
Abourezk, James (1931–2023), 145–46
Adam, Allan, 77
adoption, 34, 80–81, 144–45, 154, 156, 158–59, 161–62, 196n.12, 196n.13
Adoption and Safe Families Act of 1997, 34, 80–81
Afghanistan, 113–14
agency (exercising capacity to act), 15–16, 21–22, 71, 104, 110–11, 121–22, 154, 196n.12
allegiance, 8–9, 10–11, 14, 15–16, 40, 44–45, 46, 54, 63, 73–74, 101–3, 105, 106–9, 113, 116–18, 123–24, 190n.10
Allegiance to Australia Act, 108–9
American Samoa, 53, 54–55, 189–90n.7
Anchor Babies, 48, 58
Andersen, Chris, 156–57
Anglican Church of Canada, 132–33, 194n.2, 194n.3
Anishinaabe, 183, 196n.13
Anishinabek Nation, 148
Anti-Drug Abuse Act of 1988, 1, 78–79
Anti-Social Behaviour Orders, 16–17
Apache, 130–31
apartheid, 91–92
apology, 137–38, 152, 153, 196n.11
Arendt, Hannah (1906–1975), 128, 140–41
Ashworth, Andrew, 25
Assembly of First Nations, 136–37, 196n.11
asylum, 6–7, 8–9, 21–22, 25–27, 31–33, 35–37, 49, 59–60, 78–79, 123, 126, 141–42, 159, 165–69, 170, 171–72, 187n.6, 187–88n.7, 192n.12, 193n.3, 196–97n.15
atonement, 72–73, 89, 90–91, 127–28, 151

Australia, 11, 26, 40–42, 44–45, 52, 68, 78, 101, 103–4, 106, 136–37, 144–45
Austria, 72–73, 160–61

banishment, 10–11, 28, 29–30, 66, 82, 101, 105, 194n.4
Barnett, Randy, 191n.5
Basque Nationalism, 116–18
Beccaria, Cesare (1738–1794), 28
Begum, Jarrah, 102
Begum, Shamima, 102, 104, 111, 116
best interests of the child, 48, 96–97, 187–88n.7
Biden, Joseph, 164, 168, 169
Birth Alert, 177–79
Birthright Citizenship
    jus sanguinis, 2–4, 48, 50–51, 52, 53, 55, 62–63, 65–66, 67, 70–71, 72, 189n.4
    jus soli, 2, 9–11, 48, 49, 50, 51, 52, 53, 56–60, 62, 63–64, 65–66, 67, 68, 70–71, 170–72, 189n.4
birth tourist, 58–59
Black (African-American), 1–2, 52–53, 76–77, 87–88, 91–92, 165–66, 176–77, 179, 185n.1, 191n.8
Black (Canadian), 77, 87–88, 142–43, 185n.1, 195n.9
Black-Indigenous alliance, 142–43
Black Lives Matter, 77, 142–43
Bloom, Mia, 122
Braithwaite, John, 112
Brewer, David Josiah (1837–1910), 24
British Columbia, 129–30, 177–78, 194n.4
Brock, Gillian, 68–69
Budlakoti v. Canada (2015), 68–69
Budlakoti, Deepan, 63–64, 65
Bülow, William, 93

250   INDEX

Bush, George H.W. (1924–2018), 31–32
Bush, George W. 62

Cachagee, Mike, 132–35, 194n.5
Canada, 1–2, 11, 12, 25, 35–39, 44–45,
    49, 50, 52, 54–56, 57–58, 60, 63–66,
    67–68, 72, 77, 97–98, 101, 106, 108–9,
    127–28, 129–30, 131–33, 134, 136–
    43, 144–45, 146–51, 154–58, 159,
    161–63, 164–65, 167–68, 170–73,
    175–78, 179, 185n.1, 185n.2, 185n.3,
    186–87n.2, 187n.4, 187n.5, 188n.9,
    190n.8, 190n.9
Canada Border Services Agency (CBSA),
    36–37, 191n.4
Canada Child Benefit, 55
Canada Supreme Court, 64–65, 77, 157–
    58, 191n.6
Canada-Ukraine Authorization for
    Emergency Travel, 170
Canadian Charter of Rights and
    Freedoms, 35–36, 37–39, 171–72,
    197n.1
Canadian Human Rights Tribunal, 175
capacity, 15–16, 21–22, 45–46, 67–68, 69–
    70, 71, 82, 94–95, 104, 113, 121–22,
    123–25, 127–28, 158–59, 185–86n.4,
    192–93n.2, 192n.9
care, 2–4, 5–6, 12–13, 31, 34, 36–39, 47, 48,
    55, 62–63, 66, 68–70, 80–81, 82, 85,
    86–87, 89–90, 92–93, 94–97, 98–99,
    101, 105, 121, 123, 133, 141, 145–49,
    152, 153, 154, 158–59, 165–66, 171–
    72, 173, 177–81
care ethics, 82, 86–87, 96–97
caregiving, 10, 12–13, 16, 60–61, 78–79,
    80–81, 85–86, 89, 96–97, 99–100,
    154, 171–72, 174–75, 180–81,
    185–86n.4
Carlisle Indian Industrial School, 130–32
Chaidez, Natalie, 92–93
Charkaoui v. Canada (2007), 37–39
Chauvin, Derek, 87–89, 91
Cherokee Nation, 141–42
Chiarelli v. Canada (1992), 35–36
child custody, 16, 34, 62, 78–79, 80–81, 97,
    128, 144–45, 171, 172–73, 174–75,
    177, 178–79

child development, 29, 69–70, 121–22,
    124–25, 149–50, 179–80
child labor, 2–4, 77, 129, 131–32, 133, 136,
    193n.5
children's rights, 37, 69–70, 110–11, 123
child welfare, 128, 137–38, 139–40, 144–
    47, 148, 149, 154, 161–63
China, 164, 195n.7
Choctaw Nation, 141–42
Chow, Olivia, 65–66
Chrétien, Jean, 137–38
Christie, Nils (1928–2015), 85–86, 113, 117
circles of care, 82, 86–87, 89–90
citizenship, 2–4, 9–13, 14, 26–27, 28,
    34–35, 36, 40–42, 46, 48–74, 82, 89,
    99–100, 101–3, 104, 105, 106–9, 111,
    112, 119–20, 123, 124–25, 126–28,
    140–42, 153, 154, 155, 156, 157–
    62, 164–66, 170–72, 173, 180–81,
    185–86n.4, 189n.3, 189n.4, 189n.5,
    189–90n.7, 190n.8, 190n.9, 190n.10,
    190n.13, 196n.15, 197n.17
Citizenship Act (Canada), 52, 55, 63,
    64–65, 72
Citizenship and Immigration v. Vavilov
    (2019), 64–65
civic republican, 82, 160
civil disobedience, 7, 21–22
civilian, 7
Civil War (U.S.), 52–53, 57–58
Coates, Ta-Nehisi, 76–77
coercion, 26–27, 37, 119–20, 121–22, 123
Cohen, Elizabeth, 82, 193n.4
collateral consequences, 1, 2, 8–9, 164–65,
    172–73, 190–91n.1
collective punishment, 14–15, 44–45,
    76–77
colonialism, 10, 53, 75, 87–88, 131–32,
    133–34, 136–38, 144–45, 152–53,
    154, 164, 176, 178–79, 189–90n.7,
    194–95n.6
combatant, 64, 113–14
Condry, Rachel, 94–95
consent, 103–4, 110, 120, 121–22, 128,
    129, 156, 160, 161, 185–86n.4
consular services, 44, 63, 101–2, 118–19
corrections, 84–85
corruption of blood, 102, 129

counter-radicalization, 42, 45–46, 102–3, 105, 111, 114–15, 116–19, 121–22, 174–75, 185–86n.4

Counter-Terrorism, 40–42, 107–8

COVID-19, 12, 17–19, 26, 33–34, 51, 79–80, 94–95, 164–65, 167–69, 176–77, 183, 185–86n.4, 186–87n.2, 187n.5, 190n.9, 191n.3, 191n.4, 197n.1

Cowessess First Nation (Saskatchewan), 129–30

Crampton, Paul, 197n.1

Cree Nation, 159, 161

crime, 4, 5–6, 8, 14–16, 18, 22–23, 24, 25–26, 27, 29, 30–31, 36–37, 39, 40, 44, 60, 78, 81, 84, 85–88, 90–92, 94–95, 99–100, 105, 114–15, 119–20, 122, 172–73, 191n.5, 191n.7, 193n.8

criminology, 1, 8–9, 14

crimmigration, 8–9, 14

Daniels v. Canada (2016), 156–57

Davis, Angela Y. 87–88

Deferred Action for Childhood Arrivals (DACA), 60–61, 190n.11

Deferred Action for Parents of Americans and Lawful Permanent Residents (DAPA), 60–61

denationalization, 61–62, 82, 101, 102–3, 104, 105–11, 112, 113–15, 119–20, 125, 185–86n.4, 187n.4

Denmark, 108–9

deontological, 4

dependent, 2, 4, 5–6, 8–9, 10–11, 12–13, 14–15, 16, 19–20, 21–22, 27, 28, 34, 47, 50, 66, 70, 75, 80–81, 84, 92–97, 99–100, 101–2, 104, 105, 118–19, 129, 161, 164, 166, 170–71, 172–74, 180–81

deportation, 1, 2, 9–10, 12–13, 17, 23, 24, 25–26, 27, 29, 30–31, 33, 34–36, 46, 60–61, 66, 69–71, 95–96, 97, 98–99, 106, 119, 164, 170–71, 185–86n.4, 188n.8

deradicalization, 12–13, 102–3, 118–19, 174–75, 180–81

descendant, 67, 74, 176

Designated Foreign National (Canada), 36–37

detention, 75, 78–80, 93, 95–96, 101–2, 109

civil, 25, 30–32, 33–34

foreign terrorists, 101–2, 109, 113–14, 164–65

immigration, 1, 11–13, 17, 23, 25–26, 27, 29–30, 31, 33–35, 37–42, 46, 58, 78–79, 164–65, 170–71, 187n.3, 187n.4, 187n.5, 187–88n.7

pretrial, 16–17

deterrence, 4–5, 12–13, 27, 29–30, 31–33, 35–39, 46, 49, 59–60, 93–94, 99–100, 102–3, 105, 109–10, 111, 112, 113, 114–15, 124, 126, 143, 164, 166, 167–69, 187n.6

disloyalty, 10–11, 44, 102–3, 105, 108–9, 120

dissent, 7, 21–22, 111, 185–86n.4, 188n.12

Dixon, JoJo, 103–4

doli incapax, 121

DREAM Act, 60–61

Duceppe, Gilles, 137–38

Dumbrava, Costica, 71

duress, 70, 109–11, 123

education, 9–10, 22–23, 34–35, 47, 55, 60, 62–63, 69–71, 87–88, 90–91, 94–95, 115, 125, 126, 130–31, 133–34, 137–38, 146–47, 151–52, 157–58, 193n.4, 194–95n.6, 195n.7

Elk v. Wilkins (1884), 53–55

Ellison, Keith, 88–89

Enriquez, Laura, 170–71

entrapment, 45–46

equal protection, 9–10, 60

Espionage, 10–11, 64–65

European Union, 72, 115

execution, 10–11, 123

exile, 25–26, 29, 40, 64–65, 66, 72–73, 110–11, 115, 160–61

family separation, 1–2, 6–7, 11–12, 27, 31, 32–33, 35–39, 60–61, 76–77, 78–79, 80–81, 93–94, 97–98, 126–27, 136, 137–38, 140–41, 144–46, 148, 149–50, 154, 158–59, 162, 163, 164, 165–68, 172, 175, 176–78, 180, 185n.2, 185n.3, 192n.12

252 INDEX

Fauci, Anthony, 168–69
Femmes Autochtones du Québec, 178–79
Ferracioli, Luara, 68–70
fetal alcohol spectrum disorder (FASD), 149–50, 179–80
fetus, 48
Field, Stephen Johnson (1816–1899), 24
Finnis, John, 120
First Nations, 11, 54–55, 127–28, 134–35, 136–37, 138, 140–42, 147, 148, 151, 152, 153, 158–59, 160, 161–62, 176, 177–79, 196n.11
Fitisemanu v. United States (2021), 54–55
Fletcher, Bill, 132–33
Flint, Michigan, 22
Florida, 130–31, 187n.6
Floyd, George (1973–2020), 86–88, 91, 191n.7
Fong Yue Ting v. United States (1893), 24
Fontaine, Phil, 136–37
foreign fighters, 2, 11–12, 101–2, 103–4, 108–9, 116, 123
forgiveness, 153, 196n.11
foster care, 31, 34, 36–37, 80–81, 145–47, 148–49, 196n.10
Fourteenth Amendment (U.S. Constitution), 50, 52–53, 54, 57–58, 171–72
France, 40, 108, 115, 122, 189n.5, 192n.1
Francis (Pope), 152–53, 196n.11
free-will skepticism, 21, 22
Fuller, Melville Weston (1833–1910), 24

generations, 11, 52–53, 65, 72, 128, 137–38, 139, 140–41, 151–52, 158–59, 162–63
Geneva Convention, 4–5
genocide, 2–4, 139–40, 151–52, 165–66, 195n.7, 196n.11
Germany, 72–73, 160–61
Gheaus, Anca, 121
Gilmore, Ruth Wilson, 17
Global War on Terrorism, 12, 101, 173
Gonzalez, Juan, 62, 196–97n.15
Graham, Lindsey, 59–60
Graham, Lorie, 146
Guatemala, 154, 196–97n.15
guilt, 5–6, 8, 18, 22, 25–26, 28, 29–31, 36–39, 43, 44–45, 83, 86–87, 93, 96, 104,

109–10, 151, 166, 174–75, 188n.12, 192–93n.2

Haaland, Debra, 131–32, 176
Haiti, 31–32, 168–69, 187n.6
Harper, Stephen, 55, 137–38, 195n.8
Harris, Kamala, 53–54
Hart, H.L.A. (1907–1992), 4, 14–16, 18, 59–60, 81, 125
healing circles, 12–13, 97–98, 163, 172–73
health care, 55, 141
Hicks, David, 107–8
Holder v. Humanitarian Law Project (2010), 43
Horgan, John, 122
humanitarian law, 4–5, 43
human rights, 123, 147, 154–55, 173, 175, 195n.8

Idle No More, 138, 195n.8
immigration, 1, 2, 6–7, 8–10, 11–13, 14, 15–17, 18, 23–28, 29–31, 32–42, 43, 46, 47, 48, 49–50, 51, 52–53, 55, 56, 58–62, 63, 64–66, 68–69, 71, 72, 74, 76, 78–80, 95–96, 97, 99, 106, 109–10, 119–20, 126–28, 129, 155, 161–62, 164–66, 170–71, 180, 185n.3, 187n.3, 187n.5, 187–88n.7, 188n.9, 190n.8, 191n.4, 192n.12, 193n.5, 196–97n.15
   permanent resident, 29–31, 44–45, 49, 52, 55, 56, 58, 67–68, 70–71
   undocumented or irregular, 8, 9–10, 21–22, 31, 35–36, 48, 49–50, 51, 56–57, 58–61, 62, 63, 70–71, 122, 164, 170–72, 185–86n.4, 187–88n.7
incapacitation, 12–13, 17, 20, 29–30, 33, 35–36, 37–39, 42, 46, 49, 64–65, 89, 102–3, 105, 108–10, 112, 115, 124, 143
incarceration, 1–2, 12–13, 16, 17, 20, 22–23, 29–30, 34–35, 75, 76–77, 78–79, 80–81, 83–84, 85–89, 90–94, 95–96, 98–100, 113–15, 138, 142–43, 149–50, 162, 164–65, 172–73, 175–76, 180, 192n.11
inchoate offenses, 8–9, 14, 15–16, 39–40, 46, 102–3, 113, 119–20
India, 65

Indian Adoption Project (U.S.), 145–46
Indian Child Welfare Act of 1978 (U.S.), 145–46
Indigenous, 1–4, 11–13, 31, 52, 54–55, 77, 78, 87–88, 91–92, 97–98, 126–28, 129–34, 135, 136–39
innocence, 5–6, 19–20, 39, 40–42, 94–95, 104, 127, 188n.12, 192–93n.2, 194n.5
INS v. Lopez-Mendoza, 30–31
intergenerational care, 12–13, 180–81
intergenerational cycle of offending, 83–84, 172–73
intergenerational cycle of victimization, 171, 194n.4
intergenerational diasporic citizenship, 72–73
intergenerational harms, 2–4, 28, 49, 75, 83–84, 88, 123, 126–27, 128, 131, 133–34, 140–41, 143, 144, 146, 149–50, 154, 163, 171, 175, 176–77, 180–81, 194n.4
intergenerational institutions, 127–28, 131, 154, 156, 161–62, 165
intergenerational punishment, 10–11, 12, 105, 123, 129
International Court of Justice, 50
Inuit, 140–41, 151, 152, 177–78
Iraq, 17, 101, 108–9, 173–74
Ireland, 44–45, 72, 188n.13, 196n.12
ISIS (Islamic State in Iraq and Syria), 10–11, 17, 44, 64, 101–4, 105, 107–9, 110–11, 112–19, 121, 122, 123, 173–75, 190n.12, 192n.1
Israel, 7, 16

Jacobs, Margaret, 146
jail, 19–20, 76, 79, 103, 132–33
Jakobs, Gunther, 24
Jay Treaty, 155–56, 161–62
Johnson, Jeh, 31–32
Joppke, Christian, 185–86n.4
Jordan's Principle, 147
jus nexi, 67–68

Kamloops, British Columbia, 129–30, 131–32
Kavanaugh, Brett, 48
Kennedy v. Martinez-Mendoza (1963), 29, 33, 57–58

Kenney, Jason, 65–66
Khadr, Omar, 113–14
Korematsu v. United States (1944), 44–45
Kukathas, Chandran, 59–60
Kurdistan, 108–9

language, 62–63, 73–74, 77, 129, 131–34, 137–38, 140–41, 156–57
Lavi, Shai, 119–20
Leach, Brittany, 48
Lenard, Patti Tamara, 26–27, 82
Letts, Jack, 44
Levinson, Daryl, 4–5
Lindblom, Lars, 93
Lippke, Richard, 93–94
lockdown, 17–19, 183
Lovelace v. Canada (1979), 158
loyalty, 122, 123, 131

Magdalene Laundries, 196n.12
Manitoba, 146–47, 156–57, 177–78
Matos, Yalidy, 60–61
McAlinden, Anne, 98
McCandless v. Diabo (1928), 155
McIvor v. Canada (2009), 158
mens rea, 22, 60
mental health, 22–23, 90–91
Métis, 151, 152, 156–58, 159, 177–78
Mexico, 31–32, 62–63, 126, 155, 159–60, 167–69, 171–72, 193n.1, 196–97n.15, 197n.16, 198n.2
Miller v. Alabama (2011), 121–22
Miller, David, 16–17, 170
Miller, Marc, 148
Minority Report, 39
Minson, Shona, 92–93, 94–95
Missionary Oblates of Mary Immaculate, 153, 194n.2
Moose Factory, Ontario, 132–33
Morrison, Scott, 103–4
Muthana, Hoda, 64
Muthana v. Pompeo (2021), 64

NAACP v. Claiborne Hardware Co. (1982), 43
Nationality Act of 1940 (U.S.). 107–8
national security, 8–9, 14, 16–17, 39–42, 48, 106–7, 108, 120
Newfoundland and Labrador, 177–78

254 INDEX

New Jersey, 64
New Zealand, 44–45, 52, 136–37, 149, 171, 185n.3
nonimmigrant visa, 56, 59–60
Northern Ireland, 116–18, 188n.13
Norway, 103, 108–9
Nova Scotia, 177–78
Nunavut, 148

Obama, Barack, 31–33, 53, 60–61
Office of the Correctional Investigator (Canada), 149–50
Ontario, 177–79
outbreak, 33–34, 168–69, 191n.4

Padilla v. Kentucky (2011), 30–31
Palestinian, 7, 16
Palk, A. Naomi, 109
paper sons, 31
parenting, 97, 133
Pasternak, Avia, 5–6
Patel, Priti, 26–27, 43
Patriot Act, 43
penitence, 89, 192n.9
Pennsylvania, 130–31
Pereboom, Derk, 20, 21
personal responsibility ideology, 22–23
Pettit, Philip, 26–27
Plyler v. Doe (1982), 9–10, 60
Pratt, Richard Henry (1840–1924), 130–31
pre-crime, 40–42, 43, 46, 47
preventive justice, 1, 4–5, 8, 14, 15–16, 39, 40–42, 44–45, 46, 101, 106–7, 119, 179–80
Prince Edward Island, 177–78
prison, 1, 2–4, 17, 19–20, 23, 25–26, 27, 29–30, 33–34, 42, 44, 46, 69–70, 75, 76, 78–80, 82, 84–85, 87–89, 90–91, 92–93, 94–95, 96, 99–100, 108, 112, 113–15, 118–19, 120, 121–22, 130–31, 149, 164–66, 172, 185–86n.4, 186–87n.2, 190–91n.1, 191n.3, 191n.4, 192–93n.2, 192n.9, 192n.10, 192n.11, 193n.5
proportionality, 19, 112
protest, 18, 24, 77, 138, 143, 154, 183, 194n.2, 195n.8
public health, 17–20, 21–22, 69–70, 164–65, 167–69, 186–87n.2, 190n.9

Pueblo Laguna Nation, 176
punishment, 2–6, 7, 8–9, 10–11, 12–13, 14–20, 21–24, 25–27, 28–30, 31–39, 40, 42, 44–45, 46–47, 48–50, 59–60, 68–69, 75, 76–77, 78, 80–81, 82, 83, 89, 92–96, 98–100, 101, 102–4, 105–6, 109–10, 112, 114, 119–20, 123, 124–25, 129, 136, 143, 150–51, 160, 166–68, 170–71, 172, 179–80, 186n.1, 187n.4, 188n.11, 189n.2, 189n.3, 197n.1
punishment drift, 36, 81, 92–97

quarantine, 18, 19–23, 25, 164, 187n.3, 197n.1
Québec, 137–38, 161, 178–79

R. v. Bissonnette (2022), 89
R. v. Gladue (1999), 77
R v. Ipeelee (2012), 77
R. v. Powley (2003), 156–57
racism, 1–4, 24, 26–27, 52–53, 59–61, 77, 86–88, 91–92, 139–40, 142–43, 147, 151, 152, 156, 176, 178–79, 189n.4
radicalization, 42, 45–46, 64, 105, 108, 111, 112, 114–15, 116–19, 121–22, 125, 173–75
Reagan, Ronald (1911–2004), 31–32
recidivism, 22–23, 34–35, 90–91, 98, 112, 149–50, 172–73, 174–75
reconciliation, 11, 77, 78, 86–87, 89–90, 91, 126, 127–28, 131–33, 135–36, 139, 140–42, 143, 144–45, 146–48, 149–51, 152–53, 157–58, 160–61, 162–63, 172–73, 175–76, 183, 197n.16
Red Army Faction, 116–17
Redfield, Robert, 167–68
refugee, 17, 26–27, 28, 32–33, 35–37, 49, 123, 170, 187–88n.7, 188n.9
rehabilitation, 2–4, 12–13, 17–18, 19, 21–22, 23, 33, 34–35, 43, 46, 47, 78, 80–81, 82–84, 85–87, 89–91, 93–96, 99–100, 102–3, 109–10, 114–15, 116, 121–22, 123–24, 142–43, 153, 163, 174–75, 177, 179–81, 191n.6, 192–93n.2, 192n.10
reintegration, 4, 8, 10–11, 12–13, 23, 34–35, 46, 48, 75, 82, 84, 90–91, 94–95,

97–98, 99–100, 114, 115, 116–17, 174–75, 180–81, 192n.9
reintegrative shaming, 85–86, 90–91
reparations, 7, 76–77, 91–92, 127–28, 141–42, 154–55
repentance, 19, 118–19, 191n.6
republicanism, 82, 160
residential school, 128, 129–30, 131–34, 135–38, 139, 141, 144, 146–47, 148, 149–51, 153, 163, 194n.3, 194–95n.6
responsibility, 4–6, 7, 8–9, 11, 14–15, 17, 21–23, 36–37, 40–42, 43, 44–45, 47, 60, 72–73, 78, 81, 85–86, 89–90, 92–93, 97, 104, 112, 113–14, 117, 120, 121–22, 123–25, 126, 127, 128, 129, 135–36, 140–41, 143, 144, 147, 153, 160, 162–63, 192n.10, 193n.6, 194–95n.6
restitution, 89–90, 152–53, 191n.5, 191n.7
restorative justice, 10, 12–13, 34–35, 75, 78, 82–83, 85–87, 89–92, 97–100, 102–3, 112, 114–15, 116–18, 121–22, 123–25, 143–44, 149–51, 163, 172–73, 187n.4, 191n.5, 192n.10
retribution, 10, 12–13, 17, 29–30, 31–32, 33, 75, 80–81, 82, 86–87, 88–89, 91–92, 93, 97–98, 99–100, 102–3, 105, 108–10, 111, 121–22, 124, 142–43, 150–51, 166, 192n.1, 192n.10
retributivism, 80–81, 90–91
risk, 4–6, 7, 8, 19–20, 22–23, 33–34, 37–39, 40–43, 45–46, 50–51, 59–60, 67–68, 70–71, 79, 82, 84, 94–95, 99–100, 102–4, 106, 107–10, 111, 112, 119, 120, 123, 125, 147, 149, 164–65, 168–69, 171, 172–73, 174–75, 177–78, 179–80, 185–86n.11, 188n.11, 191n.4, 197n.1
Roman Catholic Church, 129–30, 152–53, 194n.2, 194–95n.6
Roper v. Simmons (2004), 121–22
Rudd, Kevin, 137–38
Russia, 7, 24, 26–27, 64–65, 170, 195n.7
Ryo, Emily, 59–60

sanctions
    individual, 85–86, 90–91, 93–94, 95–96, 99–100, 105, 114–15, 149–50, 170–71, 172–73
    international, 4–5, 101, 126

Sanctuary Movement, 21–22
Saskatchewan, 129–30, 177–78, 187n.4
Sault Ste. Marie, Ontario, 132–34, 194n.3
Scales v. United States (1961), 43
Schuck, Peter, 56–57, 67
Section 8 Housing, 6–7, 78–79
segregation, 87–88
sentencing, 5–6, 10, 12–13, 75, 80–81, 82, 83, 87–88, 89, 93–94, 97–98, 99–100, 120, 121–22, 163, 172–73, 175–76, 180–81
September 11, 2001–C2P1, 16–17, 39–40, 43, 106–7, 188n.9
Sessions, Jefferson Beauregard, 32–33
settler state, 4, 126–27, 140–42, 154–56, 158, 159, 160, 161–62, 185n.3, 196–97n.15
Shachar, Ayelet, 67–68, 70–71
Sharrouf, Zaynab, 103–4
Shingwauk Residential School, 132–34, 183
Six Nations of the Haudenosaunee Confederacy, 161–62
Sixties Scoop, 144–45
slavery, 87–88
Smith, Rogers M. 56–57, 67, 157–58
Song, Sarah, 24
South Africa, 91–92
sovereignty, 126–28, 146, 154–56, 158–60, 161–62, 171–72, 176, 185n.3, 196–97n.15
Spain, 72–73
Spallumcheen First Nation (British Columbia), 148
Spanish-American War, 54
Special Court for Sierra Leone (SCSL), 115
Spencer v. Canada (2021), 197n.1
Sri Lanka, 36–37
Standing Bear, Luther (1868–1939), 131
statelessness, 50, 51, 65, 70, 102–3, 104, 108–9, 165–66
Statistics Canada, 56, 175–76, 196n.10
sterilization, 139–40
Straehle, Christine, 121
substance (Drug) Abuse, 6–7, 16, 23, 76, 78–79, 133–34, 146–47, 177
suicide, 131, 147
Supreme Court of Canada, 35–36, 37–39, 64–65, 77, 149–50, 152–53, 172–73, 191n.6

256 INDEX

surveillance, 42, 44–45, 59–60, 195n.7
Syria, 17, 44, 64, 101–2, 108–9, 112, 173–75, 188n.8, 190n.12

Tadros, Victor, 119
Ten, Chin Liew, 19
terrorism, 1, 2, 7–9, 10–11, 12–13, 14, 15–16, 39–40, 46–47, 101, 105, 106–9, 111, 113–14, 116–17, 120, 121–22, 164, 173–74, 180, 185–86n.4, 192–93n.2
Texas, 79–80, 155, 159–60, 168–69
Texas Band of Kickapoo Indians, 155, 159–60
Thomson, Vannette, 84–85
Thunder Bay, Ontario, 178–79
Title 42 (United States), 167–68, 169, 198n.2
Towes, Victor, 36–37
Trail of Tears, 141–42
treason, 101, 102–3, 106, 120, 130–31, 192n.1
Trop v. Dulles (1958), 28–29, 106
Trudeau, Justin, 148
Trump, Donald, 6–7, 31–33, 37–39, 56, 59–60, 165, 167–68, 190n.11, 192n.12, 198n.2
Truth and Reconciliation Commission (Canada), 77, 91–92, 127–28, 132–33, 136, 175–76, 177–78, 194n.5, 197n.16

Ukraine, 7, 26–27, 170, 195n.7
United Church of Canada, 152, 194n.2
United Kingdom, 8–9, 23, 26–27, 40–42, 44, 102, 106, 107–8, 193n.8
United Kingdom Counter-Terrorism and Border Security Act, 40–42, 107–8
United Kingdom Prevention of Terrorism Act, 40
United Nations Convention on the Rights of the Child (UNCRC), 37, 121–22, 148
United Nations Declaration on the Rights of Indigenous Peoples (UNDRIP), 147, 154–55
United Nations Paris Principles, 116
United States of America (U.S.), 1–2, 6–7, 17, 23, 24, 25, 27, 28–29, 30–34,
37–39, 43, 44–45, 50, 52–55, 56–58, 59–63, 64, 65, 67, 70–71, 76, 77–80, 84–85, 86–88, 95–96, 99, 103–4, 106, 113–14, 121–22, 126, 128, 129, 130–32, 133, 136–37, 139–40, 141–42, 144–46, 155–56, 159–60, 161–62, 164–65, 167–72, 176–77, 179, 188n.8, 189n.1, 189–90n.7, 190n.10, 190n.11, 191n.3, 191n.4, 193n.5, 196–97n.15
United States v. Wong Kim Ark (1898), 52–53, 189n.6, 189–90n.7, 190n.10
Uniting for Ukraine, 170
U.S. Adoption and Safe Families Act, 34
U.S. Bureau of Prisons, 23, 79–80, 191n.3
U.S. Centers for Disease Control and Prevention, 167–68, 169
U.S. Citizenship and Immigration Service (USCIS), 60, 79–80, 168–69
U.S. Citizenship Act of 2021, 164
U.S. Customs and Border Protection (CBP), 59–60, 167–68, 198n.2
U.S. Department of Homeland Security (DHS), 33–34, 168–69
U.S. Federal Boarding School Initiative, 131–32
U.S. Immigration and Customs Enforcement (ICE), 34, 37–39, 79–80
U.S. Immigration and Nationality Act (INA), 52–54, 155
U.S. Interior Department, 131–32, 176–77
U.S. State Department, 57–58, 155
U.S. Supreme Court, 25, 28–31, 37–39, 43, 52–54, 106, 121–22, 190n.11
utilitarian, 14–15, 16, 28, 81, 83–84

vaccine, 79–80, 168–69
Vancouver, British Columbia, 55
Vatican, 152–53, 196n.11
Vavilov, Alexander and Timothy, 64–65
vengeance, 5, 91–92, 192n.10
vicarious punishment, 2–7, 12–13, 14–16, 21–22, 37, 48–49, 59–60, 103–4, 105–6, 111, 116–17, 125, 129, 137–38, 150–51, 166, 172, 180
victim, 2–4, 17, 18–19, 37, 77, 78, 81–84, 85–93, 96–100, 101–2, 110–11, 114–15, 116–18, 121, 122, 123–25, 128, 133–34, 138, 141, 143, 144, 146–47,

151, 152–53, 172–73, 175–76, 178–79, 191n.7, 192–93n.2, 192n.10, 193n.3, 194n.3, 194n.4, 194n.5
victim-offender mediation, 82, 89–90, 91, 114–15, 117–18, 191n.7
Virginia, 79–80
visitation, 10, 12–13, 16, 25, 34–35, 47, 75, 84–85, 92–93, 94–95, 96, 172–73, 180–81
vulnerability, 5–6, 12, 22, 31, 45–46, 50, 68, 71, 72–73, 96–97, 112, 114–15, 121, 158–59, 164–65, 180, 193n.4, 195n.7

Wagner, Richard, 191n.6
war crimes, 7, 101–3, 109–10, 121, 123, 163, 174–75
Warren, Earl (1891–1974), 28–30, 106, 188n.12
World War I 44–45, 54
World War II, 44–45, 106

Yaqui Nation, 159

Zadvydas v. Davis (2001), 39–40
Zedner, Lucia, 25–26